Contents

The European Union and Migrant Labour

Edited by
Gareth Dale and Mike Cole

BERG
Oxford • New York

First published in 1999 by
Berg
Editorial offices:
150 Cowley Road, Oxford OX4 1JJ, UK
70 Washington Square South, New York NY 10012, USA

Berg is the imprint of Oxford International Publishers Ltd.

Library of Congress Cataloging-in-Publication Data

A catalogue record for this book is available from the Library of Congress.

British Library Cataloguing-in-Publication Data

A catalogue record for this book is available from the British Library.

ISBN 1 85973 960 1 (Cloth)
1 85973 965 2 (Paper)

Typeset by JS Typesetting, Wellingborough, Northants.
Printed in the United Kingdom by WBC Book Manufacturers, Bridgend,
Mid Glamorgan.

Acknowledgements

We would like to thank I.B. Tauris and Penguin UK for permission to publish Chapter 10 of this volume. A version of it first appeared in Nigel Harris's book, *The New Untouchables*.

Preface

One need only glance at the mainstream press in most European societies to realize that, both in terms of the movement of labour and with respect to 'moral panics' over refugees and asylum seekers, migration is firmly on the political agenda. The contributors to this volume draw on socialist, and particularly Marxist, theory, in order to analyse migration, immigration control and racism in the European Union (EU).

Such analyses have a number of dimensions. First, they entail a consideration of the dynamics of capital accumulation – local, national and international – which in turn influence spatial movements of capital and labour. Second, they examine the interrelationship of these various movements. Third, they consider the role of individual capitalist states in controlling migration. Fourth, they look at the role of EU as a whole (a conglomeration of capitalist states) in the formation, legitimation and implementation of migration policy. Finally, as Marxist analysis focuses upon the effects which production relations generate across the social formation as a whole, and given that the whole process of migration is permeated by racism, a central concern is the role that social class plays in the reproduction of racism, and in its contestation.

While Part I looks at migration policy and the EU as a whole, Part II examines migration with respect to some of the nation states within the EU, the major countries and a representative sample of smaller states: England, Ireland, Germany, the Netherlands, France, Austria and Italy. The book concludes with discussions on the relationship between migrant labour and modern capitalism (Part III).

Mike Cole and Gareth Dale

Introduction

Gareth Dale

Throughout the European Union, the politics of immigration and, more broadly, of 'ethnic minorities' comprising recent immigrants and their descendants, have become highly contentious.[1] The chapters in this volume narrate some of the major recent developments. On the one hand they give evidence of substantial levels of immigration. On the other, they present a picture of national governments outbidding one another in the imposition of harsh conditions to control entry and in their mean treatment of the few who are allowed in. They describe refugees dying *en route* to Western Europe, or arriving to face imprisonment or deportation. They also discuss the continued prevalence of xenophobia and racism, not only as expressed by extreme racist parties that call for discrimination against and 'repatriation' of immigrants – such as the 'National Front' in France, the 'Freedom Party' in Austria, and the 'Italian Social Movement/National Alliance' – but also the racism of mainstream political parties and the media, which together ensure that the public arena is supplied with a regular diet of scare stories about the 'threat' of undocumentated immigrants and the dangers of 'floods' of refugees 'swamping' the nation.

Fears of immigration are entirely groundless, as several contributors explain, yet their prevalence is striking. Even plainly ludicrous anxieties can gain a serious airing – for example, where, as Kieran Allen (Chapter 4) relates, in the 1990s sections of the media claimed that Ireland, 'one of the most sparsely-populated countries in Europe, was about to be "flooded" with hordes of refugees'. If the paranoid discourse of immigration control is based upon illusion, however, how can one explain its pervasiveness, and, indeed, its influence upon policy makers in Europe and elsewhere? Is the aggressive, exclusionary approach to immigration an irrational reflex, a relic of atavistic nationalism, or is it a symptom of living contradictions of the contemporary world? The second of these views is advocated in this introduction.

The Dawn of a New Era

The view that immigration control is irrational and outmoded can be presented through several related arguments. These concern the deconstruction of national borders and a consequent relaxation of immigration control arising from (1) the consequences of free flows of trade and capital, (2) the economic irrationality of immigration control, (3) the cosmopolitan implications of strengthening liberal values and (4) European Union (EU) integration.

First of these is that global movements of capital and goods are leading to what Lester Brown (1972) envisioned as a 'world without borders'. In Nigel Harris's (1995) exposition of this thesis (Chapter 10), globalization is a progressive force. It promises not only 'a scale of growth which will allow all to get work' and 'a decreasing scale of war', but the prospect of the demise of nation states and nationalism and the birth of a truly cosmopolitan world. In part, migration will be responsible for this advance:

> World economic integration continually increases rates of mobility, so that in future it is going to be as difficult internationally to give an unequivocal answer to the question, 'Where are you from?' as it already is in developed countries.

As a result of this ongoing deconstruction of nationalities, 'world interest and a universal morality' promise to be 'reborn after the long dark night of nationalism'.

A second prong to the thesis involves an appeal to economic rationality. It is common knowledge that immigrant labour was an essential ingredient of the European post-war boom. Rapid expansion in the industrial heartlands required the tapping of new reserves of labour, largely from countries with lower costs of reproduction of labour-power. It is also widely known – and well documented in Chapters 3 to 9 of this book – that immigrant labour, being relatively mobile and 'flexible', is often crucial to sectors such as agriculture, labour-intensive industries, and the black economy. Indeed, there is a substantial body of evidence to suggest that, for employers and states in the developed world, immigration is not merely advantageous for particular purposes but is generally beneficial. As Julian Simon and Nigel Harris have shown, immigrants tend to take only those jobs that natives reject, and therefore neither depress wages nor increase unemployment (Simon 1989). On the contrary, 'there are many examples of the availability of immigrant labour *expanding* the demand for native workers' (Harris 1997, italics GD). Conversely, restrictive immigration controls may well produce a situation of 'both high unemployment and a high level of unfilled vacancies' (Harris 1997). Moreover, immigrants, far from 'scrounging' from the state, typically contribute far more to state coffers than they receive in welfare spending. If these arguments are true, surely we can rely on the self-interest of employers and politicians to perceive the advantages – to themselves, their workers, and their voters – of open borders.

If this case rests on faith in the salubrious consequence of *economic* liberalism, a related (third) argument is based upon hopes in the widening and deepening of *political* liberalism. In part this entails a belief that the freedom of movement advocated by a consistent liberalism will be taken seriously; that the contradiction embedded, for example, in the 1952 Convention on Refugees, which asserted that only the right to emigrate – and not the right to immigrate – is a universal right, will be resolved (cf. Sassen 1996: 65). Thus *The Economist* maintains that

> universal immigration controls keeping people out are tantamount to a Berlin Wall shutting them in. It is time to recognize that the right to freedom of movement implies a duty to permit immigration. (Quoted in Harris, Chapter 11)

More generally, the argument proposes that the expansion of liberal norms, together with the *de facto* persistence of settled minority communities and their integration into the 'host' society's circuits of work, education, and daily life, is bound to translate into a general recognition that rights should be granted to all residents irrespective of their origins. As evidence, advocates of this view might point, for example, to the recently promised granting of dual citizenship and voting rights to immigrants in Germany (cf. Chapter 5).

Further to these general arguments, a claim specific to Europe is sometimes voiced. European integration, it is proposed, is based upon the supersession of national borders and national particularities, as exemplified in the EU's supra-national institutions (notably the Euro) and in the freedom of movement throughout the EU granted to all citizens of its member states. In Robert Miles's version of the argument (1993: 217), European unification has 'contributed to a further decline in the significance of the nation state'. As integration proceeds the traditional national/foreigner duality is deconstructed, thus preparing the ground for a radical *detournement* of the European project. An 'emergent European space' will allow the construction of 'a new We against capital', and indeed for European integration to be recast according to 'quite different reasons and interests to those of capital and the ruling class'.

The Persistence of Exclusionary Immigration Policy

There is something seductively sanguine about these four theses, bearing as they do the promise of inexorable progress towards a cosmopolitan world order of free movement, universal rights, and open borders. However, the majority of contributors to this volume portray an EU migration regime that shows little spirit of generosity or freedom, let alone any sign of hitching itself to what Harris describes as the 'Spirit' of 'world interest and universal morality' (1995: 228). In their accounts, the European Union and its member states are resolutely committed to a restrictive immigration regime and preside over entrenched structures of institutional discrimination against immigrants and their descendants. In some respects the recent historical record even charts a shift in the direction of greater restriction and brutality. As we see in the chapters on Germany, England and France, policies that promoted immigration during most of the post-war boom were replaced by more restrictive regimes from the late 1960s onwards. Even those countries such as Italy and Ireland whose histories of mass emigration and colonization might lead one to expect a more sympathetic treatment of immigrants have tilted in the same direction. Agostino Petrillo's description of recent Italian legislation as exemplifying how 'the logic of expulsion and rejection prevails over that of acceptance' could describe any other EU state. In most cases immigration has continued unabated, but the restrictive turn has meant that arrivals are less likely to be documented workers, and more likely to be asylum seekers or undocumented workers who are denied all but the most elementary rights (see especially Chapter 9 and Chapter 7).

In face of the evidence of entrenched restrictionism, several contributors develop arguments that challenge the thesis of dawning cosmopolitanism. Chapter 11, for example, presents a critique of the notion that international migration and free enterprise herald a 'borderless world'. Despite globalization, it seems that, in Phil Marfleet's words, many major polities – including the EU itself – are actually 'reasserting old physical and cultural boundaries and establishing new frontiers' (Marfleet 1998: 68). Moreover, if the liberal position that champions open borders for capital and goods as a fundamental principle is nowadays widely held, a liberal defence of open borders for *people* remains scarce (cf. Mike Haynes and Gareth Dale in the current volume). Even Julian Simon, one of the most trenchant critics of anti-immigration paranoia, proposes that admission of immigrants should take the form of invitations to the selected few. Freedom of movement, defended as a right for capital, is seen as a privilege for labour. If the present epoch is witnessing a trend towards looser regulation of the movement of capital and goods, the international movement of labour is as circumscribed as ever. When *The Economist* asked 'has there ever been a global market for labour?' the answer given suggests that the free global labour market, which Nigel Harris prophesises, is no nearer than it was a century ago:

> During the 19th century, arguably there was. [. . .] Nowadays, there is no real market, such is the severity of restrictions in force. (*The Economist*, 1 November 1997)

International migration is strictly regulated by bilateral treaties and international conventions, not to mention the controls of nation states. In respect of migration, the modern regime of global enterprise and free wage labour is lashed to political constraints every bit as much as its predecessors. As Yash Gai observes (1997: 178):

> the market determines rights and obligations less directly than in the days of slavery and indenture. It is somewhat ironical that whereas during slavery and indenture, the movements of people were driven by the global market [. . .] in our own more global age, movements are less determined purely by market considerations.

Of course, this comparison also highlights the degree to which certain important rights and liberties have gained ground over recent centuries – the 'political constraints' referred to involve not only restrictions on movement but also the establishment of rights for immigrants. International conventions on human rights and on asylum, for instance, pose limits to the abilities of nation states to discriminate against immigrants and exclude refugees. Such conventions, reflecting the recognition by governments of their dependence on a settled, 'integrated' immigrant workforce, as well as long struggles on the part of labour organizations, immigrant groups, and liberal campaigners, express the bourgeois promise of universal human rights. As several chapters in this volume (notably Chapters 3 and 5) testify, pressure towards the expansion of immigrants' rights continues, and indeed influences government policy.

Whether this represents an irresistible tide towards truly universal rights, however, is doubtful. For one thing, citizenship, rights and liberties, although commonly framed in universal terms are in practice selectively granted by states. International conventions on human rights only have force if ratified and implemented by nation states; none challenge the right of states to deny the right to reside to would-be immigrants. In short, the particularity of nation states retains undisputed primacy over any principle of universal right. For another, political forces grounded in national particularism – conservative, nationalist, racist – actively resist the expansion of rights. Chapters 3 to 9 are replete with examples of the continued influence of conservative and racist opinion in braking (or reversing) moves towards greater juridical 'integration' of immigrants and ethnic minorities. For example, even the proposed modernization of the anachronistic 'blood-based' nationality law in Germany has provoked a virulent reaction from the conservative parties (CDU and CSU). In a highly unusual (and recklessly racist) move, these have resorted to extraparliamentary street campaigning designed to drum up *Deutschnational* Resistance to the reform.[2] In short, there are powerful obstacles to the forward march of liberal values, not least in liberalism's own marriage to the nation state system.

The final liberal proposition considered above was that European integration, through the transcendence of the nation state and nationalism, promises the dawning of a genuinely cosmopolitan Europe. Here too, most chapters in this volume offer a more critical view. To begin with, even a cursory look at EU citizenship and migration policy reveals that the major institutions are national or intergovernmental rather than transnational. Jon Gubbay (Chapter 2) points out that the EU citizenship is a derivative institution (dependent upon prior citizenship of a member state) and notes the determination of member states to maintain control over its authorization. Gubbay also emphasizes that the main bodies involved in the construction of EU migration policy – such as Schengen and the Trevi Group – are in fact intergovernmental institutions. Meanwhile, the actual policing and supervision of immigration remains essentially in the hands of national police forces and benefit and social work agencies. Ostensibly these practices are constrains by 'transitional' rights for immigrants, as asserted by international organisations such as the United Nations, International Labour Office, and the EU itself. However, as Lydia Morris has observed, these rights mean nothing unless ratified by EU member states (Morris 1997). Moreover, given that abstract rights are notoriously open to the vagaries of interpretation and implementation, even ratification is by no means a guarantee of effectiveness.

If such details qualify the cosmopolitan promise of the European project, more challenging criticisms are elaborated in the chapters by Gubbay and Haynes. Referring to Benedict Anderson's analysis of nationalism's appeal as hinging upon the construction of nations as 'imagined communities', Haynes suggests that the term can be equally applied to the formation of a European identity. The creation of a common European identity would obviously raise the possibility of the diminution of national antagonisms within the EU, but it simultaneously poses the question as to whether an 'imagined European community' would follow the example of other imagined communities, and derive its definition and appeal to a considerable degree from its definition against those excluded from the fold.

The evidence presented by Haynes and Gubbay strongly suggests that this is already the case, and indeed, that the political construction of a European 'imagined community' is intimately connected to the practice and ideology of immigration control. Just as the origins of West European integration lie in the common cause of European governments (along with the USA) in forging a bulwark against the Communist enemy, further integration in the post-Cold War epoch has been justified, in large measure, as a defensive consolidation of European 'civilization' against the peril from beyond the Mediterranean. As Marfleet notes (1998: 82),

> EU ministers have argued that [Europe's] main threat no longer comes from the communist East but from behind a "new fault line" which has allegedly replaced the Iron Curtain. This, it is said, runs along the Mediterranean, dividing southern Europe from North Africa and from the menace of Islamic societies.

This xenophobic construction of European identity is nourished by EU migration policy. The first crucial development was the emergence of a two-tier migration regime: in 1968 the free movement of labour within the EEC was formally achieved, and incorporated the principle of equal treatment for workers from other EEC countries.[3] In the process immigrants became divided into two categories: non-EC foreigners on the one hand, and EC citizens on the other. With the widening of the EC the latter category came to include the Irish, British, Spanish, Portuguese, and Greeks, among others.

In turn, the freeing of the internal labour market generated pressure towards the harmonization of immigration policy. From the late 1970s a common EC immigration policy began to emerge (see Gubbay, Chapter 2). However, as with the economic convergence that preceded the introduction of the Euro, the guiding spirit was restrictive and exclusionary. As Henk Overbeek has suggested (1995: 31), member states engaged in a 'downward harmonization' of immigration policy, pursuing a logic of 'policy competition' whereby it 'is the objective of each state to make itself at least as unattractive [to immigrants] as its neighbours'. In turn, the European Commission was able to justify its own hard-line policy by appeal to the already-existing restrictionism of its member states (cf. Brochmann 1996: 94). In Ursula Levelt's terms (1995: 210), the EU has followed a 'segmented' rather than a 'cosmopolitan' course, one centred on uncompromising division between member citizens and non-members, even where the latter are EU residents. Far from engendering supranational harmony, harmonization has led to what an EU-commissioned report (whose authors, including Lord Jenkins and Mary Robinson, could hardly be described as radicals), characterized as 'a tendency towards a Fortress Europe which is hostile to "outsiders" and discourages refugees and asylum-seekers' (*Guardian*, 9 October 1998).[4]

What do these considerations suggest for our understanding of European identity? Mike Haynes draws the strong conclusion that 'it is here in both the ideas and practice of immigration control [. . .] that the new "Europe" is being forged, just as much as in the debates and celebrations of internal unity.' It is an identity that derives much of its appeal from xenophobic paranoia; it is tightly lashed to ideologies of 'Euronationalism' and racism; and is most sharply defined in relation to immigrants from beyond the Mediterranean.[5] As such, as Jan Rath points out (Chapter 6), even those European citizens who are 'tainted' with the signs of Third World ancestry become marginalized by Euronationalism, just as much as by the nationalism of individual nation states. If the European project problematizes traditional images of 'us and them', the other side of the coin is a reaffirmation of the 'themness' of non-Europeans.

Capitalism and Racism

If the evidence brought by most of the contributors refutes the thesis that the workings of modern capitalism are rendering the discriminatory regulation of immigrants obsolescent, then the question arises as to why exactly discrimination and restriction persist?

Several contributors, including Gubbay and Dale (Chapters 2 and 11), search for an answer in the contradictions of modern capitalism. In their view capitalism, though in one sense distinctively cosmopolitan and trans-territorial, simultaneously creates and relies upon territorial structures – above all, states. These actively organize the forces and relations of production, they manage and control property and population, both within 'their' territory and, wherever possible, beyond. Capitalism engenders tendencies towards labour mobility and towards the generalization of political rights and citizenship, but simultaneously depends upon the establishment of economic, political and cultural infrastructures through which management of social reproduction occurs. These processes invariably entail the transgression of the free mobility of labour and, indeed, the limitation of rights.

As Chapters 5, 7, and 11 suggest, an inter-state system consisting of sovereign centralized states, though arising in response to crises of European feudalism, became consolidated and globalized with the rise of capitalism.[6] Adoption of the national form, entailing unification and homogenization of the interior, inevitably occasioned the fixing of insider and outsider, of citizen and alien. These developments are particularly transparent in the cases of Germany and of Austria. In the latter example (Chapter 8), it is noteworthy that it was not until the development of capitalism had spurred a decisive shift towards the creation of a homogenous, culturally German, nation state in the first decades of the twentieth century – involving the 'invention of the German race' and its identification with the nascent Austrian nation – that an exclusivist immigration policy was first instituted.

That capitalist states insist upon their 'doorkeeper' role as a keystone of sovereignty is self evident; it is a function that has become ever more regulated over the course of the last century. More importantly, they are obliged to justify their own legitimacy and to organize structures of social control. As Gubbay and Dale suggest, the first of these tasks typically occasions an insistence on the state's role as sole representative of the nation, and frames the right to citizenship as for 'nationals' only. The second invariably entails the organization of subjects into hierarchies of distinct cultural identities, historical examples of which are given by the contributors to this volume.

Several contributors point to ways in which social control and the organization of exploitation rely upon and engender racism; they examine how the racialization of immigration is at the cutting edge of these processes. Satnam Virdee explores how the racialization of immigration to England 'affected the allocation of persons to different positions in the production process and the allocation of material and other rewards and disadvantages'. For Jan Rath the focus is on the ideological construction of immigrant groups as 'deviant' and, as such, as targeted objects of social control. By exploring the analogous treatment of immigrants and other 'deviant ' groups – such as the poor and 'anti-social' – he indicates how people of Third World origin can become linked in the public imagination to a low-class and even 'deviant' status. Rath's study illuminates the way in which oppressed groups, although seemingly discriminated against as a result of their 'difference', are in fact treated in common ways because the oppression of each stems from a general logic of social control. Nowhere is the association of ethnic minorities with 'deviance' clearer than in the racist discourse that links immigration and/or minorities to crime – for example in the claim, cited by Khursheed Wadia, that the French *banlieux* are 'becoming a vast Bronx-like zone with its ethnic gangs and race riots'.

Conceived in this way, the oppression of immigrants and ethnic minorities is not a 'natural' function of innate tribalism on the part of natives, but is a product of the competitive dynamics of capitalism. This Marxist explanation of racism – as entailing above all the cultural division of workers as a means to weaken class solidarity – is expounded by several contributors.

Marx, discussing the oppression of Irish immigrants in England, made the bold – and provocative – observation that the bourgeoisie 'knows that this scission is the true secret of maintaining its power' (quoted by Allen, Chapter 4).[7] Clearly such 'scissions' are based not merely on conspiracy or illusion but rather on the fact that immigrants from poorer parts, because willing and obliged to work for poorer terms, can all too easily be depicted as 'unfair' competition on labour markets. Although studies show that this is in fact rarely the case – as immigrants generally do not compete directly with native workers[8] – several contributors (notably Petrillo, Dale and Eugene Sensenig) give examples of the strategic recruitment of immigrant workers as a deliberate means of undermining workers' combativity. Notoriously, such cases raise dilemmas for labour organizations. One possible strategy to prevent 'wage dumping' by foreign workers takes the form of support for immigration control; but if this path if followed, labour organizations themselves become wedded to the divisive logic of racism. Historically, as all contributors show, this strategy has been thoroughly tested by social democratic parties, with devastating effect. The worst case, according to Sensenig, is Austria. Austrian social democracy, around the turn of the century, fully hitched itself to the project of constructing a modern capitalist state, in opposition to the semi-feudal Habsburg Empire. In so doing, it subscribed to the shift from an imperial-based territorialism to a bourgeois territorialism based upon the marriage of state and nation. Quickly propelled to the helm of the newly defined nation state, social democracy became deeply implicated in the construction of nativist immigration control and was drawn inexorably into the perpetration of racist policies. Similarly, the other six country studies detail persistent social democratic support for (and initiation of) racist immigration regulation, and show how such measures encourage the harassment – by police, by fascists, by the media – of immigrants and minorities.

By analysing the interconnections of modern capitalism, nationalism and racism, and immigration control, a reasoned answer can be given to the question of why immigration has surged up the political agenda in Europe since the late 1960s. The 'common sense' explanation is to suggest that immigration has increased, or that economic slowdown has restricted the ability of countries to admit immigrants, but neither of these theses are tenable. Recent levels of immigration to Europe are comparable with – or lower than – those of the 1950s and 1960s. Immigration, as Harris and others have shown, brings profit to employers and revenues to states even during depressed times. A third possible explanation, advanced for instance by Naomi Carmon (1996), is that many recent immigrants are culturally ('ethnically') very different from natives. Once again, however, empirical evidence casts doubt on this assertion. For example, when the question of immigration was at its highest point on the German political agenda, in 1992, the vast majority of immigrants were from Europe, with under a quarter coming from the 'culturally different' Third World. The latter figure was considerably higher in the late 1960s, a time when immigration was not considered an urgent political issue.

A more plausible explanation is that recurrent economic crises and social polarization have intensified the contradictions faced by states – between the needs of employers (and state coffers) for immigration on the one hand, and the heightened problems of social control and of mass disillusionment in political structures on the other. Such contradictions inevitably nourish the tendency for supporters of the established order to deflect criticism and reaffirm the structures of national (and EU) power through the scapegoating of outsiders and minorities. This thesis is succinctly put by Kieran Allen, who shows that behind the recent Irish economic boom lies a story of increasing social polarization, of redistribution from poor to rich, and of cutbacks in social expenditure. In this context the racist scapegoating of immigrants was adopted by sections of Irish society as a way of 'asserting that the nation had to "look after its own first"'.

However, as Allen continues, racism is by no means an automatic reflex of economic and social contradictions. Ranged against the interests of ruling classes in perpetrating racism are the interests of immigrants and ethnic minorities in combating their oppression, and of workers in creating trans-ethnic solidarity. Although not the focus of this volume, several contributors take up the theme of anti-racism, and of its relationship to class struggle. Khursheed Wadia, for example, points to the interconnection of the generalized class struggles of 1968 and immigrant and anti-racist movements. This theme is developed at greater length by Satnam Virdee, who charts the progress of anti-racist consciousness and organization in England. Beginning with the inspiration of the American Civil Rights movement for English blacks, he then notes how anti-racism was embraced by growing numbers of 'white' workers as the industrial struggles of the 1970s undermined sectionalist consciousness and encouraged the formation of wider solidarity. It was a shift of consciousness that, although centred in workplaces, extended throughout the working class, and helps to explain the success of subsequent movements – such as the Anti-Nazi League and urban uprisings – in asserting anti-racist politics.

If these arguments carry conviction, it would seem that the dynamics of immigration control, nationalism, and racism are not mere ideological relics of a benighted age but are firmly rooted in the structures of capitalist modernity. The magnificent bourgeois promise of universal human rights and the global freedom of movement may yet be rescued, not through the affirmation but the negation of the bourgeois world order itself.

Notes

1. Thanks to Adrian Budd and Jon Gubbay for stylistic comments on a previous draft.
2. The justification given by a leading conservative is that 'The Red-Greens' policy on foreigners jeopardises security in Germany more than the terrorism of the Red Army Faction.' Other conservative leaders have pursued this paranoia even more zealously, claiming that generosity towards foreigners directly spurs terrorism (*Guardian*, 5 January 1999).
3. In reality intra-EU freedom of movement has been circumscribed. Of the 'four freedoms' (people, capital, goods, and services), the former has faced the greatest obstacles and received the lowest priority. EU citizens living in a country other than their own account for a mere 1.5% of the EU population.
4. In the light of these developments it is not far-fetched to suggest that the ideological centre of gravity of European migration policy displays an affinity with the main thrust of the racism of European New Right and fascist currents. The latter is well described by Martin Evans: 'a Fortress mentality is a central element of the current anti-immigrant racism. The racist rhetoric promoted by the National Front in France or the Republican Party in Germany lacks the expansionist element of nineteenth-century imperialism: there is no notion of France or Germany expanding outwards to dominate the world. Instead the key question is the permeability of their own borders, and how to secure them against the influx of immigrants and refugees' (Evans 1996: 45).
5. For an academic exposition of such paranoia see Samuel Huntington's

argument that Third World immigrants arriving on 'Christian' shores should be seen as *invaders* (Huntington 1997, Part IV).

6. See also Turner (1999).
7. It is worth noting that this conception marks a significant revision of Marx's earlier thinking, as exemplified in the *Communist Manifesto* (1973: 67), according to which '[N]ational [. . .] antagonisms between peoples are daily more and more vanishing'.
8. Thus *The Economist:* According to the OECD [. . .] most studies have found that the negative effect of immigration on native workers is small and short-lived (29 November 1997: 114).

Bibliography

Brochmann, G. (1996), *European Integration and Immigration from Third Countries*, Oslo: Scandinavian University Press.

Brown, L. (1972), *World Without Borders*, New York: Random House.

Carmon, N (1996), *Immigration and integration in post-industrial societies*, Houndmills: Macmillan.

Evans, M (1996), 'Languages of Racism within contemporary Europe' in Jenkins, B and Sofos, S. (eds), *Nation and Identity in contemporary Europe*, London: Routledge.

Gai, Y. (1997), 'Migrant Workers, Markets, and the Law' in Gungwu, W. (ed.) *Global History and Migrations,* Boulder: Westview.

Harris, N. (1995), *The New Untouchables,* Harmondsworth: Penguin.

Harris, N. (1997), 'Over here, overworked, overlooked', *The Times Higher Education Supplement,* February 14.

Huntington, S. (1997), *The Clash of Civilizations and the Remaking of the World Order,* New York: Simon & Schuster.

Levelt, U. (1995), 'The European Union as a Political Community through the lens of immigration policy' in Martiniello, M. Migration, Citizenship, and Ethno-national identities in the European Union.

Marfleet, P. (1998), 'Migration and the refugee experience', in Kiely, R. and Marfleet, P. (eds), *Globalisation and the Third World,* London: Routledge.

Marx, K and Engels, F. (1973 [1848]), *Manifesto of the Communist Party*, Peking: Foreign Languages Press.

Miles, R. (1993), *Racism after 'Race Relations'*, Routledge: London.

Morris, L. (1997), 'Globalization, migration and the nation-state: the path to a post-national Europe?', *British Journal of Sociology*, Vol. 48 No. 2.

Overbeek, H. (1995), 'Towards a new international migration regime', in Miles, R. and Thranhardt, D. (eds), *Migration and European Integration*, London: Pinter.

Sassen, S. (1996), *Losing Control*, New York: Columbia University Press.

Simon, J. (1989), *The Economic Consequences of Immigration*, Oxford: Blackwell.

Turner, M. (forthcoming), 'Demystifying international society and its expansion', chapter in Smith, H. (ed.) *International Theory and Historical Materialism*. Unpublished.

Part I
Migration and European Integration

—1—

Setting the Limits to Europe as an 'Imagined Community'

Mike Haynes

'Everything begins in mysticism and ends in politics', the late nineteenth-century French writer Charles Péguy once said. He was not thinking about the development of the European Union but the idea is apposite. If the European Union is to exist as a real entity, commanding popular loyalty, then its proponents claim it must be built around a 'European identity'. This idea informs particular debates such as that over a 'European defence identity' but it goes deeper still, drawing on and developing an old mystique that reaches back several centuries to embellish a developing unity project whose origins lie more in the attempt to reconstruct Western Europe after the Second World War and then to deal with the fallout of the end of the Cold War after 1989.

It is this mystique that helps to define the forms of enlargement of the European Union and the creation of new external borders around the member states. The assertion of identity implies a unity built around something that is real. Try to grasp this, however, and it dissolves before you revealing that what is really at stake is a mystique that serves to obscure a series of less pleasant issues. Consider an example from the southern fringe of this evolving 'European Union'. From the coast of Morocco it is possible to look north across a stretch of sea less than half the width of the English Channel to the shores of Spain. Standing above the shore in Spain, on the other side, you can look south, to the neighbouring coastline while listening to Moroccan radio before you return home to watch either Spanish or Moroccan TV. At one point between the two shores stands Gibraltar, the Arabic origin of its name a witness to the time in the eighth century when Arab generals crossed the straight bringing Islamic civilization to a backward Iberia to create in El-Andalus (what is now most of modern day Spain) 'one of the most advanced and tolerant societies of the medieval world' (Davidson 1984: 105).[1] It was here that the classics of ancient philosophy, physics, mathematics, astronomy and so on were preserved while the so-called 'Dark Ages' afflicted the northern lands. It was here that, by means of the work of schools of translators, often from the Arabic, the wider European 'Renaissance' would be born. So near, it seems, in physical distance and culture, and yet so far.

In the early summer of 1987 the Moroccan government caused consternation in the European Community by asking that Morocco be allowed to join. Coming fast on the application of Turkey, made in April 1987, the diplomats in Brussels and the capitals of member countries could hardly hide their smiles at the effrontery of the Moroccan regime. But, being good diplomats, they struggled not to offend when they gave their answer as a resounding 'no'. Speaking off the record, however, they were less guarded. One anonymous diplomat told *The Times*'s European correspondent, 'This is getting out of hand. First Turkey, now Morocco, who will be next to apply to join? Cyprus? Malta? Norway?' Nevertheless they briefly went through the motions of considering the application before confirming that Morocco 'clearly does not meet EEC criteria' and not least of these was that it was not in Europe (*The Times* 14 September 1987).[2]

The Moroccan government has not applied again. But, a decade later, what of the others? The EEC is now the European Union with 15 members and considering becoming more. Voters in Norway have twice rejected membership rather than the EU rejecting them. Even Malta and Cyprus have applied and have not been laughed out of court. Turkey? It still waits in the wings wondering if it is 'in Europe' and 'European' enough to join. Those considering its application say that they worry about its commitment to democracy and human rights, about its role in dividing Cyprus. There are contradictions here, however. For some things it seems Turkey clearly is both European and democratic enough to qualify – membership of NATO since 1952, a key component of the Western Alliance, a Cold War base against the Soviet bloc, membership of the Council of Europe and so on. In early 1997 Tansu Ciller, the then Turkish Prime Minister, reflecting the anxieties of a large part of the Turkish political class to join the European Union, pushed this point home 'Turkey defended European values for Europe. We have been waging a struggle for democracy within NATO for the past 45 years . . . The democratic standards of our country were acceptable at that time.'

However much we may share the distaste for the policies of successive regimes in Turkey perhaps there is another reason for the doubts about whether it qualifies to join the EU? On average its population is poor, they are 98 per cent Muslim. Why should that be a hindrance? The Rome Treaty makes neither prosperity or Christianity a condition of membership of the European Union. Indeed as early as the start of 1997 the German President, Roman Herzog, declared that 'Europe is not a Christian club' and 'Turkey belongs to Europe'. Given that Germany is Turkey's largest trading partner and the home of some 2–3 million Turkish migrants these seemed promising words. Then the mask briefly dropped creating a flurry of anger in Turkey but little comment in 'Europe'. When the leaders of the European Christian Democratic Parties met on 4 March 1997 their unguarded conversation was reported. For Wilfried Martens, a former Belgian Prime Minister and now President of the European People's Party, Turkey had no place in Europe, 'We are creating a European Union. This is a European project.' Helmut Kohl, then the German Chancellor and most powerful politician in Europe, explained to his colleagues what he thought were the first principles of geography: 'from geography lessons at school, I cannot recall being told that Anatolia was part of Europe'. Klaus Kinkel, the then German Foreign Minister came out more bluntly: despite the talk about the further enlargement of the European Union there was no prospect of Turkey joining 'in the foreseeable future'. As the furore provoked by such leaked comments grew, Wilfried Martens, something of an expert on Turkey, was forced to further clarify Turkey's status, 'Turkey should preserve and develop its place within the European forum. Neither we nor Turkey stand to gain by its incorporation into an integrated European Union'. Here, for the moment we remain. Turkey is within 'the European forum' – whatever this is – but cannot be in the 'European Union' (*European* 3–9 April 1997).

More removed still is 'the south', as one Brussels official put it – the European Union's 'vulnerable underbelly . . . a formidable challenge that exceeds by far the one that the EU has been shouldering in Eastern Europe since 1990'. For the European Union the southern Mediterranean area needs to be stabilized and held at arm's length to ensure that its countries should not 'be at war with each other; be destabilised by socio-political conflicts; export terrorism or drugs to Europe; threaten Europe's social stability by continued or sharply increased flows of illegal migrants' (Rhein 1996: 79–86). These are the blunt words with which the insider summarises the more decorous language of the 1995 Barcelona-Mediterranean Conference which was supposed to lay the basis of wider co-operation in the area. For Europe, it seems, Islam in this area remains, in Edward Said's phrase, 'a lasting trauma' (Said 1979: 59).

There is an important lesson here. In a world in which nationalism is back on the political agenda, where it is possible for the Front National in France and Jorg Haider in Austria to become major political forces and racist and xenophobic attacks to occur throughout Europe, it is tempting to see the choice between a narrow nationalism and an internationalist 'Europeanism'. Anxious to shake off the link between past nationalisms and Europe's tragic history in this century some even try to link the two perspectives – struggling peripheral nationalists whether in Scotland, Brittany, the Basque Country try to assert their 'civic nationalism' over 'ethnic nationalism' by proclaiming that what they want to be is both an independent nation and European. Beyond the borders of the European Union the idea of 'Europeanness' also plays a strategic role. Even before the collapse of the Soviet Union Gorbachev built his foreign policy around the idea of a 'common European home'. Now the debates as to who can enter the European Union and NATO and who cannot are often also built around the idea of who is European and who is not. For Milan Kundera, writing in exile, but reflecting a view dominant in the 1989 opposition and now widespread in the former Soviet bloc, 'the word "Europe" does not represent a phenomenon of geography but a spiritual nation synonymous with the word "West"' (cited in Callinicos 1991: 84). The concept in other words is explicitly set against the 'East' in general and Russia in particular. This is why so many in the region now prefer the term 'Central European' for themselves (Okey 1992: 102–33). It then becomes equally important for those excluded to assert their 'European' right to be included. For the Russian historian Tchoubarian, 'for the first time in history, Europeanisation based on democratic rights and institutions, human rights, freedom, self-determination and independence, unites all Europeans from the Atlantic to the Urals' (but not apparently from the Urals to Vladivostok – M.H.). Correctly rejecting the idea that geography can in any sense lay down where boundaries lie, he insists that 'the political aspect of the concept of modern Europe *is* much more important than these geographical disputes . . . Today plans for European development and a new European order are simply unacceptable without Russia' (Tchoubarian 1995).

Where is this Europe to be found? Not apparently in Morocco, nor in Turkey, at least for the foreseeable future. The idea of being a 'European' might imply a broader group than British or French or German, but it too is both an *inclusive* and *exclusive* concept. Just as much as the concept of 'nation', the idea of 'European' implies similarities with some and differences from others. It therefore requires those who believe in the idea of 'Europe' and the 'European', to have criteria by which some can be included and others excluded. But like the idea of nation these criteria do not simply relate to people who live on particular pieces of land. If Morocco is not European what of the Moroccans who move to 'Europe'? Can they ever become European? If Turkey as a country is on the periphery of 'Europe' – what of those who have migrated from Turkey to what is seen as legitimately Europe? Do they remain the outsiders within, just as their country of origin remains the outsider without? If they do, does not this supposedly more internationalist Europe create double standards of exclusion and marginalization, no less demeaning to both sides than the methods traditionally embodied in the nation state?

What choice do we have? 'National or European' – formulated this way we are presented with the tyranny of two choices. The third, that we need be neither but can aspire to a genuine internationalism that knows neither 'state' or 'continental limits' stands marginalized, ridiculed as pathetically utopian, the idea of the dreamer. Be a realist, accept the terms you are offered and if you are on the outside of 'Europe' looking in then show why we should accept you rather than them – how much more powerful seems this logic? The words of Tom Paine, at the end of the eighteenth century, 'my country is the world, my religion to do good' appear to crumble beneath both the weight of history and the weight of the realities of the present. However, as many travellers learn to their cost, the inviting low road that looks so much more attractive and realistic than the high mountain pass very often hides bogs and marshes that can trap the unwary before they realize what is happening to them.

What is this thing called Europe and where can it be found? In the early nineteenth century Metternich, the foreign minister of the Hapsburg empire, famously said that he could see the start of Asia when he looked eastwards from his window in Vienna. In the Czech Republic they breath a sigh of relief for they are further west. Yes take us, not them – we all know where Asia begins, at the border with the Slovak Republic. Outraged, the despised inhabitants of the Slovak Republic puff out their chests, look to the east and south east, and say 'there is Asia on our borders, take us too, take Slovakia but not them'. In the Balkans the same process is repeated, take us not them – take Romania not Bulgaria, take Bulgaria not Turkey, take the Ukraine they say in Kiev but not above all, not Russia. This is the game that 'border areas' especially must play because only if they stress their greater claim to join can they hope that they will be found on the right side of the divide. Can we not have a Europe that stretches from the Atlantic to the Urals? Of course you can; you can have any Europe you want but you will always exclude someone. To the Urals? But not beyond, and further south – the Caucuses the supposed home of the Caucasians. Well perhaps not. And Turkey, still Turkey, Morocco, Tunisia, Egypt and that invisible border that separates 'us Europeans' from 'those Africans' – no there the border must rest. We are European, they are different and it is to them we say 'they shall not pass'.

How tempting it is to agree to these terms. Yes we are the same as you because we are different from them. Where are the borders of Europe? In abstract the answer is simple – they change, they move, they fluctuate, they lie at a point nearer or further – it is usually nearer – to the south or east of whoever accepts that this is a meaningful question. In practice the answer is no less simple. The borders of Europe lie wherever those with power choose to put them and cast them in concrete and barbed wire.

We can only begin to make sense of this question of 'Europe' if we reject the idea that there is an objective geographical, cultural, linguistic, economic, ethnic or any other component that distinguishes not only national groups from one another but the European from anyone else.[3] Far from offering us an alternative to 'nation' building 'Europe' simply offers to repeat the nation-building exercise on an extended scale. To understand how this is happening we need to appreciate that the division of the world into competing nation states is not a natural part of human life but a relatively recent invention. But the power of the national as an ideology is that once in existence it makes the claim that all history as been working towards the development of the 'nation state'. In fact, in Europe, recognizable forms of nation state only came into being from the sixteenth century. In Eastern Europe their origin is even later and everywhere the establishment of national loyalty over other claims such as those of family, locality, region, Church is even more recent still and continues to be contested by other claims including those of class (see Gellner 1983). In an area like Yugoslavia we see before our eyes not only the fragmentation of an old state but the twin processes of manipulation that lead both to the building of new states and new nations around them and the defeat of other possibilities.

This, of course, is not how nationalists see it as they present us with their fictitious histories of their glorious pasts from which, they hope, will come their glorious futures. The trick that is played here by nationalists has been well put by the philosopher Jonathan Rée: 'the nation-form is a kind of false consciousness, an ideology in which the extension of the nation-form gets interpreted as an expression of the popular will' (Rée 1992: 10). The nineteenth-century Italian politician Massimo d'Azeglio put it more bluntly in his famous aphorism, 'Italy has been made; now we have to make Italians' (cited in Woolf 1969: 11). Today we might need to rewrite this, 'The Soviet Union, Czechoslovakia, Yugoslavia have been unmade; now we have to make . . .'

Nations, therefore, are not the primordial building blocks of human society. They have their origin in the development of a capitalist state system in the sixteenth century and have developed as part of it, sometimes as part of a process of unification, sometimes involving fragmentation.

As capitalist development also lays the basis for a growing internationalization of the world's population it also creates opportunities to transcend the limits of the national. However, this can be done in different ways. It could, as Marx originally argued in the 1840s, be based on a recognition that the fundamental conflicts are class antagonisms that transcend national and other boundaries, or it could involve trying to redefine national divisions of the world on a larger basis.

The idea of a continental or supranational identity plays on this tension but in such a way as to create another artificial form of human division – another 'imagined community' (Anderson 1983). Judged against the various petty local nationalisms, the 'European idea' looks attractive, but the idea of the development of a European identity involves many of the same processes that were involved in the building of 'national identity'. In this sense Jean Monnet was more correct than he imagined when he said in 1952 that, 'Europe is the bit of united Europe which we have been able to build now. It will be tomorrow that which we will be able to build tomorrow.'

Far from it being the case that there is a pre-existing 'Europe' that legitimizes the development of the European Union, the making of the European Union also requires the making of Europeans themselves. Firstly, the idea of European identity involves a class element in two senses. One is that this exercise is being carried out from above, with the people of 'Europe' very much the object rather than the subject of the creation of 'Europe'. The other is that the attempt to give meaning to the idea of Europe involves the generalization of the experience of one group to the wider whole. Nigel Harris puts the point well in respect of 'the national':

> the definition of what is the national culture is the result of a pre-emptive strike by only one group of people . . . Force is the precondition for compelling the majority of the people to accept this pretension. Thus the appearance of the nation is not the revelation of some continuous culture, but an invention of the struggle for power and prestige. (Harris 1990: 5; see also Gellner 1983)

Building a European identity since 1945 has not involved physical force in the same way that early nation building did but it is nevertheless based upon a similar assertion of power and prestige, 'a pre-emptive strike' by one group over others.

Secondly, just as with the past examples of the development of the idea of national identity, the idea of a European identity is being developed by generalizing from the features of a narrow and arbitrary geographical 'core'. However much talk there is about the need to incorporate diversity, if 'Europe' exists and is different, something must define the limits of this diversity and something must define 'the unity in the diversity'. This process involves the extension of features associated with Western Europe and even within Western Europe, an extension of a set of characteristics associated with the now dominant economic centres – London, Paris, Brussels, Berlin, perhaps supplemented by romantic gestures towards Rome, Madrid and Barcelona. If Greek philosophy, Roman law, and Christianity are used as the base for European norms this must not only exclude Islamic influence but it creates problems over how far the idea of Europe can be extended eastward.[4] It also imposes a common identity on an inner core that does little justice to the variety of cultures that exist there.

Thirdly, the building of the European idea is based just as much on myth as the national idea. The 'imagined community' of nation is imagined through the symbolic fictions to which we are supposed to attach ourselves. This searching for a mythical past to support a mythical present is evident in the renewed intensity of racism, xenophobia and nationalism that are currently sweeping the different countries of Europe, but it is no less present in the language of Europe, despite the way that this is often set against the national. The European idea needs its symbolic fictions too. According to one early writer

> The peoples of Europe share humane principles which are not found in other parts of the world . . . Christian Europeans are as ancient Greeks used to be: they may go to war with each other, but despite these conflicts they do observe the proprieties . . . that a Frenchman and Englishman and a German when they meet, often seem as if they were born in the same town. (cited in Radice 1992: 123)

The subsequent evolution of Europe hardly justified this, but myth history continues to play a central role in the idea of Europe no less than the idea of nation. The reality, however, is better captured in the words of the historian Victor Kiernan. For Europe 'it was the contrast between itself and the outer world that enabled it most fully to recognise itself and what it had in common. It saw itself as Civilisation confronting Barbarism'. But 'no civilisation has ever been more deeply divided and self-contradictory: it invented democracy and fascism, parliament house and the gas chamber' (Kiernan 1980: 47).[5]

If 'Europe' is a fiction then we should not be surprised that the irritation of those who try to grasp hold of it often shows through. For the Czech President, Vaclav Havel, 'the Europe of today lacks an ethos, imagination, generosity, the ability to see beyond the horizon of its particular interests . . . [its leaders] . . . go from conference to conference with attaché cases brimming with papers that wrap base and unimaginative interests in noble and high sounding words' (*Guardian* 8 Jan 1994). The comment is a damning indictment of the narrow vision behind the western response to the transition in the former Soviet Bloc. But the premise is flawed. It was only because Havel fell for the illusion of 'Europe', an illusion he still seeks to evoke, that he was led to think it would be any other way. The rhetoric of 'Europe', no less than the rhetoric of 'nation', has always served to 'wrap base and unimaginative interests in noble, high sounding words'.

Just how base and unimaginative these ideas are is revealed in the way that the construction of the idea of Europe serves to exclude as much as include. The idea of Europe requires an idea of 'non-Europe', an idea of the 'other'. Here, too, the high-flown myths abound, focused, as they have always been, on the notional Orient. Now, however, the suspicion of the Orient is sharpened by fears of a more assertive 'Islam' standing not only at Europe's borders but also within as a result of past migration patterns. For the American Samuel Huntington there is even a clash of civilizations, a fault line running through Europe against Islam in the south east and an orthodox Christian civilization in the East (Huntington 1993, 1997).[6]

This is the voice of respectable racism, of nationalism writ large. It is the ideology of the 'imagined community' laying down boundaries across which goods and capital might flow but people may not, or at least the mass of people may not. It is here, in both the ideas and practice of immigration control, perpetuated both at the intergovernmental level and the level of the EU, that the new 'Europe' is being forged, just as much as in the debates and celebrations of internal unity. In Britain, in 1989 Mrs. Thatcher put it bluntly, 'we joined Europe to have free movement of goods . . . I did not join Europe to have free movement of terrorists, criminals, drugs, plant and animal diseases and illegal immigrants' (cited in King 1994: 18; see also King 1993: 183–99). This language is widely echoed by less extreme politicians and governments: 'organised crime and immigration present the biggest threats to national security' says a more recent joint declaration of Swiss and Czech governments. The link is clear: people moving and especially the wrong kind of people, can be spoken of in the same breath as crime, terror, drugs, diseases.

In an age in which neo-liberalism has been adopted even by the social democratic parties that dominate European politics at the end of the 1990s, there is a paradox in the argument for economic freedom. We are supposed to see the European Union as a union characterized by the free movement of goods and factors of production, a union that is a precursor to such free movement on a wider scale, but the free movement of labour into the European Union causes difficulties even for many of the most 'liberal' of the 'neo-liberals'. In trade, the World Trade Organization polices the free movement of goods. In investment there have been arguments for a Multilateral Agreement on Investment that would effectively give 'foreign' capital the same rights as 'national' capital, but where is the liberal argument for the free movement of labour on a global scale? Whereas the buyers and sellers of commodities use neo-liberal ideology to claim the *right* to move their goods on an international scale, and whereas the owners of capital now try to stake a claim to the *right* to move capital on economic grounds to seek the highest reward without hindrance, owners of labour power are threatened with exclusion if they play the role of 'economic migrant'. In these terms labour power is not a commodity like any other – it is inferior to the tin of beans, the machine, the dollar bill.

International human rights law also lacks a properly established right to migrate. What we have is a right to leave where states are condemned for their refusal to 'let their people go', but for many this is made meaningless by the refusal to create a corresponding right to arrive. Instead, arrival, especially in the advanced countries, is treated as a crime. 'It must now be assumed that every other immigrant in the First World is there illegally', said a confidential document of the Austrian Presidency of the European Union in 1998 which implicitly defended and tried to strengthen this idea of a 'crime of arrival' (Travis 1998).

Human beings have always been mobile, migrating from place to place. Indeed if, as is now widely accepted, humanity evolved in Africa, then we are all of us, British and Bulgarian, German or Turk, the children of immigrants. Much to the horror of the white European racist, at some stage in the far distant past all our ancestors arrived as members of that most despised of groups – the black African migrant (Stringer and McKie 1997). Modern genetics supports this view showing that there is no basis to the idea that biology divides us into different racial, ethnic or national groups. Despite past and present pseudoscientific attempts to arrange humans into different groups on the basis of skin colour, head shape, brain size, intelligence quotient, genetic code humans emerge as triumphantly similar to one another (Gould 1981).

Larger scale migrations have been an ever-present factor in human history. So, too, have local movements. One of the great myths is that it has only been in the last two centuries that people have moved on a large scale; before then they were born and died within the sound of the same church bells. Historical demography refutes this. When the first local populations of seventeenth-century Britain began to be reconstructed from the historical record by the Cambridge Group for the History of Population and Social Structure it was quickly established that pre-industrial society was far from stable. Most migration tended to be local but what was striking was its scale. Villages whose population could be reconstituted showed enormous change over very short periods of time: 'people were moving to and fro, society was changing, whole households were coming and going, and . . . villages were in perpetual exchange with their neighbours' (Laslett 1985: 75).

Three aspects of the movement of people have changed in the last two to three hundred years. Firstly, this movement has become tied in much more closely to the development of the economic system – reflecting the rhythms of the growth and spread of capitalism across the world. Just as capital and goods move in response to economic stimulus, so too do people. Secondly, the technological change that capitalism has created has made it easier to move – the transport revolution and communications revolutions link us ever more closely. Thirdly, capitalism has brought with it the development of a state-based political system in which states lay claim to the loyalty of their 'own' populations, dividing us one from another while they also develop the power to control our movements, sometimes directly encouraging or discouraging movements, at other times indirectly creating them as the offspring of their wars, or crises – internal and external.

Even so, the control of movement is still more recent. During almost all of the nineteenth century there were no significant controls on movement anywhere in the world. One result of this is that we can only guess at how many people did move. Within 'Europe' national censuses give us some ideas but no one has really calculated total intra-European movements. American data give us some idea of European migration to the United States and help to produce the famous figure of some 50 million. In Asia it used to be thought that fewer moved. Now we are not so sure. Kingsley Davies estimated that, for India alone, nearly 17 million left to work in the economies of the Indian and Pacific oceans (Davis, 1974). Movement was so easy that millions moved on a seasonal basis not only between countries within Europe but even across the Atlantic, like the late nineteenth-century migrant Italian agricultural labourers who would work the harvest in South America before returning to Italy to help bring it in there.

In a world where the fruits of labour went to the few even at this time there were always those who sought to victimize and deflect tension against the migrant but what is striking is how liberal movement was and how few problems existed. It even came to be seen as a mark of the respectability of a state that it did not reduce its people to the indignity of having passports and making detailed checks on their citizens – such were the barbaric practices of a Russia or an Ottoman Empire, not of a self-respecting modern state. In the final quarter of the nineteenth century a minor British priest, Arthur Cooper, made a name for himself by walking all over Europe. The difficulties he encountered make interesting reading today. Cooper advised travellers to take passports 'despite the announcement that passports have been abolished in this country or that', but the reasons he gave were not the ones that we might imagine. A passport was helpful, he said, if you wanted to collect money or letters from the local post-office; if you got into difficulties with the local mayor and if you wanted to get into the private art gallery of an Italian aristocrat. What he did not mention was immigration control because, of course, there was none. Later, before walking through France and across the Pyrenees to Spain, he worried again about the passport and asked if he needed to obtain a visa at the Spanish consulate in Liverpool, but 'the Spanish Consul assured me I should be safe from molestation wherever I went, and that a passport was as much out of date as a blunderbuss' (Cooper 1902: 44, 321).

This began to change at the end of the nineteenth century and controls on the movement of population that we take for granted today were consolidated during the First World War and developed in the bloody practice of the next decades Capitalism might encourage movement but the 'alien' now also made a useful scapegoat for its failures, the potential enemy within, the basis of policies of divide and rule. Today these ideas help to underpin a political practice that sees Europe in danger of being swamped by outsiders.

How then do we measure these outsiders? In a world of states and passports we are either 'nationals' of the country we are in or 'non nationals'. When we consider the number of immigrants in a country or for the EU as a whole, it is this non-national population that is measured. Tables 1.1 and 1.2 show the language of 'swarms', of 'tides' and 'floods' of migrants, asylum seekers, refugees hardly bears any relationship to the composition of the population of Europe.

EU non-nationals are considered good as true 'Europeans' have the right to live anywhere in the Union and to the extent that they use this right they show the unity of 'Europe'. What the statisticians then designate as other European non-nationals are less good and, implicitly, non-European nationals even less good (unless they come from other parts of the advanced world).

There is a difficulty. For those who see the immigrant as a problem it is hardly sufficient to measure immigration in this way for what we are

Table 1.1 Characteristics of the EU Population Percentage

	1988	*1992*	*1995*
Nationals	96.1	95.7	94.7
EC foreigners	1.5	1.4	1.5
Extra EC	2.5	2.9	3.8
of which 'European'	43	68	na
non 'European'	57	32	na

Eurostat 1993, 1994, 1995, 1996

Table 1.2 Extra-European Nationals as Percentage of Population

	1988	*1992*	*1995*
EC 12	2.5		
EU 15	2.9	3.8	
of which			
Turkey	24.4	23.5	na
Yugoslavia	8.6	10.7	na
Other Europe	11.1	13.0	na
North America	4.6	3.4	na
Algeria	10.3	6.0	na
Morocco	9.7	10.2	na
Tunisia	2.8	2.6	na
Other Africa	5.3	7.5	na
Other	24.2	23.1	na

Eurostat 1993, 1994, 1995, 1996

really measuring is citizenship.[7] The harder it is to gain citizenship (as it especially is in Germany, for example) the bigger the non-national population; the easier it is to gain citizenship, then potentially the smaller the non-national population. Indeed in these legalistic terms the 'immigration' problem could be eliminated tomorrow if everyone were automatically granted citizenship.

The argument is obviously not really about this. Even if you acquire formal citizenship rights you can still be marked out as an 'immigrant', several generations on, by colour, religion, culture or whatever, as the superficial differences between people are manipulated into 'problems'. Not every immigrant is so unfortunate and it is here that the insidious racism of the immigration argument is played out, affecting even those who disclaim any racist intent. The descendants of the Marseilles born

'North African', Zinedine Zidane, will remain a 'problem' in a way that those of a New Zealand migrant to Europe, Mr John Smith, will not. There is also a gender aspect. A Russian migrant, Miss Irina Spiridonova, can begin to 'disappear' when she marries Monsieur Frank Lebeouf and her children can 'disappear' more completely still if they are named Emannuel and Laurence.

What this means is that there is no way in which the 'immigrant community' can really be tracked over time. What we really measure when we attempt this is colour, religion or some other such marker or combination of markers of difference, which define some 'immigrants' and their descendants but not others.

There is no rational basis to this, no way in which, as liberals like to think, it is possible to create 'non-racist European immigration controls'. To think otherwise is to play a dangerous game that throws you into the hands of those who have different agendas. It is just because the argument for control is built upon an irrationality that it is so malleable; at one point in time the 'problem' is one group, at another point the burden falls on another unfortunate group. It is just because the argument is built on an irrationality that when a 'problem group' becomes scapegoated its boundaries remain so unclear. Karl Lueger, the anti-Semitic Mayor of late nineteenth-century Vienna, put this well when asked who were the Jews who were the subject of his attacks. He replied that it was *he* who decided who they were.

A particular responsibility today lies with three countries – Britain, France and Germany not only because of their size but also their position in the pattern of international migration. Any economic pull in the case of Britain and France is also affected by imperial traditions of migration from former colonies, whereas in the case of Germany it is affected by Germany's location and traditional links to Central and South Eastern Europe. In 1988, although non-community foreigners made up only 3.6 per cent of their population, these constituted 81 per cent of non-community foreigners in the then EC. Britain, France and Germany also attracted 74 per cent of community nationals living abroad but within the EU in that year. However the record of these states in resisting the rhetoric of immigration control before 1988 left much to be desired and in each of them governments crumbled in the next decade before the challenge of openness and fairness encouraging a spiral of racist controls on movement which was happily taken up by similarly unprincipled governments in other countries in the European Union (see Table 1.3).

In France this process has been called the Lepenisation of politics, reflecting the way in which the fascist Jean-Marie Le Pen has been allowed to set the political agenda. In 1991 Poniatowski, then Minister of the Interior, told *Le Figaro* that 'the immigrant population, principally North Africans and Blacks, had a high propensity to commit crimes' and that he would go farther than Le Pen in immigration control. Days later the more moderate Jacques Chirac, then Mayor of Paris, but the future President, infamously took up the worst kind of racist stereotyping to build support at a political meeting, telling it that he had sympathy with the working man of poor areas of Paris

> who sees his next door neighbour – a family where there's one father, three or four wives and twenty-odd kids, getting fifty thousand francs in social security payments without going to work; add to the noise and the smell and it drives the French worker crazy. It's not racist to say we can no longer afford to reunite families' (cited in Marcus 1995: 93).[8]

The arrival of a wave of social democratic governments in the late 1990s did little to change these arguments. At best their concerns were to introduce order into the disorder of the recent past in respect of asylum laws and that, too, they often felt, was not something that could be done openly. Instead the complicity with the arguments of the right often continued. In Britain one journalist reported that 'ever since the election [of the Labour Government], planted stories have appeared in [news]papers, designed to demonstrate that Labour is tough on immigration' (Travis 1998a). If the argument went beyond this it was to integrate existing 'immigrants' with a view to establishing a firmer and more consistent line against possible new immigrants from outside the European Union.

Yet across Europe 'immigrants' bring not only variety but ironically help to maintain the basis of what many imagine to be 'national' traditions and cultures. In German factories it is Turkish and Kurdish workers just as much as 'German' ones who help to create a quality of industrial production that has been the envy of much of the rest of the world. In many parts of Britain the 'native' diet of fish and chips is only possible because the local fish and chip shop is run by a second-generation 'immigrant' family. A celebratory meal, especially for those under fifty, is as likely to involve eating Italian, Chinese or Asian – anything other than 'English'. The 'British' Sunday morning is only relieved of its local tedium by small shops similarly run by 'immigrant' families in many parts of the country.

Immigrants also bring wealth. The detailed arguments have been recently rehearsed again by Nigel Harris (1996: 6). The peculiar thing is that it should be left for someone from the left to make this case rather than the neo-classical economists who boast of their support for the free market,[9]

Table 1.3 Government Encouragement of an Agenda of Anti-Immigrant Politics

What could happen	*What governments actually do*
1. Governments attack the real causes of insecurity	1. Governments claim to be unable to deal with unemployment, poor housing, low standard of living
2. Governments keep borders open and pressure each other against immigration control and for an 'open door' policy	2. Competitive immigration restriction in respect of: 1. work 2. asylum 3. refugees legitimizes hostility: 'You see even the government thinks that they're a problem'
3. Funds made available to deal with immediate crisis	3. Pressure on budget and cuts
4. Clear orders to police and other parts of state that racism will not be tolerated	4. Institutionalized racism, tolerance of overt racism
5. Mobilization of anti-racist sentiment	5. Mainstream politicians ignore issue, accommodate to racist agenda, make links with racist parties
6. Concrete slogans for specific problems	6. Political sloganeering around abstractions (e.g. 'the inviolability of human dignity' – Klaus Kinkel)

but this has always been a theoretical Achilles' heel of so many neo-classical economists. Nevertheless, it weakens their understanding of the dynamics of capitalism. In the last two decades we have been inundated with studies of the benefits of deregulated markets included national labour markets, but how few are the studies of the benefits of free movement in the international labour market! Yet although the dynamics of the slow-down in the world economy since the golden age of the 1950s and 1960s are complicated, one wonders if at least part of the explanation does not lie in the focus on the *deregulation* of the movement of goods and capital and the attempts to increasingly *regulate* the international movement of labour?

The possible economic contribution of migration, the contribution in terms of human variety, the possibility of building on these areas of integration, are continually undercut by the language and practice of immigration control, the paranoia over the illegal immigrant, refugee or asylum seeker. This process is built into the development of 'Europe' through the concern that its external boundaries should limit the flow of undesirable movement (Butt Phillip 1994). It is there in the practice that is developing under the so-called Schengen Treaty. Schengen allowed for free labour mobility within the European Union through the elimination of passport checks and other administrative barriers, 'a Europe without frontiers', but it is a Europe with a tightening external frontier to keep out 'illegal migrants'. Moreover, in order to assist in tracking down criminal and 'illegal' elements within Europe the Schengen system is built around police co-operation supported by an international computer system allowing checking at all points of entry. The Strasbourg data bank is said to contain files for 2 million with a capacity to grow to 10 million, and there is talk now of international co-operation in the monitoring of phone, fax and computer communications. To restrict movement across Europe's outer borders is not easy, especially in the south, but the pressure is growing supported by mythologies of 'false asylum seekers', 'economic migrants', 'fundamentalist terrorists' and other 'illegals' (Baldwin-Edwards 1997).[10] Just what this can mean in practice was horrifyingly revealed at the end of 1996 when a ship with several hundred illegal immigrants from India, Pakistan and Sri Lanka was apparently deliberately rammed and sunk on Christmas Day 1996 to general indifference in Europe. Possibly as many as 280 drowned. One of the few journalists to investigate the story expressed his feelings in terms of what he felt was the widespread indifference with which the story was treated:

> many died, but they were they wrong kind of dead. Europe does not want to know what is happening on its shores; it doesn't want to accept people are dying, daily, because of co-ordinated draconian immigration laws, many drawn up in the spirit of populism rather than humanity. The dead were acting illegally, and they were black. And no one cared. (*Observor* 12 January 1997; see also chapter 10 of this volume)

Since then the pressure for tighter controls in the Mediterranean has grown still further.

What has been developing both at the level of intergovernmental co-operation in Europe and within the institutions of the EU is a process that has been called 'eastwardization' and 'southernization'. It is not simply that the external borders have to be tightly patrolled but Europe is being built in layers with the demand that the outer layers protect the inner layers. The policy is to push the control of migration, asylum seekers and refugees outwards, to the periphery of the EU itself and then to 'non-European Europe', which is expected (and assisted to) carry the burden of immigration control.

Table 1.4 The Vicious Circle of Criminalization of the Migrant, Asylum Seeker and Refugee

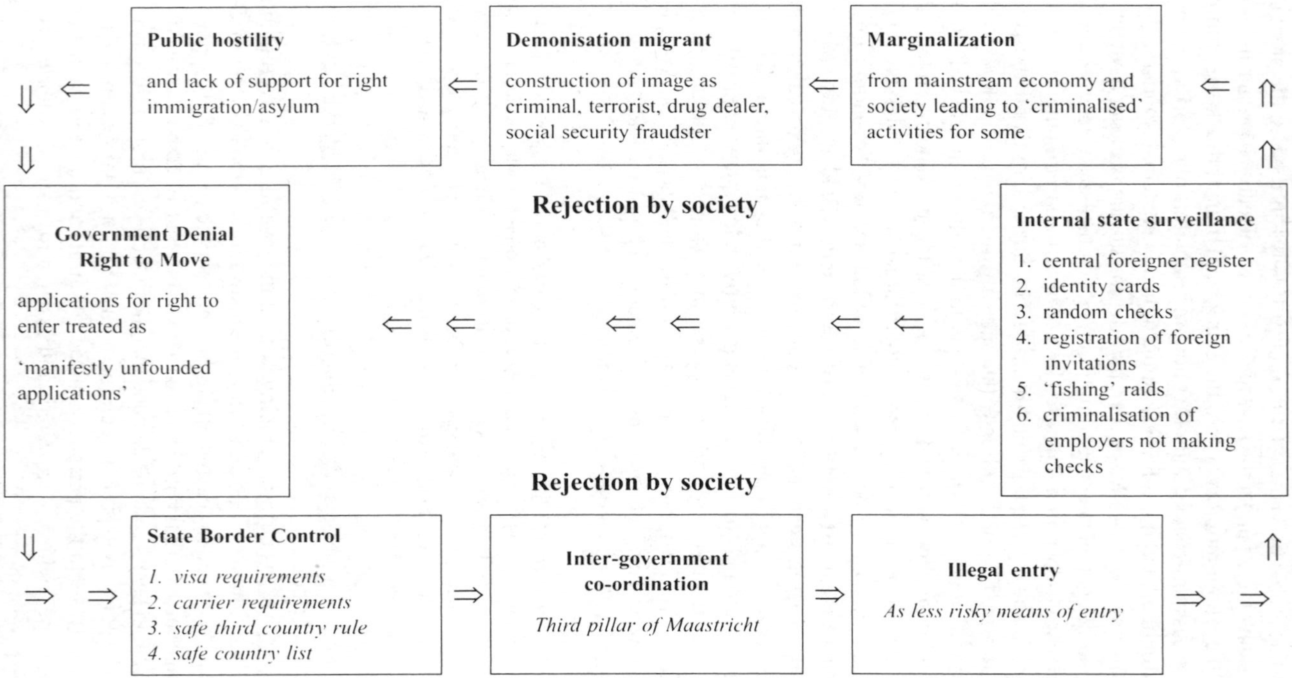

Whom are these barriers against? In the inner core the view is often that it is people from Africa and Asia, but they are set just as much against the Turk, the Bulgarian, the Romanian and the Russian or any other population that falls just outside the boundaries of where 'Europe' is said to lie. Indeed the so-called refugee or asylum crisis that evoked so much attention in Europe after 1989 was essentially a movement from the former Soviet bloc of people who in other circumstances might think of themselves as European. On one estimate of the 10 million made homeless by the disorder that followed the Soviet collapse, 4 million came to Western Europe (Travis 1998: 19). The barriers were raised not so much against 'the African' or 'the Asian', but against the former Yugoslav, the Bosnian refugee. However, they spread too. By 1991, entry to 'Europe' was subject to visa restrictions for 90 per cent of the world's population.

The Pushing Outwards of Immigration, Refugee and Asylum Control

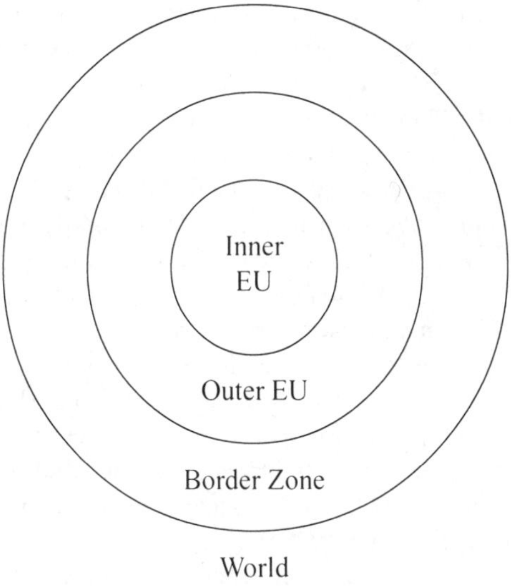

The European Commission has adopted the racist agenda of individual states arguing that external immigration control was a precondition for the internal integration of both EU migrants and existing non-EU nationals. European law is less protective of rights of illegal migrants than US law. In European law, as one commentator has put it, there is a tension between labour as a commodity and labour as a 'human being' – and a tendency to protect the former rather than the latter (Katrougalous 1995). The European Court of Human Rights, which many imagine restrains national governments, has a sorry record in defending immigrants or asylum seekers wherever they come from. Even the Eurostat statisticians happily collude with such offhanded phrases as 'the large number of foreigners in the European Union can be explained by . . .'. In what sense does the approximately 3% of non-EU nationals in the EU constitute a large number?

It must be recognized that this attempt to develop coherent structures has yet to be completely successful. This is partly because of clashing national visions, partly because of imprecision over objectives and partly because of the difficulties of rationalizing such policies. By looking only at the aspirations of these policies it is possible to derive a vision of a self-enclosed 'fortress Europe'. By looking only at the messy application on the other hand it is possible to see a still porous 'Europe' with much less precise boundaries than its leaders want. The truth is somewhere in between, which helps to further explain the irrational and frequently contradictory application of the detailed policies that flow from this.

The pressure, however, is towards a stronger system of control. Its importance in the progress of European union can be seen in the fact that the Council of Ministers adopted over seventy measures dealing with immigration and asylum matters in the years 1992–7 alone. The extent to which some are prepared to go was strikingly illustrated by the way in which the Austrian government used the first day of its Presidency of the European Union in 1998 to make a confidential proposal to revoke the right of asylum across the Union that is embodied in the 1951 Geneva Convention. Its strategy was to propose a more formal system of eastward and southwardization by creating concentric circles of Schengen states, non Schengen states effectively applying Schengen rules or even tighter restrictions, transit countries which were outside the union but had stopped migration from their populations and were now to seek to control movement across their borders more tightly and the outer circle of countries of emigration 'against which the whole range of migration policy measures need to be effective' (Travis 1998b).

However, the barriers quite deliberately do not exclude everyone. If you are part of the 'brain drain' then admission is possible for you. There is a crucial distinction here that is well made by Robert Miles:

> If a Fortress Europe is in the making, it is not only 'black' people who are to be shut out. If it is a fortress that is being constructed, it is intended to deny entry to almost all of those seeking a buyer for their semi and unskilled manual labour power, as well as those searching for sanctuary from civil conflict and

> state repression . . . there is a predominant class logic to the structure of exclusion, and racism is a secondary and contingent (although not unimportant) determinant. (Miles 1993)

This situation creates a special responsibility for intellectuals. Too often in the past, despite their pretensions to be civilized and humane, intellectuals in 'Europe' have nurtured the virus of nationalism, sung its songs, written its poems and so set the agenda that has caused so much grief. Even now not everyone recoils from these atavistic ideas of 'identity' although those that do not are rightly reviled for the way in which, harking back to the past, they offer a vision of the future that is no less destructive. For those of us who do recoil from this it is just as important that we do not run towards another fiction, become the writers of new songs and poems of identity, but that we see the world as it is, see humans as they are in their similarity. It should be our job to ruthlessly expose the absurdities, the irrationalities, the distortions and the simple lies behind these visions of difference, of insiders and outsiders.

The tide is not as heavily against us as we might imagine. For today, just as the global undercuts the 'nation', so it also undercuts the idea of the 'super-nation' and provides the basis for other identities and other potential polarizations and possibilities. How these elements will be capitalized on in the future is an open question. It would be foolish in a world that has seen a bonfire of certainties since 1989 to remain trapped in the view that politically the only choice is between 'Europe' or the nation state. It would be even more foolish to have this as an intellectual straight-jacket because this will not only prevent an exploration of other alternatives but it will debar us from an understanding of the forces that really determine the patterns of national, regional and global development and their contradictions. It will similarly prevent us understanding why the European Union will fail to uphold and deliver the humanist values of democracy, individual rights, ethnic pluralism and freedom not only beyond its borders but also within as it fails to confront the full extent of its own array of social inequalities. Two hundred years on we may look back with condescension on those words of Thomas Paine – 'my country is the world, my religion to do good', but there is also a magnificence in them that puts to shame the many greater minds that have taken a more divisive path.

Notes

1. Gibraltar is named after Jebl Tariq – Mount Tariq – itself named after Tariq Ibn Ziyad
2. This does not, of course, prevent a few remaining colonial territories, what have been called the 'confetti of empire', in places even farther distant from Brussels being represented in the EU.
3. Readers unfamiliar with this argument might consider the idea that Europe is a meaningful concept in physical geography, an idea that Helmut Kohl obviously finds attractive. Europe is no more than an appendage of Asia making up only one fifth of the land mass of Eurasia. Conventionally it is separated by a line that runs from the Black Sea to the Caspian and then turns north up the Ural River and through the Ural Mountains to the Arctic. But as one geographer puts it,

   > this utterly contrived border, which is still used by a surprising number of scholars, has no validity in either physical or human terms. It seeks out and elevates to a position of unwarranted importance an insignificant river and a low mountain ridge, the Urals, which is in no sense a barrier range or divider. It severs one of the most powerful nations in the world . . . The traditional eastern boundary of Europe is an unsatisfactory latter-day attempt to perpetuate the 2,500 year old idea of a Europe whose frontiers were physical in character. It has served to preserve the myth that Europe is a continent in the geographical sense. (Jordan 1973: 5–6)

4. Hoggart and Johnson in their account of (1987) *An Idea of Europe* conclude by arguing that 'the diversity of the *West* is its most striking characteristic: it is this which the French sociologist, Edgar Morin, has defined as the outstanding originality of *Europe*', pp. 149–50. The slippage in the argument is clear, Europe is the West.
5. The distinctions that need to be drawn were often more clearly recognized by outsiders. Consider the comment on the idea that Europe is a cultural expression of Christendom made by Charles Domingo, an African pastor in Nyasaland (Malawi) in 1911:

   > What is the difference between a white man and a black man. Are we not of the same blood and all from Adam? . . . There is too much failure among all Europeans in Nyasaland. The three combined bodies, Missionaries, Government, and Companies or gainers of money, do form the same rule to look upon the native with mockery eyes. (sic) If we had the power to communicate ourselves to Europe we would advise them not to call themselves Christendom but Europeandom. (In Davidson 1984: 209)

6. Huntington (1993, 1997). For Huntington, 'civilisations are the ultimate human tribes, and the clash of civilisations is tribal conflict on a global scale' and ' relations between groups from different civilisations . . . will be almost never close, usually cool, and often hostile'. The Gulf and Afghan Wars were 'civilisational wars'; multi-civilizational states disintegrate such as Russia and Bosnia. But what is a civilization? Huntington's list makes clear his own inability to decide between race, culture, religion since he includes (his labels) Sinic (Chinese), Western, Japanese, Hindu, Islamic, Latin American, Orthodox, African. He also recognizes a world élite culture – 'Davos culture'.
7. There are many additional problems in measuring migration. One crucial issue is the question of length of stay, which is used to separate out migrants from visitors and temporary workers. There are no rules here and the periods vary enormously between countries and so affect the overall data collected on a national and EU basis. We leave aside these intricacies here in favour of the central issue.
8. Chirac's argument involves the following assertions. That:
    1. It is the normal pattern for immigrants to have several wives.
    2. Immigrant families have 5–6 children per wife.
    3. Immigrants do not work.
    4. Immigrants make massive claims on social security – in this instance – £5,000 a week – some £200 per person!
    5. Immigrants are noisy.
    6. Immigrants smell.
    7. Hostility to immigrants is justified.
    8. Immigrants are a drain on society that cannot be afforded – especially with their large 'families'.
9. For a leading example of the contortions of a neo-classical economist trying to justify immigration restriction see Borjas (1994).
10. The Stateswatch organization in its publications and web-site monitors the underside of EU and national immigration controls. For an introduction to their work see Weber (nd 1996?).

Bibliography

Anderson, B. (1983) *Imagined Communities: Reflections on the Origin and Spread of Nationalism*, London: Verso

Baldwin-Edwards, M. (1997) 'The emerging European immigration regime: some reflections on implications for southern Europe', *Journal of Common Market Studies*, December 1997, vol. 35, (4): 497–519.

Borjas, G. (1994) 'The economics of immigration', *Journal of Economic Literature*, vol. 32, (4): 1667–1717.

Butt Philip, A. (1994), 'European Union immigration policy: phantom fantasy or fact?' *West European Politics*, 17 (2): 168–91.

Davidson, B. (1984) *The Story of Africa*, London: Beazley.

Callinicos, A. (1991) *The Revenge of History. Marxism and the East European Revolutions*, London: Polity Press.

Cooper, A. (1902) *The Tramps of 'The Walking Parson'*, London: The Walter Scott Publishing Co.

Davies, K. (1974), 'The migrations of human populations', *Scientific American*, 231 (3), 93–105.

Eurostat, (1993), 'Population by Citizenship', *Statistics in Focus: Population and Social Conditions*, no. 6.

Eurostat, (1994), 'Non Nationals Form Over Four Percent of Total Population in the EU' *Statistics in Focus: Population and Social Conditions*, no. 7.

Eurostat, (1995), 'Acquisition of Citizenship by Naturalisation in the European Union – 1993', *Statistics in Focus: Population and Social Conditions*, no. 11.

Eurostat, (1996), 'Non-nationals make up less than 5% of the population of the European Union on 1.1.1993', *Statistics in Focus: Population and Social Conditions*, no. 2.

Gellner, E. (1983), *Nations and Nationalism*, Oxford: Blackwell.

Gould, S.J. (1981), *The Mismeasure of Man*, Harmondsworth: Penguin.

Harris, N. (1990), *National Liberation*, Harmondsworth (Middlesex): Penguin.

Harris, N. (1996), *The New Untouchables. Immigration and the New World Order*, Harmondsworth: Penguin.

Hobsbawm, E.J. (1990), *Nations and Nationalism Since 1780*, Cambridge: Cambridge University Press.

Huntingdon, S.P. (1993), 'Clash of civilisations', *Foreign Affairs*, 72 (3), 22–49.

Huntingdon, S.P. (1997), *The Clash of Civilisations and the Remaking of the World Order*, New York: Simon & Schuster.

Jordan T. (1973), *The European Culture Area*, New York: Harper and Row.

Katrougalous G. (1995) 'The rights of foreigners and immigrants in Europe: Recent trends', *Web Journal of Current Legal Issues*, (5), http://www.ncl.ac.uk/~nlawwww/articles5/katart5.html

Kiernan, V. (1980), 'Europe in the Colonial Mirror', *History of European Ideas*, 1 (1), 39–66.
King, M. (1993), 'The impact of Western European border policies on the control of 'refugees' in Eastern and Central Europe', *New Community*, 19 (2): 183–99.
King M. (1994), *Fortress Europe. The Inclusion and Exclusion of Migrants, Asylum Seekers, Europe Refugees*. Centre for the Study of Public Order, University of Leicester, Occasional Paper No. 6.
Laslett, P. (1985), *The World We have Lost Further Explored*, London: Methuen.
Marcus, J. (1995), *The National Front and French Politics. The Resistible Rise of Jean-Marie Le Pen*, London, Macmillan.
Miles, R. (1991), *Racism After Race Relations*, London: Routledge.
Okey, R. (1992), 'Central Europe/Eastern Europe: behind the definitions', *Past and Present*, 137: 102–33.
Radice, G. (1992) *Offshore. Britain and the European Idea*, London: I.B.Tauris.
Rhein, E. (1996), 'Europe and the Mediterranean: a newly emerging geographical area?', *European Foreign Affairs Review*, 1 (1): 79–86.
Rée, J. (1992), 'Internationality', *Radical Philosophy*, 60: 3–11.
Said, E. (1978), *Orientalism*, London: Routledge.
Stringer, C. & McKie, R. (1997), *African Exodus*, London: Pimlico.
Tchoubarian, A. (1995), *The European Idea in the Nineteenth and Twentieth Centuries*, London: Cass.
Travis, A. (1998a), 'Playing the numbers game', *Guardian*, 12 May.
Travis, A. (1998b), 'Fortress Europe's four circles of purgatory', *Guardian*, 20 October.
Weber, F. (1996), *Crimes of Arrival: Immigrants and Asylum Seekers in the new Europe*, London: Stateswatch.
Woolf, S. (1969), *The Italian Risorgimento*, London: Longmans.

–2–

The European Union Role in the Formation, Legitimation and Implementation of Migration Policy

Jon Gubbay

> *Immigration, together with the separate but related subject of asylum, has continued to occupy an increasingly prominent place in the political agenda of the European Union and its Member States. It gives rise to public and parliamentary debate of growing intensity, and occasionally is the focus of acts of violence totally out of character with Europe's traditions and laws. There is increased recognition that the issues involved need to be tackled on a cooperative basis.* (CEC 1994, Foreward)

Notwithstanding its fatuous claims about European traditions of non-violence, the above statement by the EU Commission usefully serves to suggest a number of crucial questions. What, for the EU, are the 'subjects' of immigration and asylum? (Perhaps the 'subject' encompasses debate as to which people should be excluded and the means to achieve this). What do the member states and the EU do in defining the terms of debate? In attempting to respond to these questions, this chapter argues that the politics of inclusion and exclusion are deeply rooted in the ideology and practices of a world of capitalist states, that the tortuous development of EU immigration policy has been driven largely by economic factors but has generated predicaments and controversies around the development of EU citizenship that cannot then be avoided and, finally, that the EU has lent legitimacy to practices of excluding refugees that are incompatible with the humanitarian principles it formally espouses.

Free Movement, Territoriality, Citizenship and Nationality

In order to appreciate the fundamental sources of conflict over migration control around the project of the European Union it is necessary to recapitulate briefly some basic elements of the historically constituted practices and ideologies of territoriality, citizenship, residence and nationality. The argument is presented here in terms of the logic of capital accumulation rather than being historically specific, but it is then acknowledged that the relationship between these practices and ideologies are highly problematic.

Capitalism sundered the bonds between landlord and peasant that, in an agrarian society, were necessarily also ties across generations to particular localities. Freedom from bondage was also freedom to move, for the propertyless to sell their labour power within a wider spacial market. This freedom, however, was just one side of the class relations of capitalist society for it was also capitalists' freedom to employ, or not employ, whoever they wished. They could recruit workers from near or far and lay them off when it was no longer profitable – and set workers in mutual competition over pay and conditions. Given the spaciality of production of goods, services and transport, as firms and whole industries grew or declined and changed their relative demands for specific forms of labour, workers were attracted and repelled from one location to another to conform to the geographical aspects of capital accumulation. The synergies of industrial concentration sucked in potential workers from the countryside and from areas brought into the compass of capitalism as underdeveloping regions. In a world increasingly interconnected by modern forms of communication and travel, very many people can imagine themselves travelling to faraway places – and perhaps make a reality of it, especially in great surges following economic collapse, persecution, war or civil war. These processes correspondingly transform the built environment of transport, towns and country. Ports and shipping, canals, roads, rail and air transport successively develop – and sometimes fall into disuse – thus constituting ever-changing pathways along which people move, thereby building some settlements while depopulating others.

However, capitalist economic development is inseparable from the development of territorialized capitalist states – that is military, legal and administrative machines both regulating and representing the interests of capitals based upon their territory. Through their interaction – whether in warfare, diplomacy or colonial expansion – capitalist states carve the world territorially into countries, federations and empires. Between them, the states also carve the populations of the world, each person in principle being the subject of a single state, possessing the privilege of citizenship and the right to freedom of movement within its territory, in particular in order to sell his or her labour power within the corresponding labour market.[1] Subjects possess certain civil, political and social rights and are obliged to pay taxes to the state and be loyal to it, especially in relation to other states. (Dual citizenship is usually refused by states or only allowed in exceptional cases. Being the agent of a foreign power is a cardinal crime.) Within each country there is a single currency and free movement of capital and commodities. In practice, however, the fourfold divisions of territory, population, polity and economy have not corresponded to one another in such a simple fashion.

First, economies cannot be bounded within the territories of states. Quite the contrary. Driven by mutual competition and class conflict, capitalists are propelled all over the globe in search of cheap raw materials and labour. Capital and goods flow across borders and labour is employed by foreign capital, perhaps to produce goods for sale in yet other countries. In their outward drive, capitalists often obtain the support of their state – for example in diplomatic pressures to remove barriers to trade and movement of capital, military conquest and sponsorship of colonial settlement. (Imperial states may extend their patches whether in the form of client states, imperial possessions or imposed unification. In the latter two cases, they typically establish forms of reduced citizenship among the residents of those territories.) States cannot escape the globalizing dynamic but, within limits, they control its impact upon their territory – for example, by use of import controls, regulation of internal markets and the establishment of currency and/or trading blocs.

Second, populations cannot be neatly divided up between different states and their corresponding territories. Precisely because of the uneven and constantly changing geographical development of capitalism on a world scale, the forces pushing and pulling labour from one location to another operate across the territorial boundaries of states. Thus, there are citizens of one state who are resident, more or less securely and for shorter or longer duration, in the territory of another. Resident aliens typically pay tax in their country of residence but may enjoy relatively restricted civil, political and social rights. Marriages are contracted between citizens of different states and children born to parents of different citizenship or while residing in a country of which they are not citizens. In all these ways, as Leitner rightly argues, 'International migration poses a fundamental challenge to the division of the world into nation-states, which assume territorial, political and cultural boundedness' (1995: 261). States struggle to control these intractable realities by routinely checking on the status of individuals and by laying down rules and procedures regulating work permits, residence and naturalization.

Third, the geographic boundaries of countries shift, whether through the outcomes of war, establishment or dissolution of empires, federalizing of states or the collapse of federations. These processes create new states and destroy old ones, thus leaving many thousands of people in territories of which they are not citizens or abruptly changing or denying their citizenship. Typically, the break-up of countries generates economic disorganization and stimulates conflicts of a national or ethnic character, which then promote migratory movements. (The collapse of the Soviet Bloc and the break-up of Yugoslavia are obvious recent examples.)

This leads to the fourth point that, within many countries, populations are fragmented into groups that imagine themselves, or are treated by others, as constituting distinctive peoples, whether marked by language, religion or any other real or assumed common culture or beliefs. Such imagined communities are nations in so far as their cultural distinctiveness forms a basis for social movements demanding their own nation states. Nation states, including those formed or descended from nationalist social movements, typically adopt symbols and policies that identify citizenship with nationality, thereby promoting the idea that all subjects of the state are a single people with a common history and destiny. This is an extremely important element in the social control system of capitalist society. In multi-national states and states where there are national minorities or ethnic groups possessing a distinctive culture, the integrity of the state may be chronically challenged (for example, Basque and Catalan nationalism, Irish republicanism in Northern Ireland), continuously bargained (Walloons and Flemings in Belgium) or secured by inclusion (Polish post-war settlement in Britain) or exclusion (Roma in most European countries and confinement of Turks to 'dirty jobs' in Germany).[2] As we shall see, corresponding dilemmas of inclusion and exclusion pervade migration policy in Europe.

In conclusion, capitalist dynamics generate threefold geographic, demographic and political divisions, often supported by national identities sustained within nation states – but the global economy threatens the coherence and inter-connectedness of these divisions. In particular, the contentious and uncertain trajectory of the federalizing project of the European Union generates acute tensions around migration control and naturalization policies.

The Politics of Inclusion and Exclusion

The legitimating function of citizenship as a privilege for which its possessors should feel gratitude and pride depends in part upon the disprivileging of non-citizens and, indeed, the further buttress of finely graded rights conferred on non-citizens. Among those living in a territory there are typically a range of statuses possessing less political, civil and social rights than citizens. These include non-citizens with indefinite permission to stay, those with temporary and conditional permission to stay, and those staying without legal sanction and awaiting a decision as to whether they can stay. Those seeking to stay or staying without permission have minimal rights whereas the rights of, and conditions applied to, other non-citizens tend to vary in proportion with the period of stay, although they remain less than those of citizens. For some non-citizens, such as holiday makers, absence of such rights is not at all onerous – but it certainly is for those who wish to be employed, to be joined by family members, to be securely settled and who wish to be able to travel. Furthermore, privileges of citizenship – and the lesser rights associated with permission to stay – could not be sustained as valuable were they available just for the asking. The logic of these various statuses constituting a hierarchy of privileges is that they are progressively less easily or quickly attainable and that applicants must prove that they are worthy.

The development of the EU has compounded the complexities of these divisions because non-citizens of a particular member state possess quite different rights according to whether or not they are citizens of other member states. In particular, one of the key privileges of being a citizen is the right to enter and re-enter his or her own country but this is now a right for all citizens of member states with regard to all EU countries. Precisely because the EU is a federalizing project that is deeply contentious among and within the member states, the practical definition of citizenship and residence rights is fraught between the member states and a constant irritant to their relations with one another. As Leitner remarks, 'Debates over immigration generally start with the premise that every state has the right to control the admission of foreigners. This is seen as essential to a nation-state's sovereignty, territorial and cultural integrity' (1995: 261). With regard to naturalization, Handoll notes the determination of member states to maintain autonomous control of access to their citizenship. 'To transfer this power to the Community would, perhaps more than the transfer of any other power, sound the death-knell of the Member State *qua* independent State' (1994: 283). These views are rationalized in all sorts of irrational and racially stereotyping ways – that foreigners tend to undermine national culture, threaten security, promote crime, take scarce jobs and housing, draw on social benefits for which they do not contribute and, potentially, constitute a peaceful invasion, threatening national culture.

The recruitment of unskilled labour on short-term contracts from poorer countries is potentially a source of two kinds of benefit to capitalists in the advanced countries. First, migrant workers may be induced to work long hours in poor conditions for low wages, perhaps in order to send remittances to their families or save quickly in order to return home with relative wealth. Their precarious contracts reinforce their work discipline, again to the advantage of their employers. Second, at the level of the state, due to the age composition of migrant workers and the state's capacity to deport them if they lose their jobs or fall ill, they drain relatively less from total profits for social protection than residents generally. A further possible advantage, though this may not be consciously intended, is that the focus of native workers' discontent may be diverted away from capital towards the migrants. However, the balance of costs and benefits varies from capital to capital and generally declines when there is a high level of unemployment, reduced relative demand for unskilled labour, when migrants acquire the capacity to organize themselves in support of improved wages and conditions, or when they gain rights to settle (and thus draw social benefits). Moreover, a divided working class generates costs as well as benefits, for example in terms of policing public order and in providing a base for parties and pressure groups whose nationalist extremism is a real threat to increasingly internationally oriented capital.

Admission solely for the purposes of unskilled labour is, in principle, governed by an exclusionary rationale – minimal social and civic rights, hostel accommodation, denial of admission of dependents, deportation following on from loss of employment and admission only for the period of short-term contracts. A quite different logic operates where the aim is to generate long-term commitment and the acquisition of skills – extensive social and civic rights, family migration, resettlement assistance in normal housing and progressive stages towards naturalization. However, there is typically a dynamism about migration processes in which the purposes of both migrants and those who recruit them change over time. Many of those who came initially as guest workers in the 1950s and 1960s were able to renew their contracts successively (employers often wishing to avoid the costs of labour turnover), to be joined by family members (perhaps illegally) or to start families and become socially integrated (including joining trade unions). In short, they are not necessarily passive victims of state-sponsored social exclusion.

There are also much more socially privileged migrants, often actively recruited, who face minimal obstacles to residence and who are protected against consequences of illness or other misfortune by their own resources or insurance (Harris, this volume, Chapter 11). They include those who arrive with very substantial capital on which to live or that they can invest, expert and managerial employees of multi-national corporations where geographical movement is a characteristic feature of career paths and specialist professionals or experts hired on a contract basis.

Divisions within the working class are generated in Europe to a significant extent through its migration regimes. The interaction of immigration rules and procedures of the EU and the member states has produced an extremely complex structure of differential access to rights in seven principal dimensions – residence (indefinite, conditional, limited), employment and self-employment, welfare (for example, education, contributory and non-contributory benefits), political participation (voting, for instance), naturalization, travel within the EU[3] and whether family members can join a migrant. To compound this complexity, the rights of family members of a migrant are often less than those of the migrants themselves. (The spouse and children of a migrant may lose some of these rights, even the right of residence, with the breakdown of marriage.) Immigrant status can be ranked according to the extent of these rights, as embodied in EU rules, in the following order:

- those who are treated by their host state not as immigrants but as returnees because they already possess the citizenship of that state or it is conferred upon them automatically;[4]
- citizens of another EU state;
- those family members of EU citizens who are entitled to residence in the country where the EU citizen is legally resident;
- other legally resident third-country citizens (apart from those mentioned below);
- third country citizens who have been given leave to stay on Geneva Convention refugee grounds;
- third-country citizens who have been given leave to stay on humanitarian grounds, typically for a limited period and/or subject to specific conditions;
- asylum seekers pending a decision on their application;
- clandestine immigrants.

Differential access to rights according to migrant status tends to induce those who are least privileged to accommodate to their subordination, both because resistance appears impossible and because of the hope that compliance might earn them increased rights. However, they are forced to live in poor housing and become socially segregated, accept low pay and poor conditions or even resort to charity (or worse) – and, as such, they become prime targets for police harassment and xenophobia. The most comprehensive target of disprivileging is focused upon clandestine immigrants and supposedly bogus asylum seekers – stereotyped as driven by pursuit of personal gain, deceitful, mendacious and unable or unwilling to integrate. As will be argued below, the EU has contributed significantly to the construction of this hierarchy of migrant status and the corresponding demonization of those at the bottom of it – and thereby fostered the circumstances in which policing and information systems threatening civil liberties could be justified. Accordingly, it is utterly vain for commissioners, ministers and parliamentarians of the EU to weep crocodile tears over this outcome for it is, in part, the product of rules and practices they have themselves promoted.

Rules and Institutions

The impetus for the foundation of what was subsequently to become the EU lay in the threat that wartime destruction and the fragmentation of European capital endangered long-term international competitiveness, especially vis-à-vis the US. The central elements of the Treaty of Rome, which established the European Economic Community (EEC) in 1958, were common external tariffs and, internally, removal of barriers to trade and the movement of labour, capital and services. 'The internal market shall comprise an area without internal frontiers in which the free movement of goods, persons, services and capital is ensured in accordance with the provisions of this Treaty' (Article 8a). A recent high-level panel set up by the Commission was quite insistent on this point:

> It must not be forgotten that the free movement of persons was conceived of originally as primarily an economic phenomenon. It was the mobility of human resources as a factor of production which inspired the chapters of the EEC relating to free movement of workers, freedom of establishment and, to a certain extent, the freedom to supply certain services. (Veil 1997: 5)

The purposes of the EEC, despite the occasional high-flown rhetoric about the traditions and destiny of European civilization, were the promotion of international competitiveness and, on that basis, binding European states into an economic order that could contain their conflicting nationalisms.

Although different parties and supporters of the project had varied views as to where it might and should lead, all debate has been cast entirely within capitalist terms. On the economic side, the breadth of disagreement has been no wider than that between free marketeers and latter-day Keynesians.[5] On the political side, there is continuous controversy over the practicability, desirability and pace of federalizing processes, especially in those areas viewed as central to state sovereignty – law and order, citizenship, territoriality, defence and foreign affairs. Accordingly, the federalizing momentum has often been halted, reversed or patched up in messy compromises.[6] These controversies have also been reflected in the positions taken by the different institutions of the EU. The Commission has generally been the most pro-federal component, while adjusting its initiatives to what is likely to be acceptable to the Council. The European Parliament, by proclaiming its democratic credentials, has sought to increase its areas of intervention and urged that matters currently dealt with on an intergovernmental basis be brought into its purview. It has been sharply critical of the secrecy of intergovernmental decision making, including on migration control. The Council reflects the intractable diversity of the member states and, consequently, issues perceived to impact upon sovereignty have been reserved for intergovernmental fora where there are no provisions for majority voting. Accordingly, such treaties, conventions and resolutions as are adopted in these fields are typically advisory or qualified by opt-outs and derogations.

The right to free movement of labour and the prohibition of discrimination on grounds of nationality were written into the Treaty of Rome as fundamental to the project of constructing a common market. However, the existence of a legal prohibition does not mean that people actually abide by it and it is one thing to have a right and quite another to be able to exercise it! The Single European Act, signed in Luxemburg in 1986, did little more than reiterate the free movement commitments but they were made more effective by the Treaty on European Political and Monetary Union signed in Maastricht in 1991 and further reinforced by the 1997 Treaty of Amsterdam.

There had long been intergovernmental fora concerned with migration control. Since the mid-1970s the Trevi Group[7] had been bringing together meetings of officials and ministers of justice and home affairs for the development of common policies and measures of practical cooperation in respect of immigration, terrorism and crimes such as fraud, money laundering, drug trafficking and trade in pornography, armaments and strategic goods (Church and Phinnemore 1994: 388–9).[8] Other specialist groups have been created to complement the work of Trevi with regard to the forms of crime mentioned above, and in 1986 a meeting of interior and justice ministers established the Ad Hoc Group on Immigration. Subsequent developments have included six-monthly meetings of immigration ministers, monthly meetings of senior officials as the Coordinators on Free Movement Group and a host of working parties and specialist committees of the Ad Hoc Group (Bunyan and Webber 1995: 4–6).

Maastricht enhanced the institutional structure and mechanisms of the EEC, renaming it simply as the European Community (EC), and grafted onto it foreign and security policy (second pillar) and justice and home affairs (third pillar) – all of this constituting the European Union (EU).

Codifying previous practice, policy making in the two pillars supplementing the EC was to take place mainly through intergovernmental mechanisms. These groups and their sub-groups continued to operate on an intergovernmental basis (Bunyan and Webber 1995: 5–6). The Commission, Council and the European Parliament have only marginal powers within the second and third pillars (Hix and Niessen 1996: 20–4). The European Court of Justice has limited jurisdiction and it is very difficult to reach binding decisions in intergovernmental fora, let alone enforce them.[9] Morris neatly summarizes the Commission's view that 'there is disagreement between member states as to the nature and effects of joint actions and common positions . . . the adoption of conventions is slow and cumbersome . . . and the requirement of unanimity is a source of paralysis, preventing any outcome or reducing it to the lowest common denominator'(Morris 1997b: 202). With regard to the third pillar, the six monthly ministerial meetings were institutionalized as the Council of Justice and Home Affairs Ministers. The Ad Hoc Group was abolished and the Coordinators Group renamed K4, with Commission representation. The Maastricht Council set in train and encouraged initiatives over a wide-ranging programme for harmonizing immigration and asylum policies. This included resolutions and conventions on 'manifestly unfounded' asylum applications, family reunion and expulsion of clandestine immigrants. Article K.1 of the Maastricht Treaty states that asylum policy, controls on the crossing of external borders and policy regarding nationals of third countries are to be regarded as 'matters of common interest'.[10] As a modest first step in the direction of common action, Article 100c brought policy on visa requirements into the EC framework: 'The Council, acting unanimously on a proposal from the Commission and after consulting the European Parliament, shall determine the third countries whose nationals must be in possession of a visa when crossing external borders of the Member States.'

The Commission, with the Parliament's encouragement, evidently wished to bring items of greater substance from the third pillar into the EC but backed away from advocating it, knowing this to be unacceptable to the Council, notably to the German and UK governments. However, recognition of common interests did pose the possibility of eventual incorporation of these matters into the EC mechanisms. The Treaty of Amsterdam appears to bring this prospect nearer by setting a five-year timetable for this to happen, but exemptions for the UK, Ireland and Denmark and the reaffirmation of the principle of subsidiarity are indications that this target could be pushed yet further into the future.

Free Movement and European Citizenship

The Treaty of Rome set out to establish free movement of labour but Maastricht has significantly extended the objective to free movement of persons. That is, the aim is to give citizens of EU states the right to reside anywhere within the EU, even if they are not moving for reasons of employment. In fact, they are quite often unable to exercise that right due to administrative obstacles++++, notoriously so in the case of Roma (Morris 1997b: 199). As yet, there are significant restrictions on stays beyond three months. European Union citizens can normally gain a residence permit if they satisfy the authorities of the host country that they possess adequate resources and insurance – or are self-employed or are employed (or seeking employment or retired after being in employment in the host country). They may be excluded from areas of public sector employment in the host country and face discrimination with regard to their qualifications, though the EU has made modest progress in promoting mutual recognition. The social security systems of the member states are very diverse but the EU, while not attempting to harmonize them, has sought (through Regulation 1408/71) to coordinate them sufficiently to facilitate free movement of labour among EU citizens, for example by the provision of urgent medical treatment and unemployment benefit for up to three months while seeking work (Faist 1995: 184–7; Veil 1997: ch III). (Note, however, that in the UK unemployment benefit is denied to so-called benefit tourists.) Retired and non-active persons are not covered by Regulation 1408/71 and, indeed, there are no entitlements to non-contributory benefits.

Article 8 of the Maastricht Treaty grandly states, 'Citizenship of the Union is hereby established. Every person holding the nationality of a Member State shall be a citizen of the Union.' The Treaty also stipulates certain political rights – to vote and stand as a candidate in municipal and European Parliament elections and rights of petition to the Parliament and Ombudsman. However, as Martiniello points out, EU citizenship is derivative of citizenship of a particular state.

> The main precondition for recognition as a citizen of the Union is citizenship of a member state . . . In its present shape, European citizenship is thus a sort of complementary supra-citizenship which confirms the existence of the twelve cultural and political entities corresponding to the twelve member states of the European Union. (1995: 41)

Indeed, one of the declarations annexed to the Maastricht Treaty rules out the possibility of appealing to EU law in claiming citizenship of a member state by affirming that 'whether an individual possesses the nationality of a Member State shall be settled solely by reference to the national law of the Member State concerned' (Church and Phinnemore 1994: 432). It is thus a dubious projection of an uncertain trajectory to argue, as does Soysal, that migrants are acquiring rights and protection irrespective of their citizenship (1996: 20–1). In itself, little was created in terms of new rights of EU citizenship; rather, existing ones were packaged up for public presentation (Church and Phinnemore 1994: 76–9). However, it did serve to highlight issues of free movement and set off a new dynamic of debate and proposals for change. The citizenship articles were indeed reaffirmed in the Treaty of Amsterdam, but with the qualifying proviso that, 'Citizenship of the Union shall complement and not replace national citizenship.'[11]

Those who are not EU citizens have lesser rights with regard to travel, work and establishment. The extent to which they should be accorded such rights has been hotly disputed between states precisely because of the fundamental contradiction between individual states seeking autonomy in determining their immigration policies and yet needing collaboration to make controls effective.

The first Schengen agreement for the Gradual Abolition of Border Controls at the Common Frontiers was established in 1985, following a Franco-German initiative the previous year, between the governments of Belgium, Holland, Luxemburg, France and Germany. In fact, because of their fears about the effectiveness of border controls, implementation only began with the Second Schengen Convention in 1990, again between the same five countries. Italy, Spain, Portugal and Greece joined subsequently, delayed by reluctance to admit countries perceived as having permeable external borders; currently the only EU countries remaining outside it are the UK and Ireland. In view of the long-established Nordic passport union, non-EU Norway and Iceland have negotiated associate Schengen membership. Schengen has consistently operated at a very low level of public accountability (Curtin and Meijers 1995: 403–16).

By articles 21 and 22 of the Schengen Convention, a legally resident third-country citizen has free movement to another Schengen country for up to three months subject to certain conditions, including reporting to the appropriate authorities within three days (Hoogenboom 1992: 51).[12] This is less than the rights of free movement accorded to citizens of EU states and it justifies enforcement procedures, such as requirements to complete registration forms when staying in hotels. It also justifies police checks on whether people are EU or third-country citizens and, if the latter, whether they have reported within three days and whether they have been resident for less than three months. Once there is a responsibility for police to check on residence status, they possess grounds for targeting particular areas of residence and workplaces – and perhaps people whose appearance is foreign. The Economic and Social Committee has astutely pointed out the implications.

> As such checks could not be carried out according to objective methods, they would inevitably focus on people whose appearance suggested that they might not be nationals. In practice, this provision would smack unpleasantly of racial discrimination, at the expense of ethnic-minority EU citizens or even of those whose physical appearance differs from that of the majority of the population. (Economic and Social Committee 1996: para 7.1.4)

In its advocacy of granting third country citizens lawfully in a EU country the right to travel throughout the EU, the Economic and Social Committee argues that, 'there is the general principal of the right to travel. This is a universal human right' (Economic and Social Committee 1996: para 2.3.1). This comment unwittingly exposes the extraordinary contradiction that appeal is made to universal rights when they only apply within the EU (while restrictions on admission to the EU have been progressively tightened). The Schengen initiative has been well understood from its inception as the pacemaker for EU implementation of the freedom of movement. In effect, the aims of the Schengen Agreement are incorporated in the Amsterdam Treaty. The Treaty states the intention that, within five years, controls will be removed on both EU and non-EU citizens when crossing internal borders.

As it is difficult to enforce the conditions on movement of third-country citizens between Schengen countries, the mutual concern of those countries for restriction has prompted moves for common conditions for entry across external borders. This has not yet been achieved with regard to long-stay visits but the Schengen Convention does lay down common rules for crossing external borders for visits of less than three months. Third country citizens must possess appropriate travel documents – proof of capacity to support oneself, evidence of the purpose of the visit and, depending on the country of origin, a visa (Thiery 1997: 6–7). There is a confidential list of some 130 countries for which any member state must require third-country citizens to produce a visa as a condition of them entering by an external border (Thiery 1997: 12–13).[13] Third-country citizens seeking admission must also be rejected at the external border if any member state considers them unsuitable, for example as representing a threat to national security. This point implies the creation of an electronic database of unacceptable visitors, the Schengen Information System (developed more widely by the EC as the European Information System). Like earlier treaties, Amsterdam links immigration to terrorism and crime, now promising 'a qualitative change' in the scope and effectiveness of judicial and police cooperation, including strengthening the European Police Office, Europol (EU 1997).

Asylum Seekers and Clandestine Immigrants

The Commission and its staff are insulated from direct association with the hurly burly of party and pressure group activities and their very roles commit them to an understanding of themselves as transcending national loyalties. Accordingly, it is to be expected that their pronouncements on social conflict should be critical of what they see as chauvinistic prejudice: 'The Community has always been a multi-cultural and multi-ethnic entity whose diversity enriches the Community itself and benefits all its citizens' (Commission of the European Communities 1994: 1e). They claim that 'Western Europe has a well-established and solidly anchored tradition of respect for human values and social justice' (CEC 1994: 4)[14] but that there is an increasing problem for governments who 'must retain their credibility with moderate people' because there are 'people who are genuinely concerned by the perception that large numbers of people are immigrating to Europe in a situation where anti-democratic elements have sought to exploit the immigration issue' (CEC 1994: 4). Despite its urbane tone, this comes close to arguing that governments, and presumably the EU itself, should accommodate to xenophobia by controlling immigration and publicizing that fact in order to assuage fears of immigrants. Quite how governments are to follow the Commission's recommendation to put 'more energetic emphasis on the benefits of immigration' while also proclaiming how tightly they are controlling it is something of a puzzle! The hoary argument is rehearsed that, 'an indispensable condition for successful integration policies with respect to third country nationals resident in the Union is control of migration flows' (CEC 1994: 11). In fact, quite the reverse is true; a policy of control endorses the notion that immigrants are a problem, and thereby provides the grounds for racialist harassment and calls for their repatriation.

The Commission acknowledges that a halt to legal immigration from outside the EU 'is neither feasible nor desirable' (CEC 1994: 1e). Although governments often proclaim that they theirs is not a country of immigration, the reality is not, and is never likely to be, 'fortress Europe'. As already argued, there will be continuing demands, both from within and outside the EU, for third-country citizens to be admitted for reasons of study, business and employment within multi-national firms – and also as short term guest workers. A further flow is generated where spouses and other family members come to join those who are already resident, whether or not they are EU citizens; the principle of permitting family reunification, though often harshly implemented, is grounded in both pragmatic considerations of social integration and wider ideological commitments to 'the family'. Asylum seekers' cases have to be addressed individually – a principle often honoured in the breach, as noted below – both because member states are signatories to the Geneva Convention and because of the self-definition of Europe as committed to 'respect for human values and social justice'. Finally, as new countries in Central and Eastern Europe are admitted to the EU, old barriers will fall and people who are now prevented from migrating westwards will be able to do so freely. However, new barriers are already going up in the aspirant member states, particularly as a result of German and Austrian pressure. Thus relaxation of customs controls on the border between Poland and Germany is matched by tightening Poland's controls on the borders with Russia and Belarus. According to a *Guardian* report, 'the EU single market commissioner, Mario Monti, told Poland that its chances of joining the EU partly depended on how well it could police its border' (9 February 1998: 10). For just these sorts of reason, Slovenia is increasing its controls with regard to Croatia and the Czech Republic its control vis-à-vis Slovakia.

The Commission has urged member states to adopt 'fair' asylum procedures, but not just because of international conventions on refugees. Rather more cynically, fairness is required because the perception by potential asylum seekers that procedures are arbitrary and restrictive induces them to resort to illegal immigration. The difficulties and costs of apprehending illegal immigrants, it is argued, outweigh the costs of providing adequate hearings for asylum applications (CEC 1994: para 24).

Over the last decade there have been increasingly coordinated measures to forestall, deter and reject applications for asylum. Measures piloted in one country have been copied by others. These included requirements to obtain a visa before travel, carrier liability for passengers without proper travel documents,[15] virtually automatic rejection of applications from those coming from supposedly safe countries and those who do not apply promptly on arrival, withdrawal of social protection while applications are being considered, and even incarceration. Most EU states now have provision for fast-track expulsion without substantive investigation of applications (Santel 1995: 83). The 1990 Dublin Convention stipulates the state responsible for processing asylum applications and the 1992 London Convention agreed common criteria for 'manifestly unfounded' asylum applications.

The Dublin Convention,[16] signed by all the then twelve EU states, adopts the principle of exclusive competence in processing asylum applications, that the 'most responsible state', and only that state, should deal with an asylum application (although it may do so according to rules and procedures peculiar to that state).[17] The Convention is intended to prevent member states shuffling off their obligations to others and, overall, to save on the trouble and expense of processing applications as they share out this job between them while disallowing asylum seekers from shopping around with multiple applications. Concerns about asylum seekers making multiple applications in different EU countries – and thus prolonging their temporary stay in the EU – are addressed by requiring that, when an applicant has been rejected by one EU state, it should prevent them moving to neighbouring EU states and, failing that, other states can automatically expel the person to the country that originally considered the case (Santel 1995: 88). The spectacle of desperate people begging repeatedly for haven risks putting those who turn them away in a poor light, so what better than conspiring to prevent such a circumstance arising! Justification of this exclusionary practice is reinforced insofar as asylum seekers are painted as bogus, a charge which they can only hope to escape by revealing to sceptical officials their tortured bodies and psychological scars. Asylum seekers, understandably fearful of refusal by the 'most responsible state', thus have an interest in being anywhere but in that country. As possession of documents that indicate the 'most responsible state' makes it easier for them to be deported to it, it is obviously sensible to 'lose' them. Illegal crossing of internal borders and clandestine immigration are judged by some as preferable to the risk of deportation. In short, the Convention tends to generate common restrictive standards, while comfortably removing the onus from each individual state and placing asylum seekers in the role of supplicants or fugitives.

The Dublin/Schengen agreement is sometimes defended as being in the interests of asylum seekers because, otherwise, they might be successively palmed off to try elsewhere rather than guaranteed that one state will take responsibility for their application. As an attempt to take the moral high ground, this is a dubious argument for it concedes that member states would otherwise evade their Geneva Convention obligations to consider applications for asylum on their merits.[18]

It is quite true the Geneva Convention definition of refugee is very narrow, namely one who has a well-founded fear of persecution on the grounds of race, nationality, membership of a particular social group or political opinion. This does not include those fleeing from persecution for other reasons, let alone those unable to sustain a half-decent life for themselves in their home country as an outcome of war, civil war or economic collapse (Castles 1993: 19). In fact, the rates of acceptance under the Geneva definition are generally very low and declined sharply after 1992 – for example in 1993 reaching only 3.2% of applicants in Germany and 7% in the UK (Marshall 1996: 18; Randall 1994: 204–7). Instead, temporary permission to stay was used extensively in the case of those fleeing civil war in Yugoslavia – followed by large-scale repatriation.[19] Some states did allow those with temporary permission to stay to apply for asylum or to be granted *de facto* refugee status on humanitarian grounds. The Commission made a significant comment about this matter, to the effect that harmonization of practice would discourage such emergency migrants from concentrating their search for admission on those states with the most liberal practice (CEC 1994: 25). Germany, as by far the largest recipient of would-be refugees from Eastern and Central Europe, has persistently sought EU agreements on 'burden sharing' – but such efforts have been blocked by opposition from the UK, France and the Netherlands (Marshall 1996: 33).

Asylum seeking is a matter of 'common interest' to the EU states not just because of the administrative concern to prevent multiple applications but also because the abolition of controls on internal borders within Schengenland could allow refugees to end up in different countriesfrom those that they entered. Schengen states, although possessing the capacity for targeted or random checks, lack effective means of routine control over admission of third-country citizens across internal borders; thus they have to trust that other member states are sufficiently discriminating when people enter across external borders. Sometimes such trust is lacking, particularly where there is a sudden substantial increase in arrivals and where other states are perceived as excessively lax. For example, early in 1998 German, Austrian and French governments pressurized the Italian authorities to carry out deportations of Kurds without delay in order to avoid them going 'underground' and, perhaps, moving elsewhere in Schengenland (*Guardian*,10 Jan 1998.). Reluctantly, the Italian government agreed to speedy deportations and the detention of impending deportees.

Other things being equal, restrictions on legal migration lead to an increases in illegal immigration. Rather than contemplate the notion that it is the rules rather than the rule-breakers that are the 'problem', the EU is at one with all the member states in justifying restrictions and, accordingly, combatting those who evade them. Illegal immigration can arise in a number of ways – such as clandestine entry, entry by virtue of false documents and declaration, overstaying a temporary period of stay and becoming clandestine pending an application for permission to stay.

Immigration Ministers have resolved common strategies on preventing and identifying illegal immigrants and facilitating their deportation. The drive for similar levels of enforcement derives from each state's fear of attracting illegal immigrants because of being thought 'a soft touch' and from reluctance to establish procedures that are so blatantly inhumane as to undermine the ideological construction of Europe as a civilized community. The Commission's humanitarian sensibilities are evidently profoundly exercised by the fact that some states regularly repatriate children even where there are no relatives or guardians who will take care of them; accordingly they call for the establishment of minimum standards (CEC 1994: 9). Prevention is to be enhanced by tightening external border controls, including forestalling organized efforts to smuggle people across borders. Identification of illegal immigrants is to be achieved by states legislating to make it an offence for employers to give work to illegal immigrants and requiring them to make appropriate checks to ensure that they are not doing so (CEC 1994: 28–9). Health and social benefits also provide opportunities for detecting illegal immigrants (Morris 1997b: 205). Once illegal immigrants are detected, the Commission recommends that they should preferably be repatriated voluntarily – that is by making them an offer they cannot refuse. 'Expulsion is a necessary instrument to make it clear that illegal immigrants will not be tolerated.' (CEC 1994: 30). The process of repatriation is eased administratively, though not to the benefit of the persons concerned, where member states have agreements that, in return for cash (euphemistically referred to as aid), non-EU countries will readmit their citizens who are detected as illegal immigrants in the EU.

Conclusion

The EU is a product of, and an active agent in, the competition among capitals and states. Regulating the conditions under which capitals compete within the EU is certainly not a matter of ameliorating their competition with one another, let alone with capitals outside the EU. Rivalry between member states persists, although its form changes as the EU develops. The very project of the EU itself is a continuing source of conflict. Accordingly, although the EU may have some success in fostering a sense of European identity, it will continue to be compromised or even undermined by identities of ethnicity and nationality.

More specifically, the EU is an active agent in policy formulation, technical support and legitimation of migration control. As the EU boundaries are reconfigured (not abolished), the particular bases of inclusion and exclusion shift but their logic remains the same. The external borders of the EU will extend south and east but the member states and the Commission will be insisting all the more vigorously on rigorous policing and border checks. Governments will continue to criticize each other for being too slack in operating controls and argue over 'burden sharing'. Unfortunately, the precedents for such trends are clear.

It is not simply that a line between insiders and outsiders is periodically redrawn for there is already a hierarchy of migrant statuses ranked in terms of relative privilege and disprivilege. This is likely to be cross-cut in ever more complex ways by relative evaluations of national and ethnic groups. For example, when Poland joins the EU – and, given current Islamophobia, when Turkey does – immigrants from those countries will not be automatically welcomed in existing EU countries any more than they are now. In short, the EU, far from being a force for resolving racial and national conflicts, is part of the capitalist world system that generates them. Migration does indeed put into question both the nationality and territoriality of states; hence they struggle, in the context of an uncertain federalizing project that promotes free internal movement, to agree upon strategies that minimize the threat to these key props of their rule (Soguk 1997: 320–1). For socialists, the defence of freedom to move anywhere in the world is important not just on humanitarian grounds but also because it helps to erode these supports to the system of capitalist states and the alliances between them.

Acknowledgements

Although I am grateful for the help and advice of Sigrid Baringhorst, Paul Bellaby, John Greenaway, Barbara Marshall and the editors, I remain entirely responsible for all remaining errors.

Notes

1. Rights of movement were often qualified under autocratic regimes and during wartime.
2. There can be a self-fulfilling dynamic of accusations of disloyalty through which stigmatization of a group crystallizes its identity, in some cases as a would-be nation, and fosters their sense that they owe the state no favours.
3. The right to travel does not entail rights of residence. It encompasses 'the right to cross internal Community borders and to remain in the territory of a Member State for a short stay, or to travel onward, without the person concerned being required to obtain a visa from the Member State or States in whose territory the right is exercised'. Economic and Social Committee para 3.5.
4. Note that in Germany supposedly ethnic Germans from Eastern Europe are not counted as migrants at all but rather as returnees who are virtually automatically granted German citizenship (Faist 1995: 181).
5. Pro-EU Keynesians believe that market regulation, no longer feasible by any single state, can be effective at a European level. However, the notion that there could be socialist regulation by the EU is as fanciful as that this is possible for individual capitalist states, although there are undoubtedly those who are deluded about this matter.
6. For example, there were controversies over unanimous or majority voting in 1965, direct elections for and powers of the European Parliament in the early 1970s, powers of the Commission in the lead up to the Single European Act in 1987 and, currently, monetary union.
7. I am grateful to Barbara Marshall who, in a personal communication, has informed me that Trevi refers to the fountain in Rome, not Terrorisme-Radicalisme-Extrémisme-Violence Internationale.
8. It is surely indicative of the ingrained negative attitudes to immigration that it has been so closely associated in EU institutions with crime.
9. Article K.9 allows the Commission to take initiatives in promoting joint positions, joint actions (which are of uncertain legal status) and the drawing up of conventions (which are binding on ratification). It also allows, by a unanimous vote of the Council, for matters within the field of Justice and Home Affairs to be moved into the first pillar.
10. The areas presumed to be of common interest included conditions of entry, movement, employment, residence and family reunion of non-EU citizens – and resisting illegal immigration.
11. Note that articles 8 and 8a in the Maastricht Treaty were re-numbered as 17 and 18 in the Treaty of Amsterdam.

12. There are a range of conditions for such movement, in particular possession of appropriate residence permits or visas but, in practice, the absence of border controls in Schengenland means that these conditions are rarely checked (Thiery 1997: 8).
13. The list is drawn up without any published criteria.
14. Incidentally, this self-congratulation comes rich from a continent that pioneered colonialism, was the source of two world wars and wherein the Holocaust was perpetrated.
15. Fining carriers of travellers who do not possess appropriate entry documents effectively makes them agents for immigration control and denies people the opportunity to even apply for asylum or admission on humanitarian grounds (Morris 1997b: 198; Convey and Kupiszewski 1995: 945).
16. The Dublin Convention came into force in 1997 for the then twelve member states that signed it in 1990.
17. Six criteria are used to judge which is the most responsible state, ranging from consideration of a country where there are family links through to the country was first entered and where an application was submitted (Thiery 1997: 2).
18. According to the Commission (CEC 1994: 22), the non-refoulement principle requires states 'to be scrupulous in establishing which asylum seekers are refugees in the sense of article 1a of the Geneva Convention. Refugees are entitled to protection.' It is difficult to see how scrupulous investigation can be consistent with procedures for treating supposedly 'manifestly unfounded' applications, the presumption of safety in a pre-existing list of countries and preventing applications arising by carrier liability. In short, EU states are declaring their commitment to the Geneva Convention while actually evading its obligations. A recent attempt in K.4 to bring policy declarations into line with actual practice by calling for amendment of the Convention have so far proved to be highly controversial (Migration News Sheet, November 1998:1–2).
19. The Commission welcomed temporary protection schemes in the case of sudden influxes (CEC 1994: 25). Note that the logic of temporary protection is that such refugees should not become integrated – which entails lack of political, civil and social rights, denial of work permits, hostel accommodation etc.

Bibliography

Baldwin-Edwards, M. (1997) 'The emerging European immigration regime: some reflections on implications for southern Europe', *Journal of Common Market Studies*, 35: 497–519.

Bunyan, T. & Webber, F. (1995), *Intergovernmental Co-operation on Immigration and Asylum*, (Briefing Paper No 19), Brussels: Churches Commission for Migrants in Europe.

Castles, F. (1993), 'Migration and minorities in Europe', in J. Solomos and J. Wrench (eds), *Racism and migration in Western Europe*, Providence: Berg.

Church, C.H. & Phinnemore, D. (1994), *European Union and European Community: A Handbook and Commentary on the Post-Maastricht Treaties*, Hemel Hempstead: Harvester Wheatsheaf.

Commission of the European Communities (CEC) (1994), *Communication from the Commission to the Council and the European Parliament on Immigration and Asylum Policies* COM(94) 23 final, Brussels: Office for Official Publications of the European Communities.

Convey, A. & Kupiszewski, M. (1995), 'Keeping up with Schengen: migration and policy in the European Union', *International Migration Review*, 29: 939–63.

Curtin, D. & Meijers, H. (1995), 'The principles of open government in Schengen and the European Union: democratic retrogression?', *Common Market Law Review*, 32: 391–442.

Economic and Social Committee (1996), *Opinion Adopted at the Plenary Session on 28th February 1996*, Brussels: Office for Official Publications of the European Communities.

EU (1997), *Descriptive Summary of the Treaty of Amsterdam*
(http://ue.eu.int/Amsterdam/en/treaty/treaty.htm)

Faist, T. (1995), 'Boundaries of welfare states: immigrants and social rights on the national and supranational level' in R. Miles. and D. Thränhardt (eds), *Migration and European Integration*, London: Pinter.

Fielding, A. (1993), 'Migrants, institutions and politics: the evolution of European migration policies' in R. King (ed.) *Mass Migration in Europe* Chichester: Wiley.

Handoll, J. (1994), *Free Movement of Persons in the EU* Colorado Springs: Wiley.

Hix, S. & Niessen, J. (1996), *Reconsidering European Migration Policies: The 1996 Intergovernmental Conference and the Reform of the Maastricht Treaty* Brussels: Jointly published by the Migration Policy

Group, Churches' Commission for Migrants in Europe and Starting Line Group.

Hollifield, J.F. (1992), *Immigrants, Markets and States*, Cambridge: Harvard University Press.

Hoogenboom, T. (1992), 'Integration into society and the free movement of non-EC nationals' *European Journal of International Law*, 3: 36–52.

Leitner, H. (1995), 'International migration and the politics of admission and exclusion in postwar Europe' *Political Geography*, 14: 259–78.

Marshall, B. (1996), *British and German Refugee Policies in the European Context,* Discussion Paper 63, London: Royal Institute of International Affairs.

Martiniello, M. (1995), 'European citizenship, European identity and migrants: towards the post-national state?' in R. Miles and D. Thränhardt (eds) *Migration and European Integration*, London: Pinter.

Migration News Sheet (Monthly publication edited by A. Cruz) Brussels.

Morris, L. (1997a), 'A cluster of contradictions: the politics of migration in the European Union' *Sociology*, 31: 241–59.

Morris, L. (1997b), 'Globalization, migration and the nation-state: the path to post-national Europe?' *British Journal of Sociology*, 48: 192–209.

Randall, C. 'An Asylum Policy for the UK' in S. Spencer (ed) (1994), *Strangers and Citizens: a positive approach to migrants and refugees*, London: Rivers Oram Press.

RIMET (1996), *The EC Member States and Immigration in 1993: Closed Borders, Stringent Attitudes* Brussels: European Commission DGV.

RIMET (1997), *The Member States of the EU and Immigration in 1994: Less Tolerance and Tighter Control Policies,* Brussels: European Commission DGV, Office for Official Publications of the European Communities.

Santel, B. (1995) 'Loss of control: the build-up of a European migration and asylum regime' in R. Miles and D. Thränhardt (eds) *Migration and European Integration*, London: Pinter.

Soguk, N. (1997), 'Predicaments of territorial democracy and statecraft in Europe: how European democracies regiment migratory movements', *Alternatives, Social Transformation and Humane Governance*, 22: 313–52.

Soysal, Y.N. (1996), 'Changing citizenship in Europe: remarks on post-national membership and the national state' in D. Cesarani and M. Fulbrook, *Citizenship, Nationality and Migration in Europe,* London: Routledge.

Spencer, S. (ed) (1994), *Strangers and Citizens: a positive approach to migrants and refugees*, London: Rivers Oram Press.

Thiery, C. (1997), 'The Schengen agreements' paper presented in the workshop *Migration in the 21st century* http://migration.ucdavis.edu/mm21/Thiery.html

Ugur, M. (1995), 'Freedom of movement versus exclusion: a reinterpretation of the "insider'-'outsider" divide in the European Union', *International Migration Review*, 29: 964–99.

Veil, S. et al (1997), 'Report of a high level panel on free movement of persons, chaired by Mrs Simone Veil' EU DGXV untitled.html by search on http://europa.eu.int/

Part II
Country Studies

–3–

England: Racism, Anti-Racism and the Changing Position of Racialized Groups in Economic Relations

Satnam Virdee

Introduction

This chapter has three main aims. First, it critically assesses the economic and socio-political consequences of racism directed against migrant groups in England. Second, it goes onto investigate what organizational forms of resistance were employed to combat the impact of such racism. Third, it critically assesses to what extent anti-racist action was successful in redressing the negative effects of racism, especially the position of racialized groups in economic relations.

I limit my discussion of migrant labour to the post-war experience of South Asians and Caribbeans and their English-born children. This is not to deny that 'white' migrant groups have been subject to a process of racialization – they clearly have as Miles' (1982, 1993) discussion of the Irish and Jewish experiences during the nineteenth century and Grosvenor's (1998) reference to the Cypriot experience in twentieth century England clearly demonstrates. However, the dominance of the 'race relations' paradigms (both in its Weberian inflection (see Rex 1970, 1979) and in its black radical inflection (see CCCS 1982; Sivanandan 1982; Gilroy 1987) within post-1960s social science has ensured that a great deal more primary research needs to be carried out before one can begin to accurately map and critically assess the experiences of Irish, Jewish and other 'white' social groups in late twentieth-century England. Additionally, as should already be evident, I restrict my analysis to England. The small literature that exists on racism in Scotland (see for example Miles 1982: 121–50; Miles and Dunlop 1986) suggests that it has taken a rather different form and trajectory from that in England, which cannot be adequately assessed within the limited confines of this paper.

Racism and the Position of Migrant Labour in Class Relations in Post-War England

The demands of an expanding post-war economy meant that Britain, like most other European countries was faced with a major shortage of labour (Castles and Kosack 1985). The demand for labour was met by a variety of sources including 500,000 refugees, displaced persons and ex-prisoners of war from Europe between 1946–51 and a further 350,000 European nationals between 1945–57 (Sivanandan 1976: 348). However, the overwhelming majority of migrants who came to Britain were from the Republic of Ireland, the Indian sub-continent and the Caribbean (Miles 1989).

On the whole, the labour migration from the Indian sub-continent and the Caribbean proceeded by informal means with little 'effort made to relate employment to vacancies. Instead, it was left to free market forces to determine the size of immigration' (Sivanandan 1976: 348). However, those industries where the demand for labour was greatest actively recruited 'black' workers in their home countries (Fryer 1984; Ramdin 1987). Employers such as the British Transport Commission, the London Transport Executive, the British Hotels and Restaurants Association and the Regional Hospitals Board all established arrangements with Caribbean governments to ensure a regular supply of labour (Ramdin 1987: 197). Overall, Smith (1977: 24–5) estimated that 12 per cent of Caribbean men, 9 per cent of Indian men, 7 per cent of Pakistani men and 2 per cent of African Asian men already had a job definitely arranged before they came to England. By 1958, and after a decade of 'black' labour migration, there were 125,000 Caribbean and 55,000 Indian and Pakistani workers in England (Fryer 1984: 373).

Despite the heterogeneous class structure of the migrating populations (see Heath and Ridge 1983), they came to occupy, overwhelmingly, the semi-skilled and unskilled positions in the English labour market (Daniel 1968; Smith 1977). Furthermore, they found themselves disproportionately concentrated in certain types of manual work characterized by a shortage of labour; shift working; unsocial hours; low pay and an unpleasant working environment (Smith 1977). The causes of this position in economic relations were two fold. First, the growth of new jobs offering relatively higher rates of pay and better conditions resulted in a significant shift of 'white' labour out of the declining, older sectors of industry and into these new jobs. This, in turn, created vacancies within the declining sectors of industry, and these vacancies came to be filled by migrants from the Indian subcontinent and the Caribbean (Miles 1982; Miles 1989; Castles and

Kosack 1985). However, for Miles (1989: 125), this constituted only part of the explanation because

> Caribbean and Asian migrants were in theory free to sell their labour power to whomever they wished. They were therefore free to compete with indigenous labour for access to the expanding number of new, higher paid jobs with better conditions.

Consequently, he contended that, in practice, the racialization of the British labour market where 'social relations between people . . . [were] structured by the signification of human biological characteristics in such a way as to define and construct differentiated social collectivities' (Miles 1989: 75), ensured that migrants from the Indian sub-continent and the Caribbean were subjected to exclusionary practices that greatly prevented them from acquiring skilled manual and non-manual jobs. He is careful to stress that such exclusionary practices were motivated by the fact that these migrant groups 'had few skills relevant to an industrial capitalist economy' (Miles 1989: 126) as well as racism defined as:

> those negative beliefs held by one group which identify and set apart another by attributing significance to some biological or other 'inherent' characteristic(s) which it is said to possess, and which deterministically associate that characteristic(s) with other (negatively evaluated) feature(s) or action(s) (Phizacklea and Miles 1980: 22).

Importantly, research suggests that elements of organized labour colluded with employers to exclude South Asian and Caribbean workers from key forms of employment, especially skilled work (Fryer 1984; Wrench 1987). With little evidence of a corporate class consciousness constructed around an identity of working-class solidarity but rather a sectionalist class consciousness characterized by the primary concern of protecting the terms and conditions of immediate colleagues at work (Kelly 1988; Hyman 1972; Beynon 1984), elements of skilled organized labour, fearful of the perceived threat posed by migrant labour, colluded with employers to ensure that the trade union strategy of restrictive practices took on an added racist dimension by excluding migrant labour from skilled jobs (Virdee 1999a, forthcoming).

It was not only in the economic sphere that racialized workers found themselves discriminated against during this period. In the late 1950s, there was growing concern (informed in part by the racist violence directed against people of Caribbean origin in Notting Hill, London and Nottingham in 1958) within Parliament, the media and the major political parties, of the 'dangers of unrestricted immigration'. This contributed to an important shift in public policy towards racialized migrant labour from one of support for unrestricted immigration to one that stressed that the immigration of 'non-whites' had to be curbed if the social fabric and cohesion of the country were not to be irreparably damaged. As a result, in 1962, an Immigration Act was introduced that had as its primary objective the curbing of 'non-white' labour from the Indian sub-continent and the Caribbean, with immigration from the Republic of Ireland remaining unaffected (see Miles and Phizacklea 1984).

The consequences of this process of racialization were clear as I have already demonstrated: it affected the allocation of persons to different positions in the production process and the allocation of material and other rewards and disadvantages to groups so categorized within the class boundaries established by the dominant mode of production (Miles 1982). According to Miles (1982: 165), these different racialized groups came to

> occupy a structurally distinct position in the economic, political and ideological relations of British capitalism, but within the boundary of the working class. They therefore constitute a fraction of the working class, one that can be identified as a racialised fraction.

'Black' Self Organisation: a Strategy of Collective Anti-Racist Action

Apart from a few exceptions (see for example Virdee and Grint 1994; Virdee 1999a forthcoming), an often neglected aspect of the racialization process has been any critical investigation of the forms of resistance to it (Miles 1994; Solomos 1993). If we undertake an assessment of the 1950s and 1960s, it is clear that apart from isolated cases such as the campaign mounted by 'black' community organizations and individual 'whites' against the operation of a 'colour bar' introduced by 'white' bus workers in Bristol in 1955 (see Dresser 1986 for a detailed discussion) there is little evidence of collective resistance to such racist exclusionary practices from either racialized or 'white' workers until the mid 1960s. As Sivanandan (1982: 5) argues, 'resistance to racial abuse and discrimination on the shopfloor was more spontaneous than organised'.

However, by the mid-1960s, the discriminatory practices enforced by employers and trade unions alike came under growing pressure from a series of strikes by racialized workers working in the textile and foundry industries (Moore 1975; Duffield 1988; Wrench 1987). Importantly, nearly all these disputes were characterized by substantial support from the different racialized communities and an almost complete absence of support from the 'white' working class (Sivanandan 1982; Wrench 1987).

Drawing inspiration from the civil rights struggles in the USA and the visits to Britain of the two main leaders of the American anti-racist movement – Martin Luther King in December 1964 and Malcolm X in January 1965 (Sivanandan 1982), this period witnessed activists within the racialized community establish numerous organizations committed to challenging racism through 'black' self-organization. Importantly, and unlike in the USA, 'black' became an identity that was inclusive of all the main 'non-white' social groups subject to racism during this period. Shukra (1996: 30–1) describes how 'black' anti-racist activists set about attempting to establish a South Asian-Caribbean alliance against racism:

> The 'black' radical activist was usually an unpaid campaigner who operated intensively with a small group of like-minded people, went from meeting to meeting, distributed pamphlets, spoke at rallies, carried banners and organised demonstrations to convince what was termed 'West Indian', 'Indian' and 'Pakistani' people that their experience of inferior treatment at the hands of employers, schools, local authorities, government officials, politicians and the police was unacceptable. Crucially, they also argued that this situation could be changed through militant political activity, primarily against employers and the state . . . the black activists used the term 'black' to build a movement to mobilise and cohere self-reliant communities of resistance to racism.

Amongst some of the more prominent organizations that South Asians and Caribbeans joined to combat racism and exclusionary practices were the Racial Action Adjustment Society (RAAS), a 'black' radical organization whose slogan was 'Black men, unite, . . . we have nothing to lose but our fears' (cited in Sivanandan 1982: 16) and the Black People's Alliance (BPA) (see Josephides 1990). The outcome was that an identity previously employed to disparage particular racialised social groups was appropriated by the racialized communities themselves and infused with new meaning and an ideology of resistance – a process which Gilroy (1987) in Britain and Omi and Winant (1986) in the USA have come to define as 'race' or 'racial' formation respectively.

The impact of this anti-racist 'racial' formation project coupled with growing academic evidence which demonstrated that 'racial' discrimination in the labour market ranged from the 'massive to the substantial' (Daniel 1968) forced the state into introducing reforms to curb the worst excesses of racist exclusionary practices. One of the most important measures was the introduction of a Race Relations Act in 1968 that outlawed discrimination in the areas of employment, housing and the provision of goods, facilities, services and planning. The Race Relations Board, established in 1965 by the first Race Relations Act, was given stronger enforcement powers, and a new body – the Community Relations Council (CRC) – was created to promote 'harmonious community relations' (Wrench 1996: 24).

Consequently, by 1968, accompanying the legislation designed to curb 'non-white' immigration was the recognition by the state of the need for anti-discrimination legislation for those racialized migrants and their children already resident in Britain. These two aspects of state policy were neatly encapsulated by Roy Hattersley (a former Home Office minister) in his formulation: 'Integration without control is impossible, but control without integration is indefensible' (cited in Solomos 1993: 84).

However, for some elements of the British elite and 'white' working class, the introduction of reforms, even whilst conceding the need for racist immigration controls, was tantamount to undermining the social basis of a much revered imagined community (Anderson 1983) – the British (i.e. 'white') 'race' and its 'traditional' way of life. This current of opinion was most significantly reflected in the speeches of Enoch Powell, who, ironically, in a previous guise, as minister of health, had been responsible for the recruitment of Caribbean nurses during the post-war era of capitalist expansion (Fryer 1984). In April 1968, Powell set out his opposition to attempts by the state to curb racist discriminatory practices when he claimed that racialized migrant labour and their children should not be

> elevated into a privileged or special class or that the ['white'] citizen should be denied his right to discriminate in the management of his own affairs between one fellow-citizen and another or that he should be subjected to inquisition as to his reasons and motives for behaving in one lawful manner rather than another . . . The discrimination and the deprivation, the sense of alarm and of resentment, lies not with the immigrant population but with those among whom they have come and are still coming (cited in Miles and Phizacklea 1984: 3).

The ideological hold of such racist thought over parts of the 'white' working class was forcefully demonstrated by the marches in support of Powell by the Smithfield meat porters and the dockers of east London (Sivanandan 1982; Miles and Phizacklea 1984) who chanted 'Back Britain, not Black Britain' (The Trial of Enoch Powell, Channel Four, Monday 20 April 1998).

Racialized workers responded to this racist threat by establishing the Black People's Alliance (BPA), an organization that marked the high-point of 'racial' formation in Britain, and which included both South Asian and Caribbean activists, with Jagmohan Joshi, the leader of the Indian Workers Association (IWA-GB), becoming the BPA's general secretary (Josephides 1990). Despite such collective resistance, persistent pressure from the racist right served to forge the necessary political climate for the Labour government to introduce the Commonwealth Immigrants Act in 1968. This piece of legislation removed the right of entry into Britain from all British passport holders who did not have a parent or grandparent born in Britain (Miles and Phizacklea 1984: 60). Such racist immigration controls were further strengthened with the election of a Conservative administration in 1970, who, within a year, had introduced an Immigration Act that effectively 'marked the end of black immigration for settlement' (Gordon and Klug 1985: 7).

By the early 1970s, research conclusively demonstrated that, after being resident in Britain for over a quarter of a century and despite almost a decade of collective resistance by the racialized communities themselves, racialized workers from the Indian sub-continent and the Caribbean continued to be substantially disadvantaged in the British labour market as well as other areas of resource allocation (Smith 1977). A national survey carried out during this period demonstrated the continuing importance of colour racism in defining the life chances of these social groups:

> there is no significant difference in the level of discrimination between West Indians, Indians and Pakistanis, though we have already seen that discrimination against Greeks is markedly lower. This suggests that discrimination is based on a general colour prejudice, which does not distinguish between people belonging to different racial groups, having different religions, speaking different languages and coming from different countries. They are all lumped together as 'coloured people'. (Smith 1977: 111)

However, wider events, in particular the growing class conflict between organized labour and the state and employers (Hyman 1972; Crouch 1977) was increasingly undermining the sectionalist working class consciousness that had proved to be an important feature hindering the formation of a current of 'white' anti-racism during the 1950s and 1960s.

Growing Class Conflict in the 1970s and the Formation of a Current of 'White' Anti-Racism

The attempts to curb unofficial trade union activity by the state during the late 1960s and early 1970s served to politicize key elements of organized labour and contributed significantly to the formation of an oppositional class identity (Hyman 1972; Kelly 1988). In particular, a significant shift began to take place beyond the narrow, sectionalist class consciousness of the 1950s and 1960s to a more politicized form of corporate class consciousness that recognized the value of working-class solidarity and collective action to defend working-class interests.

This important development, coupled with almost a decade of industrial struggles against racism and exclusionary practices by racialized workers and the growing fear of far-right influence in trade unions (see Miles and Phizacklea 1978), created a more favourable ideological terrain for anti-racist ideas and an appreciation of the need for solidarity between 'black' and 'white' labour to gain a wider audience within many trade unions. By the mid 1970s, there was a growing recognition amongst key elements of the organized labour movement that racism served only to weaken the trade union movement and that it had to be actively addressed. Several major trade unions including the General and Municipal Boilermakers' Union (GMBU), the Banking, Insurance and Finance Union (BIFU), the National Union of Teachers (NUT), the National Association of Teachers in Higher and Further Education (NATHFE), the National and Local Government Officers (NALGO) and the Civil and Public Servants Association (CPSA) issued positive statements against racism and set up bodies to monitor the implementation of equal opportunity policies. Similarly, a resolution passed at the 1977 TUC annual conference called upon the General Council to conduct a campaign against racists in trade unions. This led to the publication of a General Council statement on racism in 1978, and, in 1979, the TUC sent a circular to all affiliated unions that had not adopted policies on tackling racists in their unions to do so (Labour Research 1983: 182–3).

Importantly, it was amidst this growing industrial unrest and the shift to the left amongst key sections of organized labour (Hyman 1972; Crouch 1977; Marsh 1993; Kelly 1988) that the incoming Labour government introduced anti-discriminatory legislation in the form of the 1975 Sex Discrimination Act and the 1976 Race Relations Act (Marsh 1992). The latter piece of legislation was subsequently shown to have been largely ineffective in challenging the prevalence of racism and exclusionary practices because of the sheer magnitude of the problem (see McCrudden,

Smith and Brown 1991), its introduction nevertheless represented a highly symbolic indication of the commitment to combat racism and exclusionary practices by the state under pressure from the organized labour movement and the racialized communities.

However, the most visible manifestation of the solidarity between 'black' and 'white' labour came during the course of the Grunwick dispute when thousands of 'white' (and non-white) workers including miners, dockers (including some London dockers who had demonstrated in favour of immigration controls in 1968), transport workers and post office workers undertook solidarity action to support South Asian women on strike (Rogaly 1977; Phizacklea and Miles 1978; Ramdin 1987). The dispute ended in defeat for the strikers in 1978, but it nevertheless demonstrated that amidst the growing radicalization of parts of the organized labour movement, many 'white' workers overcame the ideology of racism and acted along the fault-line of class in solidarity with racialized workers.

There is some evidence to suggest that this current of 'white' anti-racism at work was also influential in building resistance to racism outside of the workplace. In particular, primary research evidence suggests that parts of the organized labour movement played a decisive role in the formation of anti-racist and anti-fascist organizations like the Anti-Nazi League (ANL) (see for example the annual reports of the CPSA 1980: 13; CPSA 1981: 11; SCPS 1983: 26; SCPS 1984: 54; and NALGO 1981: 15). In addition to the longer established 'black' anti-racist groups, by 1973/74, many 'whites' had also begun to establish anti-racist committees supported by local trades councils. The racist pronouncements of rock stars like David Bowie and Eric Clapton led many of these activists to establish a national organization called Rock Against Racism in August 1976 (Gilroy 1987: 120–1). 1976 and 1977 were important years that saw growing confrontation between racists and anti-racists culminating in anti-racists preventing the far-right National Front (NF) from marching through Lewisham in south London – an area with relatively high 'black' concentration. In 1977, the National Front polled 119,000 votes in the Greater London Local Council elections and threatened to become the third party in British politics. The Anti-Nazi League (ANL) was established in 1977 to counter this far-right force (Gilroy 1987), and, in alliance with more locally based anti-racist organisations such as the Campaign Against Racism and Fascism (CARF) (CARF 1992: 2) they successfully undermined the National Front's electoral support by exposing them as 'Nazis' to a previously sympathetic 'white' British public (Messina 1989).

Of course, such evidence by no means suggests that the 'white' working class moved *en bloc* towards an anti-racist position otherwise, there would have been little need for the establishment of a national anti-racist organization in the first instance. Rather, this highlighted an important yet greatly neglected aspect of anti-racist politics during this period – the formation of a current of 'white' anti-racism. The consequences of such political developments were that by the late 1970s, Britain had a relatively strong anti-racist movement built around the dual ideological currents of 'racial' formation and working class solidarity.

Anti-Racism in an Era of Neo-Liberalism: the 1980s

The economic and political forces that had helped to shape the formation of an activist 'inter-racial' unity within parts of the organized labour movement was not to last long. The failure of the 1974–9 Labour government and 'left' trade union leaders to arrest the rising levels of unemployment and the decline in real wages of many parts of organized labour contributed greatly to a sense of disillusionment with such politics, which ultimately manifested itself in the return of the Conservative Party to office in May 1979 with a substantial working-class vote (Marsh 1992).

However, the introduction of neo-liberal economic policies designed with the primary purpose of curbing public spending through the stringent use of monetarist procedures served merely to accelerate the de-industrialization of Britain that had been under way since the mid-1970s (Eldridge, Cressey and MacInnes 1991). The recession was particularly marked in parts of the north and north-west of England, Scotland and many of the inner-city areas of the major conurbations (including greater London) where both 'black' and 'white' workers were laid off in large numbers (Brown 1982). Due to a complex interaction between the occupational and regional distribution of different racialized social groups, some groups were worse affected than others by the decline in manufacturing employment. Specifically, workers of Pakistani origin who found themselves disproportionately concentrated within the collapsing textile industry and residentially concentrated in the north and north-west were more adversely affected than workers of Indian and African Asian origin (or for that matter 'whites') who were more evenly distributed across several major manufacturing industries and were also more residentially dispersed (see Virdee 1999b).

It was against this backdrop of economic decay coupled with the exacerbation of more specific problems such as the growing deterioration in the relationship between the police and inner-city youth that greatly contributed to the urban unrest in many of the English conurbations during the early 1980s (Benyon 1984; Solomos 1988). Although the research evidence strongly suggests that the participants of the urban unrest comprised both 'black' and 'white' youths (see Benyon 1984; Gilroy 1987; Solomos 1988), two mutually antagonistic sets of social forces ensured that racism or more precisely, the social construction of 'race', came to dominate public policy debate about the main causes of the unrest.

On the one hand, the anti-racist movement insisted that the root causes of the unrest lay in the systematic destruction of the lives of racialized communities through the operation of racism and exclusionary practices and state (mainly police) harassment, which had served to create a 'racially defined' sub-proletariat (see Sivanandan 1993). On the other hand, the tabloid press forcefully denied that the unrest was the result of racism and instead attempted to criminalize the unrest by claiming it was the product of a 'black' criminal underbelly within society (see Solomos 1988; Gilroy 1987). In both sets of analyses, far less attention was paid to explaining the plight of 'white' working class youth who had also been active participants of the unrest (Benyon 1984).

It was amidst this highly charged political atmosphere that the results of the Scarman Inquiry into the urban unrest were published in November 1981 (Scarman 1981). The report advanced a series of recommendations including the need to introduce a more effective co-ordinated approach to tackling the problem of the inner cities; adopting a policy of positive discrimination to combat 'racial' discrimination amongst racialized social groups; reforming the police force and introducing new methods of policing (Taylor 1994: 29). However, apart from giving qualified support to the findings contained in the Scarman Report (see Raison 1984: 244–57), the right-wing Conservative administration proved to be highly averse to introducing even minor reforms necessary to tackle racism and exclusionary practices because of its disagreement with the material explanations of the unrest advanced by the Scarman Inquiry (Ball and Solomos 1990).

At this juncture, the trade unions could have colluded with employers to exclude racialized workers from the remaining areas of employment growth and stability (for example, the service sector) within the British social formation. However, they did not: the political relations in 1980s England were rather different from those during the 1950s and 1960s when the prevalence of a highly sectionalist class consciousness had greatly hindered the formation of an indigenous current of 'white' anti-racism.

Although the mass 'inter-racial' rank and file solidarity evident at Grunwick had subsided, those trade union activists that had come to prominence during the 1970s on a perspective that articulated the defence of general working class interests remained in positions of responsibility.

As a result, by the early 1980s, these activists were, in political terms at least, far to the left of their membership over a range of important issues (Marsh 1992), including the need to combat racism.

An anti-racist coalition comprising the social forces of 'racial' formation, epitomized by 'black' self-organization, trade union activists and the left of the Labour Party ensured that the recommendations of the Scarman Report, and in particular, the need to tackle 'racial' disadvantage, were forced onto the social policy formation agendas of the local state. Under such pressure, the recommendations acted as a catalyst, particularly in those local authority areas that were politically controlled by left-wing Labour parties in the greater London area where nearly half of the racialized population resided (Owen 1993) to undertake anti-racist measures (Ball and Solomos 1990).

One practical example of the kind of anti-racist initiative launched during this period was the growing recognition by some employers of the need to keep systematic data on the ethnic origin of their applicants and employees so that the extent of disadvantage could be effectively assessed and thereby more systematically remedied through the adoption of positive action programmes. Pressured by developments in parts of local government, other large public sector employers such as the British Civil Service and the National Health Service were forced to follow suit and introduce equal opportunity polices (see OMCS 1990; Beishon, Virdee and Hagell 1995), quickly followed by large private sector organizations, especially in the retail sector (Wrench 1996).

Subsequent research that has undertaken a critical assessment of the relative success of such equal opportunity policies in reducing the impact of racist exclusionary practices have shown that whereas such policies were successful in facilitating the entry of racialized social groups into non-manual forms of employment (see Jenkins and Solomos 1986; Ball and Solomos 1990), these racialized social groups remained disproportionately concentrated within the lower grades of these forms of employment (see Ouseley 1990); particularly, working within those jobs that some authors have referred to as the new working class (Hyman and Price 1980).

Despite such qualifications, by the late 1980s research evidence conclusively demonstrated that an important re-configuration in the position of racialized social groups in economic relations in England had taken place (see Jones 1993; Modood 1997). This can be empirically substantiated with reference to Table 3.1. Specifically, it shows that similar proportions of 'white' men and men of Indian origin are now represented in non-manual work whereas a slightly higher proportion of men of African Asian origin are in such work. Although men of Caribbean, Pakistani and

Bangladeshi origin continue to be significantly under represented in non-manual work compared with 'white' men, this differential has closed over recent years (Iganski and Payne 1996). On the other hand, men of Caribbean, Pakistani and Bangladeshi origin continue to be over represented in manual jobs compared to men of 'white', African Asian and Indian origin.

Detailed analysis by individual job categories reveals further important insights. Table 1 shows that the same proportion of men of African Asian origin in paid work were in professional and managerial jobs as 'white' men with only a slightly smaller proportion of men of Indian origin working in these jobs. Although men of Caribbean, Pakistani and Bangladeshi origin were significantly under-represented in this socio-economic group compared to men of 'white', African Asian and Indian origin, about one in six were professional workers and managers.

Turning to the intermediate and junior non-manual jobs, these demonstrate further the growing representation of Britain's racialized groups at all levels of the class structure. Apart from men of Pakistani origin, all the men from the different racialized groups had almost identical levels of representation in these jobs as 'white' men. The lower level of representation of men of Pakistani origin in junior non-manual jobs was almost entirely attributable to their greater representation in skilled manual jobs compared with men from the other 'South Asian' groups and 'white' men. Importantly, men of Bangladeshi origin were significantly less likely to be represented in skilled manual work than men from any other racialized social group, as well as 'white' men.

This brings us to the position in the class structure that migrants from all the different groups used to occupy overwhelmingly: semi- and unskilled work (Miles 1982). Table 3.1 shows that while men of Caribbean, Indian and Pakistani origin continue to be slightly over represented in these jobs compared with 'white' men, it is men of Bangladeshi origin who constitute the one remaining group of migrant labour that finds itself overwhelmingly located in this type of work: specifically, they were four times as likely as 'white' men to be in such work. Apart from some important differences in the economic activity rates of Muslim women (that is, women of Bangladeshi and Pakistani origin) the overall trends for women were broadly similar (see Modood 1997 for a descriptive analysis of such trends).

Overall, national survey evidence since the 1980s has consistently demonstrated that a significant percentage of migrant labourers and their children have managed to extricate themselves out of semi- and unskilled work and move into skilled manual and junior non-manual work (and

Table 3.1 Jobs Levels of Men by Ethnic Group

(column percentages)

	White %	*Caribbean* %	*Indian* %	*African Asian* %	*Pakistani* %	*Bangladeshi* %	*Chinese* %
Professional/Manager/Employers	30	14	25	30	19	18	46
Intermediate/junior non-manual	18	19	20	24	13	19	17
Skilled manual and foremen	36	39	31	30	46	7	14
Semi-skilled manual	11	22	16	12	18	53	12
Unskilled manual	3	6	5	2	3	3	5
Non-manual	48	33	45	54	31	37	63
Manual	50	67	52	44	67	63	32
Weighted	789	365	349	296	182	61	127
Unweighted	713	258	356	264	258	112	71

Base: Men in paid work

(Source: adapted from Modood 1997)

increasingly, the petty-bourgeoisie – see Metcalf et al 1996). As a result, the racialized social groups no longer occupy a homogeneous class position in the semi-skilled and unskilled section of the working class. However, as Table 3.1 clearly indicates, this process of social change has taken place at a different rate for different racialized social groups. Briefly, this has been the result of a highly complex and often contradictory interaction of several factors including the initial class origin of migrants; the restructuring of the British social formation, the political changes introduced at both national and local government level to address the worst excesses of racist exclusionary practices and the different effects of racism on different racialized social groups both in the labour market and in the wider society. These developments have served to produce a racialized population that has strikingly similar class cleavages to that of the 'white' population in England (Virdee 1999b).

Of course, by advancing such propositions, I am by no means suggesting that racism and exclusionary practices play no part in defining the economic position of racialized social groups in the contemporary social formation; they clearly do (see Esmail and Everington 1993). An additional and often neglected aspect of racism at work is racist violence and harassment (see Virdee 1995). A nationally representative sample survey of racialized social groups carried out in 1994 found that over a quarter of a million, that is, one in eight of the total adult racialized population in England and Wales, were subject to some form of racist harassment in one year (Virdee 1997). The second most likely location of such harassment was at work. More detailed evidence of the problem was gathered in the nursing profession – an occupation employing substantial numbers of racialized nurses (Beishon et al. 1995). Specifically, these nurses reported extensive racist harassment in their workplaces – sometimes from colleagues, frequently from patients. Few reported such harassment to the authorities and most felt that they had to accept it as 'part of the job' (see Beishon et al. 1995).

Conclusions

This paper has attempted to assess the manner in which racism has affected the position that migrant labourers and their English-born children occupy in economic relations. There is little doubt that during the post-war era of full employment and relatively scarce labour, the dominant strategies deployed by trade unions, especially shop stewards at a local plant level, to defend their members' interests were highly sectionalist and engendered sectionalist forms of class consciousness. Such strategies no doubt improved the pay and conditions of large numbers of 'white' workers, but they also greatly contributed to the strengthening of a racist division within the working class. The prevalence of a sectionalist class consciousness amongst elements of organized labour meant that some of them; fearful of the threat to their newly improved living standards posed by the arrival of supposedly cheaper migrant labour, instituted discriminatory practices against them, motivated by racism. In this sense, parts of organized labour were an active social agent in the manufacture of a racist division within the English working class. Such a position was reinforced by racist legislation introduced to curb 'non-white' immigration so that these racialized workers came to occupy a distinctive position in class relations during the first two decades following migration; what Miles (1982) refers to as a racialized class fraction.

It was not until the mid 1960s that collective action to confront such racist practices emerged. Due to the continued prevalence of a sectionalist class consciousness amongst elements of 'white' labour and the dominance of racist sentiment, it was racialized workers organizing independently who first began to challenge such practices. However, attempts to curb unofficial trade union activity in the late 1960s and early 1970s served to politicize key elements of organized labour and resulted in the formation of an oppositional working-class identity. This major development coupled with almost a decade of industrial struggles against racism by racialized workers and growing fear of far-right influence in trade unions created the necessary pre-conditions for the ideas of anti-racism and solidarity between racialized and 'white' labour to gain a wider audience in the trade unions. By the mid-1970s, the TUC and some of the larger affiliated trade unions explicitly recognized that working class solidarity could only be achieved through combatting racism.

However, it required the urban unrest and the political pressure that followed from organized labour and the racialized communities themselves to finally force the state to introduce reforms to curb the worst excesses of racist discriminatory practices. Specifically, non-manual forms of employment, albeit at the lower grades, were opened upto large numbers of racialized workers for the first time. This process acted as a catalyst and other large employers were forced to consider the employment and promotion of racialized workers. Despite continuing evidence of the prevalence of racism and exclusionary practices in the contemporary social formation, these developments have led to an important re configuration in the position of racialized social groups in economic relations: they no longer occupy a position in the semi- and unskilled sites of the manual working class but instead display strikingly similar class cleavages to that of the 'white' population.

Note

1. The terms 'black' and 'white' are used to signify and thereby distinguish particular social groups within England. When necessary, I also distinguish between different 'ethnic' groups by using the terms 'South Asian' and 'Caribbean'. That all of these terms are social constructions and not 'objective' categories is captured by the controversy in the USA and Britain over self-categorization (see Modood 1988; Davis 1991; Cole 1993; Roediger 1994).

Bibliography

Anderson, B. (1983), *Imagined Communities*, London: Verso.

Ball, W. and Solomos, J. (eds), (1990), *Race and Local Politics*, Basingstoke: Macmillan Education Limited.

Beishon, S., Virdee, S. and Hagell, A. (1995), *Nursing in a Multi-Ethnic NHS*, London: Policy Studies Institute.

Benyon, J. (ed.), (1984), *Scarman and After*, Oxford: Pergamon Press Limited.

Beynon, H. (1984), *Working for Ford*, London: Penguin.

Brown, C. (1982), *Black and White Britain*, London: Heinemann Educational Books.

Campaign Against Racism and Fascism (CARF). (1992), 'Where CARF Stands', *Campaign Against Racism and Fascism (CARF)*, No.6, January/February, pp.2.

Carter, B., Harris, C. and Joshi, S. (1987), 'The 1951–55 Conservative government and the racialisation of black immigration', *Policy Papers in Ethnic Relations,* No.11, Coventry: University of Warwick; Centre for Research in Ethnic Relations.

Castles, S. and Kosack, G. (1985), *Immigrant Workers and Class Structure in Western Europe*, Oxford: Oxford University Press.

Centre for Contemporary Cultural Studies (1982), *The Empire Strikes Back*, London: Hutchinson.

Civil and Public Servants Association (1980), *1979 Annual Report*, London: CPSA.

Civil and Public Servants Association (1981), *1980 Annual Report*, London: CPSA.

Cole, M. (1993), '"Black and Ethnic Minority" or "Asian, Black and other Minority Ethnic": A Further Note on Nomenclature', *Sociology*, 27: 671–3.

Crouch, C. (1977), *Class Conflict and the Industrial Relations Crises*, London: Heinemann.

Daniel, W. W. (1968), *Racial Discrimination in England*, London: Penguin.

Dresser, M. (1986), *Black and White on the Buses: the 1963 Colour Bar Dispute in Bristol*, Bristol: Bristol Broadsides.

Duffield, M. (1988), *Black Radicalism and the Politics of De-Industrialisation: The Hidden History of Indian Foundry Workers*, Aldershot: Avebury.

Eldridge, J., Cressey, P. and MacInnes, J. (1991), *Industrial Sociology and Economic Crisis*, Hemel Hempstead: Harvester Wheatsheaf.

Esmail, A. and Everington, S. (1993), 'Racial discrimination against doctors from ethnic minorities', *British Medical Journal*, 306, March, pp.691–2.

Fryer, P. (1984), *Staying Power: The History of Black People in Britain*, London: Pluto Press.

Gilroy, P. (1987), *Their Ain't No Black in the Union Jack*, London: Hutchinson.

Gordon, P. and Klug, F. (1985), *British Immigration Control*, London: Runnymede Trust.

Grosvenor, I. (1998), *Assimilating Identities*, London: Lawrence & Wishart.

Heath, A. and Ridge, J. (1983), 'Social Mobility of Ethnic Minorities', *Journal of Biosocial Science*, Supplement 8, pp.169–84.

Hyman, R. (1972), *Marxism and the Sociology of Trade Unionism*, London: Pluto Press.

Hyman, R. and Price, R. (1980), *The New Working Class? White-Collar Workers and their Organisations*, London: Macmillan.

Iganski, P. and Payne, G. (1996), 'Declining Racial Disadvantage in the British Labour Market', *Ethnic and Racial Studies*, 19: 1.

Jenkins, R. and Solomos, J. (eds), (1986), *Racism and Equal Opportunity Policies in the 1980s*, Cambridge: Cambridge University Press.

Jones, T. (1993), *Britain's Ethnic Minorities*, London: Policy Studies Institute.

Josephides, S. (1990), 'Principles, strategies and anti-racist campaigns: the case of the Indian Workers' Association', in Goulbourne, H. (ed.), *Black Politics in Britain*, London: Avebury, pp.115–29.

Kelly, J. (1988), *Trade Unions and Socialist Politics*, London: Verso.

Labour Research (1983), 'Race at work', *Labour Research*, July, pp. 182–3.

McCrudden, C., Smith, D.J. and Brown, C. (1991), *Racial Justice at Work*, London: Policy Studies Institute.

Marsh, D. (1992), *The New Politics of British Trade Unionism: Union Power and the Thatcher Legacy*, London: The Macmillan Press Limited.

Messina, A. (1989), *Race and Party Competition in Britain*, Oxford: Clarendon Press.

Metcalf, H., Modood, T and Virdee, S. (1996), *Asian Self-Employment in England: the Interaction of Culture and Economics*, London: Policy Studies Institute.

Miles, R. (1982), *Racism and Migrant Labour*, London: Routledge & Kegan Paul.

Miles, R. (1989), *Racism*, London: Routledge.

Miles, R. (1993), *Racism After 'Race Relations'*, London: Routledge.

Miles, R. and Dunlop, A (1986), 'The racialisation of politics in Britain: why Scotland is different', *Patterns of Prejudice*, 20 (1): 23–32.

Miles, R. and Phizacklea, A. (1978), 'The TUC and Black Workers: 1974–1976', *British Journal of Industrial Relations*, 16 (2): 244–258.

Miles, R. and Phizacklea, A. (1984), *White Man's Country*, London: Pluto Press.

Modood, T. (1997), 'Employment' in Modood, T., Berthoud, R., Lakey, J., Nazroo, J., Smith, P., Virdee, S. and Beishon, S., *Ethnic Minorities in Britain*, London: Policy Studies Institute.

Moore, R. (1975), *Racism and Black Resistance in Britain*, London: Pluto Press.

National and Local Government Officers (1981), *1980 Annual Report*, London: NALGO.

OMCS (1990), *Programme for Action on Race*, London: OMCS.

Omi, M. and Winant, H. (1986), *Racial Formation in the United States of America*, New York: Routledge.

Ouseley, H. (1990), 'Resisting Institutional Change', in Ball, W. and Solomos, J. (eds), *Race and Local Politics*, London: Macmillan.

Owen, D. (1993), *Ethnic Minorities in Great Britain: Settlement Patterns*, Census Paper 1, Coventry: Commission for Racial Equality, University of Warwick.

Phizacklea, A. and Miles, R. (1980), *Labour and Racism*, London: Routledge & Kegan Paul.
Raison, T. (1984), 'The view from the Government', in Benyon, J. (ed.), *Scarman and After*, Oxford: Oxford Pergamon Press Limited, pp.244–258.
Ramdin, R. (1987), *The Making of the Black Working Class in Britain*, London: Gower.
Rex, J. (1970), *Race Relations in Sociological Theory*, London: Routledge & Kegan Paul.
Rex, J. and Tomlinson, S. (1979), *Colonial Immigrants in a British City*, London: Routledge and Kegan Paul.
Roediger, D. R. (1994), *Towards the Abolition of Whiteness*, London: Verso.
Rogaly, J. (1977), *Grunwick*, London: Penguin.
Society of Civil and Public Servants (1983), *SCPS Annual Report 1982*, London: SCPS.
Society of Civil and Public Servants (1984), *SCPS Annual Report 1983*, London: SCPS.
Shukra, K. (1996), 'A scramble for the British pie', *Patterns of Prejudice*, 30 (1): 28–36.
Sivanandan, A. (1976), 'Race, Class and the State: the Black Experience in Britain', *Race and Class*, 17 (4): 348.
Sivanandan, A. (1982), *A Different Hunger: Writings on Black Resistance*, London: Pluto Press.
Sivanandan, A. (1993), *Writings on Black Resistance*, London: Verso.
Smith, D. J. (1977), *Racial Disadvantage in Britain*, London: Penguin.
Solomos, J. (1988), *Black Youth, Racism and the State*, Cambridge: Cambridge University Press.
Solomos, J. (1993), *Race and Racism in Britain*, London: Macmillan.
Taylor, S. (1984), 'The Scarman Report and an explanation of the riots', in Benyon, J. (ed.), *Scarman and After*, Oxford: Oxford Pergamon Press Limited.
Virdee, S. (1992), *Part of the Union? Trade Union Participation by Ethnic Minority Workers*, London: Commission for Racial Equality.
Virdee, S. and Grint, K. (1994), 'Black Self-Organisation in Trade Unions', *Sociological Review*, 42 (2): 202–26.
Virdee, S. (1995), *Racial Violence and Harassment*, London: Policy Studies Institute.
Virdee, S. (1997), 'Racial Harassment' in Modood, T., Berthoud, R., Lakey, J., Nazroo, J., Smith, P., Virdee, S. and Beishon, S. *Ethnic Minorities in Britain*, London: Policy Studies Institute.

Virdee, S. (1999a forthcoming) 'Racism and Resistance in British Trade Unions: 1948–79', in Alexander, P. and Halpern, R. (eds), *Labour and Difference in the USA, Africa and Britain*, London: Macmillan.

Virdee, S. (1999b in preparation) 'Racism and Class Relations in Contemporary Britain'.

Wrench, J. (1987), 'Unequal Comrades: Trade Unions, Equal Opportunity and Racism', in Jenkins, R. and Solomos, J. (eds), *Racism and Equal Opportunity Policies in the 1980s*, Cambridge: Cambridge University Press.

Wrench, J. (1996), *Preventing Racism at the Workplace*, Dublin: European Foundation for the Improvement of Living and Working Conditions.

–4–

Immigration and the Celtic Tiger: a Land of a Thousand Welcomes?

Kieran Allen

Ireland has long been known as a country of emigration, the 'human resource warehouse of Europe' as some writers described it (King, Shuttleworth and Walsh 1996). Even as late as the 1980s, when net emigration from Southern European countries such as Greece and Portugal gave way to net immigration inflows, Ireland continued to export its 'surplus' population in great numbers. The historic pattern of emigration had become incorporated into Irish life and was almost a rite of passage for many young people.

Yet by the mid 1990s, all this had changed. The influx of a small number of refugees and economic migrants shifted the political agenda and Ireland had apparently developed an 'immigrant problem'. According to some media reports, one of the most sparsely populated countries in Europe was about to be 'flooded' with hordes of refugees who would become a drain on its social services (Irish Times 25/2/1998). Even those who welcomed refugees did so within the terms of the dominant discourse. A Catholic justice commission, for example, called for a 'grasping of the nettle of expulsion' as the inevitable price that would have to be paid for a transparent, fair and speedy application process to determine who were genuine and who were 'opportunist' refugees (Irish Commission for Justice and Peace and Trocaire 1997: 4). It would seem that neither a history of colonization nor the experience of widespread emigration, some of it falling into the 'illegal category', had prevented the onslaught of anti-immigrant xenophobia.

This chapter examines how the Irish political élite used mass emigration in the past as a safety valve to relieve social tensions. It explores how the spectacular growth rates achieved in the Celtic tiger economy combined with restrictions on refugees entering Britain has brought a major reversal. Finally, it attempts to indicate how the hostility towards refugees has been functional for a political élite facing charges of corruption and a failure to spread the benefits of a booming economy.

The Safety Valve of Emigration

The absence of compulsory registration and the existence of open borders between Ireland and Britain makes estimation of Irish migration a difficult business. However there is little doubt, historically, about its overall scale. One sociologist has remarked that, 'The Irish are a people peculiarly disposed to emigration, so much so that it is easier to explain why they wander rather than remain at home'(Ryan 1990).

The tradition of emigration began when large numbers of Protestant dissenters moved to the North American colonies in the eighteenth century. It is estimated that between 1720 and 1820, 600,000 Irish-born emigrants arrived in America (O Tuathaigh 1991). However by the nineteenth century emigration took on a more Catholic and rural character. Although it began to rise rapidly with the decline of Irish industry in the early nineteenth century, the decisive event was the famine of 1847. Between 1846 and 1850, a million people left Ireland, and between 1850 and 1914 it is estimated that a further 4 million left (O Sullivan and Winsberg 1990). The vast majority went to America and, unusually, included a high proportion of single women. Later myths that the Irish female had a peculiar aptitude for domestic labour ignored how the absence of family ties compelled those women to gain access to board and lodgings in the quickest and cheapest fashion (Steinberg 1989). No other European nation lost such a high proportion of its population. By the end of the nineteenth century, for example, 40 percent of those born in Ireland were living abroad (O Sullivan and Winsberg: 116).

There is little doubt that the Irish encountered considerable hostility, religious discrimination and racism. In the 1850s, the nativist 'Know Nothing' movement won control of several state governments in the United States on the promise of anti-immigrant and anti-Catholic legislation. Denis Clark recounts an incident where plantation owners refused to supply labour for the building of the Chesapeake Canal in Virginia, arguing that 'Their slaves are worth money. Get Irishmen instead. If they die there is no monetary loss' (cited in Miller and Wagner 1994: 52).

In Britain, Marx observed that anti-Irish feeling suited Britain's early industrialists. He noted that,

> In all the big industrial centres in England there is profound antagonism between the Irish proletariat and the English proletariat. The average English

> worker hates the Irish worker as a competitor who lowers wages and the standard of life. He feels national and religious antipathies for him. He regards him somewhat like the poor whites of the Southern States regard their black slaves. This antagonism among the proletarians of England is artificially nourished and supported by the bourgeoise. It knows that this scission is the true secret of maintaining its power. (Marx 1978: 254)

Competition for jobs between Irish and British workers caused its own bitterness but assertions of Irish nationalism on the part of the emigrants only increased hostility. One journalist writing in the 1880s, noted that, 'the warmth of social welcome is reserved for those who allow the ice barrier of their nationalism to melt away'(Harris 1994: 194).

Yet if emigration brought some hardship, it was functional for both the British ascendancy and the emerging Irish élite. The British establishment viewed Ireland as an important supplier of reserve labour. Its large pool of unskilled and semi-skilled workers helped to lower wages on the mainland. Occasionally they were also used to break strikes, particularly in the mining industry. More generally, resentment against the Irish migrants helped to maintain an ideological division among British workers (Miles and Phizaclea 1984: 145). The emerging Irish élite also gained as emigration helped to smooth over the consolidation of land holdings and the commercialization of Irish agriculture. The transfer of ownership from an absentee landlord class to Irish farmers was facilitated by the exodus of landless labourers and family members who did not inherit farms. The perception that emigration was caused primarily by British involvement rather than by the development of Irish capitalism was also 'crucial in maintaining social stability and bourgeois hegemony in a Catholic society whose capitalist institutions and social relationships made lower class emigration imperative' (Miller 1990).

As Table 4.1 indicates, Irish independence in 1922 did little to stem the tide of emigration. It is estimated that between 1926 and 1986, over 790,000 emigrants left Ireland – despite the fact that the population fluctuated at around 3 million people (O Tuathaigh 1991: 11). Until recently, the only decade in which emigration stopped was the 1970s. Although the Fianna Fail leader Eamon De Valera promised that independence would bring a rural idyll where people 'should not be merely wage slaves or simply spending their lives to make money for somebody or other',(Dail Debates 1927 Col. 397 26/10/27) many found it necessary to move elsewhere to reach even this lowly station. After independence the main difference seemed to be that they migrated to Britain rather than the United States after immigration quotas were introduced there in 1924.

Table 4.1 Estimated Net Migration from Ireland (Republic of Ireland) (Inward less outward) 1911–1986

1911–26	–405,029
1926–36	–166,751
1936–46	–187,111
1946–56	–319,252
1956–61	–212,003
1961–66	–80,605
1966–71	–53,906
1971–79	+108,934
1979–86	–76,628
1986–91	–134,170

Source: Central Statistics Office, Dublin

Although emigration was often evoked as a sign of national shame, the rulers of the newly independent state continued to reap some benefits. It helped to remove a younger and restive population that might otherwise have questioned the failure of nationalist politics. It allowed a relatively underdeveloped economy to maintain a level of social spending that bore some relationship to its richer neighbour. Ideologically the argument that emigration resulted from the past wrongs of British colonialism helped to maintain a consensus for national development. The belief that emigration functioned as a safety valve was made explicit by a leading politician in a response to the 1954 report on the Commission on Emigration when he argued that,'High emigration, granted a population excess, releases social tensions which would otherwise explode and makes possible a stability of manners and customs which would otherwise be the subject of radical change'(cited in Lee 1989: 381).

However it was the return of mass emigration in the 1980s that brought the mechanisms by which emigration operated as a safety valve into a more acute focus. As Table 4.2 indicates, emigration dropped dramatically during the world recession of 1980–2 but then returned for the rest of the decade. In 1989, for example, the number leaving the state came close to the annual number being born.

The response of the political élite was to try to normalize emigration as a rational economic choice. In the past, emigration was seen as a cruel reflection on Ireland's claim to self-sufficiency and economic independence. As protectionist policies were dropped from the 1960s onwards in favour of a policy of inviting in multi-nationals, however, emigration was

Table 4.2 Net Migration from Ireland 1980–90

Year	*Net Emigration*
1980	8,000
1981	–2,000
1982	1,000
1983	14,000
1984	9,000
1985	20,000
1986	28,000
1987	27,000
1988	32,000
1989	46,000
1990	31,000

Source: Central Statistics Office Dublin

presented as an appropriate response to a globalized economy. The shift in the discussion of emigration from one that signified a legacy of shame and colonialism to a positive experience was signalled by the Deputy Prime Minister, Brian Lenehan, when he told *Newsweek* that emigration,

> is not a defeat because the more Irish emigrants hone their skills and talents in another environment, the more they develop a work ethic in a country like Germany or the US, the better it can be applied in Ireland when they return. After all, we can't all live on a small island.(Lee 1990:36)

Central to the new conception was an attempt to break the link between emigration and unskilled labour. As the official image of emigration shifted from presenting it as a painful suffering to seeing it as an exiting opportunity, the stereotype of the Irish emigrant as an unskilled navvy or a domestic servant was no longer appropriate. The 'new wave' emigration of the 1980s was supposed to be mainly based on the exodus of young graduates who were seeking skills and opportunities. As one writer put it, 'surplus highly skilled Irish labour will continue to be exported to core economies, facilitated by government initiatives, augmenting the international labour market for particular specialized non-manual skills' (Hazelhorn 1992:196).

Any notion that a social slur might attach to the status of being an 'illegal immigrant' in America was discarded. Instead the Irish Prime Ministers worked closely with US politicians in the Friends of Ireland Group to legalize their status (Mulholland and Keogh 1989: 93). The result was the creation of a special Donnelly scheme that offered 40,000 visas to the US between 1987 and 1990. Irish applicants managed to secure 41 per cent of the visas through a combination of intense lobbying and more practical arrangements to get examination results over to the US on time. According to the US Embassy in Dublin one third of the visas went to illegal immigrants already working in the US (Corcoran 1993: 9–10).

Once again this normalization of emigration disguised the benefits that flowed to ruling élites in both the US and Ireland. The export of tens of thousands of young Irish people in a period of economic stagnation and intense disputes over the dominant role of the Catholic church released damaging social tensions. At the time, the populist rhetoric of Ireland's leading party Fianna Fail was fading as it seemed no longer able to sustain the programme of national development (Allen 1997: 149–175). The exodus also helped to cement the relationship of Ireland's rulers with powerful wing of the US establishment because of the manner in which Irish migration fitted in with their domestic concerns.

The 1980s were a period of 'racial reaction' in the US where right-wing whites opposed the influx of immigrants from Asia, Latin America and the Caribbean. Typically this was done through a 're-articulation' of the discourse of civil rights to point to supposed disadvantages suffered by white ethnic groups (Omi and Winant 1986: 173). One focus for this campaign was the 1965 US Immigration Act which had abolished national quotas and opened immigration to anyone with immediate family ties in the US. As Irish and Italian immigration had mainly occurred at the start of the century, the pattern of immigration shifted towards more 'Third World' countries. The encouragement and legalization of Irish immigrants to the US coincided with pressure to secure a 'diversity programme' that would bring more Europeans to the US. As Luibhead puts it:

> The characterisation of the diversity programmes as 'affirmative action for the Irish' pointedly refers to the way that an initiative aimed primarily at white Europeans, and calling itself a 'diversity' programme, plays into dominant white reactions against efforts to achieve racial equality for other much harder pressed minority groups. (Luibhead 1997: 265)

This is not to claim that individual Irish immigrants were aware of the wider racist strategy informing the campaign to regularize their status or to suggest that they secured a privileged position because of it. Despite all the image making about the new wave immigrants being highly skilled and well paid, Corcoran found that the majority of Irish in New York were doing what they had traditionally done – working on building sites

(Corcoran 1997: 243). Nevertheless it does underline the double standards that come into play when political élites are able to 'control illegal immigration'. It also helps to explain the inconsistencies in how emigration is presented, because the very same politicians who campaigned openly for the regularization of illegals in the United States also attempted to spread fears of illegals 'flooding' Ireland when the Celtic tiger boom started. And they did so again as a way of protecting their own power and prestige within society at large.

The Celtic Tiger Emerges

On 31 August 1994, the investment bank Morgan Stanley coined the term 'the Celtic tiger' to compare the spectacular growth of the Irish economy to the then impressive Asian tigers (O Hearn 1997). In the five years to 1998, economic growth as measured by GNP averaged 7.5 per cent a year (Sweeney 1998: 14). This was all the more spectacular when compared with a sluggish rate of growth throughout the EU. The boom came as a major surprise to those who had viewed the historical pattern of emigration as conclusive proof that Ireland was fated to a 'peripheral', dependent or neo-colonial status in the world economy (e.g. Crotty 1986; Breathnach 1996).

A number of factors helped to account for the boom. One was a strategic decision made by the Irish state and its development agency, the Industrial Development Authority, in the mid 1970s to concentrate its resources on marketing Ireland as the new Silicon Valley of Europe. Since then, Ireland has become a major location for key US computer firms such as Intel, Dell and Microsoft. Another was the huge influx of EU Structural Funds designed to combat disadvantages that might arise from Ireland's underdeveloped status in a single market. It is estimated that the first tranche of these funds added as much as 3.5 per cent to Ireland's GNP in 1992 and 1993(Sweeney 1998: 78). However probably the most fundamental reason for the boom was the strategy of creating a low tax haven for companies that sought educated but cheap labour inside EU barriers. Tax on company profits from manufacturing exports stands at a mere 10 per cent whereas ample provision also exists for various 'tax efficiency measures' to reduce overall company taxation still further. As many as 40,000 foreign accounts exist as a device for avoiding taxes (Irish Times 28/2/98). As profit margins are squeezed elsewhere, companies have become more interested in gaining competitive advantages provided by the new Cayman Island of Europe.

The extensive tax avoidance measures make it difficult to assess the exact scale of the boom. In order to benefit from Ireland's low tax status, multinationals operate an extensive policy of transfer pricing. The figures on claimed output per employee offer some evidence of this. In 1990, Irish owned firms claimed a net output of £26,500 per employee in manufacturing industry. In the case of multinational-owned pharmaceutical companies it was £204,000 and in other food companies (mainly cola concentrate companies) it was £427,000 (O Grada 1997: 121). Even allowing for greater levels of technology and productivity, the figures suggest a major fictional component in the output per employee. By adjusting the pricing structure within the multinational firm, companies declare higher profits in Ireland's tax haven. One exasperated economics commentator noted that Irish economic figures had 'about the same empirical status as moving statues, flying saucers and the statue-of-Elvis-found-on-Mars-stories' (ibid.: 33).

Despite the evidence of transfer pricing, it would be wrong to conclude the Irish boom is simply artificial. Sectors such as construction, where few multinationals operate, have also shown signs of major expansion with output growing by 50 per cent between 1994 and 1996 alone (Breathnach 1998). Employment has also grown throughout the economy with the OECD claiming that total employment in Ireland rose by 26 per cent between 1986 and 1996 compared with 7 per cent in the EU and even 15 per cent in the US. More relevantly, the boom has led to a reversal of emigration and the appearance for the first time of immigration that is not based on Irish people returning to their home country.

The figures in Table 4.3 hardly indicate that a flood of people are coming to Ireland. In the five years of Ireland's greatest boom, a grand total of 23,400 extra migrants have arrived. The largest group of immigrants is classified as coming from the UK and traditionally this has largely been made up of Irish people returning for work. However, unlike previous booms a new component has been added. As the decade has progressed, the numbers arriving from outside the UK and the US – the traditional destinations of Irish emigrants – has increased. This does not automatically means that these immigrants were all 'foreigners' as Irish emigrants have also settled in countries as diverse as Germany or Australia, but it does suggest that a higher proportion of non-Irish people have moved to one of the most ethnically homogenous countries in Europe.

Refugees were one group that did arrive. After 1994, the numbers of applications for refugee status remained small by European standards but showed a dramatic increase by Irish standards. In 1992, 29 applications were made for refugee status; by 1995 this had risen to 424 applications

Table 4.3 Estimated Migration classified by Country of Origin 1992-1997. Figures in 000s.

	1992	*1993*	*1994*	*1995*	*1996*	*1997*
Immigrants from:						
UK	22.7	17.5	15.2	15.6	17.6	20.0
Rest of EU	6.5	6.6	5.8	6.3	7.2	8.1
USA	4.6	5.0	4.3	3.8	6.4	6.6
Rest of World	6.9	5.7	4.8	5.5	8.0	9.3
Total Immigrants	40.7	34.7	30.1	31.2	39.2	44.0
Emigrants	33.4	35.1	34.8	33.1	31.2	29.0
Net Migration	7.4	–0.4	–4.7	–1.9	8.0	15.0

Source: Central Statistics Office, Dublin.

and by 1997 the figure reached 3,883 (Department of Justice 1998). Two main factors seemed to account for the increase. One was the growing restriction of asylum seekers elsewhere in Europe and in Britain in particular. After the 1993 Asylum and Immigration (Appeals) Act was introduced in Britain the refusal rate for asylum seekers rose sharply, as Table 4.4 indicates. Clearly a number of refugees who did not wish to spend time in detention centres in Britain decided to make their applications in Ireland instead.

The other factor was Ireland's booming economy. Emigrants have traditionally gravitated to where economic activity is most vibrant and Ireland in the mid 1990s has proved no exception. As skill shortages developed and the pool of unskilled workers contracted, a small number of immigrants filled the gaps. One union official, for example, claimed that several thousand jobs in Dublin's catering industry were filled by immigrants (Irish Times 5/9/97).

The term 'refugee' therefore entered popular parlance as synonymous with the first wave of non-Irish immigrants who had arrived of their own accord. Small groups of refugees had arrived in the past – such as Hungarians fleeing the suppression of the 1956 uprising – but these had been housed in special army huts and had come at the invitation of the Irish state. Now, for the first time, a group on non-white people became visible in the centres of large urban conurbations.

The Political Response

The Irish state was singularly unprepared for the arrival of even a few thousand immigrants. The main law covering the entry of foreigners dated back to 1935 and was rather ominously known as the Aliens Act. The small numbers of non-EU residents who stayed in Ireland were often required to visit the Aliens Office of the Department of Justice – a department that had a long tradition of voicing suspicion about the slightest dilution of Irish culture by even the smallest trickle of foreigners. The same department had vehemently opposed the entry of Jewish victims of the Holocaust after the Second World War (Cronin 1997: 8). Although Ireland was a signatory to the UN Convention of 1951 on refugees, the procedures by which it fulfilled its obligations were only laid out in an informal agreement with the United Nations High Commissioner for Refugees in 1985 (Interdepartmental Committee on Non-Irish Nationals 1994: 8). No legislative framework existed even though it was abundantly clear that the numbers of refugees entering EU countries showed a sharp rise from the mid 1980s.

When the Irish state set about rectifying this situation, it did so at a time then 'the liberal agenda' was dominant. In 1992 the Labour Party scored its highest electoral success since 1928 and then, rather surprisingly, entered government with the conservative and right-wing nationalist party, Fianna Fail. In their joint programme for government they committed themselves to 'a policy towards the treatment of refugees, asylum seekers and immigrants [which] will meet the highest international standards' (ibid.: 3). At the same time the Catholic Church suffered a number of defeats in quick succession as the divorce, the right to travel for abortion and homosexuality were all legalized in a comparatively short space of time. To compound their difficulties, a series of scandals about priests engaged in child abuse emerged. One of the indirect effects of these scandals was the fall of the Reynolds-led coalition of Fianna Fail and Labour in 1994, after key Fianna Fail Ministers were accused of failing to extradite a paedophile priest to Northern Ireland. This in turn led to the formation of a new 'rainbow coalition' of Labour, Fine Gael and Democratic Left, which took on the task of steering the first Refugee Act through the Dail in 1996.

The debates surrounding the passage of this Act seemed at first sight to confirm the image of 'Ireland of the Welcomes' – the advertising slogan of the tourist board. The government argued that the definition of refugee should be expanded to include 'a person persecuted because of his or her gender, sexual orientation or membership of a trade union' (Dail Debates Vol. 457 Col. 706 19/10/95). The purpose of the Refugee Act was to 'safeguard the rights of applicants and to ensure that no valid application was rejected' (ibid.: Col.711). To that end it established that 'immigration officers will not have any discretion to refuse entry to asylum seekers and, accordingly, the general rule will be that such applicants will be given free entry into the country'(ibid.: Col. 715).

An independent commissioner was to be appointed to investigate each case and make a recommendation. The right of applicants for refugee status to an oral hearing before an appeal board was guaranteed (ibid.: Col. 718). Finally, the government argued that Ireland 'should be generous in relation to the provision for the reunification of families' and allowed for the entry into Ireland not only of close family members of refugees but also any relative where a dependency relationship existed (ibid.: Col. 721).

Despite the liberal rhetoric, there were serious limitations. The Refugee Act still insisted that there was a category of 'manifestly unfounded applications' formed from the considerable numbers who used false identity papers (Tormey 1996). How it was possible to escape repressive regimes without subterfuge was never explained. The Refugee Act also incorporated the provision of the Dublin Convention of 1990, which stipulated that refugees could be deported back to the first EU country they set foot on – regardless of whether that country operated a 'white list' policy or used other mechanisms to expel refugees. As Ireland is the most westerly outpost of the EU and it is difficult to arrive there from Africa without touching down in some other EU country, this gave ample provision to the government to engage in deportations.

Yet, ironically, the conservative opposition highlighted these very limitations. Drawing on Ireland's own emigrant history and experience of political repression under British rule, Fianna Fail argued for an even more tolerant approach. The future Minster for Justice, John O Donoghue, noted that

> the status of the refugee should strike a cord with every man, woman and child here who has any grasp of Irish history, our history books being littered with names and details of those driven from our country out of fear of persecution. (Dail Debates Vol.457 Col 772 19/10/95)

He attacked the provision that prevented applicants for refugee status from seeking employment and demanded free legal aid to process their claims. He sought a guarantee that if a refugee was sent to another European

Table 4.4 Adjudication of Asylum Applications In the United Kingdom 1990–1994

	1990	*1991*	*1992*	*1993*	*1994*
Accepted	1,600	800	1,900	2,900	1,400
Rejected	900	5,400	35,000	18,600	20,900
Allowed to stay	3,600	3,000	21,700	20,900	5,400

Source: UNHCR Bulletin Asylum in Europe

country there would be assurances given that the refugee could not be deported back to countries where he or she faced persecution (Dail Debates Vol. 462 Col. 874 28/2/96).

In 1996, therefore Ireland had an extremely liberal consensus on refugees. There was little discussion on deportations or detention centres and a certain pride was take in the county's 'progressive' image. It seemed the historic memory of poverty and anti-colonialism had combined to produce a greater sense of tolerance than that found in more developed countries. The more recent experience of an Irish state campaigning for its own 'illegals' in America also seemed to offer a greater realism about the issue of 'illegals'.

Reaction

Yet the liberal consensus on refugees did not last long. Within the space of a few months, the combination of a press campaign and the efforts of populist politicians helped to create a virulent anti-refugee atmosphere. Elements of racism had, of course, long been part of Irish society. Jewish immigrants were driven out of Limerick in 1904 and there was certainly no traditional Irish welcome for those who fled the horrors of Hitler's Germany (Keogh 1998). Attitudes of some Irish Americans towards black people often fed back into Irish society to create a pool of racist imagery and insults. Indigenous Irish travellers have also long been the subject of abuse and hatred. Nevertheless the rise in racism caught many by surprise and it was some time before pro-refugee organizations managed to regroup.

The shift coincided with the start of a general election that effectively began in May 1997. A minor disturbance by 300 refugees who had been forced to queue at a social welfare office for a whole day was the spark that ignited the issue for the press and the politicians. Three days after the disturbance, the *Irish Times* noted that 'not since the Celts were driven West by the Romans has Ireland seen such a large influx of refugees'

(Irish Times 17/5/97). Just over a week later the same paper ran an extraordinary story by its security correspondent claiming that 'trafficking gangs' had discovered Ireland's benefit system on the Internet and had organized an influx of refugees to arrive there. Under the headline 'Shop Keepers say Theft by Romanians growing' the paper gave a platform to an unnamed street trader to vent the emerging racist argument that, 'it's all right for the English, the French to take these people because they colonised the world. But I cannot understand why the problem is shoved onto Ireland' (Irish Times 26/5/97). This, it is worth noting, was the liberal press.

The media backlash against refugees was echoed by politicians, desperately searching for voters who would return them to office. One claimed that Ireland was being 'overwhelmed with professional beggars' (Irish Times 27/5/97). A prominent Labour candidate called for a 'crackdown' on 'welfare fraudsters traveling between here and Britain' and warned of increased tension between 'the public' and the 'international community' living here (Irish Times 24/5/97). Much of the anti-refugee rhetoric, however took place at the level of the doorstep canvass and did not reach the press through public statements. This whispering campaign was only brought to wider attention when rival politicians protested against attempts to whip up racial prejudice for electoral gain (Irish Times 21/5/97).

The racist campaign had an important effect. On the eve of polling, the Minister for Justice in the 'rainbow coalition' effectively abolished the common travel area between Ireland and Britain. Immigration officers were given powers to prevent people entering Ireland and return them to Britain or Northern Ireland without any investigation or right to appeal. However, this ruling posed a considerable dilemma. Until the recent Belfast peace agreement the Republic of Ireland claimed jurisdiction over Northern Ireland and is still officially opposed to the partition of the country. How was the Irish state to screen people who were not regarded as 'foreigners' and deny them entry? The right to a common travel area is also valued by many who have traditionally journeyed to Britain without bureaucratic restrictions. Again, how could this convenience be maintained while screening for illegal immigrants? The informal solution that was promoted by the Department of Justice was to pick out black faces from crowds crossing the borders while maintaining lax passport controls for those who had a more standard Irish appearance.

When a new Fianna Fail government took office after the General Election, in June 1997 the difficulties for refugees seemed to increase. In July, a legal injunction was taken out by a former Minister for Justice which had the effect of suspending the implementation of the Refugee

Act. In September the provisions of the Dublin Convention were implemented and refugees who were known to have come from another EU country were refused entry to Ireland. Later that month government funding for a legal service to refugees provided by the Irish Refugee Council was withdrawn. The new justice minister, John O Donoghue, who had previously called for a more tolerant policy began issuing regular figures about the number of immigrants who had been turned back, claiming major cost savings for the state. Soon afterwards a policy of deportation began and O Donoghue refused to assure Amnesty International that detention camps would not be opened (Amnesty International Irish Section 1997: 4). In March 1998 he turned down a request from opposition parties for an amnesty for refugees claiming, in a gross exaggeration, that it would cost up to £250 million. An Immigration Bill was brought in to make deportations easier and to pressurise doctors, teachers and social workers to report on 'illegals'. Finally a new Illegal Immigrants (Trafficking) Bill was introduced providing for ten-year jail sentences for those who help bring illegal immigrants into the country.

It was clear that key sections of the Irish establishment looked with disquiet on the possibility of Ireland moving towards a multi-ethnic society. One government backbencher voiced this crudely when he claimed that refugees were 'carrying on in a culture that is not akin to Irish culture'. When asked what this other culture might imply he mentioned begging from neighbours and 'bleeding lambs in the back garden' (Irish Times 26/10/97). In many ways the new emphasis was far closer to previous periods in Irish history when groups such as Jewish people were excluded because they were viewed as a threat to Irish culture. Yet how is it possible to account for this reversion to xenophobic practices? Why did such a minuscule number of refugees and immigrants provoke such a fury? More specifically, why was the tolerant language of 'progressive legislation' dropped so quickly?

When the Rising Tide did not lift all Boats

It has often been argued there is a link between hostility to migrants and economic conditions. During periods of economic boom, the presence of immigrants meets little response and extreme right-wing politics are marginalized whereas in periods of recession and insecurity racist feelings are more intense. In Germany, for example, a significant section of the population expressed indifference to the presence of 'guest workers' during the booming 1960s. Yet after the first economic crisis, in 1969, a new political language about the burden of 'alien employees' began to grow.

Later this expanded into a claim that different cultures could never integrate (Schonwalder 1996). At first sight, a similar relationship between racism and an economic downturn is not to be found in Ireland. As we have seen, hostility to the first small wave of immigrants occurred in boom conditions where employment prospects rose. Moreover, although a small number of migrants found work in areas such as catering and telesales, the most visible group were refugees who were excluded from access to the labour market while their applications for asylum were pending.

However the divergence of the Irish case from the general norm is more deceptive than it might first appear. The Irish boom of the late 1990s developed under quite different conditions from those that had occurred previously. In the 1960s, an economic boom was associated with a rising standard of living and a considerable expansion of social spending. Free education, free hospital treatment, extended pensions emerged with the economic advance of that period. However the Celtic tiger economy of the 1990s had a quite different character. If anything it polarized society still more as major inequalities of wealth became more visible. 'Social partnership' arrangements concluded between employers and union leaders meant that wage increases were kept low while profits boomed. Between 1993 and 1995, profits for all firms averaged an increase of 27.8 per cent whereas wage rises in manufacturing were pegged to a mere 5 per cent (Sweeney 1998: 92).

The boom led to a new concentration of wealth on one hand and an intense feeling of relative deprivation on the other. The earnings ratio of the top decile of the male working population to the bottom decile grew from 3.5 times to five times between 1987 and 1994(ibid.: 157). The numbers who found themselves in low-paid employment grew as a proportion of the workforce. By the mid 1990s Ireland had the second highest proportion of its labour force on low pay in the industrialized countries (Economic and Social Research Institute 1997). The growing polarization of incomes was strengthened by a state strategy of cutting taxes on the wealthy in order to 'attract' foreign industry and to encourage indigenous entrepreneurs. Paul Sweeney, a relatively uncritical apologist for the Celtic tiger, noted that

> Every week there seems to be a new tax scheme proposed to help an area or industry, which proposers know will at least be heard. Ireland is one of the world's tax havens for the corporate sector. Therefore, as the state must raise taxes for its daily activities, it does so mainly on labour and consumer spending. (Sweeney 1998:161)

This comment relates only to the official tax reduction schemes. A spate of scandals also showed that tax evasion is deeply embedded in the culture of the Irish wealthy. The revelation that a former Prime Minister was paid a regular income of £20,000 a month from an offshore bank account held by 39 leading industrialists showed not only the close relationship between business leaders and key politicians but that tax avoidance was the norm in élite circles.

The experience of a boom that polarized society provided the context in which the racist propaganda against refugees was developed. The radical redistribution of resources from the poor to the rich via tax cuts meant that far less was available for social spending. The issue of housing is particularly relevant here. The number of new local authority house completions dropped by a half between the mid eighties and the mid nineties (Bacon 1998). As more people were forced into private accommodation, they found that houses prices and rents increased dramatically. One factor that had added to the increase in house prices was the greater amount of spare cash in the pockets of the wealthy. By purchasing property for investment income they squeezed many first-time buyers out of the market (Sunday Tribune 15/3/98). The housing shortage provided racist politicians and the press with a handy stick to beat refugees. They were presented as 'spongers' who were taking accommodation that might have gone to Irish people, even depriving the homeless of their access to guest house accommodation. By focusing on refugees, politicians were able to ignore the wider problems that had arisen from their own economic strategy.

Racism, however, does not function just at an economic level. As Du Bois pointed out, it provided a 'psychological wage' that can compensate for the lack of material gains (Du Bois 1969:700–1). As the benefits of the Celtic tiger remained with the few, politicians needed a scapegoat for the bitterness that emerged in society. During the election of 1997 this was even more urgent as the 'golden circle' that tied business leaders to politicians in schemes of tax evasion and bribery became more visible. When the former leader of Fianna Fail was accused of corruption and bribery it was necessary to replace the rhetoric of understanding with one that denounced 'spongers'. The new intolerance found a hearing as many sought an outlet for their sense of relative deprivation. The talk about the success of the Celtic tiger quite simply clashed with the lived experience of the majority. The anger against refugees was therefore a means of asserting that the nation had to 'look after its own first'. Indeed it was a bitter cry of anger about the failure of that imagined community to do just that.

Of course this reaction was by no means automatic. As Gramsci pointed out, working class consciousness can often be highly contradictory – mixing elements of class solidarity with the common sense of the street (Gramsci 1978: 333). Which element is uppermost often depends on a variety of factors from political leadership to the experience of struggle and solidarity – or the lack thereof. In Ireland in the mid 1990s there was both a profound shock about corruption within the nationalist élite and a feeling that nothing could be done. Although opinion polls showed overwhelming support for the jailing of those found guilty of corruption, no politician or business leader was even charged. As the labour movement was tied into social partnership agreements, it too failed to organize significant protests. Yet when it seems that 'nothing can be done' about those on high, this only adds to the temptation to kick out at those on the bottom of the pile. The structure of the nation-state usually means that 'foreigners' are most likely to feel the boot first.

Conclusion

The reaction that developed against refugees in Ireland indicates that racism is not confined to colonial countries. Despite its own history of mass emigration and political persecution, Ireland produced a response that was little different to its European neighbours. Non-governmental organizations such as the Irish Refugee Council saw these developments as confirmation that a fear of 'the Other' is central to the construction of identity of Western Europeans (Bhabha 1993: 112–25; see also Said 1985). More crudely, it is claimed that suspicion of outsiders is an emotion which is virtually innate, particularly to those who were uneducated. Thus the combined influence of post-colonial theory and more traditional forms of social Catholicism helped to shift discussion about Irish racism onto a social psychological level where 'fears had to be dealt with'. The solution, it appeared, was to lobby the state to educate its citizens by presenting positive images of refugees. This, it was argued, needed to be combined with assurances that controls would be implemented against 'illegals'.

This chapter has argued that this approach was limited in three important respects.

Firstly, by reducing racism to a generalized psychological feeling, there is a failure to analyse the specific historical circumstances in which racism is created and triggered off. As Callinicos has argued, racism has its historic origins in ideologies that legitimize slavery and imperialism, and it draws sustenance from the competition for resources inherent in a market-based society (Callinicos 1994). Although Ireland did not share the same colonial history as other European countries, this never prevented Irish people drawing on the general stock of racist arguments. The anti-black riots staged by Irish people during the US Civil War bear ample testimony to this (Ignatiev 1995). Despite appeals from nationalist leaders such as Daniel O Connell to support the abolitionist movement, many Irish Americans were often co-opted via the Tammany Hall network to align themsleves with the Democratic Party and the pro-slavery rebellion (Allen 1994). Unfortunately those who are oppressed in one social sphere do not automatically link up with the oppressed in another. Equally, it should be understood that Irish nationalism, which was originally developed in opposition to colonialism, is not more especially more prone to racism than say British or French nationalism. It has been necessary to look at the specific context where the Celtic tiger failed to deliver benefits for the many to understand the fertile ground that had been created for racist arguments.

Second, the assumption that the state could help to educate its population away from racism ignores the direct interest that political élites have in finding scapegoats. The presentation of refugees as 'spongers' took place against a wider framework whereby welfare spending was depreciated in order to make way for further tax cuts. By focusing of refugees as the cause of issues such housing shortages, politicians could avoid questions about the implications of their policy of tax cuts. The sharp turn taken by Fianna Fail between their period of opposition and government indicates the opportunist manner refugees were used to divert bitterness from the élites themselves.

Lastly, the belief that fears need to be appeased by seeking more immigration controls can only add to the belief that immigration itself is a problem. This ignores the hypocrisy with which the whole issue shrouded. Despite lamenting the curse of emigration, the Irish state viewed it both as a release against damaging social tensions and a means of cementing their relationship with the rulers of Britain and latterly America. They never had any difficulty in accepting that Irish illegal immigration to America was necessary so that tens of thousands could gain work. Indeed, they encouraged it as a rational modern response to a globalized world, but whereas they encouraged the exodus of their own citizens as an economic safety valve, they equally sought to use the tiny influx of migrants into Ireland as a political safety valve to divert attention from problems of their making.

Despite the sustained campaign by the media and populist politicians, many have resisted a racist response. Anti-racist demonstrations have won official backing from some of the major unions. Refugeee organizations have also emerged, challenging the Irish state to give them a right to work.

Nevertheless there is sometimes a reluctance to defend economic, as against political, migrants. The Irish government has exploited this gap, claiming that they have no problem with 'genuine' asylum seekers but arguing that they need a battery of repressive measures to establish who is 'genuine' and who is not. An acceptance that immigration is normal and that workers have every right to move around the world could only add to the intellectual coherence of anti-racists.

Bibliography

Allen, K. (1997) *Fianna Fail and Irish Labour,* London: Pluto Press.

Allen, T. (1994) *The Invention of the White Race*, London: Verso.

Amnesty International (1997) *Refugees in Ireland*, Dublin: Amnesty International.

Bacon, P. (1998) *An Economic Assessment of Recent House Price Developments*, Dublin; Stationery Office.

Bhabha, H. (1995) 'Remembering Fanon: Self, Psyche and the Colonial Condition' in P. Willimans and l, Chrisman (eds) *Colonial and Post Colonial Theory: a Reader*, London: Routledge.

Breathnach, P. (1996) 'Uneven Development and Irish Peripheralisation' in P. Shirlow (eds) *Development Ireland* London: Pluto Press.

Breathnach (1998) 'Ireland: Europe's Tiger Economy' unpublished paper Department of Geography, N.U.I. Maynooth.

Callinicos, A. (1994) *Race and Class*, London: Bookmarks.

Corcoran, M. (1993) *Irish Illegals: Transients between Two Societies*, Wesport, Connecticut: Greenwood Press.

Corcoran, M. (1997) 'Clandestine Destinies: The Informal Economic Sector and Irish Immigrant Incorporation' in J. MacLaughlin (eds) *Location and Dislocation in Contemporary Irish Society*, Cork: Cork University Press.

Cronin, D. (1997) Refugees are Welcome Here, *Dublin:* Bookmarks.

Crotty, R. (19860 *Ireland in Crisis: A Study in Capitalist Colonial Development*, Dingle: Brandon.

Du Bois, W.E. (1969) *Black Reconstruction in America 1860-1880*, New York: Russell and Russell.

Economic and Social Research Institute (1997) *The Earnings Distribution and Return to Education in Ireland 1987–1994*, Dublin: ESRI Working paper No 85

Gramsci, A. (1997) *Selections from the Prison Notebooks of Antonio Gramsci*, London: Lawrence and Wishart.

Harris, R. (1994) *The Nearest Place that wasn't Ireland: Early Nineteenth Cenury Irish Labour Migration,* Ames: Iowa State University Press.

Hazelhorn,E. (1992) 'We Can't All Live on a Small Island:The Political Economy of Irish Migration' in P.O Sullivan (eds) *The Irish in the New Communities*, Leicester: Leicester University Press.

Ignatiev, N. (19950 *How the Irish Became White*, London: Routledge.

Interdepartmental Committee on Non-Irish Nationals (1994) *Interim Report on Applications for Refugee Status,* Dublin: Stationery Office.

Irish Commission for Justice and Peace and Trocaire (1997) *Refugees and Asylum Seekers: A Challenge to Solidarity*, Dublin: Trocaire.

Keogh, D. (1998) *Jews in Twentieth Century Ireland,* Cork: Cork University Press.

King, R. Shuttleworth, I. and Walsh, J. (1996) 'Ireland: The Human Resource Warehouse of Europe' in P. Rees, J. Stillwell, A Convey and M. Kupiszewskie (eds) *Population Migration in the European Union*, Chichester: John Wiley.

Lee, J. (1989) *Ireland 1912–1985: Politics and Society*, Cambridge: Cambridge University Press.

Lee, J. (1990) 'Emigration: A Contemporary Perspective' in R. Kearney (eds) *Migrations*, Dublin: Wolfhound Press.

Luibhead, E. (1997) 'Irish Immigrants in the United States Racial System' in J. MacLaughlin (eds) *Location and Dislocation in Contemporary Irish Society*, Cork: Cork University Press.

Marx, K. (1978) *Ireland and the Irish Question*, Moscow: Progress Publishers.

Miles, R. and Phizachlea, A. (1084) *White Man's Country: Racism in British Politics*, London: Pluto Press.

Miller, K. (1990) 'Emigration, Capitalism and Ideology in Post-famine Ireland' , in R. Kearney (eds) *Migrations,* Dublin: Wolfhound Press.

Miller, K. and Wagner, P. (1994) *Out of Ireland: The Story of Irish Emigration to America*, London: Aumum.

Mulholland, J. and Keogh, D. (1989) *Emigration, Employment and Enterprise*, Cork: Hibernian University Press.

O Grada, C. (1997) *A Rocky Road: The Irish Economy since the 1920s*, Manchester: Manchester University Press.

O Hearn, D. (1997) 'The Celtic Tiger: The Role of the Multinationals' in E. Crowley and J. MacLoughlin (eds) *Under the Belly of the Tiger*, Dublin: Irish Reporter Publications.

Omi, M. and Winant, H. (1994) *Racial Formation in the United States*, London: Routledge.

O Sullivan, P. and Winsberg, M. (1990) 'Ireland' in W. Serow, C.Nam, D.Sly and R. Weller (eds) *Handbook on International Migration*, New York: Greenwood Press.

O Tormey, R. (1996) 'Exodus: Migrants, Refugees and Development' in C. Regan (eds) *75/25: Ireland in an Increasingly Unequal World*, Dublin:Development Education Commission of CONGOOD.

O Tuathaigh,M.A.G. (1991) 'The Historical Pattern of Irish Emigration: Some Labour Aspects' in Galway Labour History Group (eds) *The Emigrant Experience*, Galway: Galway Labour History Group.

Said, E. (1985) *Orientalism*; Harmondsworth: Penguin.

Schonwalder, K. (1996) 'Migration, Refugees and Ethnic Plurality as Issues of Public and Political Debates in West Germany' in D. Cesarani and M. Fulbrook (eds) *Citizenship, Nationality and Migration in Europe*, London: Routledge.

Steinberg, S. (1989) *The Ethnic Myth: Race, Ethnicity and Class in America*, Boston: Beacon Press.

Sweeney, P (1998) *The Celtic Tiger: Ireland's Economic Miracle Explained*, Dublin: Oak Tree Press.

–5–

Germany: Nation and Immigration

Gareth Dale

Introduction

Since 1945 over thirty-five million people have migrated to the Federal Republic of Germany (FRG).[1] In the decades between the fall of Berlin and the fall of its wall, net immigration exceeded eighteen million – higher than the figure for the US. A tenth of the population are first-generation immigrants. Almost a tenth of the population are 'foreigners'. Many of the latter were recruited as *Gastarbeiter* (guest workers) by German employers and state officials. Their presence has transformed German society. 'German-built' Mercedes and Volkswagens are manufactured in large part by foreign labour; 'German' streets have taken on the colours of foreign immigrants and their descendants.[2]

Yet the consensus amongst the political establishment is an attitude of denial. 'Germany', they say, 'is not a country of immigration.' These lines are written in 1998, a year that saw the major parties of the right place that denial in the forefront of electoral campaigning. Helmut Kohl, leader of the Christian Democratic Union, presented his government as the sternest of hosts: 'Foreigners are guests in our country. If they do not behave like guests, they should be kicked out' (in *Socialist Worker*, 2 February 1998). Theo Waigel, leader of the Bavarian Christian Social Union, declares that 'We [sic] are not a multicultural society – we are a German nation', whilst his lieutenant in Munich sought to realize the rhetoric by attempting to deport foreigners convicted of crime – *and their families*! Trumping such 'Christian' neighbour-loving, the fascist German Peoples Union, campaigning on a nationalist and racist platform in Saxony-Anhalt, achieved the highest vote of any fascist party in Germany since the war.

These clips from an election year attest to a wider development of the 1990s: questions of race, nation, immigrants and 'minorities' have remained high on the political agenda. The decade began with German unification, swiftly followed by moral panics over impending 'floods' of asylum seekers from Eastern Europe and beyond. Murders of foreigners in several towns shocked millions and provoked mass anti-racist protests. Behind the scenes, measures for the 'processing' and deportation of refugees were tightened, while patrols on the eastern borders were bolstered and equipped with spy helicopters and infra-red devices, turning the Oder-Neisse into Europe's Rio Grande.

With the election of a Social Democrat-Green government hopes were raised that the oppression of foreigners would end. A major reform of citizenship law was promised, offering German citizenship to children born in Germany and easing naturalization for adults. However, naturalization is to remain a longer process than in most other European countries. Moreover, the new government has shown itself to be as adamantly opposed to further immigration as its conservative predecessors, and is committed to a similarly punitive treatment of asylum seekers.

What are the roots of these phenomena? Are they emanations of a peculiarly German *Geist*? Or merely the symptoms and outgrowths of a 'normal' state sustaining the health of its nation by controlling foreign bodies? Or something else entirely? This chapter approaches the question through a historical survey, and suggests that post-war issues of *Gastarbeiter* and refugees can best be understood in the light of preceding developments, above all the formation of the German nation, and pre-war systems of regulating foreign labour.

Paupers and Citizens

Our story begins with a summary of the awesome transformations of the nineteenth century, including the vigorous growth of commerce and industry and the restructuring of myriad dynastic principalities into a sovereign nation-state.

Central to these changes was agrarian revolution. With the freeing of the land market, enclosures of communal land, and commutation of peasants' servile status (usually into economic dependency), a rapid commercialization of agriculture and differentiation of the peasantry occurred. At one pole, prosperous peasants ascended towards the class of landowning *junkers*; at the other, vast masses of landless labourers were produced that outnumbered proprietors in many regions as early as 1800 (Hochstadt, in Hoerder and Moch 1995). Particularly in the West, manufacturing surged, generating enormous demand for labour. Rural-urban migration accelerated, with swathes of peasants transmuting into relatively mobile proletarians. The old feudal structures – whose endurance had resulted

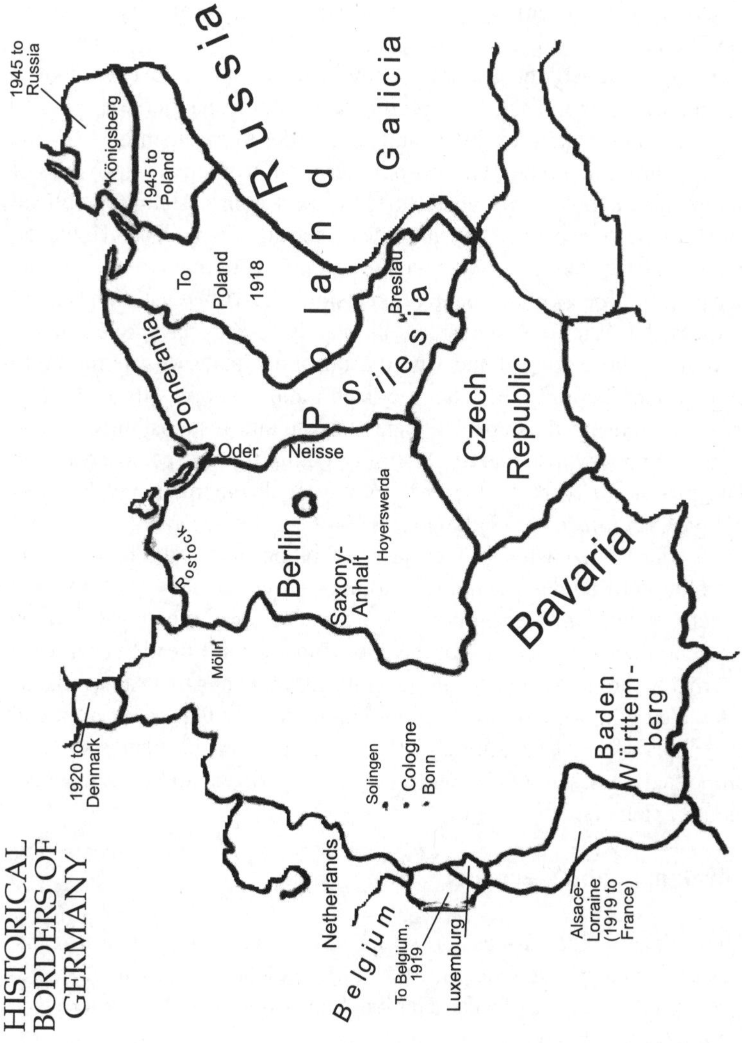
HISTORICAL BORDERS OF GERMANY
1945 to Russia
Königsberg
1945 to Poland
Russia
Poland
Galicia
To Poland 1918
Pomerania
Breslau
Silesia
Oder
Neisse
Czech Republic
Berlin
Hoyerswerda
Rostock
Saxony-Anhalt
Bavaria
Möllr
1920 to Denmark
Solingen
Cologne
Bonn
Baden Württem-berg
Netherlands
Belgium
To Belgium, 1919
Luxemburg
Alsace-Lorraine (1919 to France)

precisely from their ability to arrest peasant mobility in the context of labour scarcity – began to crack.

A juridical correlate of these transformations was the gradual dissolution of rank distinctions. Legal privileges and disabilities eroded, and the rank of *Bürger* (citizen) evolved into the universal legal category (Brubaker 1992: 60).

Emancipation of the peasantry, combined with the impoverishment of its majority part, raised the spectre of migrating pauperized masses. Parishes attempted to exclude paupers in order to rid themselves of the costs of providing relief, but this only resulted in an unviable process of competitive expulsions (Dohse 1981: 14). In response, states felt obliged to intervene, to codify citizenship rules at the communal level. However, even while regulating communal membership, states themselves engaged in a parallel process of competitive exclusion. The early nineteenth century witnessed a series of disputes that ultimately forced states to legislate – to define who belonged and who did not. Each state was permitted to expel to another only the latter's citizens, and was obliged to admit its own. Citizenship thus enabled states to disclaim responsibility for the 'foreign' poor whilst enabling mobility within their respective borders. This process marked the first firm, formal-legal demarcation of *Inländer* (native) from *Ausländer* (foreigner).

In short, citizenship in Germany developed upon the basis of the dissolution of feudal hierarchies and the *embourgeoisement* of political structures, with the appropriation by central states of municipal powers, the centralization of control of the poor, and the solidification of unitary internal sovereignties. It became generalized when inter-state antagonisms interacted with a 'domestic' contradiction, namely that between liberal principles of legal equality and free mobility, and the interests of the propertied classes in stability and 'security', which demanded the management of paupers.

Foreigners and Germans

The citizens under discussion so far are not Germans but Prussians, Bavarians and the like. The German/foreigner dichotomy remained imprecise until the creation of a pan-German State (*Reich*) in 1870–1, to which we now turn.

The infrastructure of the *Reich* was forged through a standardization and nationalization of social institutions, including customs union, an integrated market (and labour market), a unitary legal code and uniform currency. The 'material' (economic and geopolitical) forces promoting unification were given dramatic expression in the form of nationalist movements. Significantly, whereas nationalism in France and England inscribed itself within already-sovereign centralized states, German nationalist consciousness was potent long before an adequate state had formed; hence the nation was set more in a cultural than a political mould.

When it did come, unification was narrow. Arrived at through imperial war, it was largely shorn of the popular content that the nationalist revolutionaries desired. A product of Prussian hegemony, it excluded Austria, leaving the concept of 'German' to harden around 'lesser Germany'.

By no means atypically, a geographical mismatch between nationalism and the nation-state had occurred. However, the new polity quickly put material power to the service of resculpting German identity, moulding 'scattered tribal and cultural identities into a homogenized ethnocultural ensemble that became known as the German nation' (Kurthen 1995: 916). Like any nationalism in power, it set about promoting the fusion of its subjects into an imagined trans-class community, suppressing domestic struggles and mustering majorities behind central power. State-backed nationalist movements – with the inevitable paraphernalia of monuments, national holidays, national anthems and so forth – strove to weld together the cultural and political dimensions of nationhood, to generate conformity between German people and German state. The German racial recipe, a melting-pot stewed from ages of migration, was relabelled as pure stock. Partly due to the precedence of cultural nationalism, citizenship was given a pronounced 'ethnic' edge, as exemplified in the foundational law of 1870, which legislated Germans as a community united through 'blood' (*jus sanguinis*) rather than birthplace.

This process of the cultural nationalization of Germany was hardly seamless. Prussian land-grabbing had developed during an epoch in which state power was relatively remote from daily life, with sovereignty defined dynastically and territorially. The emphasis of Prussification had not been the imposition of German culture on non-German minorities, but simply securing obedience to the Prussian state. Now, with unification, Prussian territories entered an age in which sovereignty became reinterpreted in uniform and popular terms of nation and citizenship.

Initially, the Prussian tradition of unintrusive assimilation reigned, but this quickly ceded to intensely divisive policies. From the 1870s the assimilation of minorities took on a coercive cultural edge, aiming at integration into 'Germandom'. German was decreed the only language for use in primary schools, commerce, and law. With some minorities Germanization was successful, but others, notably the Poles – who comprised a tenth of all Prussians – resisted. In response, state policy towards the (geopolitically vital) Polish areas turned increasingly 'dissimilationist' (Brubaker 1992: 131). In the 1880s coercive 'ethnodemography' was pursued. The state purchased Polish-owned land for settlement by German colonists; Bismarck forbade the naturalization of Russian subjects (most of whom were Poles and Jews), and ordered mass expulsions of Poles.

It may be that the oppression of Slavs was aimed at strengthening the state's basis in German nationalism. Certainly, Bismarck is famous for his strategic skill in targeting enemies with foreign ties, real or imputed. However, if the purpose was to forge an ethnically homogenized national realm, it was doomed. For there was, as a commentator of the time put it, a 'force of circumstances in face of which all the hatred of Poles of the cabbage *junkers*, these "ever steadfast protectors of our Eastern frontiers" was rendered powerless.' And what was that force? Quite simply, 'the demand for cheap Polish workers' (Karski 1901: 723).

Gastarbeiter

The aforementioned transformations, including the freeing of employment relations and emigration to the cities of the West (and beyond), together with new methods of production that heightened seasonal fluctuation in demand, left landowners threatened by labour shortages, especially at harvest time. Many responded by recruiting foreign labourers – mainly from territories of the Habsburg and Tsarist empires (such as Poland and Galicia).

The large-scale recruitment of Slavs provoked campaigns by militant nationalists – including Max Weber – against 'Pole-ization' and '*Überfremdung*' (which translates as 'overwhelming by/infiltration of foreigners'). Weber saw Pole-ization as a threat to German national power; he called for 'an absolute exclusion of Russian-Polish workers from the German East' (in Herbert 1990: 27). Others echoed such calls, rallying to the cry of 'Germany for the Germans'.

The regime was thus caught between rival pressures, which expressed a contradiction between the ideological basis of national power and the material sources of agricultural profit. In response it edged towards a fateful finesse: the *Gastarbeiter* stratagem of permitting the import of sufficient workers to meet demand, whilst preventing their settlement. This latter qualification, the Interior Ministry believed, was 'the only means to repeatedly impress upon both foreign workers and the local German population that such workers were merely aliens whose presence was tolerated and that their permanent settlement . . . was out of the question' (in Herbert 1990: 19).

The *Gastarbeiter* policy had three dimensions of particular salience. Firstly, it allowed employers to recruit, whenever required, from a comparatively low-paid and flexible 'external reserve army'. Immigrant labour-power was reproduced at costs well below the German average, and immigrants were often willing, at least initially, to take inferior jobs at subnormal wages. They were, then as now, relatively responsive to the imperatives of capital, as Nigel Harris has explained (1980: 46):

> Workers who grow up in a particular social environment tend to absorb the defensive ethics developed by preceding generations to protect themselves from the ravages of capital. There are jobs they will not do, paces or hours or conditions of work they will not accept, moves from one locality to another they will not make for the sort of wages and terms on offer. A worker torn out of this environment is much more appropriate to the needs of capital, much more ruthlessly driven to earn at whatever the wages on offer are. Such a worker is less able to support himself during unemployment by borrowing from local networks of relatives and friends, and less likely to have reserves on which to fall back in hard times, less likely to have possessions that can be sold or pawned. Such workers are likely to be much more responsive to differences in wages – regardless of conditions – and, lacking local social ties, much more geographically mobile in response to changes in the labour market.

Such 'flexibility' was not natural but was produced by the second dimension of the *Gastarbeiter* policy: the intensive political management of the labour market. For in so far as the pliancy of immigrants depends upon their lack of 'roots', continued pliancy is ensured through ongoing deracination, which brings the forestallment of any upward levelling of aspirations. The state accorded itself the tasks of enforcing the annual deportation of foreign workers and regulating immigrants' conditions of work and life. State power was deployed towards skewing the terms of the labour contract. Work permit systems were constructed to discourage immigrants from breaking contracts and moving to greener pastures, whereas employers were granted a free hand to break their side of the bargain – virtually any conceivable grounds (even the 'lack of enthusiasm for work') was enough to justify the immediate dismissal of a foreign worker (Herbert 1990: 36).

Moreover, the state engaged in disorganizing resistance to exploitation by utilizing the foreigner/national distinction. Foreign workers were imported to act as scabs, and deported if militant. Even union membership could be grounds for deportation (Dohse 1981: 75). Employers could thus circumvent collective agreements by employing foreign labour on individual contracts. The state did not rest at the simple creation of divisions between nationals and foreigners but proceeded to erect a carefully calibrated hierarchy of distinctions that governed the treatment of each type of foreign national. Such strategies testify to the commitment of the state, during this period, to politicizing and 'nationalizing' the labour market, presumably in order to bolster the wage-depressing effect of immigrant labour.

Third, and largely as a consequence of the first two aspects, the system served to promote xenophobia, nationalism and reformism amongst sections of German workers. With foreigners permitted entry only at the bottom of the labour market, and being the first to be laid off during recessions, the social security and occupational advancement of 'German' workers could appear as if actively promoted by the state. As the Ministry of Commerce argued (in Herbert 1990: 50):

> If you limit industry to German workers alone, a larger number of such domestic workers would be laid off during a recession, thus increasing the ranks of the disgruntled. On the other hand, it would be no problem in such an eventuality to rid oneself of foreign workers.

To some extent, institutional xenophobia cut with the grain of uneven economic development. Most foreigners came from economically backward countries, were less likely to be skilled, and would tend to be employed at lower grades. That they performed lowly tasks, with corresponding lifestyles, was seen, in a circular argument, as proof of their cultural (and/or racial) backwardness (Herbert 1990: 67). German workers saw the *Gastarbeiter* in 'inferior' positions. The two groups possibly competed directly on the labour or housing markets. Alternatively, Germans felt secure in their superior status. Either way, exacerbated by problems of communication and ethnically divisive strategies of employers and the authorities, the *Gastarbeiter's* social status could easily become racially reified. In the process the low value of foreign labour-power could appear as a product of 'natural' backwardness rather than uneven development and institutionalized racism. *Gastarbeiter*, branded as an inferior group, can thus function as a living reminder to nationals of their good fortune in belonging to their nation. In John Berger's succinct words (1989: 140):

> The indigenous worker sees the migrant in an 'inferior' position, and what he sees and hears emphasizes how the migrant is different. . . . And then the inverted commas around inferior disappear: what has become the migrant's intrinsic inferiority is now expressed in his inferior status. What he is paid to do reflects this. . . . The presence of migrant workers, seen as intrinsically

> inferior and therefore occupying an inferior position in society, confirms the principle that a social hierarchy . . . is justified and inevitable.

From the above, it appears that the intertwining of nationalism and racism within the very structure of the labour market was made hard and fast during the late nineteenth century. It was not deliberately planned as a racist strategy of 'divide and rule'. But in practice it was precisely that, and those in power came to realize its potency, and were to consciously apply that knowledge to future immigration policy. The *Gastarbeiter* strategy was not dictated directly by the class position of its authors. Rather, they groped towards it, experimenting, evaluating the results, and disputing about which course to follow. It was, as Ulrich Herbert suggests, 'a learning process, the final outcome of which remained uncertain' (1990: 67).

The recruitment of (mainly Slavic) *Gastarbeiter* accelerated enormously in the decades at the turn of the century, precisely during the heyday of chauvinism that arose on the back of the failure of strategies of assimilation. It was against this background of ebullient opposition to Slavic immigration that 'blood-based' citizenship was entrenched in law in 1913. Citizenship law was framed explicitly to keep the Eastern provinces German by preventing the permanent settlement of 'ethnonationally undesired migrants' (Brubaker 1992: 134). As one government official put it in a parliamentary debate on the issue, the ethnically restrictive policy was 'in the national interest, because it erects a barrier to the stream of foreigners flooding our country from the East' (in Joppke 1996: 468). Despite such provenance, the law is still in force.[3]

War, Revolution, and Weimar Corporatism

The regulation of immigrant labour was not a major political question during the decade after 1914. However, it was inevitably remoulded by the conflagrations of war and revolution, both of which witnessed the deepening incorporation of social democrat and union élites into government.

The war witnessed the wholesale extension of the state's role in administering labour – including the conscripted labour of 'hostile aliens' in Germany and the occupied zones. It also saw the labour movement polarize into a minority internationalist wing (which faced harsh repression) and a nationalist majority concentrated in the Social Democratic Party (SPD). In 1914 the latter consummated its rapprochement with the Wilhelmine régime and was, along with union officials, rewarded with incorporation into several vital organs of administration of the war economy.

With the revolutionary overthrow of the Wilhelmine *Reich* in 1918, the SPD entered governmental office, only to face an upsurge of protests, strikes, and revolts, which approached civil war at times. In tackling these movements it deployed raw repressive force, for example, in calling on a volunteer army (the *Frei Korps*) to vanquish Polish risings in the East. But its characteristic method of drawing the sting of revolt was to grant cautious concessions to workers' demands, calibrated in negotiations between officials of business, government and unions, with the exclusion of 'unofficial' representatives of the protest movements.

Two great packages of reforms were constructed. The first occurred during the 1918 revolution itself, during which the SPD government, unions, and employers formed an *entente cordiale* to shore up the authority and legitimacy of bourgeois order against the ongoing challenges from below. As one business leader said, 'harmonious cooperation with the unions' was imperative, 'before the torrent of events drowns us all.' (in Deppe 1989: 182).

The second came in response to the mass uprisings that defeated the attempted *putsch* by the *Frei Korps* in 1920, and which developed into a serious challenge to 'law and order'. Once again, government strategy was to brutally repress challenges from the left, but simultaneously to further entrench the structures of nationalist corporatism, in particular by drawing union leaderships more closely into administration, as a concession to the widespread calls for 'workers government.'

The 1918 agreements conceded the eight-hour day, plus guarantees that demobilized soldiers could return to their former jobs. However, the latter promise meant little but an employment reshuffle in which the régime favoured one group (German soldiers) at the expense of youth, women, and, of course, foreigners, who were deported wholesale without so much as a 'thanks for your war effort'.

The 1920 deal agreed three principles, which the employers' associations had proposed. Firstly, the principle of 'primacy for nationals' – that foreigners may be hired only when no domestic workers are available. Secondly, that foreign and German workers be placed on equal wage scales. Thirdly, that admission of foreigners be monitored by commissions made up equally (*paritätisch*) by representatives of management and unions (Herbert 1990: 123–6).

In both cases the employers, on the defensive, made concessions. They restricted their rights to hire from extranational labour markets, and accepted the longstanding demand of the unions for equal wage scales. However, the deals also entailed the SPD and unions explicitly accepting and enforcing the principle of labour market discrimination against all foreigners – the 'primacy of nationals' – which has remained enshrined in law ever since. More importantly, the deals were instituted in such a way as to tie the unions, especially their upper reaches, more closely into the workings of the state. By lashing the official representatives of workers' demands into a corporatist scaffold (known as the *ZAG*, or 'labour community of employers and employees'), organized reformism was bolstered and the business community appeased.

In this way, the creation of a patriotically patrolled labour market became intimately bound up with the progressive principle of equal pay for equal work. Thus, as Knuth Dohse has suggested (1981: 116), the reforms seemed to be largely at the expense of employers, but in the long term they actually undermined the interests of workers by incorporating trade unions into the institutions of discrimination, and by strengthening one major pillar of the division between foreign and national workers (primacy of nationals) even as the other (unequal pay for equal work) was weakened. The result of the agreements was hailed by an employers' leader in unmistakeable terms:

> the *ZAG* has, in the first year of its existence, saved Germany from chaos, and from a Bolshevik revolution. While all the authorities were collapsing: monarchy, state, military, and bureaucracy, it, by way of the alliance of employers and unions, created a power which kept the economy and workplaces in a state of order.' (In Deppe 1989: 186)

'The Russians are our Negroes'

The next twist in the history of foreign labour in Germany occurred with the momentous defeat of organized labour, and of the Weimar republic itself, by Nazism.

The politics of Nazism in power may be summarized as a series of attempts to hurdle the consequences of economic crisis and to suppress class conflict through racism, conquest and state-forced industrialization. Growth was essentially state-led, and took place against the background of catastrophic decline in international trade and the implosion of the world economy into involuted fragments. Germany's arms-led expansion of the 1930s, argues Chris Harman, 'depended upon imports – especially of raw materials – which could not be financed by exports because of the stagnation of the world economy' (1984: 67). This contradiction, ultimately, underlay the geo-political 'flight forwards' in which the compass of Berlin's direct rule was forcibly expanded to incorporate neighbouring economies and subordinate them, *including their workers*, to the German military drive.

The political formulae of Nazi imperialism included the strategies of reforming Europe in a racially based 'New Order' under German hegemony, and colonial land-grabbing to the East. The latter was a highly compressed reprise of the pioneering examples of other European powers, whose expansion had entailed colonial settlement and the extermination and enslavement of indigenous peoples. As Hitler saw it, 'Russia is our Africa and the Russians are our negroes' (Craig 1981: 745). Military and population policies were harnessed together in a monstrous geo-racial engineering project. Ostensibly to conquer *Lebensraum* ['inhabitable space'] for Germans, over nine million people were resettled. German overlords were moved in to occupied areas, while 'ethnic' Germans were brought *Heim ins Reich* ['home into Empire'] following the Hitler–Stalin pact. Poles were ordered from one part of Poland to another, and millions of other Slavs, and Jews (including German Jews now redefined as foreign), were forcibly resettled. For these groups resettlement was a stepping stone to genocide.

The expansive empire, however, depended upon economic growth, which further exacerbated the labour shortages that had already arisen in the mid 1930s. As early as 1936 senior Nazis had discussed, and rejected as unpopular, such methods of expanding the workforce as recruiting women, or the forcible conscription of German men. This left only one other option: immigrant labour. In 1937, treaties were signed with Italy, Yugoslavia, Hungary, Bulgaria and the Netherlands for the recruitment of their citizens. In the following year the annexation of Austria facilitated the import of some 100,000 Austrians. Despite these efforts, by the outbreak of war there were few foreign workers relative to the number of vacancies.[4]

War exacerbated the labour shortage, but it also offered new means to its solution, namely forced conscription of foreign labour on a historically unprecedented scale. When the *Wehrmacht* marched eastwards it was accompanied by Labour Administration officials, whose methods of conscription included 'the most brutal forms of compulsion, rounding people up in the market place or during church services or in cinemas, burning down villages that did not meet the demands made on them, inflicting merciless punishment on recruits who tried to escape' (Craig 1981: 746). Such accomplished recruiting led, by the war's end, to foreigners comprising over a quarter of the German workforce, and fully a third of workers in agriculture and the arms industries. Many of modern Germany's leading firms, including Siemens, BMW, Volkswagen, Daimler-Benz and MAN, employed slave labour. In all, about twelve million foreigners were drafted during the war. Without them, Herbert claims (1990: 153), Germany would have already faced defeat by the summer of 1943.

Although vital to the war machine, foreigners imported into the German heartlands overtly undermined the Nazi ideal of the obstipated *Volksgemeinschaft* ('national community'). They were seen as a danger to the desired racial stasis, a direct challenge to the purity of Germandom. As one Nazi intellectual exclaimed, the 'German soil would only be preserved for the German people as long as it was worked and cultivated by people of German stock' (in Herbert 1990: 133).

The contradiction between the perception of foreigners as urgently required workers and as racial pathogens was reflected in differing treatment by different institutions. Representing one extreme was SS leader Himmler whose goal, suggests Detlev Peukert, 'was a racial war of annihilation against the peoples of Eastern Europe, and he decreed that their labour effort must be "exhaustive in the truest sense of the word"' (1989: 126).

However, for technocrats in the Ministry of Labour, and for many employers (most famously the NSDAP member Oskar Schindler), foreign workers were desired in their traditional role as flexible reserves, or even as a permanent (and perhaps skilled) section of the workforce. These, writes Tim Mason (1993: 350), 'began to learn that they could obtain quite high levels of production from the rapidly growing slave population, if the latter were given minimal standards of food and accommodation and the smallest monetary incentives'. Some even conceived of the exploitation of foreigners as beneficial in the long term. For example, the Ministry of Labour envisaged a post-war hegemonic Germany which would rely upon 'the importation of supplementary labour from the continental states' as well as a considerable expansion of 'so-called "visiting workers" [*Gastarbeiter*]' (Peukert 1989: 126). That these employers required 'unexhausted' workers, however, did not lessen their objective interest in the steep slope of the racial hierarchy. For example, whatever his personal attitudes to Jews, Schindler's armaments profits derived largely from a Jewish, and therefore systematically intimidated, workforce.

At the upper end of the employment hierarchy a section of the German population occupied superior positions and relatively high living standards, even as the war entered its final phase. These, as Mason observes, formed a 'sub-élite' performing a social control function:

> Numerous groups in the German working population, especially foremen, skilled workers, farmers and lower-level management . . . suddenly became in effect a supervisory corps, organizing and controlling the labour of "inferior" foreign workers; . . . It was [an] apparently seductive form of social mobility [and] was accompanied and given specific form by the massive official encouragement and enforcement of racial prejudice (1993: 351).

With state power reorganizing society in such fearsome and insidious ways it is not surprising that racism grew rank in popular consciousness. Nonetheless, it is quite striking what a small proportion of Germans viewed foreign workers, through truly Nazi eyes, as despicable slaves. Peukert (1989: 142) judges that

> the attitude of the great majority of Germans cannot be characterized either as spitefulness towards the 'aliens' or as solidarity. The most common attitude was indifference tempered by occasional sympathy. During the war people had enough worries of their own; the hardships of the foreign workers were of no especial significance.

Sympathy was generally strongest where the conditions of work and barter brought Germans and foreigners together. Despite severe legal and administrative barriers, solidarity and friendship could arise. The security services, according to Herbert, were concerned at the 'numerous reports' they received every day 'regarding overly friendly behaviour on the part of a portion of the population toward such Polish prisoners [i.e. workers]' (1990: 136). Most remarkably of all, German and foreign workers were able (admittedly in extreme circumstances) to unite in overt resistance. Peukert depicts quasi-partisan battles in late 1944

> when foreign workers, escaped prisoners of war, German anti-fascists and young anti-regime members of the 'Edelweiß Pirates' came together, carried out surprise attacks on military supply sites and high-ranking NSDAP and Gestapo officials, and mounted full-scale assaults on units of the Gestapo, Wehrmacht and police. (1989: 134)

Reinventing the Race of the Nation

Anti-fascist movements were not responsible for the overthrow of Hitler. However, with the fall of the régime a markedly anti-fascist mood arose, manifested in a widespread hope in a 'new beginning', popular demands for sweeping 'denazification', and movements for workers' control of industry. The radical and socialist demands of these movements, however, were opposed by the occupying powers. Their concerns lay elsewhere, in reconstituting the shredded fabric of the European states-system. Germany was to be recreated but reduced, with much of its territory annexed by the USSR and Poland (as 'punishment', the Allies claimed). Following the carve-up the ensuing mess was to be 'cleansed', ethnically speaking. As early as 1942 the Allies had begun to plan large-scale population transfers in the event of victory, including the expulsion of Germans from annexed territories and from elsewhere in Eastern Europe. The main justification was to eliminate the 'problem of minorities': ethnic groups collide, it was argued, and such clashes endanger international stability. Winston Churchill, putting this case to the House of Commons in 1944, declared that 'expulsion is the method which . . . will be the most satisfactory and lasting. There will be no mixture of populations to cause endless trouble . . . A clean sweep will be made' (in De Zayas 1979: 1). In 1945 this strategy was enshrined in the Potsdam Agreement.

The population movements involved were vast. Some ten million foreigners in Germany returned to their homelands, either voluntarily or under Allied orders. Meanwhile the westwards sweep of the Soviet Army triggered the flight and expulsion of Germans, known as *Vertriebenen* ('expellees') and *Flüchtlinge* (refugees). Some were POWs, some were ordered by the German authorities to decamp, others were Nazi officials fearing for their lives. Some were indubitably fleeing Communism, although as a comparatively high number ended their flight in the Soviet zone (the precursor of East Germany) this can hardly have been a prevalent motive (Niethammer, in Grebing 1987). By 1950 over twelve million had reached Germany; some two million had died *en route* (Benz, in Bade 1992: 381).

The net effect of the post-war migrations, notes Charles Tilly (in McNeill/Adams 1978: 62), was 'to homogenize nation-states and probably to increase their capacity for nationalism'. Ironically, the Allies' strategy of 'population transfer' trumped Hitler in creating an artificially 'homo-ethnic' Germany. In Herrmann Kurthen's words (1995: 918), 'after unconditional surrender, expulsion of millions of German ethnics from former Eastern territories, and years of occupation regime, a partitioned country evolved under the supervision of the victorious allies that represented a nation "ethnoculturally homogenous" to an extent even the Nazis had not dreamed about.'

This reconstitution of the race of the nation thus developed upon a basis laid by foreign powers. Its prime juridical manifestation was the FRG's founding constitution (*Grundgesetz*) of 1949, which declared unified Germany as its ultimate goal, with the pragmatic adjunct that in the meantime the FRG act as the 'core' of the future Germany, the state that speaks for *all* Germans. Denying Communist rule in the East as un-German, it was a credo that perfectly suited both Western Cold Warmongers and German nationalists. The *Grundgesetz* defined its scope as Germany in its 1937 borders. The FRG was, thus, a state founded upon a pair of transcontinental phantom limbs, stretching out through Berlin to Königsberg, through Hoyerswerda to Breslau. The denial of their amputation impinged directly on the definition of citizenship. For, with the loss of German land and population in the East, granting citizenship according to birthplace would have appeared as national ignominy. Rather, a 'law of return' extended the proprietorial claim of the German state to all 'ethnic Germans' to the East. Germany was refounded as a culturally and linguistically defined *Volksgemeinschaft*, with citizenship determined by ancestral 'blood', a definition that still holds in today's 'modern' Germany.[5]

Once in place, this legal-cultural apparatus of differential racialization served to divide immigrants into different groups, branding some as 'foreign', to be herded into separate pens. This can be seen clearly by contrasting Bonn's treatment of 'ethnic Germans' with that of immigrants from the Mediterranean.

'Ethnic Germans'

The bulk of the immigration of Germans from the East took place during the latter stages of the war and in its immediate aftermath, during which time about one in two Germans, including soldiers and evacuees, were moving residence (Von Plato, in Niethammer and Von Plato 1985: 177). The experience of being uprooted and the need to reorient to a new society was a general one; the immigration of the Easterners was partially submerged within this process. Nevertheless, they can be discussed as a distinct group.

To a large extent they filled employment positions vacated by foreign conscripts, and attitudes towards them were often strikingly similar to attitudes towards their predecessors (Herbert, in Grebing 1987: 172). This is hardly surprising, for most Easterners were similarly branded by poverty, often lived in the Nissan huts or bachelors hostels only recently vacated by 'genuine' foreigners, and spoke in strange-sounding tongues (such as Silesian). Even the term of abuse for Poles (*Pollacken*) was freely applied to these 'Germans' from the East.

However, the prevailing attitude of the indigenous population seems to have been tolerance, particularly, argues Von Plato (in Grebing 1987: 267), where the common identity in employment usurped the ulterior identity of 'expellee'. Moreover, the dominant attitude of the authorities was assimilationist. Officials, with only few exceptions, welcomed Easterners as compatriots. They automatically received full citizenship rights, training, language tuition (for the non German speakers), and assistance in finding accommodation. They enjoyed full political rights and exerted influence at all levels of the public arena. Whatever the motives of their migration, they were automatically identified as refugees; to look after their interests Chancellor Adenauer appointed a 'Minister for Refugees'.[6] For decades Bonn persistently demanded that Moscow grant any remaining 'Germans' the right to emigrate. In short, their case became an instrument of Cold War with which Bonn portrayed itself as the humanitarian champion, providing refuge from communist tyranny.

Alongside such political functions, the Easterners provided an ideal influx of 'flexible' labour to feed the ballooning labour demand. They became vital to branches such as agriculture and mining. In the 1950s they were followed by 3.5 million East Germans, fully 20 per cent of the German Democratic Republic's (GDR's) population, and mainly young and skilled. It is not far fetched to conclude that the German 'economic miracle' was made possible by immigration from the East.

That these mass migrations, lasting some sixteen years, were composed largely of Germans had important ramifications. In particular, they functioned, in Herbert's words, as a 'partitioning factor' (1990: 201), which served

> to isolate the mass utilization of forced labourers between 1939 and 1945 in public consciousness as a special case closely associated with the war effort. . . . Consequently, it proved possible to resume recruitment and employment of large numbers of foreign workers a decade and a half after the end of the war relatively unencumbered by misgivings about its implications.

Rediscovering the Gastarbeiter System

The 'economic miracle', facilitated by competitively priced and skilled Easterners, saw the unemployment rate plummet from 11 per cent in 1950 to 1.3 per cent a decade later, even as the workforce swelled from fourteen to twenty million. From the late 1950s demand for new sources of workers became urgent, preferably ones willing to take low-grade jobs that were being refused by indigenous workers. Labour shortages were exacerbated by rearmament, which deprived the labour market of half a million workers (Thränhardt 1992: 169), and by the closure of the Berlin Wall, which stemmed immigration from the GDR. As before, the solution for employers lay in reaching out to tap the labour markets of peripheral economies.

Contrary to common misconceptions, the *Gastarbeiter* did not migrate as an automatic 'economic' response to the demand for labour. In the absence of a free international labour market the tasks of organizing immigration were appropriated by the state. Bilateral treaties were negotiated: with Italy in 1955, then with Greece, Spain, Morocco, Portugal,

Turkey, Tunisia and Yugoslavia in the 1960s. These not only established a legal framework for the recruitment of foreign workers, they also laid down their conditions of work. At first, most *Gastarbeiter* were recruited by the state on behalf of individual employers – their work permits were contracts with the state as well as the employer (Hollifield 1992: 60). However, once inter-state frameworks had been constructed, employers tended to develop direct relations with foreign labour markets.

Although, like the 'ethnic Germans' of Eastern Europe, *Gastarbeiter* immigration was instigated by Bonn, they were received not as fellow citizens but as coolies for stoking the furnaces of economic expansion. Their migration would begin in a queue, lasting years. At its end would come screenings for physiological and political maladies; German employers had the pick of the healthiest. These were the lucky ones, yet they had to leave spouses and children behind – until the 1970s family reunification was almost impossible.[7] Their admission into Germany was almost completely determined by the demand for labour. One study showed that 96 per cent of any variation in numbers admitted from one year to another was due to changes in the number of unfilled vacancies (Böhning 1984: 141).[8] *Gastarbeiter* quickly became indispensable. During the upswing of 1963–5 they supplied almost 70 per cent of employment expansion; this figure reached 85 per cent in 1969–73 when 500–1000 arrived every day (Giersch 1992: 128). By 1973 their share in the total workforce had soared to 12 per cent.

Often intending to remain for only a brief term most *Gastarbeiter* were prepared to suffer atrocious conditions, with poor diet, wages and terms of work. They occupied the despised jobs, replacing upwardly mobile nationals. Of the 1.1 million Germans who left manual for white collar jobs between 1961 and 1968, half were replaced by *Gastarbeiter*. Generally, they were employed on assembly lines in the automobile industry, in hotels and catering, and in dirty and/or dangerous sectors such as construction, foundries, asbestos, mining, fish processing, cleaning, and refuse collection. Such work was usually highly routinized, and with disproportionate levels of shift work and piece work (Bech and Faust 1981: 51).

As with their nineteenth-century predecessors, the Mediterranean *Gastarbeiter* provided a workforce that would readily adapt to the changing needs of capital. Comparatively mobile, it could move to where vacancies beckoned, and would seldom refuse employment. Aiming to accumulate savings as quickly as possible in order to return home to a life of security, most of these 'lazy foreigners' actually worked harder than 'diligent Germans' (Bech and Faust 1981: 64).[9] Comparatively willing to work shifts and overtime, and move from one job or location to another, they were perfect for maximizing the employment of industrial capacity and for lubricating structural change.

Immigrants' qualities of tractability and temperance are determined at one level by structures of world capitalism. The system of competing nation states mapped onto an economically uneven world directs foreigners from 'backward' societies, traditionally defined by imperialist practices and ideologies as inferior, towards the lower end of the labour market. As in earlier periods, however, the state actively organizes this process, entrenching the ethnic hierarchization of the workforce through various forms of institutionalized discrimination.

The state creates and polices the boundaries of the nation, with Germans granted citizenship and others denied it; foreign immigrants are thus defined as separate from (even a potential threat to) the nation. The denial of citizenship rights is bound up with the state's consistent opposition to foreigners settling permanently on 'German soil'. Naturalization is an extremely difficult process. To naturalize, foreigners must prove their 'Germanness': they must have resided in Germany for a minimum of eight years; demonstrate the capacity to support themselves and their families; lead an 'irreproachable' way of life; be 'integrated into' and show a 'lasting orientation to' Germany and German culture; demonstrate knowledge of the German state, and show an active commitment to the constitutional order of the FRG. In short, they have to be more 'German' than most Germans. Most seriously of all, they must give up their previous citizenship. If all these hurdles are cleared, they must then pay a hefty sum of money for the privilege. And even then, nationality is granted only if it is perceived as being 'in the interests of the German state'. No wonder Germany has one of the lowest rates of naturalization in Europe.

Juridically, *Gastarbeiter* entered Germany, initially, on the basis of the *1938* 'Foreigners Police Decree'. Needless to say, this gave them no political rights. Nor was the situation greatly improved with the 'Foreigners Law' of 1965. Its aim was to provide government with a flexible means of meeting the changing needs of the labour market. Accordingly it maximized the authority of the relevant bureaucracies, giving them immense power over the lives of *Gastarbeiter*, and leaving the latter, as far as possible, segregated, rightless, and insecure. They remained excluded from many of the rights that the constitution reserves for Germans, including freedoms of movement and occupation, not to mention protection from extradition abroad.

As a result, foreigners have a 'dual' legal status. In many areas they do indeed possess the same rights as natives; but these can, at a stroke, be rendered meaningless when the police and courts order deportation (Dohse 1981: 419). Notoriously, the 1965 law laid down eleven grounds for the deportation of foreigners, including any violation of German law (even petty crime) and 'the endangering of public health or morality' – with the definition of the latter left to the ethics of the 'Foreigners Police'. Concealed within the velvet glove of civil rights lies the iron fist of executive power.

In addition to the restrictions of civic and political rights, *Gastarbeiter* were legally oppressed on the labour market. Initially, they were tied to particular employers, usually for one year at a time. If they changed employer or were laid off, they could – and often did – have their residence permit withdrawn. The overt purpose underlying this unfreedom was the principle of 'rotation': *Gastarbeiter* were expected to come for several years only. This discouraged permanent settlement, and tended to sequester them as a special sort of reserve army, one that would dutifully return home during recessions and thereby act as a 'conjunctural shock absorber'.

Of the grounds for deportation mentioned above, the most important was redundancy. Accordingly, employers possessed enormous influence over immigrants' lives, not just their labour power. Juridical restrictions armed employers with fearful weapons. For example, striking *Gastarbeiter* were threatened with deportation (Dohse 1981: 296). Such legal intimidation gave (and gives) employers a license to subject foreigners to the most dirty and dangerous jobs, at indecent rates of pay, with safety regulations ignored. Even worse off are undocumented immigrants, who can be deported at the nod of their employer. Advising a prospective foreman on how to deal with 'unruly' foreigners, one employer insisted: 'Just tell me their names. I've got a direct line to the Foreigners Police. Then they're gone, before they even know what's hit them.' (Wallraff 1985: 167).[10]

For a host of reasons, then, modern *Gastarbeiter*, like their nineteenth-century predecessors, are branded different and inferior; obliged to enter German society at the bottom, they generally find themselves forced to live in overcrowded ghettos in the inner cities. Thanks to the inertia of disadvantage (exacerbated in epochs of sluggish growth), but thanks also to juridical discrimination and to prejudice in personnel departments and elsewhere, social mobility is very low. Only a small proportion of *Gastarbeiter*, perhaps 11 per cent, have achieved any upward mobility during their stay (Herbert 1990: 241). Their children are in many ways worse off, with limited prospects on the labour market, and caught between two cultures, sometimes fluent neither in German nor in their mother tongue.

Settlement and Struggle

The story of the Mediterranean *Gastarbeiter*, fortunately, did not rest with rightlessness, racism and 'rotation'. In countless ways, many have come to strike roots, gain rights, and assert identities. Several 'unfreedoms' lessened over time. The heaviest chain – forced rotation after one year – was abandoned in 1964, and although work permits still had to be regularly renewed, against a background of economic expansion this became almost automatic. The end of rotation was one symptom of the deeper process whereby the majority of *Gastarbeiter* became a core section of the workforce, with an increasing blurring of the boundaries of occupational segregation. Even after the end of the 'economic miracle' employers still required immigrant labour; for example, of the more than six million requests for the issue of work permits in 1974–8, only 2.4 per cent were refused (Böhning 1984: 127). Meanwhile, spouses began to arrive in greater numbers, often through workers asking employers to specifically request them to fill vacancies. The proportion of women in the foreign population rose (from 31 per cent in 1961 to 41 per cent in 1981). Children, inevitably, followed and the 'minority' population grew steadily, from 1.2 per cent of the total in 1960 to 7.2 per cent in 1985. By 1993 over half had resided in Germany for over ten years, and of these, over half had resided for over twenty years (*Der Spiegel* nr. 26, 1996). Increasingly, *Gastarbeiter* entered into many of the institutions of welfare and education, and in this sense became *de facto* members of the state, in a process that implicitly 'undermined the ethnically founded national regulation principles of citizenship.' (Bommes, in Martiniello 1995: 126). During the 1990s the strict rules of naturalization were more leniently interpreted, enabling some hundreds of thousands of foreigners to gain German citizenship.

Associated with these objective developments was a growing public self-confidence on the part of foreign immigrants. Although generally expressed in the small change of everyday life, this did occasionally hit the headlines, notably through participation in strike action. Already in 1963, and despite the lack of citizenship rights that had underwritten the deportation of leaders of previous strikes, thousands of foreign steel workers took strike action. Six years later *Gastarbeiter* struck against pay discrimination during a wave of mass unofficial strikes, which was followed by four years of 'almost crescendolike development of foreign worker strike actions and labor militancy before the explosion of foreign worker strikers onto the German political scene in August-September of

1973' (Miller 1981: 106). Most militant of these was the unofficial strike and occupation at Ford in Cologne by most of the plant's 12,000 Turkish workers; but several strikes that same summer, in which Germans participated, and which were led by their foreign colleagues, were more successful. As Mark Miller points out (1981: 106), radicalized German workers 'undoubtedly played an important role in the development of foreign worker wildcat strikes in the FRG'.

One outcome of the upturn in industrial action of 1969–73 was a greater concern shown by trade unions towards *Gastarbeiter*. Following the pattern of the Weimar period, unions had tended to oppose immigration (as 'dilution of labour'), whilst campaigning for equal pay for equal work so as to prevent immigrants being used to undercut prevailing conditions. But in the wake of the militant strike waves, which threatened their grip on labour organization, they turned their attention to recruiting and representing immigrants. From 1973 to 1978 the number of foreign trade unionists rose by 40 per cent, even as the foreign workforce declined by a quarter; since that time the union density for foreigners has hovered at around 33 per cent, only a little lower than the figure for Germans.

The Politics of Immigration

A running theme of this chapter has been that the political treatment of foreign labour develops within a framework formed by multiple contradictions: between economic growth and slump; between the instrumental requirements of individual employers and the social control interests of their class as a whole; between immigrants as a disposable 'reserve army' and as a mainstay of the economy; between foreigners suffering oppression and resisting it; and between German workers as racist, and as anti-racist. In different phases of the post-war period, these contradictions have taken varying forms.

Bonn's first policies towards foreign immigrants were primarily instrumental: establishing the framework for recruitment and rotation. Public debates on the question were low-key. Even right-wing newspapers carried arguments justifying the *Gastarbeiter* programme as a means of stabilizing the economy, braking wage growth, and countering restrictions on labour mobility. At the official celebrations held for the arrival of the one millionth post-war labour migrant the Minister for Labour delivered a speech which crowed that '[t]hese one million persons on the job in Germany help contribute to maintaining production growth while keeping prices stable and maintaining our [*sic*] reputation on world markets' (in Joppke 1996: 466). *Gastarbeiter*, as the name suggests, were 'invited' as only a short-term measure, and the public mood towards them, at least as recorded by opinion surveys, was indifference.

However, from the earliest phases, discussion of the question was marked by xenophobia. For example, in 1964 Christian Democratic Union (CDU) Chancellor Erhard explicitly appealed to German workers to work longer and harder in the cause of expurgating foreigners from the land. Towards the end of the long boom foreign immigrants increasingly came to be defined as a 'problem'. During the recession of 1966–7 the first major public debate, though centring on the economic utility of *Gastarbeiter*, witnessed a xenophobic tone, most obviously in the shape of fascist election victories but also in the press, CDU speeches, and so forth. The xenophobic tone intensified in 1971, in the context of the strikes referred to above, which were accompanied by a virulent media campaign against the militancy of foreign workers. Xenophobic opinion next concentrated on a law being introduced that enabled long-term *Gastarbeiter* to receive five-year work permits. In response to such campaigns, which raised the spectre of militant 'guests' becoming permanent settlers, the government began to restrict new entries of foreign workers. In 1973 such moves culminated in a ban on all further recruitment, which the SPD government under Willy Brandt insisted was necessary in order to prevent 'social conflict'.

In this period the existence of ethnic minorities in Germany was firmly branded a 'problem' and a remorselessly increasing one at that. This shift in political climate occurred contemporaneously with the subsidence of the economy into a protracted period of slow growth and repeated crises. In such periods states tend to shift their focus to managing crisis, or 'public order'. As Stephen Castles has pointed out (in Cross 1992: 47), the stricter control of immigration and of minorities in Germany is directly connected to these economic and political developments.

In the autumn of 1973 the economy entered recession. Unemployment soared from 1 per cent in 1973 to 4.7 per cent in 1975. Once again, politicians and media pundits loudly scapegoated foreigners. For example, the left-wing minister Egon Bahr claimed that 'about 500,000 of the jobs occupied by *Gastarbeiter* could be taken over by German employees'. This was not intended as a serious proposal. Even had deportations been attempted, few unemployed Germans would have accepted such jobs. The intention instead was simply, as a commentary of the time pointed out, to deflect 'the domestic pressure felt by a government faced with rising unemployment' (Gauer and Schloesser 1975: 6).

From this period onwards, immigration and ethnic minorities became increasingly politicized and polarized themes. On the one hand, society passed through a series of economic and political crises, which often saw those in positions of power resort to xenophobic scapegoating. On the other hand, foreigners were striking strong roots. As a proportion of the population their numbers continued to grow. Reflecting accelerating levels of contact, larger sections of the national population came to accept their presence and defend their rights. For the latter reasons governments felt obliged to mitigate some of the more draconian discriminatory legislation, with gradual improvements on some fronts, for example, by easing renewal of residence permits. However, this never led to a change in the guiding principles of policy. Governing parties always remained opposed to the permanent settlement of immigrants and to the extension of citizenship rights to foreigners.

The Kohl Decades

In 1983 the incoming Kohl government loudly reaffirmed the principle of opposition to immigration, introduced measures to prevent family reunification, and even pandered to racist voters by setting up a programme for repatriating immigrants. These latter measures were economically irrational, for, as Giersch et al. argue (1992: 218), 'despite chronic unemployment, there were also supply-side constraints to economic growth from the labour side'. Though barely implemented, they did symbolize an ideological reframing of the immigration debate. The 1980s witnessed a reemergence of strident nationalism into mainstream public debate, in particular around the question of how to heal Germany's supposedly 'sickly' national identity. Concepts that reeked of Nazism, such as *Überfremdung*, were championed by a coalition including CDU Chairman Alfred Dregger and columnists of the *Frankfurter Allgemeine Zeitung*. Against the prevailing consensus that Germany was capable of assimilating small numbers of immigrants, Dregger and his co-thinkers introduced a new theme, centred on the claim that particular types of immigrants (especially Turks, other Asians, and Africans) are irremediably and eternally different from Germans, and therefore 'unintegrable'. This current exemplifies what Martin Barker (1981) has termed 'new racism', whose proponents argue not in the language of racial superiority but in terms of *nation*, understood as the essentialized *Volk* with a common culture the supposed homogeneity of which must be defended against infiltration from outsiders.[11]

Such racism, linked to bullish nationalism, gained ground in the 1980s thanks partly to the FRG's increased stature on the world stage, and presumably also due to the ebb of the workers' movement during that decade. In resurrecting the pre-1945 principle of differentiating foreigners between decent West Europeans and loathsome 'Others', it provided a rationale for a discerning xenophobia that could accept the stubborn fact of immigration from EU countries, and target instead those incomers who lacked such backing from Brussels – typically refugees.

Asylum had already arisen as a major issue in 1980–1 during the dying days of Helmut Schmidt's SPD-FDP government. The CDU-CSU had instigated a campaign, eagerly taken up by the mass media and fascist parties, which pilloried as 'bogus' and 'welfare scroungers' those refugees who were fleeing Turkey following the 1980 military coup. Schmidt had readily acceded to such 'public pressure', taking measures to restrict Turkish immigration and expressing deep sympathy with his beleaguered voters, claiming for example that '[i]t's not easy for Germans who live in an apartment house and do not like the smell of garlic to have to put up with it and even to have a lamb slaughtered in the hallway' (in Cornelius 1994: 206).[12]

Under Kohl's prefecture refugees were repeatedly the butt of organized racism. A series of measures were introduced, mostly with the support of the SPD, to reduce asylum and deter refugees. The motto 'the boat is full' – which had been coined in 1930s Switzerland as the justification for refusing asylum to German Jews – was recycled and popularized by the CDU-CSU. Each successive scare was followed by stiffened policy. The state increasingly resorted to such restrictive measures as redefining refugees as 'economic migrants' (and hence deportable), reducing the numbers allowed to stay in Germany, and insisting that visas be carried. Only a tiny proportion, usually around 4 per cent, are recognized as refugees. They are treated as the lowest of all immigrants. Applicants are kept in overcrowded conditions, often in huts surrounded by high fences. They are banned from work for at least a year, even though most are of working age. Such conditions serve to emphasize the government's tough stand. As argued by Lothar Späth, when head of the CDU government in Baden Württemberg, in an attempt to seduce racist voters disguised as a message to refugees, 'The bush drums will say: Stay out of Baden Württemberg. There you are put in a camp and given terrible things to eat, little money and no work permit' (Räthzel 1991: 34).

Having become contrived in the 1980s as a virulent threat to the German nation, refugees were then served up, in the 1990s, as scapegoats for the failures of German unification. The unification process had, of course, begun with mass immigration of East Germans; who were accompanied, as the Soviet Bloc broke apart, by 'ethnic Germans' from the USSR, Poland and Romania.[13] These immigrants were, of course, welcome; the proverbial 'boat' was suddenly no longer full, for here were long-lost brothers back in the bosom of the happy homogenous family.

And yet, no sooner had the unification celebrations died down than the myth of national unity began to be shaken. Germany lurched onto a more crisis-ridden and unstable trajectory. Although bringing glory to Kohl and a surge in profits to West German business, unification brought wage cuts and tax rises to workers in the west and acute crisis to the east. Social unrest began to grow, with miners' protests in the west and a wave of factory occupations and demonstrations in the east. Kohl's election promises – 'no tax rises' in the west, 'blossoming landscapes' in the East – turned to dust. In this climate, with unification euphoria turning rapidly into a mood of malaise and bitterness, and with polls showing an extraordinary slump in voters' confidence in government and parliament, how tempting it must have been for governing politicians to divert public attention onto other issues.

In mid 1991 an anti-refugee campaign was organized, with military diligence, from the office of CDU general secretary Volker Rühe. Germany was being swamped by 'phoney asylum-seekers' who were out to 'scrounge' from its 'generous' welfare system.[14] Media coverage of the issue was thorough, and contributed to a sharp shift in political climate towards the racist right. Racist attacks rocketed to ten times the average of the preceding three years, and included pogroms against asylum seekers' hostels in Hoyerswerda and Rostock. The CDU-CSU kept the heat on the issue, pressing the SPD to agree to tougher measures to control the arrival of refugees. Typically keen not to alienate xenophobic voters, SPD leaders such as Oskar Lafontaine and, above all, Gerhard Schröder, steered a majority of their parliamentary party sharply towards agreement with the CDU-CSU, championing the latter's insistence that the right to asylum should be drastically restricted. This consensus found expression in a constitutional amendment, in 1993, which sharply raised barriers to the entry of refugees by excluding from refugee status all applicants who had arrived overland as well as any from countries where it 'appears that political persecution or degrading punishment does not occur'. In effect, the amendment turned the ability even to apply for refugee status from a right into a privilege.

The 1991–3 'asylum debate' was accompanied by further waves of racist violence, including the murders of Turks in Mölln and Solingen. A report by Helsinki Watch (in Laster and Ramet 1998: 82) pointed the finger of blame not simply at the perpetrators but also at 'government officials [who] failed to address the underlying economic and social problems that . . . contributed to the dramatic rise in anti-foreigner violence, and instead . . . used the violence to further the political goal of a restricted right to asylum.' Indeed, the decision to amend the constitution was justified by an implicitly xenophobic argument: because racism is a response to 'floods' of non-German immigrants, a decline in their number will precipitate a decline in racism. Although common sense (especially in élite groups) this assumption that immigration generates racism is demonstrably false. As Wesley Chapin's research has demonstrated, 'in areas where relatively more foreigners live, the vote for the [racist] New Right is actually lower than in areas where relatively few foreigners live. This suggests that additional contact with foreigners reduces xenophobic tendencies and also reduces electoral support for the New Right' (1997: 83). In Germany, racism in the virtually foreigner-free east is at least as rife as in the west.[15] There is also evidence that violence against foreigners does not correlate with numbers of foreigners in a given region (Laster and Ramet 1998: 84). Levels of racist violence, moreover, have actually risen since the constitutional amendment, and in 1997 they reached their highest level since 1990 (*Guardian* 7 May 1998). As *Human Rights Watch* has argued (1995: 6), 'The asylum debate has left a legacy that continues to have a negative impact on foreigners . . . It explicitly put the burden of right-wing violence on the victims – the asylum seekers – rather than the perpetrators.'

The trouble is, playing the 'race card' designates foreigners as a 'problem' that the government must then remedy or else risk seeming impotent. But the logic of defining immigrants as a major 'problem' is, ultimately, repatriation, which is inevitably an economic own-goal. As Miles suggests (1993: 206),

> Every official statement expressing support for the 'principle' of increased [immigration] control therefore legitimates political opposition to immigration within the electorate in circumstances where the state faces structural constraints on its ability to deliver what it promises.

The logic of this contradiction is to encourage the rise of parties which are consistently hostile to immigration and ethnic minorities. Xenophobic policies and campaigns of the established parties are invariably justified as ways of undermining racism, but in fact pour petrol on the flames. A vicious circle can ensue, with established parties attempting to undermine fascist rivals by championing 'tough' anti-immigration policies, but which actually serve to position such issues ever more firmly on the political agenda, putting wind in the sails of the extreme right, which, in turn, places the main parties under yet greater pressure. Thus, in the 1998 general election the *Republikaner's* campaign posters proclaimed menacingly 'We deliver what the CSU promises'.

A Liberal Turn?

The 1990s has witnessed a persistent and polarized debate over questions of immigration and ethnic minorities. On the one hand, governments have doggedly stuck to the mantra that 'we [*sic*] are not a country of immigration'. Kohl's governments reinforced the prevailing ethnic hierarchy with a decree that job vacancies must first be offered to 'domestic' Germans, then, if none apply, to German immigrants, next to EU nationals, and only lastly to 'other foreigners'. In 1998 the government, with SPD support, passed further legislation to worsen the conditions and reduce the rights of refugees. It repeatedly pressed other EU states for a tough common policy on immigration, and for 'porous' borders to be more thoroughly policed. In line with the government's 'tough' stance, SPD leaders directed their fire towards Italy's offer of asylum to Kurdish refugees (*The Guardian*, 6 January 1998).

On the other hand, a variety of interests – in addition to immigrants themselves, their friends and colleagues – benefit from continued immigration. For reasons outlined above, the advantages to business, even in recession-ridden periods, continue to be enormous. The state benefits too: absolved from many of the costs of the reproduction of immigrant labour-power, and with immigrants tending to be of working age, the balance sheet for the state is very positive. For example, in 1989 foreigners contributed 7.8 per cent of total payments to the state pension fund, but only 1.9 per cent of payments went to foreigners. One economic institute has calculated that, in 1991 alone, immigrants netted the state coffers a profit of DM 41 billion (Cohn-Bendit and Schmid 1992: 341).

Despite the unfriendly political climate, immigration actually increased under Kohl, reaching historically high levels in the early 1990s. Between 1988 and 1992 gross immigration was particularly high, at 4.3 million.[16] This figure included about 2.5 million Germans from East Germany and Eastern Europe; non-Germans, including refugees from Yugoslavia, arrived too, raising the percentage of foreigners in the total population to 8.8 per cent in 1995. Meanwhile, Bonn quietly created a new *Gastarbeiter* system geared to tapping traditional sources of labour in Eastern Europe. Bilateral agreements were signed to enable the recruitment of East Europeans on a rotation basis, on a seasonal basis (mainly for the construction industry), and as commuters from adjoining areas of Poland and the

Czech Republic. Together, these sources of immigration led to the rate of economic growth being almost double that which otherwise would have occurred, and filled state coffers with hundreds of billions of Marks (for detailed estimates, see Gieseck et al., 1995).

However, with rising unemployment and increasing restrictions on entry, net migration declined from 1992 onwards, reaching negative figures – for the first time since 1984 – in 1997 and 1998. Despite this decline, and official rhetoric to the contrary, Germany is a 'country of immigration', and looks likely to remain so for years to come. It has an ageing population and one of the lowest fertility rates in the world. From 1990 to 2010 the number of salary earners is expected to decrease by nearly four million, while unfilled vacancies will in all likelihood rise. The German Economic Institute estimates that 300,000 immigrants per year will be necessary for the next thirty years merely to maintain the existing size of the workforce (Wingen 1995: 713). Despite the recreation of *Gastarbeiter* systems, many foreigners will settle and 'integrate' and, accordingly, pressure for upgrading the rights of non-EU immigrants will continue.

Reflecting the contradiction between settled minorities on the one hand, and xenophobia and intensified restrictions on entry on the other, the politics of immigration have become highly controversial. On the right, the *Deutschnational* wing of the CDU-CSU favours restricting immigration, with stepped up controls and policing of borders. Particular hostility is directed at immigrants from non-Christian cultures who, supposedly, cannot assimilate. The moderate right favours limited immigration, and assimilation, while sharing the *Deutschnational* paranoia that immigration may impel 'society toward disintegration into various groups and communities and toward the loss of unity based on the binding character of commonly shared values' (Max Wingen, Ministry for Family and Senior Citizen Affairs, 1995: 716).

These currents, however, were dealt a severe blow in the general election of 1998. The acid drizzle of racism that emanated from the CDU-CSU camp was rewarded with its worst election result since the 1940s, while the Left scored its highest vote ever.[17] The incoming SPD-Green government is committed to significant reform. Citizenship law is to be based upon *jus soli*, dual citizenship is to be permitted, and the process of naturalization eased. These reforms will convert many immigrants into Germans (and, quite possibly, into supporters of the SPD and Greens). They will narrow the gap between the treatment of 'ethnic Germans' and 'foreigners' that had traditionally meant that, for example, 'immigrant Polish speakers who could produce a grandfather's Waffen-SS papers were already almost Germans [whereas the] vast majority of an ever-growing number of German-born, German-speaking, German-educated Turks were not' (Schoenbaum and Pond 1996: 56).

However, liberal reform of citizenship law is coupled with a continuation and deepening of the conservative treatment of asylum seekers and a xenophobic scapegoating of immigrants, particularly on the part of leading SPD politicians such as Gerhard Schröder and Otto Schily.[18] On the good ship Germany, a number of third-class passengers are to be moved into more secure second class accommodation, but those who misbehave are to be dealt with sternly; boarding passes will be even more scarce and nearly all those who appeal for rescue will be thrown back over the rails. The illiberal countenance of the new government was highlighted only a matter of weeks after its assumption of office when the Home Secretary, Otto Schily – to loud acclaim from representatives of CSU and *Republikaner* – declared that there were too many foreign immigrants in Germany, and called for draconian tightening of the grounds for which asylum may be claimed.

If this is an indication of the temper of the SPD leadership, who will speak out against illiberal immigration policy? The most obvious answer would be the Green party, which was for a time justly famous for its liberal policy on immigration. This was, however, jettisoned in 1991, as the culmination of a decade-long rightward shift, the most prominent exponents of which were Otto Schily (before he joined the SPD) and Joschka Fischer. The key theoretician of the Green's shift on immigration policy, however, was Daniel Cohn-Bendit. Against its previous liberal commitment to the right of residence for all, Cohn-Bendit argued for strictly monitored immigration control. Basing his argument on the conservative axiom that human nature is inherently tribal, he concluded that immigrants generate 'problems and conflicts' in host societies and their numbers must therefore be limited. His preferred solution is a quota system, with numbers fixed annually by agreement amongst corporate bodies (employers organizations, economic institutes, trade unions, and representatives from the minority communities), whose decisions should be guided by the demands of the labour market, as well as 'available admission capacity' (existing provision of housing, schools, hospitals and so forth). Cohn-Bendit's argument served well as an apparently 'fair' rationale for the deportation of immigrants (including Kurdish refugees) by Green regional state politicians in the 1990s. Its acceptance by the party leadership marked a lurch backwards from a position of innovative liberalism to one rooted firmly in the corporatist-patriotic tradition as institutionalized in the Weimar years. Over a hundred years after the construction of the first systematic regulation of foreign labour in Germany the policies of even the most liberal of the established parties remain, ultimately, wedded to the utilitarian interests of German-based business, and geared to policing the walls of the nation. Given the indissoluble ties between them, an enduring challenge to xenophobia will only occur through effective opposition to the practice and principle of immigration control.

Notes

1. As this volume deals only with the EU, we are here concerned only with the FRG, not the GDR.
2. I use the term 'foreign' as it is defined by states. For discussion of the problems of such terminology, see Haynes in this volume.
3. This chapter was largely written before the 1998 election of the SPD-Green government, which is committed to reforming the 1913 law.
4. Not surprisingly, given the treatment they could expect (cf. Dohse 1981:120).
5. See note 3.
6. Ironically, the first occupant's previous post had been in the SS.
7. Even today, family unity comes second to 'foreigner law': if a foreigner with residence permit has a spouse whose application for asylum is denied, family unification can be, and often is, denied.
8. The same applies today: foreign workers only do jobs where domestic workers are in short supply (cf. *Der Spiegel*, nr. 48 1998: 27).
9. Indeed, they sometimes attracted resentment as rate busters on piece work.
10. This is not the place to list the cruelties perpetrated by German employers and foremen. For a flavour of this modern, institutionalized sadism read Wallraff (1985).
11. In fact, cultural racism is not 'new' to Germany. For example, in the 1930s the arch fascist Ernst Jünger espoused a particularly virulent variety thereof. However, he was in a minority amongst racists of the time; prevailing prejudice was 'biologically' cast.
12. Unsurprisingly, the campaign against refugees encouraged racism of all sorts. Surveys indicated a steep rise in support for the idea that immigrants should return – from 39 per cent in 1978 to 67 per cent in 1982.

13. Annual arrivals of 'ethnic Germans' rose from 39,000 in 1985 to 397,000 in 1990.
14. Needless to say, the scare was artificial. In 1990 only 193,000 refugees arrived, of which a mere 8,500 were granted the right to stay. Compare that to the late 1940s when the FRG absorbed two million refugees per year, or the early 1950s when the figure was 220,000. In those days the FRG was desperately poor; today it is among the richest countries in the world.
15. The basis of racism in East Germany was not the presence of foreigners but their oppression. *Gastarbeiter* in the GDR could envy those in the West. They were subject to the strictest rotation, received lower wages than Germans, and were generally confined to ghettoes. Pregnant women were given the 'choice' of abortion or deportation.
16. *Net* documented immigration from 1985 to 1995, however, was only 2.4 million.
17. Although the fascists (and sundry extreme right) performed better than in the previous general election – 3% in the West and 5% in the East – these figures were lower than expected, so did not temper the victory of the left.
18. Schröder even resorted to xenophobia in the 1998 election campaign, attacking East European immigrants for 'stealing German jobs' (cf. also *The Times* 28 August 1998).

Bibliography

Bade, K. (ed.) (1992), *Deutsche Im Ausland, Fremde in Deutschland*, München: Beck.

Barker, M. (1981), *The New Racism*, London: Junction.

Bech, R., and Faust, R. (1981), *Die sogenannten Gastarbeiter*, Frankfurt: VMB.

Berger, J. and Mohr, J. (1989), *A Seventh Man*, Cambridge: Granta.

Böhning, W. (1984), *Studies in International Labour Migration*, London: Macmillan.

Brubaker, W. (1992), *Citizenship and Nationhood in France and Germany*, Cambridge: Harvard.

Chapin, W. (1997), *Germany for the Germans? The Political Effects of International Migration*, Westport: Greenwood.

Craig, G. (1981), *Germany*, Oxford: OUP.
Cohn-Bendit, D. and Schmid, T. (1992), *Heimat Babylon,* Hamburg: Hoffmann + Campe.
Cornelius, W. (ed.) (1994), *Controlling Immigration*, Stanford: Stanford University Press.
Cross, M. (ed.) (1992), *Ethnic Minorities and Industrial Change in Europe and North America*, Cambridge: CUP.
de Zayas, A. (1979), *Nemesis at Potsdam*, London: Routledge.
Deppe, F. (ed.), (1989), *Geschichte der deutschen Gewerkschaftsbewegung*, Köln: Pahl Rugenstein.
Dohse, K. (1981), *Ausländische Arbeiter und bürgerliche Staat*, Königstein: Hain.
Fullerton, M. (1995), *Germany for Germans*, New York: Human Rights Watch.
Gauer, C. and Schloesser, J. (1975), *Die ausländischen Arbeiter in der Krise*, Frankfurt: SAG.
Giersch, H., Paque, K-H., Schmieding, H., (1992), *The Fading Miracle*, Cambridge: CUP.
Gieseck, A., Heilemann, U., Von Loeffelholz, H., (1995), 'Economic Implications of Migration into the FRG', *International Migration Review* 29 (3): 693–709.
Grebing, H. et al. (1987), *Flüchtlinge und Vertriebene in der westdeutschen Nachkriegsgeschichte*, Hildesheim: Lax.
Harman, C. (1984), *Explaining the Crisis*, London: Bookmarks.
Harris, N. (1980), 'The New Untouchables', *International Socialism* 8: 37–63.
Hoerder, D. and Moch, L. (eds) (1996), *European Migrants*, Boston: Northeastern.
Herbert, U. (1990), *A History of Foreign Labour in Germany*, Ann Arbor: University of Michigan.
Hollifield, J. (1992), *Immigrants, Markets, and States*, Cambridge: Harvard.
Joppke, C. (1996), 'Multiculturalism and Immigration', *Theory and Society* 25: 449–500.
Karski, J. (1901), 'Die polnischen Wanderarbeiter', *Die Neue Zeit*, 19 (1): 722–36.
Kurthen, H. (1995), 'Germany at the Crossroads', *International Migration Review* 29 (4).
Laster, M. and Ramet, S. (1998), 'Xenophobia and Rightwing Extremism in Germany', in Smith, P. (ed.) *After the Wall*, Boulder: Westview.
Martiniello, M. (ed.) (1995), *Migration, Citizenship and Ethno-national Identities in the European Union*, Aldershot: Avebury.

Mason, T. (1993), *Social Policy in the Third Reich*, Oxford: Berg.
McNeill, W. and Adams, R. (1978), *Human Migration*, Bloomington: Indiana University Press.
Miles, R. (1993), *Racism After 'Race Relations'*, London: Routledge.
Miller, M. (1981), *Foreign Workers in Western Europe*, New York: Praeger.
Niethammer, L. and von Plato, A. (1985), *Wir kriegen jetzt andere Zeiten*, Bonn: Dietz.
Peukert, D. (1989), *Inside Nazi Germany*, Harmondsworth: Penguin.
Räthzel, N. (1991), 'Germany: One Race, One Nation?', *Race & Class*, 32 (3): 31–48.
Schoenbaum, D. and Pond, E. (1996), *The German Question and Other German Questions*, Houndmills: MacMillan.
Thränhardt, D. (ed.) (1992), *Europe: A New Immigration Continent*, Münster: Lit.
Wallraff, G. (1985), *Ganz unten*, Cologne: Kiepenhauer.
Wingen, M. (1995), 'Immigration to the FRG as a Demographic and Social Problem', *International Migration Review* 29 (3): 710–24.

–6–

The Netherlands: A Dutch Treat For Anti-Social Families And Immigrant Ethnic Minorities

Jan Rath

Introduction

Social science research into migratory and post-migratory processes in Europe deals to some extent with the way in which certain categories of immigrants are ideologically problematized and are excluded from regular social resources. A key concept here is *racism*. What racism really is – that is, what phenomena can be indicated by the concept – and how racism is embedded in its social environment, has for years been the subject of heated theoretical debate. That debate is, among other things, about whether racism is a matter of ideology or of (intended or unintended) practices. It is also about whether racism revolves round the signification and negative evaluation of phenotypical racial characteristics or those of cultural traits; about how far the colonial project is essential for the development of racism; and what impact racism has on class relationships. So far this debate has not led to any unequivocal conclusions. In so far as tendencies do appear, they are contradictory.

On the one hand there is the current tendency to label as racist discourses which have so far not been considered to be racist. The introduction of the concept of *neo-racism* is significant here. According to Barker (1981), with whom the concept became identified, racism is now expressed in cultural terms and no longer in biological ones. The concept of neo-racism should express both the continuity and the renewal of the phenomenon. Moreover it is the case that few students of racism today still assume that racism denotes a simple and static complex of beliefs and values. Following in particular Hall (1989: 917; see also 1980: 336) they start from the assumption that racism 'is historically specific, and applies to the period, the culture and the type of society in which it occurs'. Consequently they no longer talk of racism, but – in the plural – of *racisms*.

On the other hand there is a tendency to localize racism exclusively in colonial and post-colonial relationships. The occurrence of racism in European centres is then directly related to the migration of black people from former colonial territories. The title of the otherwise fascinating collection of papers, *The Empire strikes back. Race and racism in 70s Britain* illustrates this tendency in full. This theoretical demarcation has the consequence that other types of racism are excluded in advance from the researchers' field of view, or are defined as non-existent.

In this chapter these contradictory tendencies are discussed in the light of the theoretical insights of Robert Miles, the British sociologist, and as such this chapter can be considered as a critical appraisal of his work. In several publications he calls for theoretical and empirical research to be done into instances of racism outside the colonial context (Miles 1991a, 1991b, 1993a, 1993b). Miles argues that such exercises put us in a better position to identify, understand, and explain racism. The evidence he offers is so far rather thin, but that fault is easily remedied by carrying out more research. More problematical is the suggestion that all discourses of problematizing sections of the immigrant or native population should be labelled without hesitation as instances of racism or racialization. This chapter is a plea for not starting from such an assumption *a priori*, and substantiates this suggestion by empirical data from the Netherlands. Before discussing the specific case of the Netherlands, however, the definition of the concept of racism and the context within which the phenomenon should be analysed will be examined more closely.

Racialization and Racism

In his book *Racism*, Miles (1989: 41–68) dwelt at length on the definition of racism. He derides the trend of many modern students of racism to stretch definitions so that all kinds of other specific discourses – such as cultural or nationalist ones – can be included in the concept. Nor is he happy about the tendency of other students to relativize the social significance of ideologies or intentions, and to label the origin or the maintenance of black disadvantage as racism. Miles belittles these developments as 'conceptual inflation', and he is right in doing so. With all these increasingly broad definitions it becomes steadily less clear what the essence of racism is.

Miles himself describes *racism* as a specific form of evaluative representation, analytically distinguishable from exclusionary practices. He considers racism as an ideology of dominance, grounded but not determined by a specific combination of political and economical relations. As an ideology racism gives direction, or legitimacy, to a certain inequality in the distribution of class positions and social resources. According to Miles (1989: 79) it is racism when collectivities identified as 'races' are 'attributed with additional, negatively evaluated characteristics and/or [are] represented as inducing negative consequences for any other'. Racism thus implies the ranking of social collectivities.

Miles puts forward an important idea when he says that racism is a specific articulation of a wider (descriptive) process of *racialization* and that it is consequently of essential importance to get a hold on that process. After all, the ideological construction of collectivities – in fact thinking in terms of 'race' – logically precedes the construction of a hierarchy of these collectivities. Miles (1989: 70) describes the process of racialization as the process of attributing meanings 'to particular objects, features and processes, in such a way that the latter are given special significance, and carry or are embodied with a set of additional, second order features'. It should be noted that Miles is not quite clear as to the nature of the characteristics signified. In his book *Racism* (Miles 1989) on page 76 he restricts the concepts of racialization and thus of racism to instances of signification of 'biological features of human beings' only, whereas on page 79 of the same book he argues that those characteristics may be 'either biological or cultural'. In the light of the position he takes in Miles (1993b), I take it that racialization and racism refer to instances of signification of real or alleged biological characteristics of people or of cultural characteristics that are considered as fixed or naturalized as 'the criterion by which a collectivity may be identified.[1] In this way, the collectivity is represented as having a natural, unchanging origin and status, and therefore inherently different' (Miles 1993b: 79). The logical consequence of this strict definition is that the signification of characteristics other than those mentioned cannot be included as instances of racialization. Even less, then, can that process lead to racism.

How racism is manifested cannot be foreseen. Miles (1993a; see also 1992) writing about British literature, but also referring to other literature (for example, Van Dijk 1991: 26–7; Essed 1991: 39) suggests, however, that students of racism mainly treat this concept in an unidimensional and monocausal sense. He argues that they often start from the assumption that 'the only or the most important racism is that which has "black" people as its object'.[2] The use of such a concept excludes to a greater or lesser extent the notion that any non-black population can be the object of racism. Wrong, thinks Miles. He ascribes the popularity of this theoretical assumption to the predominance of the colonial paradigm of racism and to the influence of political and academic discourses in the United States. The colonial paradigm of racism is founded on the empirical data of the history of (British) colonialism and the subsequent immigration of black immigrant workers and others from former colonial territories (to Britain). Though in themselves undeniable, these data are fairly specific. Miles (1991b: 538) suggests, therefore, that 'theories of racism which are grounded solely in the analysis of colonial history and which prioritize the single somatic characteristic of skin colour [have] a rather limited explanatory power'.

The limitations are revealed when the historical development of various European nation states is compared. For instance, the existence of racism in Luxembourg, Germany, Poland or Switzerland can hardly be explained by the colonial history of these respective nation states, though some have in fact made an attempt in this direction (Castles, Booth and Wallace 1984; see for a critical view Bovenkerk, Miles and Verbunt 1991: 382). Moreover, the ideological representation of some categories of non-black natives sometimes shows remarkable congruence with those of some categories of black immigrants, an empirical fact that in the British context can only with difficulty be shown as being inherent in the colonial scheme. For the record: it has never been denied that in specific cases there can be a link between racism and colonialism. What is in question is whether the history of colonialism is a sufficiently adequate starting point for theoretical discussion about the nature and significance of racism in present-day Europe.

How can the problem be solved? Miles (1991b; see also Bovenkerk, Miles and Verbunt 1990; Schuster 1999) suggests as an alternative starting point the formation and continued existence of nation states. In a general sense it is a question of the demarcation of an area of territory within which their own forms of citizenship and of political representation are valid, and within which a state apparatus operates that contributes to the continuity of the dominant means of production, the reproduction of class relationships, the distribution and redistribution of social resources, and the maintenance of the unity of the nation as such. More particularly it is a question of defining the boundaries of the nation, that is to say the processes that continually define and confirm who belongs and on what conditions, and who does not belong to the 'imagined community' (Anderson 1983) called nation, thus the processes which define the 'self' and the 'other' and the differences between them. In every case there is the idea that those who belong to the nation have some specific common attributes regardless of social class, sex or anything else. It must be quite clear that this ideological representativeness is specific and – if only because of existing class differences – is inherently contradictory.

The Interrelationship between the Interior and Exterior 'Others'

Racialization and racism belong to the processes that, in certain circumstances, can be part of the process of forming a nation state. This is, for example, the case in Great Britain. The black population in the colonial territories of the British empire – later the black immigrant workers in Britain from former colonial territories – were in this way ideologically isolated from the dominant majority of the population: there is a widespread idea that blacks do not belong to the British race. However, if we do not concentrate only on colonial relationships and on black people, other modalities come into the picture. For instance, in the last century some fractions of the white working class inside the nation state became problematized on almost identical grounds.

What had happened? In previous times, the bourgeois class, eager to safeguard their privileged and dominant position, looked for ways to distinguish themselves from common people. This was done among other things by a refinement of their own values and manners. Paradoxically enough they also aimed at forging the nation of which they were a part into a homogeneous unity – on their own civilized terms, be it understood – without wanting to remove the differences between and within classes. In this process the bourgeois class identified all kinds of 'unsound' elements, people who in their eyes did not fit into the image of a civilized nation. In this way they constructed within the bounds of the nation state two dialectically connected categories of people: the 'civilized self' and the 'uncivilized other'. This second category – also so called 'dangerous class' – consisted mainly of members of the subordinate classes such as the rural peasantry and the expanding urbanized working class. It is of importance theoretically that the various categories of people were represented as *races apart*. On the one hand the bourgeoisie thought 'that its values and manners were more a matter of *inheritance* than a social construction' (Miles 1991a; author's italics). On the other hand 'the "backwardness" and "insularity" of rural peasants, and the "savagery" of the urbanized working class [were] often interpreted as *biological attributes* which obstructed their incorporation as "races" into membership of the nation' (Miles 1993a; my italics). For these reasons Miles identifies and labels this model as *racism of the interior*[3] as opposed to the better known *racism of the exterior*.

The parallels and even the historical linkages between these interior and exterior processes are remarkable. Miles (1991a) refers emphatically in this connection to the ideology of the *civilizing mission*. The colonial project claimed as one of its objectives the civilization of 'backward races'. This civilization came down to 'in varying combination, conversion to Christianity, the provision of elementary education (to teach "good manners" and to ensure at least some degree of literacy [. . .]) and the organization of labour order to ensure commodity production'. Within the boundaries of the nation state a similar civilizing mission was carried out, this time directed at the interior 'others'. This scheme was 'logical' because it fitted smoothly on to 'a preceding signification of these interior Others as inferior Others'.

Miles' contribution to the theoretical debate – fitting racialization and racism into the continuous formation of nation states, and the congruence between interior and exterior processes that could be distinguished analytically – is in any case interesting and valuable. However, I cannot help wondering whether a new unidimensionality is hidden in an approach within which the problematizing of specific categories of the population – of the exterior or the interior, and irrespective of their colour – is invariably analysed in terms of *race*. The reference to phenotypical and naturalized cultural characteristics applies perhaps to the specific empirical instances of Great Britain or France, but not necessarily to other nation states. Miles (1989: 119; see also Bovenkerk, Miles and Verbunt 1990) usually recognizes this, but seems sometimes to do so rather inconsistently. For instance, he suggests that in certain European countries (notably Germany, the Netherlands and France) the notion of race 'has largely disappeared from official and much public discourse. Explicit references to human differentiation in terms of a fixed biological ranking, and sustained by assertions of congenital inferiority, are equally rare (*although belief in the existence of "races" remains widespread*)' (Miles 1991a; my italics). Elsewhere he says that 'the history of nation state formation in Europe, is a history of a multiplicity of *interior* processes including those of *civilization* and *racialization*' (1993a; author's italics). It seems to me that Miles, in the absence of empirical research, is somewhat too definite here. At least, he does not mention what possibly equivalent processes might look like.

I would like to investigate further how far it is necessary to speak of racialization and of racism, or of such functionally equivalent ideological representations of interior 'others', by looking at the specific example of the problematizing of native 'anti-social families' (*onmaatschappelijke gezinnen*) in the Netherlands. The struggle against anti-socialness, waged mainly and most intensively in this century – but never with complete success – is particularly interesting because it demonstrates striking similarities, both ideologically and practically, with the present-day approach to 'immigrant ethnic minorities'.

The Problematizing of Interior Others: the Anti-Social Families Approach

For at least a century there have been intensive efforts in the Netherlands to absorb families into the life of the nation or at least to discipline them. This has particularly been the case with families who over the years 'have been described variously as inadmissible, anti-social, socially ill, unsocial, socially maladjusted, deprived, underprivileged, and problem and multi-problem families' (Van Wel 1992). The state and a great many private social institutions have tried in many ways to intervene in the life of these families. In doing so they went further than would have been thought possible in any other nation state. Until late in the 1950s whole families were transferred for treatment into separate hostels or encampments in the countryside far from the conurbation. A broad outline of the development of this unique example of social intervention is given below, together with the ideological representation of the interior 'others' affected by this intervention. The outline is inevitably a very broad one.

Up to the Second World War

For a good understanding of the situation we must go back more than 100 years. In the late nineteenth century, when industrialization was finally getting into its stride in the Netherlands, a social class of proletarian factory workers came into existence. The members of this class were recruited from the rural areas round the industrial centres. The inhuman living conditions under which the proletarians existed provoked a reaction from enlightened liberals among the bourgeoisie. They mobilized their forces from moral repugnance, but also from fear of revolt by the impoverished mob. They pressed for laws and measures to protect the socially and economically disadvantaged and to raise them from their pitiable condition (De Regt 1984: 243; see also Roes, Veldheer, De Groot, Dekker and Castenmiller 1987). It was not long before the state followed in their footsteps. It unfurled a range of initiatives in the fields of poverty relief, unemployment relief, education, social housing and health care. This was particularly the case around the turn of the century in municipalities dominated by the democratic socialists.

These socialists hoped to accelerate the defeat of capitalism by the working class by social and economic improvements, but also by moral improvement (*zedelijke verheffing*) of the working class. Although this was primarily regarded as an essential part of the collective emancipation of the working class, it also had practical motives. In the eyes of the socialist vanguard self-discipline, devotion to duty, and class consciousness encouraged willingness to take collective action. The moral improvement was achieved by (socio-cultural) education of the working classes; for this purpose workers' evening classes, libraries, outdoor pursuits, theatrical and singing groups, and youth organizations were established (Dercksen and Verplanke 1987: 42; De Regt 1984). In practice the moral improvement came down to a 'civilizing offensive' (*beschavingsoffensief*) based on such themes as order, neatness, industriousness, thrift, and devotion to duty. This offensive was, for that matter, not exclusively restricted to the democratic socialists. The Christian Democrats also played their part in the fight against moral depravity, by which they understood primarily the slide into godlessness and socialism.

The ideals of culture and civilization seem to have caught on mainly with the educated, better-paid and better-organized workers (Leydesdorff 1987). De Regt (1984: 242–3) and Van Wel (1992: 149) suggest that this is the result of the search for distinction of the upwardly mobile groups of workers. They did not want to be identified with the working population lagging behind in the slums, the rough mob of illiterate, casual, unorganized labourers. They distinguished themselves from them by assuming a more respectable and socially respected lifestyle, by which they in fact meant the lifestyle of the middle class. In this respect it is significant that the Social Democratic Labour Party (SDAP) and the trade unions linked to it were mainly organized by educated workers who had succeeded in rising socially. Meyer, Kouprie and Sikkens (1980) believe, in this connection, that the socialist leaders were not sure what to do about the unorganized workers whom they feared because of the risk of spontaneous go-slows, wildcat strikes, riots and brawls, which ran counter to the civilized parliamentary strategies of the SDAP and the unions.

As time went on the emancipating groups had less and less sympathy for the 'unrespectable' behaviour of those 'left behind' (De Regt 1984: 202–5). Gradually their moral improvement acquired a less voluntary character. For instance, municipal authorities used their responsibility for social housing to come to grips with 'socially weak families'. In Amsterdam, where the socialists dominated local politics, housing officials identified these families as a problem group and attached the term inadmissible (*ontoelaatbaar*) to them. They next denied 'inadmissible families' access to normal council housing. They could go straight into housing schools (*woonscholen*), special residential areas under the supervision of wardens, who educated them into being respectable people. Partly because psychiatrists applied themselves to the problem, the counselling of the residents was to some extent focused on to their psychological state. The struggle against anti-socialness gradually became institutionalized, while the approach to it increasingly became a professional one.

Inadmissible families were defined as a problem, because they neglected their accommodation, were destructive, made a mess, caused trouble among themselves or with their neighbours, and failed to pay their rent on time (De Regt 1984: 205–12). This deviant behaviour was increasingly associated with characteristics like drunkenness, child neglect, crime and mental deficiency. It was not only the way they lived, but the total functioning in society of those involved that became the problem. By this definition all the characteristics combined to form a syndrome dominating the lives of these people and damaging for society.

Anti-socialness is more than a socio-cultural or moral problem: it is in all its aspects a problem of class. Its existence is inseparably linked to the growth of the modern capitalist mode of production and the accompanying development of social classes. The anti-social behaviour of the lowest fractions of the working class bring painful memories of their own origins to the higher fractions (De Regt 1984: 199–203). The latter clearly experience the changed relations of production and the emergence of class differences in terms of respectability and culture. In one sense the civilizing mission against anti-socialness can also be regarded as a struggle for the socio-cultural hegemony of the middle class, sanctioned by the state.

In the inter-war years several academics looked for the cause of anti-socialness in mental incapacity and suggested that this was a question of temperament and heredity. The supporters of eugenics who put this point of view forward believed that lower classes and races should not be given the chance to reproduce themselves, as otherwise the whole population would degenerate. The eugenic point of view can plainly be characterized as racism of the interior. However, Dercksen and Verplanke (1987: 53–67) suggest that the adherents of eugenics in the Netherlands were not successful in gaining wide acceptance for their ideas (see also Noordman 1990).[4] On the contrary, another ideological tendency became dominant. In this period most people came to accept that the 'problem of anti-social families' could be traced back to wretched living conditions that had existed for generations. They believed that long-term deprivation led to backwardness and degeneration of character, which were perfectly curable. The dominant ideological representation of anti-social families depended on the whole not on people's racialized traits, but on the signification and the negative evaluation of socio-cultural features of people from the lowest social classes without these features being classified as either unchangeable or natural.

The 1940s and 1950s

During the Second World War and for a short time afterwards the civilizing mission went ahead undiminished (Dercksen and Verplanke 1987: 89–104). Reconstruction was taken seriously in hand and the Dutch economy was set on its feet again. However, reconstruction was not just a matter of economics. During the war morals values were relaxed and disturbed, and everywhere there was concern about social upheaval and moral degradation (Neij 1989: 41). Some people lacked any moral substance and suffered from loss of religious faith and broken families: the anti-socials.

The socialists pointed to the dark side of modern society (Meyer, Kouprie and Sikkens 1980: 56–60). Its massiveness and its large scale led in their opinion to depersonalization, to a dulling of social relations and to undermining the community spirit. The 'socially elusive' were particularly susceptible to this: they thought only of their own interests, did not take part in social, cultural, political or religious organizations and so escaped their influence, lived on their emotions, were uncritical, were unconscious of moral values and social norms, and as a result were an enduring hidden danger (Hoekstra: 1950).[5] The Christian democrats also pointed to the crying need for moral and cultural improvement as well as for economic progress. They primarily regarded moral reconstruction in terms of a sound religious and family life.

But what was to be done with those who ignored conventional morals? Not three months after the liberation, experts came to the conclusion that anti-social families had to be put under supervision and re-educated. They advised that this would have to be compulsory. However, the legislation did not authorize compulsory residence in special institutions for families. Amendments were considered but in the end were not implemented because of the ethical implications of deprival of liberty (van Wel 1992: 152). 'Voluntary' residence did come within the law.

Almost the only people to go to the Family Institutions for Socially Maladjusted Families (*Gezinsoorden voor Maatschappelijk Onaangepaste Gezinnen*) were those living in great poverty, who had little education, were not in regular work, and whose living conditions were very poor (Van Wel: 105–87). In the eyes of contemporaries they had only themselves to blame for these distressing circumstances, and they were not yet capable of catching up with the rapid developments in society. The men were said to lack responsibility, hardly cared for their wives and children, and failed to make a living properly. Their re-education was directed at giving them a sound work ethic, meaning that they had to learn to turn up for work regularly and on time, work properly, behave correctly towards their superiors and their fellow workers, recognize their place in the hierarchy of power, and so on. The women had to cope with other problems. They were supposed to have discarded their natural responsibility as mothers, neglected their children, wasted money and were unhygienic. Their re-education concentrated on housework and motherhood. They learned housework skills, such as washing up, cooking and cleaning, and also tasks involved with bringing up and caring for children. They also (like the men) learned to cut their coat according to their cloth. Finally there were special programmes for children who were rude and aggressive, had no standards, were socially inhibited and inarticulate, and who distrusted the world outside. Only when their total behaviour had been adjusted might the family return to 'normal' society.

Private institutions and local authorities set up a series of institutions for special family and neighbourhood work for anti-social families. Particularly after the creation of the Ministry for Social Work in 1952, social work expanded enormously (Dercksen and Verplanke 1987: 86). The same applied to sociology and psychology, whose practitioners discovered an interesting and lucrative area for research in anti-socialness. The increasing professionalization of the civilizing work continued, one expression being the growth of the number of Schools for Social Work. In some of these schools 'the asocial family' or the 'socially maladjusted family' made up a separate section of the curriculum.

As was the case before the war, anti-socialness was regarded in this period primarily as a socio-cultural problem. It was generally seen as involving people who had a deviant life style from that of the middle classes and who therefore deteriorated. The diagnosis was now often couched in epidemiological terms: anti-socials were socially diseased and threatened to affect the stability of the whole of society. They were seen as standing in the way of the development of society. They lowered standards, undermined law and authority, and made up 'centres of infection for moral deterioration' (Dercksen and Verplanke 1987: 92). This could be cured by means of social isolation of the family and by work therapy.

It was accepted that maladjustment can in principle apply to all social classes. Despite this only the maladjustment of the lowest fractions of the working class were defined as a problem. For instance, around 1960 a state advisory committee stated that maladjusted behaviour could also occur in 'higher circles' (Dercksen and Verplanke 1987: 224). The committee gave an extremely *positive* evaluation of this: 'The lack of adjustment of artists, philosophers, inventors, can be of essential importance for the whole of society. The deviant and alienating behaviour of heroes and saints, which leaves the average man somewhat at a loss, can arouse and inspire'. The tone alters sharply when it discusses 'inferior' people:

> There are people, families, groups of the population found, among others, in the bottom layers of society, where deviance from the rules of the game is obviously more frequent, more disturbing, more deep-rooted and more manifest. This section of the population is so prominent that it has been labelled with the terms 'anti-social' and 'asocial'.[6]

The committee therefore found that the deviant behaviour of the bottom layer had a disturbing influence on society, believing particularly that this bottom layer made demands on institutions for social relief and was dependent on the state. These associations assumed a life of their own. As Milikowski (1961: 124–6; see also Van der Valk 1986: 164–6) later demonstrates, some people went so far as to identify socio-economic weakness as a sign of anti-socialness. For instance, for the purposes of a research report on anti-socialness (in 1950) people were only investigated who were on the files of the social services or of some more or less philanthropic institution.

The 1960s and Afterwards

In the 1960s there was a change of approach. The family institutions were abolished, and the special department in the Ministry of Social Work reorganized. Its central objective was no longer to fight anti-socialness, but to arrange conditions in which everyone could deploy their own capabilities (Dercksen and Verplanke 1987: 225). Social work expanded from socially backward areas to cover the whole population. In complete conformity with assumptions transferred from the United States about community organization, institutions applied themselves to the improvement of peoples' social environment. In this view society is not a static entity, to which anti-socials must adapt themselves, but the producer, and reproducer, of this socio-economic backwardness and inequality of opportunity. In this period the discourse gradually changed (Dercksen and Verplanke 1987: 206–49). 'Anti-social families' became 'deprived or underprivileged families'. However, these underprivileged were categorized on the basis of more-or-less the same characteristics: if anything their low social class was given more emphasis. The broader perspective, however, from which these characteristics were viewed was fundamentally different. The causes of the behaviour of the underprivileged were considered more in their politico-economic context. Moreover, the evaluation of this behaviour became less negative; deviation deserved understanding and acceptance, even if there were limits to this acceptance. According to Dercksen and Verplanke (1987: 225) 'other norms could be accepted as long as they did not come into conflict with the general norms of society. [. . .] If there is conflict then it will be necessary to try and correct the deviant norms'.

At the end of the 1980s the discussion about problem families flared up again. Again the question became topical of whether people with maladjusted or deviant behaviour should be housed in segregated areas. For instance, in 1989 a conference of a thousand practitioners in the field of social housing discussed *Neighbour Nuisance – From Taboo to Policy*. Van Wel (1990: 146; 192: 160) points out that this increasing intolerance of deviant living and lifestyles now particularly involves ethnic minorities.

The Problematizing of Exterior 'Others': the Ethnic Minorities Approach

Van Wel's observation indicates that there is a congruence between the way in which interior and exterior sections of the population are problematized. The process of problematizing ethnic minorities has been discussed elsewhere (Rath 1991, 1993a). It is only necessary here to summarize two historical examples: the forced assimilation of the Indonesian Dutch in the 1950s and the social assistance to guest workers from the Mediterranean in the 1960s.

The Forced Assimilation of the Indonesian Dutch

In the course of the 1950s, as a consequence of the independence of Indonesia, approximately 300,000 Indonesian Dutch settled in their *patria*, the Netherlands. Officials, members of state advisory committees, and private institutions for the reception of the Indonesian Dutch had previously worried a great deal about 'those rooted in Indonesia' (Schuster 1999). Would they be able to cope adequately with the pattern of life in the Netherlands? The yardstick applied here by the Dutch policy-makers and social workers is the cultural pattern of the 'Dutch middle class' (Godeschalk 1988: 90). The policy makers and social workers attacked the problem of 'maladjustment' by falling back on a familiar solution: the anti-social family approach (Schuster 1992: 54–6). To keep everything on the right lines, the Ministry of Social Work set up the Special Care Commission. The objective of this commission was 'to prevent social degradation as much as possible, and if possible to cure it' (quoted in Godeschalk 1988: 62). The commission included several people who played a leading role in the struggle against anti-socialness. Soon the Special Care Commission joined the Central Committee of Churches and Private Initiatives for Social Care of Repatriates (CCKP) which co-ordinated the implementation of policy on behalf of the Ministry. The CCKP pulled out all stops to effect the adjustment of the repatriates as quickly and completely as possible. Numbers of social workers and house visitors started work under its aegis. They concentrated particularly on the cultural characteristics of the 'lower segments' (Godeschalk 1990: 43–4) which might obstruct their adjustment to Dutch society, and in doing so used schemes originally developed for anti-social families (Godeschalk 1988: 67). Those repatriates who were housed in hostels had particular difficulty in escaping from them. They were instructed in the Dutch style of housekeeping, bringing up children, budgeting, cooking, dress, language, home furnishing and so on.

Social Assistance to Mediterranean Guest Workers

Since the end of the 1950s and early 1960s, hundreds of thousands of foreign workers from the Mediterranean countries have found work in Dutch industry. As soon as the first few hundred Italians arrived, almoners, social workers, academics, officials and others came forward to point out the 'other' nature and lifestyle of 'the' guest worker, their alienness and their southern mentality, their difficulty in acclimatizing, and their problems of adjustment (see, among others De Graan 1964; Simons 1962). The Dutch experts were quite sure that society was faced with a special category of people with special problems. Their message was that social assistance and other measures to encourage integration were essential if disorientation and rejection were to be prevented, and if conflicts with the Dutch caused by cultural differences were to be avoided. From the start they opted for a group-specific approach. In many places welfare institutions were set up on a corporate base, which could provide for more indirect and more uniform adjustment of the guest workers into Dutch culture. These welfare institutions applied to the Ministry of Social Work for a structural subsidy, drawing comparisons with their social work among caravan dwellers. An important factor is that, in this period, the struggle against anti-socialness began to subside and a need for new target groups began to grow among the specialists. 'Initially, that is in the late 1950s, mainly professionals from the private sector – particularly Roman-Catholic almoners and social workers – interfered in the life of the Mediterranean guestworkers. At that time, the government declined any responsibility for the guestworkers. This changed rapidly when it became clear that the presence of these migrant workers would in one way or another affect the life of the Dutch. The national government then decided to support the private initiatives morally and financially. This happened soon after violent clashes between local rowdies and Italian and Spanish guest workers (in the Eastern region of Twente in 1961, caused by the exclusion of Italians from a dance, see Groenendijk 1990: 82), and after the arrival of the first guestworker families.' Within a few years the government assumed all responsibility, and was in complete charge of the reception of guest workers, and later also of other categories of immigrants such as those from Surinam. In view of the assumption that they would eventually return home, there was as yet no excessive pressure for their adjustment, and they had scope to develop their own communities.

It is these categories – caravan dwellers, immigrants from Mediterranean countries, Surinam, the Netherlands Antilles, the Molucca Islands, and a few others – which have later been labelled as 'ethnic minorities'. In an advisory note to the government in 1979 the Scientific Council for Government Policy (WRR) emphasized the specific nature of the problems of many members of ethnic minorities. These came down to 'problems of backwardness, of their own cultural identity, and encounters with a different type of society' (WRR 1979: viii). For instance, they have a relatively low level of education, limited skills and training, and hardly any economic power (WWR 1979: xii). They also cherish their own ideas of the relationships between the sexes, family relationships, the work ethic, eating habits, attitudes of citizens vis-à-vis the authorities, and so on. 'This confrontation of ethnic minorities with their new environment can *obviously* lead to great tension', declared the WRR (1979: x; my italics). The advice of the WRR appears to have been very influential in the establishment of the Minorities Policy in the 1980s that is a policy programme designed by the National Government and aimed at the integration of immigrant ethnic minorities.

Socio-cultural Maladjustment

These examples illustrate the extent to which specific 'others' become problematized on the grounds of their socio-cultural maladjustment compared with the Dutch middle class ideal type. This applies particularly to the lower social classes. The idea is that their presence in society 'obviously' leads to 'great tensions'. Measures to encourage integration, that is measures designed to adapt them, should prevent 'conflicts caused by cultural differences'. At this ideological level the parallel with the problematizing of anti-social families is unmistakeable (see further Rath 1991: 142–4).

It is important to understand that socio-cultural non-conformity does not *necessarily* lead to the construction of problem categories. The socio-cultural non-conformity of American or Japanese immigrants, for instance, is commonly approached with a highly positive attitude, but they are predominantly higher class people. The Japanese immigrants in the town of Amstelveen – which is adjacent to Amsterdam – constitute the largest immigrant community in the place. They are concentrated in a number of apartment blocks, send their children to Japanese schools, spend their free time in Japanese clubs, have little proficiency in the Dutch language, and do not show a great interest in learning the language or interacting with the Dutch. Contrary to what usually happens with regard to Turkish, Moroccan or Surinamese immigrants who live their lives separated from the native Dutch, the Japanese way of living is not defined as a problem. As a matter of fact, the opposite is the case. A commercial bank in Amstelveen has even opened a Japanese desk to cater for its Japanese clientele (*Intermagazine*, November 1991). How different is the situation a few miles north, in south-east Amsterdam. This relative new neighbourhood needs to be profoundly renewed, so the authorities have decided. A number of high rise buildings have been torn down to make place for luxury and expensive apartments. The tenants of the high rise buildings – predominantly immigrants from Surinam and African countries – accused the authorities of having racist motives when designing their plans. The responsible Alderman of Housing and the director of the housing corporation involved strongly denied these allegations. But, interestingly enough, they also claimed this:

> A continuing concentration of poor minority groups in one neighbourhood is not good. This is not because cultural diversity does not have attractive aspects, but because it concerns low income groups with little or no education and a high rate of unemployment. Problems accumulate, the tenants are stigmatized and confronted with the prejudices of others (*De Volkskrant*, 22 September 1992).

In my view, this is an exemplary case of how socio-cultural non-conformity in combination with low socio-economic status is problematized.

The ideological representations of anti-social families and immigrant ethnic minorities show remarkable similarities. There are nevertheless differences. The non-conformity of anti-social families was negatively evaluated without any hesitation. Their identity had to be mercilessly moulded into what was considered as a 'normal' identity. The identity of ethnic minorities, however, is treated somewhat more cautiously. Particularly in the 1970s, immigrant ethnic minorities were give the right and facilities to maintain their cultural identity in one way or another. This was to prevent them from becoming alienated from their cultural roots and was considered important for those who would return to the home country. This basically served to confirm their exclusion from the Dutch mainstream. Furthermore, social pressure against engaging in racism has become more prominent during since the 1960s, partly due as a reaction to the experience during the Second World War. Finally, unlike anti-social families, immigrants and ethnic minorities do have their own associations that have been recognized as partners in the political process. Particularly since the democratization movement in the 1960s, the government has a greater need to co-operate with target groups and to legitimize its policies (Compare Rath and Saggar 1992) . The co-operation of ethnic minorities can be enhanced by providing subventions and facilities. These subventions and facilities seem like a blessing, but then one ignores the hidden political agenda.

The Roles of the State and Academia

Let us return to the interior 'other'. The reproduction of the ideology of anti-socialness is largely to be ascribed to the reckoning of the state. The state may not determine this ideology, but it certainly sanctions this type of thinking about socio-cultural maladjustment by applying all kinds of political measures, which in their turn reinforce the dominant ideology. It was officials who first used the term 'inadmissible', it is the state represented by municipalities that uses its authority to exclude 'inadmissible families' from normal social housing, and so on. With the expansion of the welfare state in the 1950s the involvement of the state with 'anti-social families' also grew. In this way the state intentionally or unintentionally reinforced the assumption that there was something wrong with these working-class families. The bureaucratic apparatus, the nimbus of welfare institutions, the educational institutions, training skilled professionals, and researchers who produced reports, together formed an institutional complex that gave the 'problem family' approach its own dynamic: everyone justified each other's ideological representations of the maladjusted 'other' and each other's actions. Incidentally, all those involved were in their own way progressive. They were inspired by the wish to help society and believed that people could be changed for the better, and in the importance of their civilizing work.

In accordance with the empiricist tradition of Dutch social science (Rath 1991; 2000), researchers carried out practical social research into the extent and nature of the phenomenon of anti-socialness. The family institutions were true laboratories where researchers could experiment to their hearts' content (Dercksen and Verplanke 1987: 107). Researchers, policy makers and practitioners met each other regularly in conferences and took part together in working parties and committees, and some academics even became officials in the Ministry of Social Work. Dercksen and Verplanke (1987: 188–9) go so far as to say that the broadening of the views on anti-socialness can be ascribed to the emergence of the social sciences.

Not until 1960 did more critical studies appear, of which the most well known is Milikowski's (1961). He accused the academics of lack of objectivity. They gave *common sense notions* about anti-socials an academic cachet, without worrying about whether they had any scientific basis. Blinkered by the cultural patterns of higher social classes they claimed that in the interests of their emancipation everyone should conform to these patterns. According to Milikowski those who make such claims allow themselves to be used by the higher classes to defend the existing social order. Milikowski is, in fact, drawing attention to the existence of an organized consensus built round the paternalist treatment of specific interior 'others'.

Civil servants of the Ministry of Welfare, later the Ministry of Culture, Recreation and Social Work (CRM), who played first fiddle in the struggle against anti-socialness, then started looking for new target groups and new activities. Later, when it became evident that the post-migratory 'problems' went beyond their bounds, they tried to win other ministries for the cause of the integration of ethnic minorities. In so doing, they mobilized social researchers. In 1978, the ministry establish the Advisory Committee on Research of Cultural Minorities. In its very first advice, the committee stated that members of ethnic minority groups were fundamentally different from native Dutch in similar inferior positions, due, amongst other things to: 'the sometimes strongly different cultural orientation of those minorities' (ACOM 1979: 9–11). Like the Scientific Council for the Government Policy (WRR), which published its report on ethnic minorities in the same year, the ACOM was quite influential because it designed and implemented an ambitious research programme on 'ethnic minorities'. Numerous researchers embarked on this programme, thereby following the ACOM's definition of the situation.

Conclusions

In various publications the British sociologist Miles has opposed the unidimensional and monocausal use of the concept of 'racism'. Many students of racism assume wrongly that the only or the most important racism is that which has black people as its object, as if any non-black population cannot be the object of racism. According to Miles this is because they put the colonial model central in their considerations. The formation of the nation state is in his view a better starting point for theoretical consideration of the nature and meaning of racism in present-day Europe. It implies the construction of the imagined community of the nation. Racism is one of the ideologies that are involved in that process, as is plain from the French and British cases. According to Miles this does not just involve *racism of the exterior*, the ideological process that is specifically relevant to black immigrant workers. There is also the question of *racism of the interior*, the problematizing of specific categories of non-blacks such as the 'dangerous class' of urbanized proletarians. These two modalities are closely linked to each other. In each case they involve sections of the population that are ideologically excluded from the imagined community on the grounds of the negative evaluation of racialized features, whereas the remaining members of society are ideologically included on the grounds that they are evaluated positively. Those affected are all represented as *races apart*, that is to say, as collectivities that exist as the result of the signification of real or alleged biological characteristics of people or of cultural characteristics that are considered as fixed as a consequence of the ideological process of *racialization*.

The process of nation-state formation, however, is historically specific. In each nation state there are specific criteria that determine who does and who does not belong to the imagined community. So it is premature to assume that the ideological construction of interior and exterior 'others' in all cases that may arise, are necessarily modalities of racism. In this respect the Dutch case is interesting. On the one hand it shows Miles to be right that the problematizing of exterior 'others' and interior 'others' are congruent. The way in which, nowadays, immigrant ethnic minorities (the exterior 'others') are ideologically represented displays remarkable similarities with the way in which anti-social families (the interior Others) were represented in an earlier historical phase. In one sense there is even historical continuity. Research into the struggle against anti-socialness certainly gives us a better understanding of the current problematizing of ethnic minorities.

On the other hand the Dutch case also shows that problematizing anti-socials or ethnic minorities is not necessarily an expression of racism of the interior or, as the case may be, of racism of the exterior. Anti-social families and ethnic minorities – both constituting fractions of the lowest social classes – are seen by the rest of society as people with a lifestyle that deviates from that of the middle-class ideal type, as people who do not adequately conform to the dominant norms of normal behaviour, as backward people with a lifestyle of an earlier pre-industrial period. To pick out some of the characteristics ascribed to them: they show insufficient respectability, neatness and hygiene; they don't housekeep properly; they are noisy; are a nuisance to their neighbours; are difficult socially; settle conflicts by violence; show criminal tendencies; go in for alcohol or drugs abuse; run into debt; do not have a sound work ethic and are often unemployed; are dependent upon the state and hardly capable of standing on their own feet; have enjoyed little education; don't speak proper; don't care much for parliamentary politics; don't base marriage on romantic and affectionate relationships; give a low status to women; don't bring up their children properly, letting them stay up late and not being supportive of their education; *and so on*. The predominant ideological representation of these collectivities on the whole revolves round real or alleged *socio-cultural features* of human beings. That's why the 'others' are not represented as *races apart* but as *minorities apart*. There is no question of racialization, and so not of racism in Miles' sense. The crux is that in the Dutch case – with the exception before the Second World War of a small number of supporters of eugenics with little influence – the signified socio-cultural features are *not* regarded as *fixed or naturalized*. As a matter of fact, the state and private institutions have done their utmost to get these 'others' to adjust to the dominant lifestyle, in other words, to change them.

As the problematizing of interior and exterior 'others' in the Netherlands does not begin with the ideological process of racialization, we must have recourse to a neologism: minorization, a concept that refers to the ideological construction of minorities (Rath 1993b). It goes without saying that racialization and minorization are theoretically distinguishable but functionally equivalent concepts.

Some critics may argue that this view is at odds with the prevailing image of the Netherlands as a country that has deliberately chosen a 'multicultural minorities policy' and which, in doing so, has shown its progressive and humanistic stand (cf. Strijbosch 1992). They may furthermore claim that the Dutch approach takes more account of cultural diversity than the German or French approaches do. These distinctions, however, are only relative. What is more important is that those who herald Dutch multiculturalism are often reluctant to go beyond its fancy image and to face its ideological foundations and its perverse exclusionary effects.

Notes

1. This is still a matter for debate. Schuster (1999), for example, concludes that Miles take the more narrow position.
2. This does not necessarily imply that these authors consider racism as something exclusively associated with phenotypic characteristics.
3. Balibar (1991: 204–16) speaks in this connection of 'class racism'.
4. An additional reason for the religious denominations to oppose possible eugenic legislation, such as compulsory sterilization, is that this would imply state interference. They tried to prevent this as much as possible.
5. In addition to 'anti-socials' Hoekstra (1950) includes those 'honest citizens' who are 'unaware' of their social environment and who duck out of the control of the latter. In reaction to this Kaan (1950) calls this lack of social awareness the core of the 'problem'.
6. *Sociale integratie probleemgezinnen* (Social integration of problem families). Report of the Advisory Commission on the Prevention of Anti-socialness. The Hague, 1961. (Quoted in Dercksen and Verplanke 1987: 224).

Bibliography

ACOM (Adviescommissie Onderzoek Minderheden) (1979), *Advies onderzoek minderheden*, The Hague: State Publishers.

Anderson, B. (1983), *Imagined communities. Reflections on the origin and spread of nationalism*, London: Verso.

Balibar, E. (1991), 'Class racism', in E. Balibar and I. Wallerstein, *Race, nation, class. Ambiguous identities,* London: Verso.

Barker, M. (1981). *The new racism. Conservatives and the ideology of the tribe*. London.

Bovenkerk, F., R. Miles and G. Verbunt (1990), 'Racism, migration and the state in Western Europe. A case for comparative analysis', *International Sociology*, 5 (4): 475–90.

Bovenkerk, F., R. Miles and G. Verbunt (1991), 'Comparative studies of migration and exclusion on the grounds of "race" and ethnic background in Western Europe. A critical appraisal', *International Migration Review*, 25 (2): 375–91.

Castles, S., H. Booth and T. Wallace (1984), *Here for good. Western Europe's new ethnic minorities*, London: Pluto Press.

Dercksen, A. and L. Verplanke (1987), *Geschiedenis van de onmaatschappelijkheidsbestrijding in Nederland, 1914–1970*, Meppel: Boom.

van Dijk, T. (1991), *Racism and the press*, London: Routledge.

Essed, Ph. (1991), *Understanding everyday racism. An interdisciplinary essay*, Newbury Park, CA: Sage.

Godeschalk, M. (1988), *Assimilatie en heropvoeding. Beleid van de overheid en kerkelijk en particulier initiatief ten aanzien van gerepatrieerden uit Indonesië, 1950–1960*, MA-Thesis, Nijmegen: Catholic University Nijmegen, Department of Economical and Social History.

Godeschalk, M. (1990), 'Het assimilatiebeleid voor Indische Nederlanders. De overheid en het maatschappelijk werk gedurende de eerste jaren van de repatriëring', *Janbatan*, 8 (1): 39–48.

de Graan, N.F.A. (1964), 'De buitenlandse werknemer en zijn aanpassing aan de Nederlandse samenleving', *Maatschappij-Belangen*, 128 (7): 350–357.

Groenendijk, C.A. (1990), 'Verboden voor Tukkers. Reacties op rellen tussen Italianen, Spanjaarden en Twentenaren in 1961', in F. Bovenkerk, F. Buijs and H. Tromp (eds), *Wetenschap en partijdigheid. Opstellen voor André J.F. Köbben*, Assen/Maastricht: Van Gorcum.

Hall, S. (1980), 'Race, articulation and societies structured in dominance', in *Sociological theories. Race and colonialism*, Paris: UNESCO.

Hall, S. (1989), 'Rassismus als ideologischer Diskurs', *Das Argument*, 31 (6): 913–21.

Hoekstra, A. (1950), 'Enige sociologische aspecten van het vraagstuk van de "maatschappelijk ongrijpbaren"', *Socialisme en Democratie*, 44–53.

Kaan, A. (1950), 'De "maatschappelijk ongrijpbaren" in de grote stad', *Socialisme en Democratie*, 611–20.

Leydesdorff, S. (1987), *Wij hebben als mens geleefd. Het Joodse proletariaat van Amsterdam 1900–1940*, Amsterdam: Meulenhoff.

Meyer, H., R. Kouprie and J.R. Sikkens (1980), *De beheerste stad. Ontstaan en intenties van een sociaal-demokratische stadspolitiek. Een kritiek*, Rotterdam: Futile.

Miles, R. (1989), *Racism*, London: Routledge.

Miles, R. (1991a), 'Die Idee der "Rasse" und Theorien über Rassismus. Überlegungen zur britischen Diskussion', in U. Bielefeld (Hrsg.), *Das Eigene und das Fremde. Neuer Rassismus in der Alten Welt*. Hamburg: Junius Verlag.

Miles, R. (1991b), 'Migration to Britain. The significance of a historical approach', *International Migration*, 29 (4): 527–44.

Miles, R. (1992), 'Einwanderung nach Großbritannien. Eine historische Betrachtung', in A. Kalpaka and N. Räthzel (Hrsg.), *Rassismus und Migration in Europa. Argument-Sonderband AS 201*, Hamburg/Berlin: Argument Verlag.

Miles, R. (1993b), 'The articulation of racism and nationalism. Reflections on European history', in J. Wrench and J. Solomos (eds), *Racism and migration in Western Europe*, Oxford/Providence: Berg.

Miles, R. (1993b), *Racism after 'Race-Relations'*, London: Routledge.

Milikowski, H.Ph. (1961), *Lof der onaangepastheid. Een studie in sociale aanpassing, niet-aanpassing, onmaatschappelijkheid,* Meppel: J.A. Boom en Zoon.

Neij, R. (1989), *De organisatie van het maatschappelijk werk. Voortgang zonder samenhang I,* Zutphen: De Walburg Pers.

Noordman, J. (1990), *Om de kwaliteit van het nageslacht. Eugenetica in Nederland 1900–1950*, Nijmegen: SUN.

Rath, J. (1991), *Minorisering: de sociale constructie van 'etnische minderheden',* Amsterdam: Sua.

Rath, J. (1993a), 'La construction sociale des minorités ethniques aux Pays-Bas et ses effets pervers', in M. Martiniello and M. Poncelet (eds), *Migrations et minorités ethniques dans l'espace européen*, Bruxelles: De Boeck.

Rath, J. (1993b), 'The ideological representation of migrant workers in Europe. A matter of racialisation?', in J. Wrench and J. Solomos (eds), *Racism and migration in Western Europe*, Oxford/Providence: Berg.

Rath, J. (2000), 'Anti-Marxism in Dutch ethnic minorities studies', in P. Ratcliffe (ed.), *Sociology, the State and Social Change*, Houndmills, Basingstoke, Hampshire: Macmillan. (Forthcoming).

Rath, J. and S. Saggar (1992), 'Ethnicity as a political tool in Britain and the Netherlands', pp. 201–221 in A. Messina et al. (eds), *Ethnic and racial minorities in the advanced industrial democracies*. Wesport, Connecticut: Greenwood Press.

de Regt, A. (1984), *Arbeidersgezinnen en beschavingsarbeid. Ontwikkelingen in Nederland 1870–1940. Een historisch-sociologische studie*, Meppel: Boom.

Roes, T., V. Veldheer, H. de Groot, P. Dekker and P. Castenmiller (1987), *Gemeente, burger, klant*, Rijswijk: Social and Cultural Planning Office (SCP).

Schuster, J. (1992), 'The state and post-war immigration into the Netherlands. The racialisation and assimilation of Indonesian Dutch', *European Journal of Intercultural Studies*, 3 (1): 47–58.

Schuster, J. (1999). *Poortwachters over immigranten. Het debat over immigratie in het naoorlogse Groot-Brittannië en Nederland*, Amsterdam: Het Spinhuis.

Simons, M.S.M. (1962), 'Italiaanse arbeiders in de Limburgse mijnstreek en in Twente. Aanpassingsproblemen en sociale begeleiding', *Mens en Maatschappij*, 37: 233–46.

University of Birmingham, Centre for Contemporary Cultural Studies (1982), *The Empire Strikes Back: Race and Racism in 70s Britain*, London: Hutchinson.

van der Valk, L. (1986), *Van pauperzorg tot bestaanszekerheid. Een onderzoek naar de ontwikkeling van de armenzorg in Nederland tegen de achtergrond van de overgang naar de Algemene Bijstandswet, 1912–1965*, IISG Studies + Essays 2, Amsterdam: International Institute for Social History.

van Wel, F. (1990), 'Asociale gezinnen, van woonschool naar degradatiewoningen?', *Jeugd en Samenleving*, 20 (3): 131–47.

van Wel, F. (1992), 'A century of families under supervision in the Netherlands', *British Journal of Social Work*, 22 (2): 147–66.

WRR (Scientific Council for Government Policy) (1979). *Etnische minderheden. Reports to the Government No. 17*, The Hague: State Publishers.

–7–

France: from Unwilling Host to Bellicose Gatekeeper

Khursheed Wadia

Introduction

Over the last 150 years and until relatively recently, France has promoted itself as Europe's main country of immigration and asylum. It is the only European country to have rivalled the United States as far as immigration and the long-term settlement of migrants[1] is concerned. Immigration began to exceed emigration from 1800 and took on larger proportions during the second half of the nineteenth century (Cipolla 1976: 63), at a time when industrial development and economic growth coincided with a sharp decline in France's birth rate[2] and an equally sharp increase in its ageing population.[3]

This combination of factors meant that, earlier in the history of immigration, successive French governments appeared to place a greater emphasis, at least in their articulation of the issue, upon the role of immigration as a demographic regulator rather than as a means of responding to immediate labour shortages and the needs of the economy. It should be noted that 'demographic' concerns were deliberately disassociated from 'economic' ones and population expansion was often presented as essential in maintaining a physical presence within the Empire, in order to continue France's universal civilizing mission (*mission civilisatrice*) and in further acquiring *grandeur* and independence on the international stage (especially vis-à-vis Britain and the United States). Hence, this logic dictated that population growth contributed to a strong empire that, in turn, enabled France to remain free and to uphold freedoms universally. The concern about population was expressed in the elaboration of relatively broad nationality legislation, which aimed at breaking down the differences between French nationals and migrants in order to promote national unity. For instance, the nationality law of August 1927, passed in response to the immigration waves of the 1920s, provoked an almost threefold increase in the number of naturalizations in the following decade.[4]

However, if anxiety about population and early policies relating to migrants were presented in terms of maintaining French grandeur, then it quickly became clear that it was an economic logic that had driven immigration and nationality legislation since the beginning and in the long term. For instance, the introduction of a number of restrictive decree laws during the crisis period of the early to mid 1930s, meant that the number of naturalizations fell by 35 per cent (Viet 1997: 1). Furthermore, in August 1932, a law setting out work quotas for immigrant workers, was introduced in a xenophobic climate that had produced calls for national preference policies and subsequently for the repatriation of migrant workers. The effect of this was that the population of 2.7 million immigrants in 1931, had decreased by 450,000 by 1936 (ibid: 3; see also Insee 1997: 16). From 1936 to 1939 immigration figures increased again, mainly through the arrival of Spanish refugees but the socio-economic and political upheaval of the war years led to the departure of hundreds of thousands of immigrants so that by 1946, the migrant population in France stood at two million (Insee 1997: 16).

It was only after the Second World War that the pre-eminence of economic logic became clear as the French State undertook a more dirigiste organization of immigration, dictated by the insufficiency of French labour in meeting the demands of restructuring a war-torn capitalist economy and of sustaining its growth. The creation of the Office National d'Immigration, (ONI),[5] in 1945, signalled a new politics of immigration, the aims of which were to plug the labour deficits in various branches of industry, to select those migrants most likely to be drawn to France and to put into effect a programme of settlement and assimilation of newly arrived groups of migrants. However, just as immigration was encouraged during a time of economic growth, so it has been vigorously discouraged since that growth ended and recession set in after 1975.

From the mid 1970s onwards, successive French governments have put into effect restrictive laws in order to achieve 'zero immigration' and have come to define immigration as one of the most pressing 'problems' facing French society today.

This chapter aims, firstly, to examine the factors governing immigration flows to France in the post-war period, concentrating on the legacy of French colonialism, on the role of migrant labour in the restructuring and development of the post-war economy in France, particularly from the 1950s, and on the new international division of labour between North and South that has provoked 'a new phase of mass population movements'

(Castles 1993: 17) in the 1980s and 1990s. Secondly it aims to demonstrate that the issue of immigration, bracketed with those of unemployment and social problems leading to disorder, has been used by French governments and oppositions of right and left, to give the appearance of being able to manage society and to provide national solutions which, in reality, have never been possible.

Immigration and its Contributory Factors: 1945–98

After the Second World War until the mid 1970s, immigration to France increased at a relatively rapid rate with the introduction of two ordinances of October and November 1945, which fixed, quite loosely, the conditions of entry and settlement of immigrants. Table 7.1 shows that the main migratory flows into France originated in Southern Europe and North Africa.

Immigration, Repopulation and Cultural Preference

In the first decade following the war, the largest groups of immigrants originated from Italy, Spain and Algeria. Immigration from Italy and Spain had been actively encouraged by the ONI, which, theoretically, was under the supervision of the Ministère du Travail et de la Sécurité Sociale (Ministry of Employment and Social Security) and of the new post-war Ministère de la Santé Publique et de la Population (Ministry of Public Health and Population) but whose senior officials (drawn largely from the old Ministries of Labour and Foreign Affairs), maintained, in practice, a distance from their new political bosses. Unlike any other public authority in the history of immigration, the ONI claimed and was, by default, allowed to operate within a vast field of social action. Within the ONI, the main preoccupation of senior officials was the repopulation of France which, as far as they were concerned, had to be achieved without risk of diluting the French 'ethnic character' (*l'éthnie française*). Criteria for 'assimilable' and 'desirable' migrants had been established immediately after the war (but subsequently vetoed by the Conseil d'Etat)[7] by demographers such as Georges Mauco of the Haut Comité consultatif de la Population et de la Famille[8] and an unofficial policy of 'cultural preference' was evidenced by the choice of locations of ONI offices outside France (in border countries, especially Italy and later Spain and Portugal), by the implementation of the *Plan Culture Famille* in 1948 (whereby war-displaced families were brought to France) and by the financial incentives that were offered from 1947 to Italian, German, German-speaking and Yugoslavian

Table 7.1 Distribution of Immigrants According to Country of Origin: 1962 to 1990 (in percentage).[6]

Country of origin	*1962*	*1968*	*1975*	*1982*	*1990*
Europe:	**78.7**	**76.4**	**67.2**	**57.3**	**50.4**
Portugal	02.0	08.8	16.9	15.8	14.4
Spain	18.0	21.0	15.2	11.7	09.5
Italy	31.8	23.9	17.2	14.1	11.6
EU states (12)	10.6	09.5	07.4	07.1	07.3
E. Europe	12.3	11.2	08.8	07.3	06.2
Other	04.1	02.1	01.7	01.2	
Africa:	**14.9**	**19.9**	**28.0**	**33.2**	**35.9**
Algeria	11.6	11.7	14.3	14.8	13.3
Morocco	01.1	03.3	06.6	09.1	11.0
Tunisia	01.5	03.5	04.7	05.0	05.0
Other	00.7	01.4	02.4	04.3	06.6
Asia:	**02.4**	**02.5**	**03.6**	**08.0**	**11.4**
Turkey	01.4	1.3	01.9	03.0	04.0
S.E Asia	00.4	00.6	00.7	03.0	03.7
Other	00.6	00.6	01.0	01.9	03.6
Americas and Pacific:	**03.2**	**01.1**	**01.3**	**01.6**	**02.3**
Origin undeclared	**00.8**	**0.1**	–	–	–
Total (percentage)	**100.0**	**100.0**	**100.0**	**100.0**	**100.0**
Total (figures)	**2,861,280**	**3,281,060**	**3,887,460**	**4,037,036**	**4,165,952**

Source: Insee (1997)

families who settled in France.[9] From the 1960s Spanish and Portuguese families were also offered financial inducements to settle in France.

Clearly then, within the logic of immigration as a means of repopulating France, emphasis was placed upon family migration and those migrant groups tempted to settle in France as a result of the family benefits offered to them included a higher proportion of women and children than was true of migrant groups which had entered France during the inter-war period (with the exception of groups which had fled the Spanish Civil War in the mid to late 1930s).[10]

In addition to encouraging families from European countries to settle in France, efforts were stepped up to accept asylum-seekers. In 1952, France became a signatory of the Geneva Convention. The Geneva Convention, drawn up in July 1951 and enshrining the definition and rights of the refugee and of states offering asylum, addressed the problems of persecuted and/or displaced persons in the context of a post-Yalta Europe and the East–West conflict.[11]

In France, a department for refugee affairs (Office Française de Protection des Réfugiés et Apatrides – OFPRA) was established to ensure implementation of the Geneva Convention which widened the commitment to asylum already included in the preamble of the 1946 Constitution and later in the constitution of the Fifth Republic, in 1958. Within the terms of the Geneva Convention, a place was made for political refugees from East and Central Europe, also considered to be relatively easily 'assimilable' and, therefore, to be useful contributors to the repopulation effort.

This unofficial policy of cultural preference had been pursued by ONI civil servants (not so by OFPRA as far as evidence suggests) in a bid to counterbalance the flow of Algerian migrants into France, which had begun to take on mass character.[12] North and sub-Saharan Africans and, to a lesser extent, Asian populations were considered to be culturally less able or unable to assimilate and, hence, likely to dilute the French 'ethnic character'. However, considerable tension was generated between this line of thinking, which saw immigration as a means to repopulate France with 'culturally assimilable' peoples, and that which saw immigration as a necessity for the development of the post-war economy and that, therefore, was less willing to operate distinctions between immigrants based upon their ethnic origin. Eventually, it was the 'repopulationists' who were compelled to compromise and to consider the recruitment of 'economic migrants' from beyond the boundaries of Europe, especially as the latter was proving to be an ungenerous source of immigration. Other European countries were also in the process of economic reconstruction and modernisation and were unwilling to allow mass emigration. Some countries (such as Poland and Italy), even made patriotic appeals for their nationals, in France, to return and help rebuild their home economies. By 1966, the replacement of the Ministry of Public Health and Population by the Ministry for Social Affairs indicated that policies of repopulation combined with those of cultural preference were finally renounced in favour of economic immigration coupled with the theme of social integration of non-European migrants.

However, while the ONI was to turn towards Africa and Asia, cultural preference or racism that may have become officially and publicly less admissible persisted stubbornly within institutions responsible for implementing policies with regard to immigrants and this was to become amply clear after 1975.

Migrant Labour and the Development of French Capitalism

At the end of the War, France was facing ruin as economic activity had almost ground to a halt. The causes of this ruin can be attributed to: the heavy exploitation of the French economy by the Germans (draining of currency reserves, imposition of levies amounting to 75 per cent for the most productive industries); trade blockages; physical destruction (bombardment, wilful sabotage); the inactivity of French workers either because of the *Service du Travail Obligatoire* (STO), which forced a significant proportion of the working population to work in Germany or because of low morale of industrial and agricultural workers. An increase in production levels, in 1944 barely reaching 40 per cent of those of 1938 (Trotignan 1985: 227), and industrial modernization were seen as the key to economic revival.

However, the scarcity of labour proved to be a major stranglehold on development. France was simply unable to provide the labour power required. Not only was the demographic shortfall, in relation to the working population, a historical problem but the end of the war also saw the departure of many previously settled groups of migrants, answering appeals for labour from their countries of origin. Thousands, it seemed, preferred to suffer poor housing and food shortages in their countries of birth. For example, 1945 saw an exodus of Polish mine workers for reasons just outlined.

Throughout the period 1944 to the late 1960s, French employers[13] put enormous pressure upon government to organize mass recruitment of migrant labour for a number of reasons. First, during the early post-war years, the use of migrant labour, apart from plugging the skills gap, would solve the major wages problem. In 1944, the scarcity of labour had driven up employers' wage bills by up to 50 per cent, depending on the economic sector (Trotignan 1985: 270). This had led to, or threatened to lead to, bankruptcy as investors saw profits plummet in the face of wage inflation. The employment of migrant labour would break this spiral as it would avoid having to hire French workers at the lowest levels of the job pyramid, at higher costs, which then pushed up wages correspondingly, throughout the pyramid, as workers fought to maintain wage differentials and job status. Furthermore, in 1947, employers, shaken by strike waves and trades-union militancy,[14] wanted access to a pool of migrant workers who could be used to flout union agreements and break strikes because the lack of strong social ties between the immigrant and host communities often placed the former outside the labour movement. In 1947, René Pleven estimated that a million extra workers had to be recruited in order to ease pressure on employers (ibid.: 315). A consultation of sixteen European countries by the 'Manpower Committee' of the 'European Council for Economic Cooperation' revealed that France had the highest requirement for foreign labour (Bize 1947: pp 876–902). Thus, for example, Italian workers were recruited to the iron and steel industry in the north-eastern region of Lorraine, to the coal mines of the Nord-Pas-de-Calais (whose workforce also included Poles and war-displaced ethnic Germans), to agriculture in the regions around France's south-eastern borders with Italy and to various small and medium-sized enterprises) (SMEs) and the car industry in the Paris region. Spanish migrants, on the other hand, settled in southern France providing agricultural labour and in the Paris region, working in small commercial enterprises and in the service sector.

By the late 1950s, France had achieved stable economic growth, sustaining approximate annual increases of 3.5 per cent in productivity and 4.5 per cent in GNP between 1950 and 1960 (Trotignan 1985: 436). Furthermore, the 1960s represented a decade of economic development unfettered by the financial difficulties of previous years. During this period of rapid growth, the necessity for migrant labour continued although the reasons for its requirement changed.

First, as the economy and job market expanded, particularly in the burgeoning tertiary sector,[15] then acute motivational problems occurred at the bottom of the employment pyramid. The most precarious and unpleasant of jobs, at the bottom, were left unfilled as they did not allow for acquisition and preservation of social status. In order to maintain productivity levels, employers were forced to seek a workforce for whom the wage rather than job status or prestige was a prime consideration. Migrant workers, who did not envisage long-term settlement in France, filled this gap perfectly. Algerian men, in particular, who arrived in France in the 1950s and the 1960s without their immediate families, often worked in 'rotation' – whereby one man would work for a period of time and then return home to be replaced by another male member of his family or village.

Second, this period of growth witnessed a sharp bifurcation of the French labour market. This was due to the fact that employers had increasingly sought to meet demand for materials and goods through investment and use of fixed capital rather than labour in the primary and certain secondary sectors of the economy. Hence, semi-automated and automated techniques, which helped to meet the needs of expansion more efficiently than mechanization, were first introduced in the 1950s, in energy production (nuclear and electronic), petrochemical and oil refining industries. Gradually, automation was extended to those sectors where machines began to replace, amplify and standardize the functions normally performed by the worker (automobile and machine-tools, transport, communications amongst others). This led to the creation of a capital-intensive sector where complex tasks requiring special training and experience were relatively well paid and where workers acquiring sector-specific and often even firm-specific expertise enjoyed stable employment conditions hence often becoming a fixed factor of production in the same way as the capital equipment with which they worked.[16] This sector was clearly distinguishable from a labour-intensive sector (light manufacturing and services) within which semi-skilled and unskilled jobs, in poor, increasingly casualized working conditions, attached to low pay and low status, multiplied in response to rising demand for goods and services but which could be sharply reduced during periods of economic stagnation. Skilled French and European workers tended to shun employment in the labour-intensive sector as, in the 1950s and 1960s, they were able to secure jobs within the capital-intensive sector. Moreover, the most highly skilled could offer their skills elsewhere in the industrialized world, within a progressively internationalized labour market. The shortfall of labour within the labour intensive sectors of the economy was then made up by migrant workers.

Third, the necessity for migrant labour to fill the most unpleasant jobs had become particularly great in the 1960s because women and teenage children who, in the past, had fulfilled this role, were no longer willing to do so. Expanding education and tertiary sectors began to provide these two groups with opportunities previously unavailable.

In the 1950s, 1960s and until the mid 1970s, the range of migrant labour sources increased with the arrival of immigrants from Portugal, Algeria, Morocco, Tunisia, Yugoslavia and Turkey under agreements signed between the French government and those of the countries mentioned. Senegal and other sub-Saharan countries also became smaller contributors of migrant labour.[17] Unlike the groups of Italian and Spanish migrants that had arrived in the early post-war period, these groups, in particular Portuguese migrants, tended to form more scattered communities throughout France, although urban, industrialized centres were inevitably favoured. Although Portuguese migrants were recruited primarily by construction firms and the service sector,[18] migrants from the Maghreb and Turkey filled the most physically demanding jobs within the construction and automobile industries and those from sub-Saharan Africa entered the light manufacturing and service industries at the bottom of the employment hierarchy in those sectors.

So far, immigration to France has been explained mainly in terms of the labour requirements of French capitalism. However, it is equally important to examine factors that have provoked movements of peoples from migrant exporting zones. Among the factors worthy of consideration are colonialism and its legacy and the new division of labour within the global economy.

Immigration: Colonial Legacy

One of the main legacies of colonialism, during which time local modes and relations of production were replaced forcibly by capitalist ones, is that the economies of ex-colonies have been unable, in the long term, to support growth and meet the needs of their populations. Even after decolonization, production within the young independent states of Africa and Asia was geared to the needs of the French (and Western) economy and consumer and, to a lesser extent, the needs of the new 'Francisized/ Westernized' bourgeoisies of those states. The development of cash crop farming, mining/refining and other industries of importance to developed countries led to the breakdown of traditional societies, which in earlier times were able to subsist. The development of such industries, by colonial powers, ruptured a centuries-old link between colonized peoples and their land, in that raw materials extracted had, previously, directly served the communities that had lived and worked on the land even though established socio-economic hierarchies prevented such raw materials, and the wealth created from them, from being equally distributed. After colonization, such populations were to find that with the gradual expropriation of land by the colonizer and the resulting social disintegration, the only thing that allowed them to satisfy their needs was paid labour. However, either paid labour gave them insufficient buying power to sustain their families or few jobs were available. This led them to find work elsewhere, first in the large urban centres of their own countries but inevitably in the colonizing country where even the most difficult working conditions were preferable to unemployment and the levels of immiseration in the underdeveloped world. This process of emigration from ex-colony to ex-colonizing state is amply demonstrable through the example of Senegal.

During colonization, Senegal's traditional but diverse economy based on food crops (such as millet), fishing and the long-established craft of ebony carving was replaced by an economy based on groundnuts and groundnut products (mainly oil). Senegalese peasants representing 70 per cent of the population (N'Dongo 1976: 90), had been persuaded that their soil was best suited to groundnut production. Even after Senegal's independence in 1960, 65 per cent of peasant land was allocated to cash crop cultivation (compared with 29 per cent of land used for the needs of

Senegalese peasants) (Ibid.: 91) and the majority of this production was exported to France, from where it went elsewhere. Moreover, Senegal, in common with other ex-colonies was locked into the *Zone Franc*, a monetary union based on the principle that currencies issued by the central banks of the Franc Zone countries, other than France, carried no international value. This meant that ex-colonies were unable to make any transactions without passing through the Bank of France and the control of exchange rates and of credit policy remained entirely in French hands. Hence, if France proverbially sneezed, it was the Franc Zone countries that caught a severe cold, and the process of economic deterioration, in ex-colonies, commenced from the time of independence. In Senegal, the total income of peasant farmers from groundnut production fell from 18.5 (US) billion francs in the financial year 1965/6 to 9.9 billion francs in 1968/9 (Ibid.). This severely limited their buying power at the same time as prices of food, clothing and the most basic farming equipment mounted. As farmers became more indebted and were threatened with impoundment of equipment or imprisonment, they made their way, in their thousands, towards Dakar hoping to gain employment in the railways and dockyards, in local government or domestic service. When Dakar failed to provide solutions, they set their sights on France in the late 1960s and early 1970s. The example of emigration from Senegal to France is typical (see also Landor 1997). In general, French neo-colonialist policy in Africa and Asia proved to be undynamic and short-termist within the logic of capitalist competition and failed to resist other industrialized countries (such as the USA, Japan and Germany) keen to gain influence in France's former colonial preserves.[19] Consequently, France failed to invest in the infrastructures necessary for the efficient exploitation of natural resources. Conversely, emphasis upon the development of post-colonial financial institutions and mechanisms (often grafted onto archaic colonial structures) and upon 'indirect investment' in French armaments zealously used in military interventions all over Africa, from the 1960s to the late 1970s, had the most deleterious effect on the populations of ex-colonies. Eventually their long-standing educational, cultural and politico-administrative links with France, logically, pushed them towards that country. Maghrebian and sub-Saharan immigration to France more than doubled between the early 1960s and the 1990s (see Table 7.1).

France and Immigration in a Globalized Economy

The spectacular economic growth experienced by Western countries in the 1950s and 1960s provoked profound structural changes within the world economy. Industrialized economies became highly competition-oriented as governments were compelled to open their markets to foreign suppliers due not only to greater demand for materials, goods and services but also to the fact that consumers (individual, collective and corporate) became more selective in seeking cheaper sources of materials and other requirements beyond national boundaries. Although the oil crisis of 1974 had a dampening effect on economic growth, the process of market deregulation had, by the late 1970s, acquired its own dynamic and continued uninhibited, during the 1980s, spreading from the industrialized West to the less developed economies of Eastern Europe, the Middle East and the southern hemisphere. The pressures created by market deregulation and high competitiveness produced varying effects within national economies. In Eastern Europe it contributed (along with other factors) to the implosion of state socialist economies and to the establishment of capitalist relations of production while South-East Asian economies boomed as industrialization led to rising production levels and to the emergence of the so-called 'tiger' economies. In other less-developed countries, with rapidly expanding populations, the continued imposition of Western models of development exacerbated the negative social and economic effects that have already been described in the section on immigration and the colonial legacy.

The changes described above have necessarily affected immigration flows globally, leading to greater east-west and south-north movements.[20] In the newly industrializing countries (such as the Asian 'tigers') rapid industrialization has led to outflows of people, both of 'dying' class groups (peasants and artisans) and of ascendant class groups (possessing specialized technical knowledge and skills). East-west migration has been caused by the restructuring of frontiers and the social and economic disorder ensuing from the fall of state socialist economies, whereas outward movements from the less developed countries of Asia and Africa have been caused not only by the growing socio-economic and demographic inequality between south and north and but also, often, by the breakdown of political order and of cultural identities due to the development of capitalism.

As far as France is concerned, new waves of immigration continued from the mid 1970s, countering the belief that mass migrations would cease after measures to halt migrant labour were adopted, following the oil crisis of 1974. Between 1975 and 1985, the number of geographically distanced sources of immigration increased and groups of immigrants began arriving from a number of Asian countries, notably, Lebanon, Iran and China[21] as well as from sub-Saharan countries that do not have long-standing colonial links with France, such as Zaire and Mauritius.[22] These new waves of immigration unfurled alongside existing ones. In the late 1980s and 1990s these patterns have remained more or less unchanging although the number of admissions decreased after 1993 when new legislation, further restricting immigration, was introduced. Hence, 1995 figures, indicating the breakdown of immigration flows to France, show that: by far the largest group of immigrants (44 per cent of the total) granted rights to long-term residence in France came from Africa (of which 75 per cent from the Maghreb). Europeans, including Turks, constituted 32 per cent of the total number (of which 13 per cent came from Eastern Europe and the CIS).[23] The third largest group came from Asia (14 per cent of total) and the smallest (10 per cent) from the Americas (Insee 1997: 28; Tribalat 1997: 184). Furthermore, after 1974, family reunion became the principal reason for immigration to France with 63 per cent of all immigrants entering the country in order to join families while about a quarter (of which 60 per cent from the EU or European Economic Area) came to find permanent employment. The fastest growing category was that of refugees accounting for 9 per cent of all immigrants entering France in 1995 (Insee 1997: 28–9). The demand for asylum had risen from 2,000 applications in 1972 to 20,000 at the beginning of the 1980s to a peak of 61,372 in 1989 after which time there followed an uninterrupted drop to 17,405 in 1996 (Tribalat 1997: 186; France Terre d'Asile 1997: 1). This rate of demand was paralleled by the rate of recognition of refugee status until the early 1990s when the rate was significantly lowered in order to discourage asylum seekers.[24] Alongside the diversification of reasons for and sources of immigration, the mid 1970s onwards also saw the emergence of a different sociological profile with the arrival of larger numbers of women and children and more heterogeneously qualified groups of immigrants. In the first case, the majority of women and children were either joining husbands/fathers (already working in France) and this was particularly true of those from the Maghreb and sub-Saharan Africa or they were part of a family group including the adult male member of family, for example, in the case of refugees from Asia and Eastern Europe. As far as the occupational profile of new immigrants is concerned, especially that of refugees from Asia and Eastern Europe, the skills and qualifications brought ranged from intellectual and highly technical ones to commercial and managerial ones, although also present alongside these was the experience of semi-skilled or unskilled labour.

The Problematization of Immigration

Historically, a weak system of immigration control has operated in France due to the fact that immigration has provided a useful instrument by which to regulate the labour market and to increase the population stock. Hence, the ordinances of 1945 that provided a basis for French immigration policies until the mid 1980s, deemed that permission to reside in France should not be contingent upon permission to work. The separation between work and resident permits was designed to encourage families of immigrant workers to settle in France. Further encouragement was given through relatively open nationality law, privileging *jus soli* (nationality gained through place of birth) over *jus sanguinis* (nationality obtained through blood or descent), dating from 1889, which allowed for the incorporation into the national community, of any individual born in France, of foreign parents, who elected French nationality on reaching the age of majority.

A number of other conditions also applied to this rule of which assimilability (leading to successful integration) was an important one. Assimilability was taken to mean acceptance of and identification with the values of French Republicanism and culture (deemed to be universal but which, at the same time, produced and represented 'Frenchness') and, by virtue of this, the putting aside, publicly, of one's potentially divisive original cultural, ethnic and religious beliefs and values. In return, the conferment of French nationality opened access to rights of citizenship, namely political rights, the absolute right to enter and remain on French territory without fear of expulsion or extradition, the right to certain social benefits reserved for nationals and so on. The question of assimilability, nationality and citizenship caused few problems while immigration to France consisted of mainly Europeans who were considered to be eminently assimilable due to their geographical proximity to France, to their sharing of common socio-cultural, politico-juridical Christian-based values and after 1957, due to the fact of European construction or privileged bilateral agreements with other non-EC European countries.

The Republic versus Non-European Immigrants

It was only with the mass migration of non-Europeans from geographically distanced areas of the world, whose non-Christian cultures and value systems appeared to challenge the universality of Republicanism (and 'Frenchness'), that the hitherto comfortable connection between immigration, nationality and citizenship came to be called into question and, in contrast with Europeans whose status had, through the European integration process, evolved from that of 'absolute foreigners' to that of 'relative foreigners', decolonization changed the status of those from France's ex-colonies from that of 'relative [inferior] Frenchmen/women' to that of 'absolute foreigners'. However, as long as economic expansion reinforced the competition between countries of immigration for labour power sought so desperately by French employers, then the immigration of non-European migrants remained relatively unproblematic. The problematization of immigration emerged after the entry of Western economies into recession in 1974, which revealed the degradation of social conditions and strife and the inadequacy of state measures to alleviate these conditions in France.

The sentiment that non-European migrants (mainly from France's ex-colonies in Africa and Asia) were either resistant to or incapable of assimilation, according to the French model of integration, and that they should therefore not be encouraged to enter and settle in France, began to be expressed strongly from the mid 1970s onwards. The French Republican model of integration (as that of citizenship) is based upon four main elements: employment, nationality, compulsory schooling and equal rights for legal immigrants. It was increasingly being argued that although this model had worked well from the beginning of the Third Republic (1871) to the immediate post-war period, it was rendered unworkable by non-European immigrants. What was not being recognized was that the evolution of the French economy and society in the post-war period was merely exposing the weaknesses of a republican model that was neither universal nor timeless and that, in turn, was challenging the basis of 'Frenchness'.

Employment. First, employment, which was considered an important factor of socialization (as an area in which immigrants forged their first links with the host community) and emancipation (for children of immigrant parents permitted, by wages earned, to leave the parental home and familial culture to live amongst the host community) was no longer easily available. Unemployment of immigrant workers, (almost twice the national average)[25] pointed, therefore, to their increasing ghettoization from French society and led to a widespread but false perception that unemployed youth from immigrant communities did little other than engage in criminal activity (such as drug smuggling and trading in drugs) and public disorder, which destabilized French society. The emergence of what appeared to be ethnic gangs in the 1980s and outbreaks of violence involving youths from North African and other African communities in the early 1990s, in cities such as Paris and Lyon,[26] provided ammunition to anti-immigrant propagandists who claimed that the French *banlieue* (inner and outer ring city areas) was 'becoming a vast Bronx-like zone with its ethnic gangs and race riots' (Etchegoin et al. 1990: 47). Furthermore, if employment, also a key component of citizenship, conveyed a sense of identity and self-worth, then the lack of employment opportunities coupled with continuing immigration meant that immigrants (formerly colonized people whose position had been more servile than that of even the most disadvantaged Frenchman or woman) were seen to be responsible for 'invading' France and usurping the jobs of French workers and for robbing them of their sense of identity and even 'Frenchness'. Either way, non-participation as well as participation of immigrants in the labour market was seen as a challenge to national unity and identity.

Nationality. Second, access to French nationality has been progressive: automatic for third-generation immigrants, elective at the age of majority for the second-generation and by naturalization for the first generation. Such a system, it is argued, allows time for a process of individual socialization to take place. However, those most keen to problematize immigrants have pointed to the fact that naturalization rates amongst first-generation migrants have often been very low. Algerian immigrants, in particular, are held up as examples of those who appear to have refused naturalization and incorporation into the national community. For the majority of first generation Algerian immigrants, memories of the Algerian War and the part they may have played, even indirectly, in the formation of a new Algeria, in 1962, make acceptance of French nationality a betrayal of the struggle for independence. Besides, as far as this generation was concerned, ties with family and community in Algeria were extremely strong and their stay in France was envisaged as temporary. As there was always the intention to return to Algeria (and many did before 1974) then the acquisition of French nationality made little sense. For instance, between 1966 and 1969 only 0.5 per cent of successful applicants (through naturalization or election at majority age) for French nationality were Algerian (previous nationality) compared with the 33.9 per cent who were of Italian origin (Insee 1997: 39). However, it should be noted that there is no indication of the number of rejected applications, which, if added to those that succeeded, would give a more accurate picture.

Descendants of immigrants, on the other hand, often hold dual nationality, where permitted, or retain that of their parents' country of birth for practical rather than ideological reasons but are nevertheless regarded as outsiders (hence a threat), not fully committed to France. The idea of the outsider representing a threat is further reinforced in the case of many young, second- and third-generation Algerian men who hold dual nationality and who can, under the terms of a bilateral Franco–Algerian agreement of 1983, choose to do their military service in Algeria. Suggestions that young Arab men, in particular, represent a threat to the security of France have surfaced periodically but most vociferously during the time of the Gulf War, in 1991, even though France had signed both bilateral and multilateral agreements on military service with other countries and even though the majority (70 per cent) of young men in this situation choose military service in France (Hargreaves 1995: 136). Furthermore, political upheavals which have shaken Algeria in the 1990s and which have seen the rise of Islamic fundamentalist groups such as the Front Islamique du Salut (banned in Algeria since 1992) have contributed to the demonization of young North African immigrants with even the most liberal of mainstream magazines and newspapers running headlines like 'Terrorism. How the Islamists are recruiting in France' (Raffy et al. 1994: 40) and making statements such as 'If increasing numbers of young people of immigrant origin are on the side of religion, it is because they see it as a last anchor of hope against a hostile environment. However, the communitarian protest which they are being led into by Islamic movements is incompatible with the integrating spirit of the Republic' (Etchegoin 1994: 29).

Education. Third, it is considered that compulsory schooling plays an indispensable role in the formation of potential citizens because it teaches a common language, culture and history. However, a significant number of (non-European) immigrants are past the age of compulsory schooling when they arrive in France so that, it is argued, they never achieve the level of language necessary for their integration into French society. If, in addition to that, they are unemployed then the chances of them catching up are slim and they remain on the margins of society. Furthermore, while French-born descendants of immigrants will have attended school, opponents of non-European immigration complain that first generation parents and grandparents will reinforce the importance of their own language, cultural and religious practices above those of France in order to protect their children from what they view as negative 'Western' influences.[27] Muslims, in particular, are accused of 're-Islamizing' young people of North African origin and of posing obstacles to their integration into French society. This line of argument was most evident in what became known as the *affaire du foulard* or 'headscarf affair', which began in October 1989 and which created a controversy lasting five years. The 'affair' surrounded the exclusion of three Muslim girls from their school, in the town of Creil, for refusing to remove headscarfs worn in accordance with Islamic dress codes of modesty. The media attention given to this provoked a national debate, polarizing into opposing camps (which cut across traditional politico-ideological divisions) those who argued that the schoolgirls, instigated by Islamic fundamentalists ('The wearing of the headscarf appears today as one of their [fundamentalists'] main battle-horses') (Ibid.) posed a direct challenge to the secularism (*laïcité*) upon which the French Republic was founded and which had, at all costs, to be defended and those who argued for a more tolerant version of secularism given the pluri-ethnic nature of French society.[28]

Equal Rights. The fourth element, equality of rights (except voting rights) between legal immigrants and French nationals, aims to provide an egalitarian and individualist model of integration whereby each individual stands in exactly the same relationship to the French state as far as rights and obligations are concerned (regardless of attributes such as class, sex, or religion). Once again, though, the 'difference' between non-European immigrants and the French is emphasized as an obstacle to integration. Immigrants and their descendants, and Muslims especially, have been variously accused of wanting special rights and treatment (for example regarding school attire, places of prayer in schools and work-places) in addition to social benefits without wanting to fulfil certain obligations to the French State (for example, by choosing to carry out military service in their countries of origin). However, it must also be remembered that the notion of equal rights sits uncomfortably, in the thinking of many French people, with immigration from ex-colonies. One of the reasons put forward by rulers of the Third Republic in favour of colonialism was that France, with its universalist thinking, could (more than any other colonial power) pass on the values of progress, culture, reason and education to colonized people. However, values were separate from rights and there was no question that colonized people would enjoy rights in the same way as the colonizers. For many this idea persists in any discussion of the rights of non-European immigrants in France today.

Illegal Immigration. The discussion above has focused upon the process of problematization of legal immigrants. However, this process has been extended to highlight a specific category of immigrants that, it is argued, remains outside the framework of integration and that, therefore constitutes a particular cause for concern within French society. The category in question is that of illegal immigrants. Illegal immigration was not regarded as a problem until after 1974. During the expansion period of the 1950s and 1960s, large numbers of immigrants entered France as 'false tourists' and overstayed to find employment, encouraged by the French state, in the context of bilateral agreements (waiving visa requirements) with countries of emigration. What were exceptional procedures for the regularization of illegal immigrants became generalized as thousands were issued with work and residence permits well after their arrival.[29] During this period the state's attitude to illegal immigration was summed up by Jean-Marcel Jeanneney, the Minister for Social Affairs, as: 'illegal immigration is not without its uses, because if we were to comply strictly with international regulations, we would perhaps face labour shortages' (*L'Humanité* 21 March 1969: 5). However, after 1974 and the onset of economic recession, one of the principal targets of the opponents of immigration was illegal, non-European immigration. Illegal immigration has come to be regarded as a major danger to French society and as such immigrants are unable to find legal work, become naturalized, claim social benefits or participate in the education system. Illegal immigrants are then accused of creating 'black markets' of labour, goods and services, and the social relations that arise from this can create a counter-society that can ultimately have a destabilizing effect.

The accusations levelled at non-European immigrants, of unwillingness or inability to adapt to French society, its ('unique' and 'universal') culture and laws, in the context of the economic and social degradation in France since the 1970s, have led to extreme hostility towards them which has manifested itself at the level of political institutions, in discriminative public policy, through racial violence and harassment and to calls for 'zero immigration' and the repatriation of 'unassimilable' immigrants. The following section will consider the politicization of immigration and the responses of major political players.

The Emergence of Immigration as a Pivotal Issue in French Politics and Political Responses

Prior to the 1980s, legislation relating to immigration was scanty. Immigration policy was almost a private affair of governments, executed through circulars, decrees and ordinances. The main reason for this was that the majority of policies that were executed in this way were regarded as uncontentious by deputies and senators and prior to 1974 there had been no question about the need for migrant labour. Even in the mid 1970s, when the damaging effects on the French economy, of the oil crisis prompted the government of Jacques Chirac to impose restrictions on immigration, there was little or no opposition from the parliamentary parties so that measures to halt labour migrants of non-EC nationality (July 1974) and to exercise stricter border controls (October 1974) were introduced in an atmosphere of relative consensus. It was at the end of the 1970s, as economic recession set in and as the issue of soaring unemployment reactivated 1930s type discussion and proposals over repatriation[30] that immigration became an important political issue.[31]

The Emergence of Immigrant Activism after May 1968

However, the process of politicization of immigration cannot be explained without some reference to the cultural changes taking place in French society, exposed by the protest movements of May 1968, until which time the subject of immigration had been subsumed under questions of law or economics. One of the smaller movements of this period was that of immigrant workers (mainly African) who had, during the 1960s, organized themselves into workers' associations[32] to fight against poor wages, conditions of work and insalubrious housing conditions. The events of May 1968 contributed to an increase in the political awareness of immigrant workers and accelerated their social movement. The 1970s witnessed a number of highly visible actions on the part of immigrant workers; for instance, rent strikes carried out by residents of a number of hostels or *foyers* including forty-seven hostels run by the state accommodation agency SONACOTRA (Société Nationale de Construction de Logements pour les Travailleurs). Many of these strikes represented long and protracted battles between immigrant workers and hostel owners or agents and ended only when the occupants were forcibly evacuated by riot police (N'Dongo 1976: 114–40). These events made non-European immigrants highly visible through media coverage. Their image as agitators and their demands for better treatment, far from drawing sympathy, brought them hostility from large sections of French society, which entertained a different image of non-European immigrants from ex-colonies – that of simple, hard-working people who were generally submissive and grateful to be offered (any kind of) work and board. The events also drew attention to the presence of illegal immigrants resident in the seediest of hostels. Their status was such that little housing provision (or other social aid) had been set aside for them through the Social Action Fund (*Fonds d'Action Sociale*), run by the state with the aim of integrating legal immigrants into French society. The general attitude of the government, from the mid to late 1970s was to brand those evacuated from their hostels as troublemakers who posed a threat to law and order, to encourage employers to lay off such troublemakers and to then imprison or expel the latter from

French territory for 'security' reasons. In the run-up to the 1981 presidential elections, the government of Raymond Barre and the left opposition were playing the game of who would best control immigration and lead the fight against illegal immigration.

The Development of Anti-Immigrant Politics

It was in this context, with immigration already identified as a problem, that the emergence of an anti-immigration party, the Front National (FN)[33] and its clearly racist programme, took place and that, as a result, immigration became a key item on the programmes of all the mainstream parties. The FN, formed in 1972 under the leadership of Jean-Marie Le Pen, made its first electoral breakthrough in 1983 when a municipal by-election, in the town of Dreux, gave it a first-round vote of 16.7 per cent. This success was then followed up in 1984 by a vote of 11 per cent at the European elections (Mayer 1993: 331). The timing of this electoral breakthrough is unsurprising given first, that immigration was already perceived as a 'problem'; second, that the Socialist government, which had arrived in power in 1981 on a Keynesian programme of wealth redistribution, had by 1983 started to reverse many of the wealth-distribution policies designed to alleviate social problems; third, that unemployment was becoming a more entrenched feature of the socio-economic landscape; fourth, that working people felt unable to undertake collective, proactive struggle to bring about change due to the declining power of the labour movement and the disintegration of strong workplace and neighbourhood networks. Furthermore, the combination of the above factors contributed to a crisis in French Republicanism and identity that has permitted expression of racist logic and upon which the FN has capitalized. The party has maintained between 10 per cent and 15 per cent in national elections as well as in local and regional elections (of which the significance and impact extend beyond the level of municipality or region) over the past fifteen years.

The growing assumption that the FN can no longer be considered a temporary aberration within the party system is borne out by the fact that it has been gaining support in every social class, and in a growing number of occupational groups (see *Le Nouvel Observateur* 1996, 'Enquête sur les réseaux Le Pen' no 1669: 4–13) so that one in three voters does not exclude the possibility of voting for the party in future (Mayer 1993: 333). This level of support gave the FN its second breakthrough in 1995 when it won control of the southern town councils of Orange (35.93 per cent of second round vote), Marignane (37.27 per cent) and Toulon (37.2 per cent), followed by Vitrolles in a municipal by-election of 1997 (52.04 per cent). For the FN, these towns represent 'points of support and show cases for national reconquest' (*Le Monde Diplomatique*, March 1998: 10) in which the four main priorities are national preference,[34] security, low taxes and the restoration of French culture. Although many of the policies that have emerged from these priorities are contested at the political and legal levels and in some cases are ruled illegal,[35] their announcement during periods of election have, nevertheless, made an impact and increased tensions, in particular within the two mainstream right-wing political formations, the Gaullist Rassemblement pour la République (RPR) and the Union pour la Démocratie Française (UDF).[36] It is the mainstream right that has sustained the most contamination by FN ideas so that, for example, 46 per cent of the right's sympathizers agree with the FN's ideas (compared with 16 per cent of the Left's sympathisers) (*Le Nouvel Observateur* 1996, No 1669: 6). The extent of this contamination was most evident during and immediately after the regional council elections of 15 March 1998 when the FN gained a vote of 15.27 per cent (*Le Monde* 17 March 1998: 5), making significant inroads into the constituency of the mainstream right and placing itself in the position of 'kingmaker' as far as a number of incumbent regional council leaders of the RPR and UDF were concerned. Following the regional elections, the FN leadership issued a challenge to RPR and UDF regional council leaders to choose between entering into alliance with the FN and retaining leadership of their councils or allowing the Left to take further control. The challenge has caused the most damaging splits within the RPR and the UDF from which, it is predicted, the mainstream Right is unlikely to recover in its present configuration (*Le Monde* 26 March 1998: 12–13 'Les dix jours qui ont déchiré la droite').

Although the main parties of the Left, the Parti Socialiste (PS) and Parti Communiste Français (PCF), may be less infected by the FN's agenda, no less than 24 per cent of their sympathisers agree with FN views on immigration (*Le Monde* 17 March 1998: 5). This has produced a discourse and policies from the Left, especially when in power, which has often positioned it on the side of xenophobes. For instance, one shameful incident, according to PS militants, was the occasion of a televised debate, during the 1983 municipal elections campaign, which saw Gaston Defferre, (then Socialist Interior Minister and Mayor of Marseille) and Jean-Claude Gaudin (contending Marseille's mayorship) in competition over whether left or right had deported the greatest number of illegal immigrants (*Le Nouvel Observateur* No 1684, 1997: 32. 'Le désarroi et l'amertume des militants'). The left, in common with the right, has pursued immigration policy focusing on illegal immigrants although, arguably, the principles underlying this policy are different as demonstrated by the immigration and nationality legislation each side has introduced.

Immigration and Nationality Legislation in a Xenophobic Climate

Legislation introduced by the Left is marked by two principles: the dominance of legality over administrative procedure and the integration of immigrants. On the other hand, the right has placed emphasis on the absolute power of administrative structures and procedures relating to immigration and upon measures of exception.

Socialist Legislation. The Left's reforms, especially between 1981 and 1986, have led, firstly, to acknowledgement and acceptance of legal expertise and rulings. For instance, the 'Questiaux' law of October 1981 obliged government to accept rulings of the then newly configured Deportations Commission. Secondly, the application of common-law guarantees to police procedures and operations were emphasized; for example, the October 1981 law specified that the detention of immigrants had to be supervised by judicial authorities to ensure that the detainee's right to an interpreter, doctor, lawyer and diplomatic consul was protected. Thirdly, limiting the measure of threat possibly posed by certain categories of immigrants to public order has also formed part of the left's reforms. Again, in 1981, deportations were limited to 'very serious' threats to public order. Fourthly, the left has legislated in favour of special protection for immigrants with certain family connections and in 1981; for instance, specified categories of immigrants to be protected from deportation (examples include spouses of French nationals, the parents of children resident in France since the age of ten years or who had lived in France for a minimum of fifteen years).

As far as integration of immigrants is concerned, The 'Dufoix' law of 1984 introduced the automatically renewable ten-year resident permit (incorporating both work and residence permits), which spared thousands of legal immigrants the experience of complicated renewal procedures and the unhelpful and often hostile attitudes of the bureacrats in charge.

However, as the stakes have increased in immigration politics, the left has become less 'generous'. Legislation presented to Parliament at the end of 1997, by Jean-Pierre Chevènement, Minister of the Interior, adopted definitively by the National Assembly on 8 April 1998 and approved almost entirely by the Constitutional Council on 5 May 1998 (*Le Monde*

7 May 1998: 7) may have softened some of the right-wing legislation, passed in the early to mid-1990s, but has not returned to the more flexible Socialist positions of the early 1980s. For example, where the detention of immigrants is concerned, the Chevènement law has increased the number of days during which time a detainee can be held by police from ten to twelve. It increased from one to two days the leave for appeal against a deportation order (http://www.liberation.fr...n/semaine/cjeu1204b.html, 8 December 1997). On the question of residence permits, the Socialist government settled on compromise in the face of criticism from the right. Whereas the original text of the Chevènement Bill allowed residence permits to those able to prove 10 years residence in France, the amended version increased the time period to 15 years (ibid.). Similarly, the 1998 changes to the nationality law, originally conceived to soften the Pasqua-Debré laws (see below) of 1993 and 1997, have been subject to compromise (following over a thousand amendments to the original proposals made by the Opposition) during parliamentary debate. Hence, while the Socialist government has re-established the automatic acquisition of French nationality at the age of 18, for children (of immigrant parents) born in France,[37] it has refused to reinstate the pre-July 1993 right that allowed non-French parents to obtain French nationality for children born in France.[38] The 1997–8 parliamentary debates on immigration and nationality have clearly demonstrated the unwillingness of the Socialists to stand firm in the face of xenophobic sentiments (http://www.liberation.fr...n/semaine/bven1205h.html, 8 December 1997).

The Right and Immigration Law. The key piece of legislation introduced by the right, in July 1993, was a set of laws referred to as the 'Pasqua' laws after the then Minister of the Interior.[39] These laws, introduced in a climate of mounting xenophobia and after what was dubbed as years of Socialist 'laxness' in immigration matters, were aimed at producing a 'poster effect' (Dreyfus-Schmidt 1998: 25), to warn potential immigrants as well as those already resident in France that long-term settlement was not an attractive option. At the same time, they represented a call to the voters, who had deserted the mainstream right over the issue of immigration, to return to the fold. Thus the Pasqua laws were the first, since 1889, to call into question the principle of *jus soli*. Although eventually, the principle in itself was not revoked, aspects of it were questioned and adjusted.

The main adjustments related to access to French nationality and hence to the long-term settlement and integration of immigrants. A number of restrictions were imposed on the automatic acquisition of nationality so that children born in France of foreign parents could no longer expect to gain French nationality automatically unless they signalled their intent to do so between the ages of sixteen and twenty-one. In cases where intent was not signalled, nationality could be denied on grounds of a criminal record gained after the age of eighteen or if a young person had been subject to a previous deportation order due to the status of his or her parents. In addition, parents no longer had the right to claim nationality on behalf of children who were minors. The intention of such measures was to mark a symbolic separation between an entire generation of young people of immigrant origin and their French counterparts. Secondly, and more importantly, the measures were designed to stop parents of French-born children from claiming guarantees (such as protection from deportation and the right to resident permits). These changes to the French Nationality Code were accompanied by anti-immigration measures that reinforced administrative powers and procedures relating to border controls and to police checks on immigrants suspected of illegal entry and residence or of crime and which severely restricted the rights of asylum-seekers in line with the Schengen (1985) and Dublin agreements (1990). The Pasqua laws were further tightened by the 'Debré' law (after Jean-Louis Debré, then Minister of the Interior) of April 1997 (see Julien-Laferrière 1997).

The effect of these laws was an increase in police harassment of immigrants and of their descendants, severe restrictions on asylum seekers and the creation of an entire category of immigrants referred to as 'sans-papiers' (people without legal resident documents). The latter category was created as a result of the changes to the Nationality Code, which prevented parents of minors born in France from obtaining nationality on behalf of their children but who were protected from deportation orders under Article 8 of the European Convention of Human Rights. Although many of these immigrants have since acquired legal status, following the election of the Socialist government in June 1997, large numbers amongst them have suffered severe infringements of their social and human rights (see Agalarrondo 1996: 30–1 and Monnin 1996: 32–3).

While recent Socialist measures may have eased the situation of certain categories of immigrants,[40] the course pursued by both left and right has been one of curbing immigration in order to give the impression of dealing with the problems of French society.

Conclusion

This chapter has argued that immigration to France has been dominated by an economic logic relating, on one hand, to the need of post-war French capitalism for immigrant labour in order to ensure its survival and expansion and, on the other hand, to the globalization of markets that has led to the increased circulation of materials, goods and services and, inevitably, that of persons. Although changes in France's economic landscape, which accelerated after the oil crisis of 1974, may suggest that there is no longer need for immigrant labour, population movements, provoked by the effects of globalization, continue despite government measures to halt them outside or within national boundaries. In any case, while successive French governments continue to undertake such measures in order to appear to be tackling economic and social problems, there is little evidence to show that they seriously expect or even wish to achieve the 'zero immigration' talked about by Charles Pasqua in 1993. In 1996, Jean-Louis Debré suggested that what is really meant by 'zero immigration' is in fact 'zero illegal immigration' accompanied by controlled legal immigration to meet continuing labour needs within the economy. Furthermore, it is interesting to note that Charles Pasqua's most recent statements on the issue of illegal immigrants, more specifically the 'sans-papiers' (in the wake of France's football World Cup victory), call for the legalization of an entire category of migrants created by his law of 1993. Pasqua's reasoning is that 'when France is strong, she can be generous' (*Le Monde*, 17 July 1998: 1 and 6).

However, the pursuit of illegal immigrants is a convenient measure of appeasement to xenophobic opinion and masks the fact that illegal immigrants are sought out by French employers in much the same way as they prefer, in the 1990s, to employ workers on part-time or short-term contracts and to employ young people or the long-term unemployed on so-called work training or experience programmes. The needs of French capital (as in other industrialized countries) dictate the creation of a dual economy of labour whereby a division occurs between workers in secure long-term jobs and those whose conditions of work are precarious. Illegal (as well as legal) immigrants simply belong to the latter category from which employers select according to their short-term needs. While this situation persists within national economies and while socio-economic and demographic disparities persist between North and South and East and West, then movements of populations will continue from South and East to North and West. In this context French governments will be obliged to introduce increasingly complex measures in order to appear to address the contradictory needs of the economy and those of society (while maintaining their own political interests in balance) in which the degradation of living conditions and the breakdown of 'Frenchness' give rise to racism amongst other expressions of fear and discontent.

Notes

1. Firstly, 'immigrant' or 'migrant' will refer to people settled but not born in France and will include those who have subsequently acquired French nationality. It will not include children born in France. Secondly, it will refer to the following: 'economic' immigrants, those who entered France within the framework of family reunion, illegal entrants and refugees. It is recognised that previous categorisations of immigrants become increasingly meaningless today as migratory patterns, established according to national policies and/or international conventions of the past, have continued in spite of recent socio-economic transformations.
2. France's demographic decline began a century earlier than in other industrialised countries. While France headed the population league table of European countries in 1800, it had dropped to bottom position by 1908. See Cipolla (1976) p.56.
3. By 1911, France was leading other European countries in terms of its over-sixty age group. Ibid., p.56.
4. The number of naturalisations for the period 1889 to 1927 totalled 164,000 while the figure for the period 1927 to 1940 had increased to 452,000. See V.Viet (1997) p.1.
5. The ONI processed, for a per capita fee, applications from employers who required foreign labour. Note that the ONI was renamed Office des Migrations Internationales (OMI) in 1987.
6. These figures are extracted from 1990 census data which constitute the most recent, public data from which (limited) quantitative comparisons between migrant groups can be made. Historically, there has been a lack of public statistical data relating to migration flows and migrant groups in France. This lacuna has been filled by surveys of limited interest or by qualitative studies on very small migrant population samples. For a discussion on the paucity of statistical data see M. Tribalat (1996), 'L'enquête MGIS: une anomalie dans la statistique française ou un changement de cap', *Journées européennes "Démographie, statistique et vie privée", cinquantenaire de l'INED*, Paris.
7. A principal organ of state, the Conseil d'Etat advises the government on each parliamentary bill and ordinance to be introduced.
8. This was established in 1945 and attached to the presidency of the Provisional Government of the Republic.
9. For a fuller discussion of 'cultural preference' policies see P.Weil (1995), 'Racisme et discrimination dans la politique française de l'immigration. 1938–1945/1974–1995', *Vingtième Siècle*, July–September, pp.77–102.

10. Whereas the proportion of women had not exceeded 44 per cent of the total migrant population in the inter-war period, by 1954 it had reached 46.5 per cent. After the mid-1950s it declined again until the 1990s, by which time it was the difference between male and female mortality rates which accounted for the higher proportion of women within the migrant population. Insee (1997), *Les immigrés en France* p.21.
11. For a comprehensive discussion of this subject see D. Joly (1996), *Haven or Hell: Asylum Policies and Refugees in Europe*, London. Especially Chapters 1 and 2.
12. A law of September 1947 had applied a special statute to Algeria, allowing French Muslims from Algeria (*Français Musulmans d'Algérie* – FMA), unimpeded movement between France and Algeria. The number of FMA, in France, had increased from 22,000 in 1946 to 209,000 in 1954. M. Tribalat (1997), 'Chronique de l'immigration', *Population*, no.1, p.173.
13. The Conseil National du Patronat Français (CNPF) was formed in 1946 precisely to unify the dispersed *chambres patronales* and to resist the tripartite government (including Communists) and which was regarded as too pro-trades-union.
14. In 1947, the number of workdays 'lost' due to strikes totalled 23, 361,000. Trotignan (1985) p.259.
15. Between 1954 and 1964, jobs in the tertiary sector increased at an annual rate of 2.4 per cent while the whole working population expanded at a yearly rate of 0.2 per cent during the same period. Ibid. p.439.
16. For the effects of capital intensification within the production process see R. Northrop, 'Automation: Effects on Labour Force, Skills and Employment' *Industrial Research* (Annual Proceedings Report), 1958.
17. France had waived entry visa requirements from 77 countries, including ex-colonies, under various conventions and agreements signed between 1957 and 1972. See Viet, *Migrations Etudes*, no. 84, p.5.
18. Almost half of the male population worked in the building and construction sector while women, forming a large proportion of the Portuguese migrant labour force, worked within the services sector including private domestic labour.
19. Unlike its competitors, French capital seemed incapable of pretending to conceive and implement an autonomous strategy to resist the dominant Germano-American vision for Europe's relations with the South and also failed to exploit inter-imperialist tensions and contradictions between the USA and its German or Japanese allies.

20. For a comprehensive account of new patterns of migration see S. Castles and M. J. Miller (1993), *The Age of Migration*. London.
21. Migrant numbers from these three countries had risen from 90,000 in 1982 to 159,000 in 1990, representing a 77 per cent increase. Tribalat, 'Chronique de l'immigration', p.175.
22. The number of Mauritians and Zaireans entering France had doubled between 1982 (37,928) and 1990 (78,474). Ibid. p.177.
23. Predictions of the arrival of large numbers of East and Central European immigrants were not borne out in reality as there were insufficient reception facilities in France and because France had few (temporary and/or sectorial) bilateral agreements with East and Central European countries.
24. For recognition rates between 1981 and 1994 see Tribalat, 'Chronique de l'immigration', p.187.
25. Between 1973 and 1976, out of the 265,000 industrial workers made redundant, 64 per cent were immigrants. Furthermore, the rate of unemployment for immigrant workers increased by 400 per cent from the mid-1970s to the early 1980s to reach 14 per cent of the total unemployment rate in 1982 (compared with 8.4 per cent of French workers), 18.6 per cent by 1986 (9.6 per cent for French workers) and 20 per cent by 1995 (eight points above the national average). See Landor, 'North African Workers in France', pp.392–393 and Insee, *Les immigrés en France*, p.85.
26. Between the end of 1991 and the end of 1994, over 45 outbreaks of collective violence had taken place in or around the outskirts of French cities. See G.Denis (1994), 'Cinquante émeutes en trois ans', *Le Nouvel Observateur*, no.1568, pp.10–11.
27. Recently, increasing numbers of Muslim applicants have been refused French citizenship because of their obvious adherence to their culture. In November 1997, a Moroccan woman who had lived in France for twenty years, was refused naturalisation by the Department of Naturalisation in Rezé (Loire-Atlantique) because 'It transpires, from the examination of your dossier, that your behaviour, notably where your choice of clothing is concerned, shows a refusal to integrate into the French community.' See *Migration News Sheet* (1998), no.180, p.11.
28. For a summary of this debate see Hargreaves, *Immigration, 'Race' and Ethnicity*, pp.125–31.
29. According to figures published by the Direction de la Réglementation, 43 per cent of foreigners had partly or completely bypassed the provisions of the November 1945 ordinance. Viet (1997), p.5.

30. Repatriation aid was introduced in April 1977. Proposed legislation on forced repatriation fell through in 1979 due to the Left's opposition.
31. Between 1978 and 1983 unemployment became the main concern of voters. From 1984 onwards, up to seventy per cent of voters felt that it constituted the absolute priority for government action. See O. Duhamel and J. Jaffré (1987), 'L'Opinion publique et le chômage: réflexions sur trois courbes', *Les Temps Modernes*, vol. 42, no. 496–7, p. 310.
32. Some of the most militant of these were: Association culturelle des travailleurs d'Afrique noire en France, Mouvement des travailleurs ivoiriens en France, Union générale des étudiants, des élèves et des stagiaires sénégalais, Union générale des travailleurs sénégalais en France and Union nationale des étudiants camerounais.
33. Although immigration formed the main plank in the Front National's programme, voters were also attracted to the party for other reasons: generally because of its self-proclaimed role of 'tribune of the people' (previously fulfilled by the PCF) and because voters wanted to protest against the inability of the main parties to solve social problems but more specifically, for instance, because of the FN's objection to the Single European Market.
34. National preference policies would reserve political, socio-economic and cultural rights for French citizens alone.
35. For example, the announcement made, in January 1998, by the Mayor of Vitrolles, Catherine Mégret, that couples of European origin (taking into account the large numbers of voters and FN representatives, in Vitrolles, of Italian, Spanish and Potuguese origin), who produced children would receive a payment of 5000 Francs per birth ('local maternity benefit') as reward for adding to the indigeneous population.
36. The theme of national preference was taken up more recently, in a Europe 1 radio interview, of 21 June 1998, by former RPR Prime Minister Edouard Balladur, who argued that the issue of national preference should be discussed openly by the mainstream Right.
37. They are no longer required to prove five years' continuous residence in France prior to their eighteenth birthday.
38. The only exception to this rule applies to children of whom one parent at least was born in Algeria prior to 1962 (independence).
39. For a summarised review of these laws see D. Lochak, (1998), 'La nationalité Française en débat', *Après-Demain*, no. 400–401, pp. 13–17.

40. For instance, the move to legalise the position of the 'sans-papiers' through the granting of residence permits. Approximately 64 per cent of the 150,000 applications for legalisation received have been treated favourably. See *Le Monde*, 22–23 Feb. 1998, p.8.

Bibliography

Algalarrondo, H. (1996), 'Sans-papiers: les secrets d'un fiasco' *Le Nouvel Observateur*, 1660: 30–1.

Après-Demain (1998) , Special issue on 'Immigration', no.400–401.

Bize, P. (1947), 'Les problèmes de main-d'œuvre à la conférence des Seize', *Revue Française du Travail*, 19: 876–902.

Castles, S. (1993), 'Migrations and Minorities in Europe. Perspectives for the 1990s: Eleven Hypotheses', in J. Wrench and J. Solomos (eds), *Racism and Migration in Western Europe*, Oxford.

Castles, S. and Miller, M.J. (1993), *The Age of Migration*, London: Macmillan.

Cesarini, D. and Fulbrook, M. (1996), *Citizenship, Nationality and Migration in Europe*, London: Routledge.

Cipolla, C.M. (1976), *Fontana Economic History of Europe: The Industrial Revolution*, 3rd edn, Glasgow: Fontana.

Dreyfus-Schmidt, M. (1998), 'Droits des étrangers: régime d'exception attenuée ou d'égalité partielle?', *Après-Demain*, 400–401: 25.

Dubet, F. (1989), *Immigrations: qu'en savons-nous? Un bilan des connaissances*, Paris: La Documentation Française.

Etchegoin, M.-F. *et al* (1990), 'Les casseurs', *Le Nouvel Observateur*, 1359: 46–52.

Etchegoin, M.-F. (1994), 'Beurs: pourquoi les islamistes marquent des points', *Le Nouvel Observateur*, 1562: 29–31.

European Council on Refugees & Exiles (1997), *Minutes and Conference Papers from the ECRE Biannual General Meeting*, unpublished papers, ECRE.

Gaspard, F. and Khosrokhavar, F. (1995), *Le foulard et la République*, Paris: La Découverte.

Harris, N. (1995), *The New Untouchables*, London: Penguin Books.

Hargreaves, A.G. (1995), *Immigration, Race and Ethnicity in Contemporary France*, London: Routledge.

INSEE, (1997), *Les immigrés en France*, Paris: INSEE.
Joly, D. (1996), *Haven or Hell? Asylum Policies and Refugees in Europe*, London: MacMillan.
——, (1997), 'A New Asylum Regime for Europe', unpublished paper, Centre for Research in Ethnic Relations (CRER), University of Warwick.
——, (1997), 'Temporary Protection within the Framework of a New European Asylum Regime', unpublished paper, CRER, University of Warwick.
——, Kelly, L. and Nettleton, C. (1997), *Refugees in Europe: the Hostile New Agenda*, Minority Rights Group: London.
Julien-Laferrière, F. (1997), 'La "loi Debré" sur l'immigration', *Regards sur l'Actualité*, 232: 27–39.
Landor, J. (1997), 'North African Workers in France: Processes of Integration and Exclusion', *Contemporary Politics*, 2 (4): 381–99.
Massey, D. *et alia*, (1993), 'Theories of International Migration: a Review and Appraisal' *Population and Development Review*, 19 (3): 431–66.
Mayer, N. (1993), 'Le Front National', in D. Chagnollaud (ed.), *La vie politique en France*, Seuil, p.329–343.
Migration News Sheet (1998), 180: 11.
Miles, R. and Thränhardt, D. (eds.), (1995), *Migration and European Integration: the Dynamics of Inclusion and Exclusion*, London: Pinter Publishers.
Monnin, I. (1996), 'Lois Pasqua? Non, lois Ubu!', *Le Nouvel Observateur*, 1660: 32–3.
N'Dongo, S. (1976), *Coopération' et néo-colonialisme*, Paris: Maspero.
Raffy, S. *et al* (1994), 'Terrorisme. Comment les islamistes recrutent en France', *Le Nouvel Observateur*, 1560: 40–44.
Samuel, M. (1978), *Le prolétariat africain noir en France*, François Maspero: Paris.
Schor, R., (1996), *Histoire de l'immigration en France de la fin du XIXe siècle à nos jours*, Paris: Armand Colin.
Tribalat, M. (1996), 'L'enquête MGIS: une anomalie dans la statistique française ou un changement de cap', *Journées européennes "Démographie, statistique et vie privée", cinquantenaire de l'INED*, INED: Paris.
—— (1997), 'Chronique de l'immigration', *Population*, 1: 163–219.
Trotignan, Y. (1985), *La France au Xxe siècle – tome 1: jusqu'en 1968*, 2nd edn, Paris: Dunod.
—— (1984), *La France au Xxe siècle – tome 2: depuis 1968*, 2nd edn, Paris: Dunod.
Viet, V. (1997), 'Le cheminement des structures administratives et la

politique française de l'immigration (1914–1986)', *Migrations Etudes*, 84: 1–7.

Vincent, C. & Grossin, W. (1958), 'Les conséquences de l'automatisation pour les travailleurs dans les pays capitalistes', *Economie et Politique*, 42: 1–29.

Wrench, J. and Solomos, J (1993), *Racism and Migration in Western Europe*, Oxford: Berg.

—8—

Social Democracy in One Country: Immigration and Minority Policy in Austria

Eugene Sensenig-Dabbous

Austria is an immigrant nation. Taking the current borders as a point of reference, between 20 and 40 per cent of the population in the major Austrian urban centres was ethnically foreign immediately prior to the First World War. Non-nationals were employed by the hundreds of thousands during both major European wars in this century. During the inter-war period, the Republic of German-Austria, or the First Republic as it was later called, clamped down on labour migration. Following the Second World War, occupied Austria (1945–55) was forced by the occupying Allied forces to integrate several hundred thousand *Volksdeutsche* German refugees from Czechoslovakia, Hungary and the Balkans. The Second Republic's economic miracle (*Wirtschaftswunder*) years, from the late 1950s to 1973, saw the massive immigration of guest workers increase the total presence of foreign labour from 0.5 per cent to 8.7 per cent of the total workforce, only to be reduced by nearly half (5.1 per cent) by 1984. The economic boom, following the political reunification of Central Europe in 1989, led to an increased demand for cheap labour in Austria. Today, close to 10 per cent of all legally employed workers in Austria are foreigners. Over 90 per cent of these employees are not from the European Union – third-country nationals, mainly Slav, Albanian, Roma or Magyar natives of the post-communist southern Slav republics.

Viewed demographically and economically, migration to Austria parallels developments in many other centres of mass immigration throughout this century. Politically, however, the Austrian experience is an exception. Unlike other continental countries of immigration such as Switzerland, Germany, France or the Netherlands, Austria experienced severe alterations in labour market size and policy. This occurred a total of four times in the last 80 years. In 1918 the vast, unrestricted, multicultural Austro-Hungarian labour market was dismantled. In 1938 Austria was integrated into the racist labour market of the German Reich. Between 1945 and 1955 developments in the Allied-occupied Austrian Republic were dominated by the hostilities emanating from the Cold War conflict between the United States and the Soviet Union. Finally, after joining the European Union in 1995, a 40-year period of Austrian labour market protectionism (1955–95) came to an end.

Overlapping these various fractures in Austrian history, the ultimately successful attempt of the labour movement to structure immigration flows provided the country with a surprising level of continuity. The fact that, by 1946, the national trade union federation and the semi-official Chamber of Labour had achieved hegemony over access to employment in the non-agricultural segments of the economy sets Austria apart from all other European nations. To fully appreciate the unique effects of the Austrian concepts of social partnership (*Sozialpartnerschaft*) and active labour market policy (*aktive Arbeitsmarktpolitik*) one must take a closer look at the origins of this distinctly Central European phenomenon.

Historical Overview

During the last 50 years of the Habsburg era, the empire was divided into the German-dominated sphere of Austria (Cisleithania) and a Magyar-dominated sphere of Hungary (Transleithania). Both 'Austria' and 'Hungary' were merely geographical terms designating a far-flung set of loyalties to the Habsburg dynasty and its Kaiser Franz Josef, rather than to a specific nation or race. There were no limitations on migration within this labour market, either for citizens of the two constituent parts or for non-citizens, mainly natives of the German Reich, the Kingdom of Italy and the Russian empire. Following the break-up of Austria as a multinational dynastic entity in 1918, the Germans in Austria formed the Republic of German-Austria as a nation state. Between 1918 and 1934 Austria was a democracy. The difficulties stemming from the disintegration of the Habsburg empire were aggravated by the world wide recession that had spread to Central Europe by 1930. During a brief civil war in 1934 the authoritarian Fatherland Front (Vaterländische Front), supported by the Catholic Church and allied with Mussolini, outlawed the leftist parties and trade unions and introduced a brief period of clerical fascist rule, only to be overthrown by Hitler's Nazi party in 1938. Following the liberation of Austria in 1945, the country was occupied and divided into four zones for 10 years. Following full independence in 1955 Austria has remained a neutral country, run, with brief exceptions, by coalition governments uniting parties of the centre-left and centre-right. Austria joined the EU, along with Finland and Sweden, in 1995.

From the 1890s to the 1990s, the Social Democratic movement attempted to gain and consolidate control of labour market policy. This they considered an absolute prerequisite to the introduction of a truly democratic society based on social solidarity of all its members. The two major conservative political camps – the Christian Socials and German Nationals – never developed coherent labour market or migration policies. Following their political instincts to secure a large pool of unprotected and flexible labour, the centre-right successfully frustrated the attempts of the trade unions and Social Democrats to engineer a comprehensive system of migration control during the inter-war period. Because of this policy vacuum on the right, the Social Democrats were the only political force to have a clear idea of which type of labour market set-up they wanted in 1945. The German Nationals were outlawed at this time because of their support for the Nazis. The Christian Socials were discredited and weakened because of their role in undermining democracy in 1934 and because of the fact that the Nazis had nationalized large segments of the economy during the war; these remained state controlled under Allied directorship and later became the property of the Austrian Republic. Enjoying the support of both the Social Democratic ministers of Social Affairs and of the Interior, the national labour organizations, Österreichische Gewerkschaftsbund (ÖGB) and Arbeiterkammer (AK), were informally integrated into the directorship of the national employment agency (Arbeitsamt) in 1946. By the late 1950s this control had been formalized; by 1961 it had been consolidated by a broad-based agreement between the Christian Social Party and Chamber of Commerce, on the one hand, and the ÖGB, AK and Social Democratic Party on the other.

In view of the deep-seated national and ideological traditions of migration policy consensus, a portrayal of Austrian migration and minority measures is only possible following an in-depth presentation of their historical background. In this first section of the chapter a chronological overview of Social Democratic migration policy development will be superimposed on the various fractures in Austrian history during the first half of this century. In the second section, the actual application of social partnership and active labour market policy will be presented in detail.

Austria – Half an Empire

Migration in the Habsburg empire was mainly an internal affair. This meant that immigration was left mainly to the whims of the capitalist market. In comparison to other major countries of immigration within Europe, the Habsburg Empire had a totally open labour market and an 'open doors' immigration policy. The concept of migration was indeed heatedly debated prior to World War One, but only as it related to emigration from Austria and Hungary to the Americas, the German *Reich* and Switzerland. One issue that was of immanent importance to post-war immigration discourse, though not considered a related topic at the time, was the establishment of labour referral services, then being propagated by leftist-liberals, right-wing Social Democrats and other social reformers. Their goal was to establish a network of government sponsored Arbeitsnachweise or Arbeitsämter, which would be placed directly under the supervision of parity control commissions. The concept of Parität, or equal representation of big business and organized labour on social policy governing boards, went back to the continental revolutionary period of 1848. By the turn of the century liberal Viennese Kathedersozialist (Fabian) academics, politicians and bureaucrats such as Eugene von Philippovich, Social Democrat intellectuals like Karl Renner, and Christian Socials including Leopold Kunschak, had reached agreement on the desirability of class co-operation. The term *Mitbestimmung* or co-determination became the predominant symbol of practical and non-revolutionary social reform (Boyer 1988; Filla 1981; Weidenholzer 1985).

Prior to the First World War, little progress was made in the field of labour market engineering. Increasingly, however, this became one of the central demands of the Social Democratic leadership, both in Vienna and in the provincial industrial centres. By the outbreak of hostilities in 1914, nine *Arbeitsnachweise* existed within the borders of present-day Austria, but only two – Linz and Wiener Neustadt – had parity governing boards. In order to regulate the labour market during the war, the government began introducing a tightly knit system of *Arbeitsnachweise* in 1914. Extreme pressure from the Social Democrats and the trade unions, and fear of the spontaneously organized workers councils then being set up along the lines of the Russian model, led the Habsburg government to establish full parity in the field of labour market planning and referrals in 1917. As late as the summer of 1918 these *Arbeitsnachweise* were still working on plans to co-ordinate the demobilization of the military workforce in all of Austria in order to guarantee a speedy and orderly reconversion to a civilian, peacetime economy. With the collapse of the Monarchy in November of that same year, the new Social Democratic Minister of Social Affairs, Ferdinand Hanusch, simply took over and expanded this existing network from his imperial predecessor, Victor Mataja (Schmidt 1991). Following the political crisis immediately after the war, unemployment dropped from 18.4 per cent in 1919 to 4.2 per cent in 1920. By 1921 the newly founded German Republic of Austria was suffering from an over-employment crisis, with only 1.4 per cent of all residents registered as unemployed. The resulting attempts by both employers and the Ministry of Social Affairs to encourage immigration and cross-border commuting from the traditional employment markets – now parts of Italy, Yugoslavia, Hungary and Czechoslovakia – were seen by a significant faction of the Social Democratic movement as an orchestrated attempt to undermine trade union influence over the recruitment process, then controlled by the newly founded Industrielle Bezirkskommissionen (district industrial employment boards), or IBK. Thus the immigration, parity and labour-referral issues became tightly interrelated. As shall be demonstrated below, this policy link has remained in place until the present.

The Origins of Nationalist Immigration Policy

The social reform strategies propagated by centre-left bureaucrats, politicians, and labour leaders during the last decades of the monarchy interacted with internal ideological debate amongst the academically educated and intellectual members of Social Democratic Workers' Party of German Austria (SDAP) at the time. Although revolutionary activists would retain a degree of significance up until the outbreak of civil war in 1934, by the turn of the twentieth century the truly anti-capitalist wing of the party had lost its influence in all significant areas of decision making. According to Wiedenholzer (1985) and Talos (1981), Austrian Social Democrats had, on the whole, reconciled their policy, if not their rhetoric, to a consolidation of capitalist democracy prior to the First World War. Assuming the eventual collapse of capitalism under its own weight sometime in the future to be self-evident, Austro-Marxists concentrated on the expansion and perfection of their own mass organizations. Starting with the base – the shop steward councils, ward party organizations and local consumer co-operatives – paid and volunteer party functionaries were encouraged to learn the skills necessary to enable them to rise in the ranks and conceivably play a leading role in the future Social Democratic bureaucracy of socialist society in their own lifetime. This emphasis on dual administration led to the need to invest the majority of Social Democratic resources in organization building and organizational skills. Unfettered labour mobility often clashed with these goals because of the need to constantly incorporate new and predominantly foreign (non-German) migrants.

Internationalism versus Demographic Luddism. Along with the purely structural and organizational challenges that migration presented to labour internationalism, rank-and-file nativism also proved to be increasingly virulent. Despite the official internationalist proclamations of the union and party leadership, local craft union and ward leaders tended to reject the multi-ethnic solidarity approach. This inherent conflict within the labour movement appears to have a variety of causes based on the very nature of industrial capitalist development.

According to Fuchs (1993), nineteenth century labour organizations were confronted with three challenges simultaneously: the abrupt liberalization of the labour market, the continuous deskilling of production and a gradual improvement of transportation services for the poor. Slowly, the quantitative increase of labour mobility into the respective markets that these skilled trade organizations individually controlled threaten to take on a qualitative nature. The main issue in this context became the prevention of wage dumping, in general, and strike breaking and the replacement of locked-out workers, in particular. The Central European Social Democratic leadership recognized that the historical ability of the guilds to control access to the workplace and thus protect their living standards was becoming a thing of the past. Luddite (*Maschinensturmer*) tendencies were therefore considered not only impractical, but hazardous to the success of strike action because they improved the ability of employers and the state to split the ranks of the working class. German labour activists within the German Confederation or Deutscher Bund (until 1866), Austria or Cisleithania (as of 1867) and the German *Reich* (as of 1871) were not only confronted with a rise in native labour mobility, but also an increase in the migration of foreign labour into the German lands. Parochial demographic Luddism turned nationalist and anti-Semitic. The revolutionary and modernist thinkers within the movement expanded their inclusionary strategy from the regional to the national level, opening local labour organizations to foreign language and Jewish workers. Despite certain setbacks, this policy succeeded on paper. German nationalism was declared anti-socialist. Contemporary government-sponsored research on the subject reveals a Social Democratic bureaucracy in tune with the multi-ethnic nature of its constituency (Mataja 1898).

The German-Austrian (and Czech-Austrian) champions of internationalism on the European level demonstrated, however, an extremely parochial and nativist slant to their thinking and policy in respect to the actual implementation of domestic politics. According to Löw (1984: 14), the German-Austrian workers had traditionally been internationalist for the simple reason that their mother tongue was the *lingua franca* of the monarchy. Nationalism and the issue of national rights was seen as a reactionary strategy of the bourgeoisie.

> This naive cosmopolitanism was a product of the relative national disinterest of the German working class which can be explained by the dominant position of the Germans within Austria. For the workers belonging to the other nationalities (of the Monarchy, E.S.), this meant the de facto exertion of German hegemony within the movement. (Löw 1984: 15)

With 6.4 million inhabitants, the Czechs in Cisleithania were by far the most important non-German nationality. The last census during the monarchy (1910) counted a total population of 28 million. This included 9.9 million Germans, 5 million Poles, 3.5 million Ruthenians and 1.2 million Slovenes. Together, the Slavs outnumbered the Germans one-and-a-half to one (Volkszählung 1912: 59). Until the late 1880s there was practically no debate about the language issue. As the Czechs started suing for equal rights within the Austrian party, the Germans first responded by declaring their demands reactionary and in violation of revolutionary proletarian internationalism. By the mid 1890s, however, the conflict had escalated considerably. Setbacks during major strikes and a lack of progress on the voting rights issue convinced the Czechs that years of struggle would be necessary until socialism was achieved.

> Now that victory for the working class in the near future, through the introduction of universal suffrage, no longer seemed probable, it became obvious that a long, drawn-out and strenuous process of organisation building would be necessary. The issue of national rights could therefore no longer be postponed until after the working class became victorious. The nationalisation of Czech Social Democracy took a huge step forward. (Löw 1984: 24)

The Czech challenge to German hegemony led to an organizational division of the so-called Little International in 1899 along ethnic lines. The Austrian Social Democratic Party formally split into a Czech-Austrian and centralist faction in 1911. German domination of the party outside the Czech lands thereby became overwhelming. This forced the issue of national rights of the circa 300,000 Czechs in the imperial capital of Vienna to the forefront. By 1914 relations between the Germans and Slavs in Austria had fully deteriorated, thus facilitating the break-up of the empire along nationalist lines in 1918.

The direct effects of war on migration and minority affairs will be demonstrated below. This brief thematic aside will be followed by a portrayal of policy development in the inter-war Austrian Republic.

Labour Mobility and War. As a traditional country of emigration, Austria-Hungary had no need to recruit foreign workers at the outbreak of the

First World War. On the contrary, during the initial year of the war the economy was confronted with widespread unemployment because of the logistical difficulties directly related to mobilization and their negative effect on heavy industry in general and the transportation network in particular. A genuine need for foreign labour only existed in the years 1916 and 1917. Research on the interrelationship between employment during the First and Second World Wars in Central Europe has until now been based exclusively on the *Reich*-German experience (Dohse 1981; Herbert 1985). Austrian studies on civilian and POW workers in the Ostmark (1938–45) deal with occupied Austria as if it were an integral part of the German *Reich*. This assumption – conceivably correct – has never been tested. In the following, the Austrian experience in both World Wars will be briefly described. It is important to note here that not only were labour conditions for foreigners different during both wars, Austria-Hungary also followed a much less aggressive policy then did the *German Reich* between 1915 and 1918.

The First World War. Austrian emigration figures skyrocketed in the decade prior to the outbreak of war. Not only did the Empire replace Italy as the main source of transatlantic migration, but Austria also contributed over 300,000 workers to the labour market of the German *Reich*. The hundreds of thousands of POWs from Russia, Italy and Serbia that began to be transported to the German-speaking region of Austria, following the major victories of the Central Powers in 1915, were seen as more of a nuisance than as welcome manpower by the military, heavy industry and the local authorities. The main rationale behind employing POWs in 1915 was to help alleviate overcrowding in the camps. Russian and Italian workers were needed desperately by mid 1916, however, because of the unexpected length of the war. The impending crisis on the home front (*Heimatfront*), because of a severe lack of manpower in the coal mines and in agriculture, was to be met by supplying the peasants and the mining industry with free POW labour. Malnutrition, underheated barracks and the gradually developing revolutionary workers' movement led to rebellion within the ranks of the POWs, which by late 1917 could only be brought under control with great difficulty. The First World War represents the first attempt by the Austrian authorities and industry to employ forced labour in large numbers. It was seen as a limited success (Aggermann 1927; Sensenig, 1998).

The Second World War. On paper at least, Austria and the Sudeten region of Czechoslovakia were just as much a part of the German *Reich* as Bavaria or Prussia between 1938 and 1945. There were, however, major differences between the disparate cultural and economic traditions of the various regions of the *Reich* proper (*Altreich*), on the one hand, and its newly acquired south-eastern territories, on the other. Although the German and Czech regions of the Habsburg empire had formed an alliance with the rest of Germany within the Holy Roman Empire and German Confederation until 1866, the *kleindeutsch* solution had permanently separated the German *Reich* from Austria in 1871. The massive voluntary and forced recruitment of friendly *Gastarbeiter* – from Italy, Hungary, Slovakia, Croatia and the Netherlands – and enemy *Fremdarbeiter* – from Poland, Belgium, France, Yugoslavia and the Soviet Union – began shortly after the *Anschluss*. When war broke out, the National Socialist re-education programme in the Austrian and Sudeten territories was by no means complete, considering the fact that the authorities had needed six years of peace in which to train the Reich-German population. Most Austrians reconciled themselves to German occupation because they had no other choice. The improvement in living standards that occupation brought was short lived. As the German invasion of the Soviet Union was halted in 1942 and the repressive Nazi regime could no longer deliver on it promise of prosperity, Austrians began to discover, or rediscover, their distinct national identity. The limited documentation dealing with this topic indicates that this development had a positive effect on the treatment of the civilian and POW workers in anticipation of *Reich*-German defeat (Gatterbauer 1975: 256).

Social and Democratic Nationalism

The effects of wartime forced labour employment on immigration and minority policy in times of peace has yet to be properly researched. As a working hypothesis it will be assumed here that the mistreatment of Italians and Slavs in both World Wars tended to reinforce nationalist sentiment within the population in general, and substantiate the notion that non-national workers could be legitimately reduced to their role as labour power without individual rights. In the following, the development of nationalism within the labour movement and its effects on migration policy immediately after the First World War will be portrayed in detail.

Three developments, at the beginning of the two-decade-long lifespan of the First Republic, are symptomatic of this foundation-building period following the introduction of democracy, i.e. the so called 'Option', through which citizens of the defunct Habsburg Empire could choose the nation state to which they wished to belong, the anti-foreigner job referral policy and the passing of the Domestic Labour Protection Act (*Inlandarbeiterschutzgesetz* – IASG) in 1925, which conclusively terminated debate on freedom of mobility and equal treatment for immigrant labour. The anti-foreigner ordinances and *Inlandarbeiterschutzgesetz* are significant because they demonstrate the interrelatedness of nationalism and social exclusion; the 'Option' is significant because it not only entrenched the concept of the nation state within Central Europe, but was also openly racist and anti-Semitic in nature.

The 'Option' – Inventing the German Race. The Czech region of Cisleithania seceded from the monarchy during the last weeks of the war. The founding of the German-Austrian Republic was declared shortly thereafter. This left millions of German speakers and hundreds of thousands of Polish, Yiddish, Rumanian, Italian, Ruthenian, Slovene, Croatian, Slovak, but especially Czech speakers on the wrong side of the respective new borders within ex-Cisleithania. A top priority for both the new German and new Czechoslovak states was thus to determine who was a citizen and who was a non-national immigrant. The Treaty of Brno (7 June 1920) between Austria and Czechoslovakia determined that both countries would naturalize all members of the respective language group in a liberal manner. Anyone whose official residence or *Heimatgemeinde* was within the borders of Austria was automatically Austrian. Those legally residing in Austria before the outbreak of hostilities in 1914 received preferential treatment during the naturalization procedure. Many language groups, including Czechs, Slovaks and Italians, who had moved or were transferred to German-Austria during the war, also had no difficulty receiving citizenship. One ethnic group, however, was aggressively excluded by the authorities irrespective of their political orientation – the Jews.

Hundreds of thousands of Cisleithanian Jews had been forced to leave their homes near the Russian front during the war; many were evacuated against their will. The majority lived in the greater Vienna area at the end of the war (Hoffmann-Holter 1985). Consensus existed between the German Nationals, Christian Socials and Social Democrats on the ordinance governing the 'Option' (*Vollzugsanweisung*, 20 August 1920), requiring anyone who was planning to apply for naturalization and who had not lived in the country before the war, to prove that they met two criteria. The first and less difficult stipulation was that they spoke German as their language of choice in daily affairs and at home (Umgangssprache). Secondly, they were requested to prove that they belonged to the German race (*sic*). The race clause was used almost exclusively against Jews from Hungary, Galicia and Bucovina. The Treaty of Brno protected Jewish

Czechs. Any discrimination against the hundreds of thousands of Czechs in Austria would have had an immediate effect on the millions of Germans living in Czechoslovakia (Grandner 1995; Mussak 1995).

The 'Option' was based on a long-standing policy tradition and must be seen in this context. Only a third (98,461) of the approximately 300,000 Czechs (John 1990: 18) in Vienna had been willing to admit, during the last census before the First World War, that their mother tongue was not German. This hesitancy was the direct result of the nativist, German-nationalist policy of the Viennese Christian Social mayor, Karl Lueger. According to the Christian Social party the imperial capital was a German and Catholic city, Jews and Czechs were not welcome. In order to receive the Viennese *Heimatrecht* or right of residence, a new resident 'had to swear an additional oath that he would do his utmost to preserve the German character of the city of Vienna' (Glettler 1985: 306). Following the 'Option' the Czech ethnic group grew somewhat, reflecting the increased prestige the Czech nation now enjoyed. More than a third of the Viennese Czech minority (120,000) opted for Czechoslovak citizenship (John 1990: 16). The Social Democrats saw this group of foreigners as their natural constituency, mainly because, politically, the Czechs had nowhere else to go. They therefore encouraged them to remain active in trade union and party life. The most significant concession to Czech ethnic clout during the First Republic is the Shop Steward Act of 1919. Despite the fact that Czechoslovak (and Reich-German) policy excluded foreigners from becoming members of the shop stewards' councils, Austrian Social Democrats choose to neglect the principle of reciprocity in this case in order not to alienate a major section of the party rank and file.

National Job Referral. Following the revolutionary upheavals in 1918/1919 and the brief restructuring crisis in 1919/1920, full employment was achieved in 1921, re-establishing the traditional migration patterns common in the monarchy, as mentioned above. In the spring of 1921 skilled seasonal Slovenian and Italian brickmakers applied for positions with their previous employers in the brickworks of the southern states of Carinthia and Styria. Czech and Polish labourers were rehired by the sugar factories of Upper and Lower Austria. Slovaks and Hungarians again found work on the large plantations in Burgenland. Skilled, high-altitude Italian construction workers were recruited to head crews building dams, power-lines and railroads in the Alps, often over 3,000 meters above sea level. The Sozialministerium (Ministry of Social Affairs) – then a domain of internationalist Social Democratic reformers – initially encouraged labour mobility across ethnic lines, viewing it as a return to normality. This position was not shared by everyone in the Social Democratic Party. The labour unions, especially in the building trades, saw the new international borders as an opportunity to re-establish at least limited control over access to the workplace. Competition for the well-paid construction jobs in the western Austrian mountains served as the initial incident in a chain reaction of increasingly nativist labour market policy adaptation. By the fall of 1921 one specific incident was singled out to force the trade unions' case. Seventy Italian technicians and specialized stone masons from the Dolomites had been recruited to lead a crew of 350 workers building a hydraulic power plant in the south of the state of Salzburg. The Italian states of Trentino, Veneto and Friuli had traditionally supplied the Monarchy with these highly skilled workers. This case of ethnic infiltration led the German-Austrian Social Democratic Freie Gewerkschaften union federation in Salzburg to demand the exclusion of all immigrant labour along national lines. This initiative was supported by the newly formed Chamber of Labour in Vienna and the Social Democratic deputy governor of Salzburg.

> The Chamber (of Labour, E.S.) has complained about the hiring of Italian workers which is naturally both a national and domestic economic threat. [. . .] Effective steps must be taken to protect the native population against the threatening inundation (Überflutung) of foreign language workers. (Italiener/ÖStA: 1921)

The combined pressure of the trade unions, Chamber of Labour and State of Salzburg resulted in the first direct restriction of labour market access in the history of modern industrial Austria. An internal agreement between the Sozialministerium and Innenministerium (Ministry of the Interior) in January 1922 restricted the immigration of all foreign, non-skilled workers. This policy was extended and clarified in an ordinance in August of the same year.

> The municipal and district industrial employment offices have been informed that the unemployment registry listings are to be reordered so that when considering unemployed workers who have registered with the agency in order to find employ, the Austrians and Reich-Germans are in all cases to be treated preferentially; this policy is to be strictly followed irrespective of the length of time that these foreign (especially Czech) workers have been listed as being unemployed. (Einwanderung/ÖStA: 1922)

The position taken by the Innenministerium and Sozialministerium – that in the area of employment 'Austrians and citizens of the German *Reich* are to be treated preferentially' – is a clear concession to German-nationalist sentiment within the population as a whole and the trade unions in particular. This pan-German, anti-Slavic position was only dropped after the beginning of hyperinflation and the ensuing economic crisis in the German *Reich* in 1923. As of this point in time all major Austrian parties were forced to compromise their pro-*Reich* sentiments in order to prevent mass migration of unemployed Reich-Germans into Austria, especially to those states directly bordering on Bavaria.

De-Ethnicizing an Ideological Vacuum. The period between the introduction of the above mentioned ordinances – the anti-Semitic 'Option' of 1920 and anti-foreigner job referral policy of 1922 – and the passing of the IASG (Domestic Labour Protection Act) in 1925, is significant. For the first time, social welfare and labour market considerations became more important than German nationalism. The cities of Salzburg and Bregenz, both located directly on the border with Bavaria, were the first to feel the brunt of the wave of cross-border commuting into Austria, facilitated by the privileged treatment given to German aliens. Both state governments – Vorarlberg and Salzburg – introduced labour market ordinances in 1923 in order to control this phenomenon. These were ruled unconstitutional because they affected the sphere of international relations. The pressure exerted by these two western-Austrian state governments, the Freie Gewerkschaften and AK did, however, finally forced the federal government to take action.

In essence, the IASG, which went into effect in January of 1926, was actually an improvement for many non-German foreign workers. The employment limitations it introduced were restricted to those immigrants who had moved to Austria after the beginning of 1923. Thus, the large number of Czechs, Galician Jews, and Italians who either were not permitted or had not chosen to opt for citizenship in the German Republic of Austria now enjoyed equal labour market access with Austrian citizens irrespective of their race or ethnicity. Furthermore, all those foreign-language workers, who had returned to their places of employment immediately following the war, only to realize that – as citizens of the newly formed or expanded kingdoms and republics of Italy, Yugoslavia, Hungary, and Czechoslovakia – they were now considered hostile labour market competition by the nationalist Freie Gewerkschaften, were now protected from the threat of deportation. On the other hand, the Reich-German cross-border commuters were severely effected. The local IBK labour referral offices were required to report a foreigner to the authorities in those cases in which their employers could not prove that no equally qualified Austrian citizens could be found. If this was the case, they were subsequently deported or barred from entering Austria.

Re-Ethnicizing Austria. This policy, by which all resident foreigners were treated equally in Austria, was short lived. By the time the IASG started taking effect (spring of 1926), the economic crisis in the German *Reich* had run its course. The number of Austrians working in the *Reich* far outnumbered the Reich-German workers living or commuting daily, weekly or monthly into Austria. The IASG was modelled after the Reich-German equivalent, which had been passed in 1921 and amended in 1923 (Dohse 1981). These neighbouring countries thus had an interest in deregulating migration policy on a reciprocal basis. The Republic of Austria and the German *Reich* signed a secret agreement in mid 1926 opening their labour markets to each other's citizens. This clandestine agreement, officially titled 'Zwischen dem Bundesministerium für soziale Verwaltung und der deutschen Reichsarbeitsverwaltung aufgestellten Richtlinien', remained intact until the German *Reich* invaded Austria in 1938. In 1933 the democratically elected Christian Social Chancellor of Austria, Engelbert Dollfuss, dissolved parliament, using the powers entrusted in the head of state by the dictatorial laws passed during the First World War. The ensuing civil war of February 1934 lead to the outlawing of the democratic trade unions, the SDAP and the Communist Party of Austria. After the attempted Nazi coup in July of that same year, the NSDAP was also banned. The subsequent Catholic-oriented, corporatist-fascist regime – known as the Fatherland Front or Vaterländische Front (VF) – amended the Shop Steward Act (*Betriebsratsgesetz*) excluding non-nationals from the right to campaign in factory council elections. All other laws effecting foreigners were kept in place. Other than the newly amended fascist Shop Steward Act – now termed the *Werksgemeinschaftsgesetz* – Jewish, Czech and Italian foreigners experienced no direct discrimination from the new regime. After the Anschluss in March of 1938, Jews and Czechs were brutally persecuted. Italians now enjoyed an improvement of their status because of the various labour relations agreements between Hitler and Mussolini. The IASG remained intact in the Ostmark until the months prior to the invasion of the Soviet Union. On April 1, 1941, the Austrian Domestic Labour Protection Act was replaced by the Reich-German Ordinance Governing Foreign Workers (Verordnung über ausländische Arbeitnehmer), which had been introduced on 23 January 1933 by the last democratic government in the Weimar Republic, the centrist administration of General Kurt von Schleicher. This law would remain on the books in Austria until 1976.

Labour Union Migration Policy

The unique position that Austria found itself in during the spring of 1945 permitted it to re-establish a federal civilian government prior to the end of the Second World War. This highly fluid transition period from fascism to democracy presented the domestic labour movement with the long awaited opportunity to exert effective influence on the job referral process with respect to the local workforce. The historical goal of controlling the employment of immigrant and non-national labour had finally been achieved.

The Post-War Period (1945–61)

Vienna was liberated by the Red Army on 13 April 1945, almost a month before the end of hostilities (May 8). The Provisional Austrian Government was recognized by the Soviets on 27 April. On 1 May this new administration, including Christian Socials, Social Democrats and Communists, passed the Rechtsüberleitungsgesetz, Verfassungsgesetz vom 1. Mai, which re-established democratic rule in Austria. According to the policy of this constitutional founding Act, the only Reich-German laws that could remain in place were those of a non-fascist nature. In the field of minority policy, this rule seems to have been only partially applied. The Weimar Republic's Ordinance Governing Foreign Workers, being of democratic origin, remained in effect. It required employers, as well as employees, to apply for state permission before hiring. Thus foreigners who were turned down by the Arbeitsamt employment office could appeal to the labour referral board. After 10 years, immigrants were eligible for a *Befreiungsschein*. This work-permit waiver allowed them to work in any industry anywhere in Austria.

The Nazi Ausländerpolizeiverordnung (22 August 1938), which regulated police control of all immigrants from countries not allied with the Third Reich, was, however, obviously fascist in nature. It was, nevertheless, keep on the books. Finally, the clerical fascist Shop Steward Act (Werksgemeinschaftsgesetz) was integrated into the new Betriebsratsgesetz of 1947 in one important area. The policy, introduced by the authoritarian Vaterländische Front in 1934, barring mainly Jewish, Czech and Reich-German foreigners from running in plant council elections, remained in place. This aspect of the post-war immigration regime has proven particularly resistant to change.

Refugees and Volksdeutsche

> Ex-enemy nationals, such as Volksdeutsche, must be treated as part of the labor supply in the same manner as Austrians. [. . .] It was determined that since Austrians in that area must work or lose their food ration card rights, a food sanction must be imposed against those recalcitrant workers resident in the camp under U.S. authority. [. . .] The results of this action have not been fully reported, but initial indications are that the Volksdeutsche are recognizing that they are not in a privileged class of workers and not to be given privileges of United Nations' Displaced Persons.

This quote, taken from a report of the US Forces Austria, Labor Division (11 December 1945 Nat.Arch.Wash., Leg.& Dipl.Br.) illustrates the predicament Austria found itself in following the war. Although officially considered a victim of Nazi aggression, the federal and state authorities were nevertheless required to care for almost half a million ethnic German refugees and approximately 100,000 privileged United Nations' DPs and other foreign language refugees. During the second half of the 1940s, tens of thousands of Jews fled Poland and other Eastern Bloc countries because of the post-war pogroms. They were joined by an even larger number of refugees fleeing their countries after the communist takeovers and the establishment of people's republics. The Allied armies and the United Nations helped care for the non-German refugees. Members of this privileged group were permitted to work on the domestic economy if they so chose. The Volksdeutsche, on the other hand, were expected to carry their own weight. By 1946, the US Army had reached an agreement with the Zionist Brichah, permitting them to illegally transport eastern European Jews through Austria to Italy and on to Palestine. The Austrians were forced to comply with this policy. The Russian occupation forces, on the other hand, expected the Austrian police to help round-up and deport all east bloc refugees entering their zone from Hungary and Czechoslovakia. The Austrians cooperated under duress. Finally, the British permitted Yugoslav refugees to freely enter their zone from the south and expected the Austrians to care for them. Austria suffered from a labour shortage after the war because of the large percentage of the male population either killed, missing in action or prisoners of war. Many of the Volksdeutsche, foreign language DPs and Eastern Bloc refugees were, however, skilled labourers and artisans and were thus able to compete with the domestic population for the relatively well-paying jobs in heavy industry and the trades (Stanek 1985). As was the case after the First World War, the trade unions considered cheap foreign labour a threat to their newly won political power and demanded measures that would enable them to reduce immigrant employment to a minimum.

Labour Union Clout. Between the liberation of Austria in 1945 and the beginning of mass immigration in 1961, the newly formed and politically unified ÖGB was able to both lever and pressure the government to permit it to dominate migration policy development. Together, the Social Democrats and the Communists had received over 50 per cent of the popular vote in the first parliamentary elections in November of 1945. The SPÖ subsequently formed a grand coalition with the conservative ÖVP, emphasizing that it was the only guarantee that Austria would not follow the example of Hungary and Czechoslovakia in the direction of forming a popular front government. The SPÖ secured the leadership of the Sozialministerium and Innenministerium – both vital for control of migration – and, with the exception of a brief four-year period in the 1970s, has held on to them ever since. Finally, by undermining the massive and highly explosive leftist-led general strike of 1950, the Social Democratic faction within the ÖGB was able to break Communist resistance to the Marshall Plan. By the mid 1950s European recovery began improving working-class living standards, thus ostensibly proving the Social Democrats right.

The ÖGB faced two major challenges to its control of foreigner employment during the occupation period: the presence of hundreds of thousands of refugees in a country with a population of 7 million and the fact that the Weimar Ordinance Governing Foreign Workers of 1933 had eliminated trade union parity. An ordinance introduced on 26 April 1946 reinstituted the pre-World War Two parity enjoyed by the Freie Gewerkschaften. On 20 June 1951, a further ordinance expanded this influence, giving the ÖGB the right to veto the labour referral decisions of the Arbeitsämter and to exert decisive influence within the Sozialministerium. Along with these decision-making powers, an ordinance introduced on 9 January 1948 undermined the position of non-nationals. Now, employers alone were required to apply for permits to fill job openings with immigrant workers. They alone could appeal against a negative Arbeitsamt decision. Foreign workers were reduced to their commodity value and had no social rights whatsoever. This new ruling gave the trade unions the power to veto applications to employ the 300,000 Volksdeutsche remaining in Austria. This generally highly skilled minority was relegated to the secondary job market and forced to take unskilled industrial and agricultural positions until foreign protest – mainly from the World Council of Churches and other humanitarian organizations – forced Austria to integrate the Volksdeutsche population in the early 1950s (Stanek 1985; Wollner 1996).

The Quota System. The first major wave of immigration to Austria took place after the Russian pullout in 1955. Tens of thousands of refugees, mainly from Hungary and Yugoslavia, flooded Austria, once word spread that the Austrian border patrols would no longer send them back if apprehended. Whereas the crackdown in the Eastern Bloc countries after the uprising in Hungary in 1956 reduced immigration from these countries to a trickle, Yugoslav migration continued to increase. According to a 1957 report contained in the files of the International Organization for Migration in Geneva (IOM) for Yugoslavia, the term 'economic refugee' was introduced at this time.

> It appears that the Yugoslav Government is well aware of the fact that many thousands of Yugoslavs are leaving the country illegally for a neighbouring country in order to seek resettlement opportunities abroad. They do not consider these people as political refugees but as economic refugees.

By 1961 Yugoslavia indicated that is was prepared to drop its opposition to guest-worker emigration to the West. According to reports in the 'Liaison with Govt. Yugoslavia' collections of its archives (1957) 'the export of some manpower, [...] is presently prevented [...] by the fears of adverse political repercussions from the other communist countries.' In the same collection Yugoslav Vice-president Rankowitsch is quoted as stating in the party publication, *Politoca* (9 July 1961):

> Until now the Yugoslav authorities and trade unions showed a negative attitude towards such moves, but it seems that even in this field a new attitude is beginning. A relaxation of the current practice would be of advantage to both sides: the shortage of labor in the Western European countries could be alleviated, on the other hand many Yugoslavs could obtain technical skills which ultimately would benefit their country as a whole. As in this case the host country as well as Yugoslavia would have an equal interest to make the stay of the Yugoslav laborers abroad only a temporary one, it should be possible to find a suitable ruling amicably.

The year 1961 is also the year in which the ÖGB one-sidedly introduced the guest-worker system to Austria. Social partner negotiations on immigration strategy had stagnated during the late 1950s. By 1960 the ÖBG president, Franz Olah – who would later become Minister of the Interior – had determined to go it alone and thus force the hand of the employers' organizations. By simply announcing that the trade unions would boycott the central labour referral board meetings until a specified quota of foreign workers was filled and then veto all further immigrant employment, the

ÖGB introduced a *de facto* quota system in the buildings trades and tourism industry in the spring of 1961. In a subsequent meeting headed by Olah and the president of the Austrian Chamber of Commerce, Julius Raab – who had recently retired from his position as federal chancellor in the fall of 1961, the Raab-Olah-Abkommen was hammered out. This agreement between the leaders of big labour and big business informally transferred all decision-making in the fields of economic and social policy from the parliament to the Paritätische Kommission. This informal parity board had no legal basis and had originally been organized in 1957, under the sponsorship of the ÖVP-SPÖ grand coalition, in order to co-ordinate wages and prices on an annual basis. The Raab-Olah-Abkommen also contained an agreement by which the social partners would agree annually on guest-worker quotas. (Farnleitner 1977: 66). When the international recession became evident in 1973, the ÖGB simply reduced the quota. Within 10 years, the guest-worker population was thus reduced by almost half (Matuschek 1985; Wollner 1996).

Europeanization of Austrian Migration Policy

The recruiting system set up by the social partners in 1961 remained in place until 1976. With the passing of the Ausländerbeschäftigungsgesetz (Foreigners Employment Act) in 1975 and its implementation in the following year, the Weimar Republic's Ordinance Governing Foreign Workers and its adaptation through the Paritätische Kommission were finally replaced with an Austrian law which integrated social partnership parity, the quota recruitment system, strict foreigner employment ceilings, and the ÖGB's right to veto all employment above and beyond the annual quotas at will. This regime, however, proved to be ineffective. As soon as it became clear that the ÖGB planned to reduce sharply guest-worker employment, those foreign workers who were permitted to stay attempted to consolidate their situation in Austria. Thus, although the number of guest workers was sharply forced down prior to the fall of the Berlin Wall, the number of aliens living in Austria actually increased from 176,773 in 1971 and 291,448 in 1981 to an average of 387,183 in 1989. Significantly, the guest-worker rotation system had proven a success in the labour market sphere, but a failure when seen in a broader socio-political perspective. As a reaction to this situation, the Ausländerbeschäftigungsgesetz was amended in 1988 and 1990, reintroducing the Befreiungsschein waiver system. Foreigners who had worked in Austria for a number of years thus received a work permit (Arbeitserlaubnis), which freed them from dependency on their employers and permitted them to appeal in cases where their permit was not renewed by the Arbeitsamt referral service (Davy and /Gächter 1993/2).

The economic boom that followed the reunification of Central Europe led the ÖGB to permit a speedy enlargement of the annual employment quotas. Legal employment, sanctioned by the social partners, increased from 167,400 (5.8 per cent of total employment) in 1989 to 273,900 (9 per cent) in 1992. The number of foreign residents jumped from 387,200 to 623,000 in the same period. In 1992 the government completed a legislative reform package that completely revolutionized the guest-worker system. This regime of encouraging migration while radically curtailing immigrants' rights is part-and-parcel of Austria's active labor market policy. Following the enactment of these immigration, employment and asylum laws in 1992 and 1993, the size of the guest-worker population and foreign resident population was permitted to continue to increase and peaked in 1996 with 300,400 (9.9 per cent) and 728,200 respectively (Sopemi 1997).

A European Role Model?

Responding to a critical portrayal of Austrian immigration policy in the Social Democratic *Journal for International Policy – International* – in 1991, the Deputy to the Sozialminister (SPÖ) for Refugee Affairs, Manfred Matzka, wrote in the same magazine in 1992:

> Austrian immigration policy is an international role model (international Schule machen), and particularly in Germany, but also in other European states, it is seen in a very positive light. In Germany and Switzerland, for example, immigration policy reform measures are currently being debated that totally reflect Austrian measures such as the Asylum Reform Act and the proposed Residence Act (Niederlassungsgesetz). [. . .] Asylum debate in the Federal Republic of Germany is only now entering the phase that Austria successfully overcame more than half a year ago. Various positions have been presented, but [in Germany – E.S.] one can not speak of partisan consensus, let alone a parliamentary majority for an amendment of asylum policy. [. . .] Visionary models, such as Austria's proposed Niederlassungsgesetz, are not even on the horizon in the majority of European states.

Matzka's portrayal of Austrian policy appears indeed to be correct. Integrated into the Schengen process as an informal observer from 1985 onward, the Social Democratic Ministries of the Interior and Social Affairs, as well as the state-sponsored Chamber of Labour and the ÖGB were able speedily to implement the security target goals of this secretive organization. Labour union hegemony in the sphere of immigration policy and an almost complete lack of internal opposition within the SPÖ permitted the Austrian government to introduce a severely restrictive minority and immigration policy while at the same time allowing foreign employment to rapidly rise. This development is unique within the European Union.

Forced Complementarity

> The unstated assumption (of this study, E.S.) might be thought to have been that trade union influence would be a force for more positive policies towards migrant workers. The final example of Austria shows that, to the contrary, the consequence of the formal incorporation of a powerful trade union federation into the political process can be the bolstering of exclusionary policies which directly contribute to the exploitation of and discrimination against foreign workers. (Wrench 1996: 118)

In conclusion, an attempt will be made to demonstrate that the exploitation and discrimination which the EU Commission's Dublin Foundation attributes in part to the ÖGB's status within the Austrian political élite in the quotation taken from the study *Combating Racism at the Workplace* (Wrench 1996: 118), is indeed a product of the *Sozialpartnerschaft* system and not primarily the result of ethnically motivated nationalism or the orchestrated campaign of the radical right. Traditional wisdom and circumstantial and anecdotal evidence have led many researchers to conclude that the Austrian crackdown on asylum abuse, illegal immigration as well as the severe limitation of the rights of the immigrant minority communities is in some way a product of the reunification of Central Europe, the xenophobic reaction to this radical liberalization of migration and the ensuing nativist campaign introduced by Jörg Haider's FPÖ. According to this scenario, the grand coalition and social partners merely reacted to international developments and domestic pressure exerted by the Freedom Party and the daily tabloids allied with it.

This portrayal of events seems to appeal to critics, journalist and academics in inverse ratio to their knowledge of the subject. Chronologically, Haider's anti-foreigner campaign was initiated immediately after Matzka's interpretation of migration policy was published. More significantly, the conceptualization of the Austrian reform process was a direct result of negotiations with the Schengen states prior to the fall of the Berlin Wall. Schengen's second phase, the Schengen Implementing Agreement (Woltjer 1990), was postponed in 1989 by the end of the Cold War and not caused by it. Haider's Austria First (Österreich Zuerst) referendum –

which is traditionally considered the beginning of blatant nativism and racist violence in Austria – took place between 25 January to 1 February of 1993. Support for it was much lower than the FPÖ had expected. Finally, immigration actually picked up again after the anti-foreigner referendum. The guest-worker population increased 21.1 per cent in 1991, 6.7 per cent in 1992, 0.8 per cent in 1993, 5.4 per cent in 1994 and 3.2 per cent in 1995. It plateaued in 1996 – with an absolute increase of 100 workers or 0 per cent – three years after the referendum. The only area in which the Ausländergesetze foreigner legal reform package of 1992/1993 actually had significant numerical effect was in combating the abuse of asylum status to circumvent the guest-worker regulations. Statistically speaking, applications for refugee status began to pick up rapidly in the late 1970s after it became clear that this was the only quick method to obtain legal status in Austria, Germany and Switzerland. The Austrian Statistical Office reported massive increases in 1987, 1988 and 1989 and a sharp immediate drop off in 1993, after the new Asylum Act took effect (Sopemi 1997).

The forced complementarity concept, developed in the mid 1990s by the Viennese social scientist and Dublin Foundation correspondent for immigration and anti-discrimination policy, August Gächter, seems to offer a more appropriate explanation for the apparently contradictory development of Austrian migration policy. According to Gächter the ÖGB introduced a paradigm shift in the 1980s. Prior to this period, the trade unions and AK followed the Inländerprimat (domestic worker privilege) strategy described by Matuschek in 1985. Foreign labour was seen as a necessary evil that was tolerated or even encouraged in periods of economic expansion. Unemployment was then exported with the beginning of each recession. This classic rotation approach was abandoned after the ÖGB realized that by severely undermining the legal and economic status of guest workers, they could be forced to work at extremely low wages, simultaneously maintaining a comparatively low rate of unemployment. The result of this process has been, according to Gächter – whose statistics seem to prove him correct – a stabilization of Southern Slav and Turkish/Kurdish workers at the bottom of the income hierarchy, a high employment rate within these ethnic communities and excess revenues for the social welfare system. Foreigners are not eligible for most welfare benefits, although they pay into the system in full (Gächter 1995; Biffl 1997).

Finally, readers not familiar with the Austrian situation may wonder why the immigrant communities have tolerated this situation for so long. Here again, Austria deviates from the Western European norm. The only major country of immigration with a post-Second World War immigration tradition remotely similar to Austria is the Federal Republic of Germany.

Both countries were the recipients of large numbers of *Volksdeutsche* refugees, eliminating the need to recruit foreign labour until the late 1950s. The Weimar Republic's Ordinance Governing Foreign Workers and the Nazi *Ausländerpolizeiverordnung* (22 August 1938) remained on the books in both countries following liberation in 1945. The German labour federation DGB and Austrian ÖGB were both dominated by the respective social democratic parties. Here the similarities end. The DGB was excluded from migration policy development by its conservative government. When mass migration began in the early 1960s the majority immigrant population in Germany came from Italy, an EU member state with a long tradition of trade union radicalism in the Diaspora. In Austria, during the same period, two thirds of all immigration came from Yugoslavia, a country that to a large extent had been an Austrian colony prior to World War One. The Belgrade government and Communist trade union federation cooperated closely with the Austrian government and Social Democratic dominated ÖGB, in an attempt to prevent the integration of the Yugoslav guest workers and thus ensure their return after a limited time period. Lastly, as the international recession began to effect both Germany and Austria, both trade union federations simultaneously demanded an immigration moratorium. In Germany the government passed an ordinance stopping all foreign labour recruitment. In Austria this step was taken by the ÖGB by using its influence within the Paritätische Kommission. As opposed to the DGB, the Austrian trade unions had structurally insulated themselves against pressure from the Yugoslav and Turkish/Kurdish rank-and-file. Reintroducing the clerical fascist policy of barring foreigners from active participation in shop steward elections meant that most Slavs and Turks have no formal access to the ÖGB leadership and thus no influence on the decision-making process within the Paritätische Kommission.

Austrian Exceptionalism?

In conclusion, the Austrian experience forces the question whether the formal incorporation of a powerful trade union federation into the process of migration and minority policy making is indeed a significant cause of racism and ethnically motivated exploitation or merely a substantiating circumstance. Put more precisely, are the trade unions, the Chamber of Labour and the federal ministries and state and local governments dominated by the Social Democrats, an integral part of a broader racist phenomenon or are they – as is the case in many neighbouring countries – merely unwilling effectively to combat a problem that originates from rightist and neo-Nazi political circles, particularly unscrupulous employers and the traditions of German nationalism and anti-Semitism that pre-date the founding of the Austrian Republic in 1918?

According to domestic and EU-wide comparative studies (Cinar 1995; Wrench 1996), Austria now has the worst minorities rights record of all traditional countries of immigration within the Union. Discrimination and exploitation of ethnic minorities in Austria is driven by social policy and is not primarily nationalist in nature. To again quote the EU Commission's Dublin Foundation report on workplace racism (Wrench 1996: 72):

> Indeed, the legal restrictions governing immigrants in relation to residence, employment and works councils are so severe that it might be argued that legislation against informal discrimination would be of little value until the system of legal discrimination had been dismantled. Foreign workers are legally pressured to accept jobs with poor working conditions, and remain compliant within them. In the words of the Austrian report [from Gächter – E.S.], 'the legal regime in Austria produces racism instead of combating it'.

Despite the highly restrictive policies of the labour organizations – ÖGB/AK – and the SPÖ dominated Ministries of the Interior and of Social Affairs and the traditional bastion of Social Democracy, the SPÖ city hall in the national capital city of Vienna, Jörg Haider's ultra-rightist Freedom Party, FPÖ, has continuously been able to exploit nativist and racist sentiment and receive well over 20 per cent of the vote in local, state and national elections. Non-EU nationals are over-represented in the construction, tourist and private service industries. Companies in these sectors have definitely profited from the current legal regime in Austria with respect to Southern Slav, Albanian, Roma, Turkish and Kurdish minorities. The fact that guest workers are concentrated in the small and medium size business sector has enabled a large number of these traditionally low-wage employers to avoid costly investments in productivity improvement that have meant ruin for their competition in other countries. Finally, anti-Semitism and (Austrian) national chauvinism, which largely replaced traditional German nationalism following the Second World War, are as much a problem in Austria as they are in neighbouring states.

Specifically Austrian in nature is the interface of trade union initiated discrimination against non-EU labour and the unwillingness or inability of the majority of this population group – the southern Slavs, Albanians and Roma from ex-Yugoslavia – to resist. Both phenomena are products of the undemocratic and exploitative policies of the social democratic and communist parties and the trade union federations in the countries of emigration and immigration. Austria appears to demonstrate that the incorporation of powerful labour organizations within the dominant élites of a capitalist society can have side effects that are as negative as those of the defunct communist model. Racist exploitation and discrimination in Austria is not a product of social democracy, but social democrats clearly participate in it.

Bibliography

Franz Aggermann (1927), 'Die Arbeitsverhältnisse im Bergbau', in: Ferdinand Hanusch and Emanuel Adler, *Die Regelung der Arbeitsverhältnisse im Kriege*, Wien/New Haven, S. 83–94.

Gudrun Biffl et al (1997), *Ökonomische und strukturelle Aspekte der Ausländerbeschäftigung in Österreich*, WIFO Studie 97/063/S/3792, Vienna.

Otto Bauer (1909), Der Weg zur Macht', in: *Der Kampf*, vol. 2, Vienna, pp. 337–344.

John W. Boyer (1988), Austrian Catholics and the World, Facing Political Turmoil in the Early Twentieth Century, in: Solomon Wank, et al (ed), The Mirror of History, Essays in Honor of Fritz Fellner, Santa Barbara, CA/USA, pp.315–343.

Dilek Cinar et al (1995), *Integrationsindex, Zur rechtlichen Integration von Ausländern in ausgewählten europäischen Ländern*, Institute for Advanced Studies (IHS), Political Science Series, no. 25, Vienna.

Ulrike Davy & August Gächter (1993/2), Zuwanderungsrecht und Zuwanderungspolitik in Österreich, Teil 2, in: Journal für Rechtspolitik, Jg. 1, Heft 4, Wien, S.257–281..

Knuth Dohse (1981), *Ausländische Arbeiter und bürgerlicher Staat, Genese und Funktion von staatlicher Ausländerpolitik und Ausländerrecht, Vom Kaiserreich bis zur Bundesrepublik Deutschland*, Königstein/Ts.

(Einwanderung/ÖStA, 1922), Bundesministerium für soziale Verwaltung/ SozPol, Zl. 13699, Sammelmappe, GZ: 21391, Kt. 61, Verhinderung der Einwanderung fremdländischer Arbeiter nach Österreich: Austrian State Archives, Ministry of Social Affairs Collection.

Johann Farnleitner (1977), Die Paritätische Kommission, Institution und Verfahren, second revised printing, Eisenstadt.

Wilhelm Filla (1981), *Zwischen Integration und Klassenkampf, Sozialgeschichte der betrieblichen Mitbestimmung in Österreich*, Vienna.

Brigitte Fuchs (1993), 'Nationale Märkte, internationale Migrationen und internationale Sozialdemokratie: zur 'Frage der Ein- und Auswanderung' zur Zeit der Ersten und Zweiten Internationale (1864–1918)', unpublished masters thesis, University of Vienna.

August Gächter (1995), 'Forced complementarity, the attempt to protect native Austrian workers from immigrants', in: *new community*, vol. 21, no. 3, Oxford, pp. 379–398.

Roswitha Helga Gatterbauer (1975), 'Arbeitseinsatz und Behandlung der Kriegsgefangenen in der Ostmark während des Zweiten Weltkrieges', unpublished doctoral thesis, University of Salzburg

Monika Glettler (1985), 'The Acculturation of the Czechs in Vienna', in: Dirk Hoeder (ed), *Labor Migration in the Atlantic Economies, The European and North American Working Classes During the Period of Industrial Revolution*, Westport/London, pp. 297–320

Margarete Grandner (1995), 'Staatsbürger und Ausländer, Zum Umgang Österreichs mit den jüdischen Flüchtlingen nach 1918', in: Gernot Heiss and Oliver Rathkolb (Hg.), *Asylland wider Willen, Flüchtlinge in Österreich im europäischen Kontext seit 1914*, Vienna, S. 60–85

Ulrich Herbert (1985), *Fremdarbeiter, Politik und Praxis des 'Ausländer-Einsatzes' in der Kriegswirtschaft des Dritten Reichs*, Bonn.

Baetrix Hoffmann-Holter (1995/2), 'Jüdische Kriegflüchtlinge in Wien', in: Gernot Heiss and Oliver Rathkolb (Hg.), *Asylland wider Willen, Flüchtlinge in Österreich im europäischen Kontext seit 1914*, Vienna, S. 45–59.

(Italiener/ÖStA, 1921), Bundesministerium für soziale Verwaltung/SozPol, Zl. 13699, Sammelmappe, GZ: 27788, Kt. 61, reichsitalienische Arbeiter in Salzburg: Austrian State Archives, Ministry of Social Affairs Collection.

Michael John and Albert Lichtblau (eds) (1990), *Schmelztiegel Wien, Einst und Jetzt, Zur Geschichte und Gegenwart von Zuwanderung und Minderheiten*, Vienna.

Victor Mataja (1898), *Die Arbeitsvermittlung in Östereich*, Vienna.

Bernhard Mussak (1995), 'Staatsbürgerrecht und Optionsfrage in der Republik (Deutsch-) Österreich zwischen 1918 und 1925', unpublished doctoral thesis, Vienna.

Helga Matuschek (1985), Ausländerpolitik in Österreich 1962–1985, Der Kampf um und gegen die ausländische Arbeitskräfte, in: Journal für Sozialforschung, vol. 25, no. 2, Wien, pp. 158–198.

Manfred Matzka (1992), Betrifft: Ausländerpolitik zwischen GUS und EWR, von Eugene Sensenig, in: *International*, Zeitschrift für internationale Politik, no. 1, Vienna, pp. 43

Normalien-Sammlung für den politischen Verwaltungsdienst (1901, 1902, 1903, 1907, 1912), vol. 1–5, Vienna.
Monika Pelz (1994), 'Ausländerbeschränkungen Österreichs in der Zwischenkriegszeit', unpublished masters thesis, University of Salzburg.
Oscar Pollak (1919), 'Die Stellung der Arbeiterräte zur Parteiorganisation', in: *Der Kampf*, vol. 12, pp.637–642.
Johann Vesque von Püttlingen (1842), *Die gesetzliche Behandlung der Ausländer in Österreich nach den daselbst gültigen Civilrechts=, Straf=, Commerzial=, Militär= und Polizei=Normen, nebst einer einleitenden Abhandlung über die österreichische Staatsbürgerschaft*, Vienna.
Franc Rozman (1993), 'Etbin Kristan und seine Idee der 'Personalautonomie', in Helmut Konrad (ed), *Arbeiterbewegung und Nationale Frage in den Nachfolgerstaaten der Habsburgermonarchie*, Vienna, pp. 97–110.
Karl Schmidt (1991), Geschichte der Arbeitsmarktverwaltung Österreichs von ihren Anfängen an, Salzburg.
Eugene Sensenig (1998), 'Ein vielfach unentbehrliches Betriebsmittel, Kriegsgefangene und die Halleiner Salinenarbeiter im Krieg', in:, Ulrike Kammerhofer (ed), *Alltag und Identität der Dürrnberger Bergleute und Halleiner Salinenarbeiter in Geschichte und Gegenwart Salzburg*, forthcoming.
Sopemi (1997), Report on Labour Migration, Austria 1996/97, WIFO Studie 97/229/1/27291, Vienna.
Eduard Stanek (1985), Verfolgt, verjagt, vertrieben, Flüchtinge in Österreich von 1945–1984, Vienna.
Emmerich Talos (1981), *Staatliche Sozialpolitik in Österreich, Rekonstruktion und Analyse*, Vienna.
'Volkszählung vom 31. Dezember 1910, Die Ergebnisse der'(1912), in: *Neue Folge Österreichische Statistik*, vol. 1, no. 1, Vienna.
Josef Weidenholzer (1985), *Der sorgende Staat, Zur Entwicklung der Sozialpolitik von Joseph II. bis Ferdinand Hanusch*, Vienna.
Eveline Wollner (1996), Auf dem Weg zur Sozialpartnerschaftlich regulierten Ausländerbeschäftigung in Österreich, die Reform der Ausländerbeschäftigung und der Anwerbung bis Ende der 1960er Jahre, unpublished masters thesis, University of Vienna.
Aleidus Woltjer (1990), Recent developments in Europe: the Schengen Implementing Agreement, Eugene Sensenig (ed), in: *Fortschrittliche Wissenschaft*, Vienna, pp. 14–20.
John Wrench (ed) (1996), *Preventing Racism at the Workplace, A report on 16 European countries*, Dublin.

–9–

Italy: Farewell to the 'Bel Paese'?

Agostino Petrillo

Introduction

This chapter sets out to provide a clear picture of the transformation of Italy from a country of emigration to one of immigration, surveying the development of this recent phenomenon, a transformation that continues to be felt today. In the first part a number of historical events that were decisive in starting this process are outlined, and the immigrants' situation is analysed from a quantitative sociological point of view, especially with regard to the labour market. In these first sections the usefulness of immigrants as a floating workforce, both in the official and underground economies is clarified, as are the difficulties they meet in settling in the country. The following sections illustrate the various social, political and ideological features of immigration into Italy, such as the instruments of control established by governments over the years, the welcome immigrants receive, and their situation with regard to law and housing. Towards the end of the chapter the reactions to their presence are considered, with reference in particular to the role of the media in feeding a growing prejudice and hostile public opinion towards immigrants, and also assessing the recent importance of the problem of policing the Italian border, an issue that has been taken up at both national and European levels.

Transformation from a Country of Emigration to One of Immigration: 1975–98

Italy has traditionally been considered a country of emigration, and indeed the image of the Italian emigrant has become somewhat of a cliché. The country's political and economic history, as well as its cultural heritage, have been deeply marked by the reality of emigration and the image of the emigrant. The Italian expatriate living in New York or Sydney, Buenos Aires or Stuttgart is a familiar character in the media, cinema and literature,

as is the relative returning home speaking Brooklyn Italo-American slang. The history of Italian emigration covers more than a century and is linked to the great international migratory cycles. About 26 million Italians left the country between 1876 and 1976.[1] Emigration abroad was an important tool in the hands of the Italian élite for the regulation of the internal labour market, and as a safety valve for social problems. It created a fall in the unemployment rate and also brought in a continuous flow of hard currency. Over such an extended time span Italian emigration illustrated a wide variety of trends and cultures. Its most recent peak period was between the 1950s and the 1970s after the Marshall Plan and the creation of the European Community (EC) when Italy, together with Spain, Greece and

Portugal, was the main supplier of labour in the last great period of European migration. In these years Italian emigration came mainly from the south. The defeats suffered by the southern masses in 1958–59 in the struggle for agrarian reform, coupled with unemployment, were the main reasons for the creation of a 'push effect', driving many young people to other European countries. The Italian South, 'il Mezzogiorno', was the main source of manpower until the early 1970s. The 'Mezzogiorno' exported its labourers to countries such as Germany, France and Belgium, but the emigration of these workers within Italy was also of the utmost importance to its economic 'boom'. In the years of rapid industrialization after the Second World War, millions of people from the south migrated to major manufacturing regions of the north – Piedmont, Lombardy and Liguria. In particular, they were drawn to the three cities of the 'industrial triangle', Turin, Milan and Genoa, to work in the big factories. By the early 60s this migratory flow became an exodus of biblical proportions that changed the social composition of entire neighbourhoods and cities, completely reshaping the human geography and the territorial balance of the country. This great internal migration involved about 20 million Italians between the years 1955 and 1970. No other European country has experienced such large-scale internal migration. For most these migrants the transfer was a permanent one. Turin became the largest 'southern' city after Naples and Palermo. This internal migration was to have enormous consequences, creating a totally new kind of factory worker in the north, who would become a protagonist in the fierce struggles of the 1960s and 1970s. This large-scale transfer was linked to many social problems; in particular, prejudice and racism against southern immigrants was widespread in the 'industrial triangle' and remained a serious problem for at least a decade.

This well-established image of Italy as a country of internal and outward migration prevented migratory movements *towards* Italy from being noticed at first. The transition to a country of immigration, which attracts immigrants from poorer nations, happened gradually and silently, starting in the second half of the 1970s. It was in 1975 that Italy first presented a positive migratory balance, with more people arriving than departing, as Table 9.1 illustrates.

After the 1973 oil crisis, when other European governments tried to halt immigration (see Table 9.1, and the chapters on France and Germany in this volume), in Italy circumstances were favourable to the arrival of immigrants from abroad and their settlement in the country. The 'open doors' policy practised by the Italian government in those years allowed immigrants to enter the country without a visa, simply as 'tourists'. Before

Table 9.1 Migratory balance in selected OECD countries 1950–1984 (thousands)

Period	*Canada*	*France*	*Germany*	*Italy*	*United States*
1950–54	599	169	1,123	–496	1,896
1955–59	523	791	1,626	–513	1,859
1960–64	179	1,469	1,689	–389	1,877
1965–69	521	504	219	–560	2,263
1970–74	448	477	1,388	–81	4,081
1975–79	244	186	387	83	4,675
1980–84	438	380	–7	364	2,816

that period there were only very small groups of immigrants in Italy: among these were small settlements of Somalis around Rome (a result of Italy's colonial experience) and Latin Americans fleeing the tragic political conflicts of the 'southern cone' (Chile, Argentina and Uruguay) in the 1970s. A small migratory enclave, which predated the subsequent, larger migratory flow, was that of Tunisians who began to settle in Sicily to work in the fishing industry during the late 1960s.[2]

The start of immigration towards Italy in the 1970s coincided with a severe economic crisis: industries had to regain a competitive edge in international markets and so a series of profound transformations of not only working conditions, but also collective bargaining and the structure of the labour market began, which rendered the production process more 'flexible'. To accomplish this goal, workers' militancy, a product of the long cycle of struggles in the late 1960s and early 1970s, had to be broken. Production was thoroughly reorganized, with several new features. The workforce in the largest industries was reduced by firing 'redundant' workers, and the payment of the minimum wage was avoided by transferring a large part of production to small enterprises as these were outside the control of the unions (companies with fewer than fifteen employees were not permitted union representation).

Migratory influxes into Italy were stimulated by restrictive policies in other countries, as well as the growth of demand in Italy for irregular or illegal work that was linked to the restructuring of production. In short, immigration to Italy became a major phenomenon when a stronger migratory push met the need, on the part of several industries, for underpaid manpower – 'flexible' because it was outside the protection of the law or the unions. The ideal subjects for this kind of work are undocumented immigrants, who have few rights and very little choice about pay or working conditions.

Major immigration reached Italy later than other European countries and acquired peculiar features, coming as it did in a phase of industrial reorganization – decentralizing of production and expansion of the labour market in the direction of irregular, 'black' or part-time work (a sector that employed relatively high numbers of immigrants). In those years the 'dualization' of the labour market began, its division into a regular market, and a 'black' one, which was to become a growth-inducing feature of the next decade.[3] Voices in the business world and the press began to harp on the wonders of this informal economy.

In this first phase (up to the end of the 1970s) only the more apparent or colourful aspects of immigration were noted, such as the arrival of non-European women to work as maids and domestic assistants.[4] Union members spoke at the time of a 'demand for servile labour' as the key to the phenomenon and focused their attention only on the problems of these women. Initially, these workers were largely 'regularized' (arriving through semi-official channels), were concentrated in a few large metropolitan areas, and numbered no more than one hundred thousand, but this was only the tip of the iceberg. By the end of the decade at least 300,000 illegal immigrants were already working in small or medium-sized firms or in other service sectors – mostly restoration – with extremely skewed contracts or with none whatsoever. In 1979 a survey of several big cities brought to light the structure of the imported workforce in the Italian economy, how it compensated for the imbalance of domestic supply, occupying jobs which no native wanted to do.[5]

During the 1980s the immigrant presence in Italy grew slowly, and was principally located in a few big urban areas. Halfway through the decade Rome was already displaying the features of other European capitals, with the metropolis exercising a strong attraction and the immigrants' presence becoming more visible. In Milan the process was initially slower. Meanwhile, the immigrant presence in the smaller urban areas or small cities remained so small as to be irrelevant. Even in port cities like Genoa and Naples, which are directly linked to the North African coast by regular sea routes, there was no exceptional growth in the presence of immigrants.[6]

Only at the end of the 1980s did the media and public opinion realize that Italy had become a country of immigration (even if this was not yet numerically substantial). As immigration grew and diversified, its distinctive features became clearer. In the previous decade there had been ambiguities in the patterns of migration, making it possible to consider Italy as a place of passage, as a trampoline[7] for temporary immigrants on their way elsewhere. Now, however, it had clearly become a country of permanent residence. Italy had become a substitute for other countries that were now more difficult to enter. Its own appeal had also risen, chiefly due to the possibility of finding 'any kind of work whatsoever' following the opening up of its labour market. The reality of unemployment among natives – in the south as high as 20 per cent of the active workforce – had no bearing on the migratory flow, because of the ongoing balkanization of the labour market, fragmented into a series of enclaves between which there was little competition.

Economic growth in the 1980s was gradual but steady. Immigration centred on those places which needed workers, both in the traditional, 'Fordist' factories demanding unskilled labour, and in the new industrial districts in the north-eastern and central regions. Here, in these areas with 'diffuse economies',[8] the growth of medium and small-sized firms was at the heart of the country's economic recovery. In the south the immigrant presence was chiefly linked to seasonal, low-paid work in the field of agriculture.[9] These were also the years in which pedlars began to work the tourist areas of both the Adriatic and the Tirrenian seas, especially during the summer months. These vendors walked the beaches, selling anything from cassettes to coconuts and they became known by their familiar call *vuccumprà* (from the italian *vuoi comprare*? 'do you wanna buy?'). Later an urban street-vending scene developed, which was not dependent on the summer season. Imported from Africa, and in particular from Senegal where it is practised without restrictions, this practice of 'direct sales' is used by immigrants as a first source of income in the orientation period following their arrival in the country. It also acts as an additional income in lean times when more secure jobs, such as those in factories or in construction, are scarce. Between the late 1980s and the early 1990s an estimated 16 per cent of immigrants made a living by selling things on the streets, 20 per cent of whom worked in the cities.[10] These percentages fell quickly in the following years. Immigrants often have to switch between the roles of street vendor and factory worker,[11] pulled toward the 'safe' job when production is on the upswing and pushed back to the street during contractions.

It was however in the years 1988–90, while the Italian economy was particularly successful, that immigrant manpower was most intensively employed. On the one hand, it provided Italy with a flexible labour force at a time when flexibility was very important. On the other hand it responded to demand for permanent jobs to cover the negative demographic balance (population gap) in the northern regions (Italy has the lowest birth rate in the world[12]). The demand for illegal work emphasized the features already described, which had developed in the previous decades.[13]

With the attempt to close the national borders after the regularization of 1990–91, the number of illegal immigrants increased. These were both immigrants drawn to Italy by the regularization decree but who arrived too late, and 'illegal' immigrants who entered Italy in the following years, after the closing of the borders. During the recession of 1992–93 immigrants were badly hit, some of them losing their jobs and having to return to their own countries. However, for others illegality was perceived as an advantage, being preferable to a permanent job, particularly as the illegal immigrant had greater opportunities on the 'black' labour market. This is the reason for the apparent stabilization and even decrease of the immigrant presence around 1994, when for the first time the number of immigrants with a legal permit to stay seemed to shrink. This apparent reduction was the result of the fluctuating economic trends and the restrictive policies carried out by various governments in the first half of the 1990s. Despite their different political allegiances, these all seemed to follow a similar immigration policy: closing the borders to allow the creation of a large pool of illegal immigrants. This was clearly useful to those sectors which were most affected by fluctuations in market demand.

However, for subsequent years official figures contradicted the trend toward a decrease in the immigrant presence, showing instead a rise, due not only to new arrivals but also to a new regularization decree in 1996. This decree allowed for the emergence of a large number of illegal immigrants from the underground labour market, albeit for a limited time span only. The increase in the 1990–97 period is largely due to the 1996 regularization. In this sense the economic trend of the first half of the 1990s is faithfully mirrored in the official regularization numbers.

Foreigners in Italy: Numbers and Country of Origin

There is some confusion over the figures regarding the immigrant presence on Italian soil.[14] These are provided by the Ministry of the Interior, and they comprise all foreigners residing in Italy, from rich and poor nations alike: but they chiefly consider those immigrants who were the subjects of the various regularizations since 1986.[15] The information from the end of 1997 takes the 1996 regularization into account, and puts the number at 1,200,000 legally registered individuals, plus an estimated 250,000–300,000 illegal or 'underground' people – no more than 25 per cent of the official figures even by the largest estimate. The total foreign presence, based on the figures for work permits granted, represents just over 2 per cent of the Italian population, the latter being just below 58 million. As regards the nationalities on Italian soil, the Moroccans are the most

Table 9.2 Quantitative variations of work permits 1990–97

Year	*Permits*
1990	781,138
1991	862,977
1992	923,625
1993	987,405
1994	922,706
1995	991,419
1996	1,095,622
1997	1,240,721
1996–90	+40,3%
1997–90	+58,8%

Source: Ministry of the Interior

numerous (130,000 in total), followed by the Albanians (rapid growth in numbers has brought the figure to 80,000), then migrants from the former Yugoslavia, the Philippines, Tunisia, Senegal and Rumania.[16] However it is clear that, on this dimension, Italy is far behind many other European countries.

These figures regarding foreign residents must be integrated with other data: 168,125 are citizens of the European Community, with a further 100,131 coming from other 'developed' nations. Among the others, 292,656 are from Eastern Europe and 679,806 are from the southern hemisphere. Moreover, there is a growing female presence, due to reunion of families and the increasing demand for domestic helpers for the elderly. At the end of 1997 there were 562,470 women (98,897 from the European Union), representing 45.5 per cent of the total.[17]

Territorial Distribution and Work Patterns of Immigrants

The distribution of immigrants varies immensely from region to region in terms of the number of immigrants, the countries of origin and their occupations. Such irregular distribution is closely tied to the territorial imbalances that are characteristic of Italy today, as well as to the deep differentiations inherent in a highly segmented job market and to reduced mobility in the workforce.[18] It is precisely the migrants' high mobility within Italy – much higher than that of natives – that underlies an ever-changing distribution, as highlighted by the trend, especially in recent years, of migration to the north where job opportunities are greater.

Table 9.3 Summary of foreigners resident in Italy by country of origin (first 20) at the end of 1997

Country	*Number*
Morocco	131,406
Albania	83,807
Philippines	61,285
USA	59,572
Tunisia	48,909
Ex-Yugoslavia	44,370
Germany	40,079
Rumania	38,138
China	37,838
Senegal	34,831
Poland	31,329
France	28,333
Sri Lanka	28,162
Britain	26,271
Egypt	26,171
Peru	24,362
Brazil	23,008
India	22,620
Croatia	20,464
Switzerland	18,611
First 20 countries	830,086
Total	1,240,721

Source: Caritas 1998

Nonetheless, I will attempt to divide the country into three major areas in order to clarify the picture.[19] The first area of interest is the southern one, which includes all regions from Sicily to Lazio. Here the immigrants find highly intensive work mainly in the agricultural industry, particularly in horticulture and in the seasonal harvesting of agricultural products.[20]

It has been reported that in the southern regions the local job markets are highly segmented. As a matter of fact, the lack of a system of regulation in this market makes illegality and clandestine immigration, as opposed to having a job or an income, an 'almost normal' condition.[21] It is not surprising, then, that in such regions, where industrial jobs are scarce, the percentage of illegal immigrants is higher than where immigrant work is largely regulated.[22]

Table 9.4 Female immigrants as proportion of the total (statistics 1996)

Female foreigners	44,7
Senegal	5
Pakistan	7,7
Algeria	10,8
Tunisia	16
Egypt	17,7
Morocco	20
Albania	27,7
Ghana	34,6
ex-Yougo	35,5
Iran	36,4
India	38
Sri-Lanka	38,7
China	43
Nigeria	51,7
Rumania	55,2
Argentina	55
Chile	59
Poland	66
Somalia	66,2
Philippines	67,3
Peru	70
Brazil	70,8
Ethiopia	71
Colombia	74

Source: Ministry of the Interior

The situation in central Italy is highly variegated. On one hand there is a concentration of people around Rome, a magnet for many migrants. In fact, according to recent data, more than 210,000 immigrants live there. In this area jobs are typically related to household and restoration work. A further characteristic of the city is the great variety of nationalities represented there.[23]

There are also regional instances where a group of small businesses employs an increasing number of immigrants. The small business that 'cannot find the skilled labour in the local workforce necessary to support its expansion process and its permanent restructuring'[24] tends to attract within its orbit immigrants which were previously employed in seasonal and street-trading activities, thus transforming the 'birds of passage' into workers for the leather, marble and shipbuilding industries. In Tuscany an entrepreneurial spirit among immigrants is in evidence amongst 'ethnic businesses', mainly tied to leather processing and largely carried out by the Chinese community, and which have frequently caused scandals due to exploitation and forced labour.[25]

In the northern regions the picture of immigrant employment is also highly varied. In the whole of the north-eastern part of Italy stable forms of employment prevail, due to the fact that in the more industrialized areas of the country the presence of immigrants is needed to fill positions that are available because of the negative demographic trend. Statistics have shown that 'the reserves of the indigenous workforce are seemingly becoming exhausted'[26] in the north-central job markets, not only because of the demographic trend but also due to a higher educational level among young people. Recent research on immigration into Emilia-Romagna has shown how foreigners in these areas are by no means limited to work that is considered inferior by the native workforce. Neither are they solely employed with pay and working conditions which would be unacceptable to Italian workers. Rather, they may fill significant gaps in the job market and are employed in traditional factories carrying out blue-collar functions. As a matter of fact, the immigrant employment rate in this region is extremely high, and the percentages of illegal and unemployed migrants is very low.[27] Furthermore, in Veneto and Lombardy a large number of immigrants work in firms of varying sizes, from the small and very small to the medium large, even though their pay and working conditions are often not equal to those enjoyed by natives. In these regions, where economic development has been booming since the late 1970s, 'atypical' modes of working are becoming increasingly common. These new types of contracts are representative of the shape the post-Fordist 'new work' is taking in Italy, and include self-employment contracts, compulsory part-time contracts, and special contracts in derogation of existing laws. The pace of work and the hours, as well as the hygiene and environmental conditions, and the level of risk, vary enormously from situation to situation. In some cases contractual differentiation has even been introduced, with the employer often resorting to the regulations in force in the immigrants' country of origin in order to stipulate their contracts.

The general picture of immigrant labour in Italy, beyond the regional differences seen above, is one of a workforce that is not only mobile and 'flexible' but is also subject to real discrimination and segregation on the job market, a discrimination that varies according to the structure of the

Table 9.5 Distribution of Foreigners per Region

Region	*Foreigners 1997*	*Foreigners 1996*	*% of region 1997*
Val d'Aosta	3,352	2,976	0,3
Piedmont	81,806	72,183	6,6
Lombardy	250,400	213,747	20,2
Liguria	31,968	28,786	2,6
Trentino	39,481	32,133	3,2
Veneto	100,634	87,971	8,1
Friuli	35,893	32,186	2,9
Emilia	93,208	82,212	7,5
NORTH	**636,742**	**552,194**	**51,3**
Tuscany	94,241	72,592	7,6
Umbria	25,244	20,433	2,0
Marche	26,339	22,074	2,1
Lazio	232,611	218,978	18,7
CENTRAL	**378,415**	**334,077**	**30,5**
Abruzzo	17,127	19,920	1,4
Molise	1,699	1,377	0,1
Campania	67,433	59,792	5,4
Puglia	33,066	28,825	2,7
Basilicata	2,625	2,564	0,2
Calabria	19,856	16,874	1,6
SOUTH	**141,833**	**129,322**	**11,4**
Siciliy	71,929	68,854	5,8
Sardinia	11,802	11,175	1,0
ISLANDS	**83,731**	**80,029**	**6,7**

Source: Caritas data processing 1997 Ministy of the Interior

regional labour markets. Immigrants get the heaviest, most dangerous and wearing jobs, and the contracts and wages are significantly worse than those given to Italian workers for similar work.

Housing and Urban Life

Discrimination in the job market is closely linked to segregation and discrimination in housing. Housing, in fact, is one of the most dramatic aspects of the immigrant's present situation in Italy. There has been no sign of a housing policy for immigrants. The logic of a disposable work-force, one that may be dismissed when no longer economically necessary, coupled with the perception that immigrants are somehow always 'transient', has created an ambiguous situation, characterized by a wait-and-see attitude on the part of local administrations and by a lack of legislative provisions on the part of governments. One need only consider that the immigration centres of 'first acceptance' were only established with a decree issued at the end of 1990, and that financial support for these centres was quickly exhausted in many provinces and never renewed. A substantial part of immigrants' needs, such as lodging and socio-medical assistance, has been partially satisfied by the voluntary sector alone, both Catholic and secular. Until recently it was not possible for immigrants to be registered on council house waiting lists. In many areas this situation still exists. Hence, a dual housing market began to emerge, one for Italians and another for immigrants. The latter is separate from the former, and is characterized both by artificially inflated prices and by lower quality accommodation. The split housing market has brought about a situation of virtual housing segregation. As a result, immigrants are trapped in a spiral that combines precarious housing with precarious employment. Any inclination to settle, and/or the desire to be reunited with family members, is ultimately frustrated by the lack of an urban plan to deal with this problem. Given the absence of planning schemes that would account for the housing needs of new arrivals, for those arriving in Italy today, there is no possibility of finding accommodation other than by resorting to the parallel rent market, where the new figure of the 'tenant without rights' is emerging. Immigrants end up by being confined to degraded areas that, in turn, further degrade their occupants. Thus all the conditions that lead to permanent forms of socio-spatial discrimination are present.[28]

The Rise of a New Xenophobia: 'Citizens' Committees' and the Lega Nord

Despite all the rhetoric on this subject, the fact that Italy has become a country of immigration only recently does not make it immune to xenophobic poison. The few, and sometimes dramatic, meetings and debates that have welcomed both current and Italian ex-immigrants to the same conference table have been bitter but also exemplary in terms of what they have taught us about the diversity and the incommensurability of the two experiences. It must be added that the country's climate has changed rapidly in the last few years. The tolerance and openness that seemed to permeate public opinion in the 1980s have been replaced by prevailing attitudes of fear and prejudice toward foreigners. Sociologists have pointed out that attitudes toward foreigners have been worsening since the beginning of the 1990s, that is, in the period in which it became obvious that the new arrivals were there to stay, and when the first mass regularizations were applied.[29] It was precisely during these years that new kinds of local initiatives began to develop, which implicitly – and often explicitly expressed – dislike and hostility toward immigrants. Anti-immigrant and anti-gypsy 'civic committees' were established in many northern cities, including Milan, Turin and Genoa. Some arose spontaneously, others were inspired by particular social strata. They consist not only of the districts' 'inhabitants' but also of local politicians and tradesmen who aim to attain their own objectives through collective mobilization. The principle aim that the groups' participants share is that of vindicating the need for a tight control over the territory. By using slogans such as the 'need for security' the 'committees' push forward demands such as that of improving police patrols. More police control is intended to 'discipline' and 'domesticate' the immigrants, if not to actually expel them. There have been street demonstrations against 'immigrant crime' (which have attracted some left-wing party members, alongside other local inhabitants), and there have been riotous manifestations of intolerance, which have even been reported in the international press.[30] Among the many factors that may have contributed to such an abrupt change in public opinion is the fact that Italy at the beginning of the 1990s was wracked by significant political instability, which was in turn attributed to the so-called transition between the 'first' and 'second' Republics, a transition that brought about the dissolution of the major political forces and of the parties that had dominated the country's history after the Second World War (principally the Christian Democrats and the Communist Party). The crisis of the major parties, and of the labour movement organizations, was accompanied by their increasing inability to mediate social conflicts at a local level. New political entrepreneurs of intolerance established themselves, and proved capable of exploiting the immigration issue in order to gain political support. First among these was the Lega Nord.[31]

The Lega Nord built itself not only by expressing and voicing the symbolic need for renewal by demanding the birth of a new nation, and by supporting the judges who were prosecuting a large section of the old ruling class, but it was also the only political movement that understood the importance of creating a new political identity by identifying an enemy. At the beginning of the 1990s the Lega Nord was already arguing that 'the foreign invasion jeopardizes internal unity and the very identity of our people'.[32] From the very beginning the Lega attributed a great number of the 'new problems' that had arisen in Italy to immigrants. At the outset, its emphasis on the dangers of an uncontrolled migrational influx from the south and its vociferous campaign against Africans and 'Terroni' (the traditional nickname used by northern Italians to denote southern Italians) was not properly understood and was considered folklore, but in the course of a few years it became clear that the Lega was trying to create a precise frame of reference in which a totally new feeling of superiority would underline the distance between 'us' and 'them', between natives and immigrants, between 'padani' and southern Italians. It is obvious that this plan for the creation of a new identity was strongly motivated by economic factors (due to the growing difference between the economies of the developed north and the underdeveloped south) and implied a whole series of extremely radical political choices, first among which is that of abandoning the poorer areas of the country to their own destiny by means of political secession and the birth of a new state. The fundamental consideration behind Lega Nord's choices is that it is now time 'to leave', fully exploiting the potential of Italy's wealthiest regions, and at the same time carrying out a ruthless selection of immigrants, keeping 'all those who work' in the Po territory and 'sending the criminals home'.[33] As a matter of fact, one of the images obsessively re-proposed by Lega Nord, by the citizens' committees and by elements of the extreme right is precisely that of the 'immigrant-criminal', an evil character against which the only possible policy is that of expulsion. In 1996 a Lega MP proposed that all immigrants present on national territory should have their foot-prints filed together because, according to him, the 'immigrant-criminals' would actually resort to plastic surgery and alter their fingerprints just to be able to stay in Italy.

The mass media, especially the local press, have also played a very important role in creating the image of the immigrant 'enemy'. Alessandro Dal Lago remarked that

> the treatment of immigration in Italian newspapers ranges from the common use of stereotypes to the labelling of migrants as criminals, the production of false data about their numbers, explicit racist statements and campaigns for their expulsion . . . there is now a common targeting of immigrants as *social evils* in the local and national press, in the political system and in local initiatives.[34]

Another factor that has probably triggered this xenophobic trend of the 1990s is the general indifference to the immigration question in Italy that had so characterized previous decades. Such indifference may be attributed principally to governments, as they have not provided proper structures of admission, nor have they created a juridical framework in which immigrants could find a place.[35] During the 1990s the immigration issue in Italy has been constantly considered an emergency and has been treated as a very serious problem, in a way that is totally out of proportion to the reality of the situation. This new 'immigration emergency' is a result both of the unreliability of official statistics, which has led to wild guesses being made as to the real numbers of immigrants (the estimates for immigrant figures range from one million to several million), and also to an atmosphere of profound social alarm and political crisis in the early 1990s, for which the use of immigration as a tool for propaganda and agitation was a logical next step.[36]

Although the government and right-wing parties tend to over-estimate the phenomenon in order to introduce restrictive or repressive measures, civil rights associations and other individuals and groups favourable to immigrants attempt to minimize the phenomenon. Government agencies are usually successful in presenting immigration flows as tides menacing the frontiers and the internal stability of the country. For instance, in a statement in 1994 the Berlusconi government maintained that the number of clandestine immigrants in the country was over 700,000, when the most reliable sources at the time calculated the figure as less than 100,000, but even in the early 1990s the secret services, intent on spreading alarm, were talking of up to 1,200,000 illegal immigrants.[37] It is important to understand that this represents not only an over-evaluation of a social phenomenon but that it is also a powerful factor shaping politics and society.

The 'immigration emergency' has long been one of the foremost issues both on the political agenda and in media debates. As a result, a series of provisions, inspired by the rationale of interventionism in 'extreme' situations, was issued by governments.[38] These have constantly followed the proposals of the citizens' committees and the press, militarizing entire districts and tightening up laws targeting 'clandestine people'. A recent survey indicates that:

> It is also evident that the fear of the migrants does not depend on the quantitative dimension of the migrations, but on the political meaning which they have assumed in public opinion. If immigrants are labelled as enemies, it is not because the journalists know the data on the migrations (which are mostly fanciful or uncontrollable). The 'data' [are] nothing but symbols which are useful *for all practical purposes*, and with which public opinion searches for a confirmation of its fears. The problem is that the social definition, or labelling, of the immigration as the sign of the fear cannot but have the consequence of defining immigrants as (real or virtual) criminals. But it is important to stress

> that the characterisation of the migrant as an enemy comes logically (even if not chronologically) before the forms of devaluation, degradation and stigmatisation with which a society traditionally legitimises its actions against internal and external enemies. For example, the decision taken in 1995 to patrol Puglia's coasts with an army brigade, also had the effect of transforming the migrants and the refugees into enemies of our country.[39]

It is difficult to establish exactly why the country's climate has changed so abruptly. Moreover, it is doubtful whether we can talk about a truly racist wave in Italy in the last few years or about a more articulated and complex 'new' racism[40] in which the traditionally racist extreme right is joined by 'concerned citizens' who are convinced they are facing an 'immigrant invasion' in their own neighbourhood and journalists ready to fan the flames of fear and prejudice and thus shape a public opinion that is already largely hostile. In addition to the Lega Nord, discussed above, consolidated racist political organizations such as MSI-Fiamma Tricolore have played an important role in the organization and promotion of xenophobia in the south and in the centre of the country. This movement was born in the early years of '90 as a result of a split in the old Movimento Sociale Italiano (MSI). From this split both the MSI-Fiamma Tricolore and the Alleanza Nazionale (AN) were born, the latter being a right-wing party which aimed to be more open and modern, which had "neo-gaullista" ambitions and wanted to form part of the goverment. The 'Fiamma Tricolore', in its attempt to increase its own limited electoral basis, have used increasingly heated catchphrases against the immigrants, and youth movements linked to this party have acted as aggressors against immigrants, especially in Rome. However, even the militants of the Alleanza Nazionale, despite the declarations on the part of the leaders of the party (who propose the creation of a new right and distance themselves from Fascism and racism) have been very active in anti-immigration and anti-gypsy movements, in some cases even becoming their leaders.[41] In addition to the role played by the Lega Nord and by the two right-wing parties, the MSI and AN, the behaviour of the media, the intellectuals and a large part of public opinion is also a cause for concern. One critic notes that

> of course, explicit racist movements exist, although they comprise only a minority of the Italian population [. . .] It is clear now that migrants are not considered enemies because of the initiatives of small groups of racists. In this sense we have to speak of a 'new' racism, more articulated than before. I think that we have to look for it at the level of the organized public and political opinion.[42]

Immigrants' perceptions of the country have certainly undergone profound change. Throughout the 1980s they saw Italy as a Mediterranean country where a certain degree of tolerance or at least indifference reigned. It was perceived as fairly liberal country that did not have too many controls in place and where loopholes could be found that would permit the immigrant's integration and financial wellbeing. Today, however, the image that prevails is one of a country that is hostile to immigrants, not very hospitable and that implements strict controls. Immigrants are becoming aware that gaining legal status is becoming increasingly difficult, and even where it is secured scarcely any guarantees exist. Orientating oneself in the bureaucratic maze is an increasingly complicated task, whereas even those previously regularized constantly run the risk of falling back into an irregular status (until this day only temporary provisions and revocable permits have been issued). In defiance of official regulations, permits are issued for an astonishingly wide range of time periods, a situation made possible as the police and administration enjoy a high level discretion. On the other hand, public opinion seems to be increasingly oriented towards repression, and surveys testify to a constantly rising hostility toward immigrants. There is an almost unanimous demand for measures against clandestine immigrants, who are stereotyped as criminals.

Immigrant Legislation

Several of the problems outlined above are manifested in the evolution of immigrant legislation. This legislation illustrates the belated recognition of the transformation from temporary to permanent immigration, the slowness and prejudice characteristic of the State administration, the absolute subjection of the immigrant to the power of the police, the rise of the public's hostility towards immigrants, and finally the pressure of certain political forces and citizens' groups that have been clamouring for stricter controls. A survey of the juridical decisions of the last decade clearly demonstrates a policy to grant only minimal rights to a limited number of immigrants. The Ministry of the Interior has played the central role in the definition and drafting of the various laws and decrees, emphasizing the need for 'national defence' and for control over immigrants. The Ministry not only determined the framing of the legislation but arrogated to itself the right to decide all ambiguous cases. Local police authorities are directly dependent on the Ministry of the Interior and it is these authorities that are charged with the issuing of permits and regularizations. Immigrants are considered dangerous subjects, and are forced to submit to frequent checks by the police, who already hold ample discretionary powers over them.[43]

Legislators seem determined to establish police procedures rather than issuing a coherent policy. The strict and police-oriented nature of the legislation has been instrumental in the ongoing creation of clandestine immigration and in the maintenance of a high number of 'irregular' residents.

The development of immigrant legislation has been slow, having really only begun in 1986 at the time of the first regularization.[44] In 1986 only a third of immigrants had been regularized. It was only with the decree of 1990 that the problem of regularizing foreigners already present on Italian territory was dealt with seriously. The decree of 1990 introduced yet another new rule concerning entry and rejection at the border, residence and expulsion. Expulsion of clandestines was made easier, and an article of the law permitted detention for up to six months for aliens still on Italian soil after having being expelled: surely this is a true 'immigration crime'; it was pronounced unconstitutional in 1995 following protests from anti-racist associations. Thus, on the one hand, the decree was intended to regularize the greatest possible number of clandestine people, and on the other to introduce a criterion of 'programmed influx', that is, to establish a fixed number of immigrants that Italy could accommodate each year, a sum that was to be determined by the Foreign Ministry and by the Ministry of the Interior, after consultation of a series of other bodies. It was basically an attempt at rationalizing and disciplining the immigration issue. However it met with little success. Although, in 1991, many immigrants were finally regularized, the clandestine problem resurfaced immediately. Indeed, in the years following the enforcement of this law the attempts made to establish an annual quota of legal immigrants was utterly failed. Year after year the public administration limited itself to claiming that the number of immigrants needed by the Italian economy had to be zero. This simultaneously involved a grotesquely distorted representation of the real situation and at the same time allowed the black market to work and intensive exploitation to spread. This had already reached extreme proportions in the '*caporalato*', a southern Italian tradition of mafia management of the labour market, which had been erased by the farm labourers' struggles of the 1950s and 1960s. The 'programmed influx' theory thus transformed itself into a complete obstacle to legal immigration.

A further important piece of legislation was the citizenship law of 1992, which made the granting of Italian citizenship to EU citizens easier, but more difficult for all others. Belonging to the EU is perceived both by the general public and the media as a sign of superiority over non-Europeans and a new word, 'extracommunitarian', soon came into use. At first sight this is a neutral word, meaning only 'not from the EU'. However, it is used, usually disparagingly, as a synonym for 'immigrant from a poorer country'.

In the midst of a turbulent political climate, which was partly the result of the fiery debates over the 'immigration emergency', Prime Minister Dini's law of 1996, backed by the Democratic Party of the Left, introduced new a regularization with the apparent aim of resolving two of the major problems inherent to the Italian economy: firstly to regularize a certain number of clandestine people, and secondly to expose cases of illegal work.[45] In contrast to that of 1990–1, this regularization was characterized by its fairly strict conditions.[46] From a merely quantitative point-of-view it has been a great success, as more than 200,000 immigrants have been regularized – although a more complete analysis has shown that, 'both of the legalisation's aims were only partially and transitorily achieved'.

This sort of situation was highly predictable considering that the selection criteria for issuing permits was that one had to prove that one was working in an activity characterized by continuity and regularity. Indeed the legalization of 1996 can be considered only relatively successful if its aim was truly that of driving the immigrants out of the underground economy. For many of them it was only a matter of uniquely formal and transitory regularizations, destined to be effective only for a limited time, still characterized by that status-shifting, periodic oscillation between regularity and irregularity that – as we have already seen – marked immigration in Italy up to the present day.[48]

In 1998 a very controversial comprehensive law on immigration was approved, its aim being to do away with the idea of emergency measures. It was conceived and overtly supported by the centre-left 'Ulivo' government, but its operative details were almost entirely drafted by the Ministry of Interior, and they appear to be largely inspired by the Schengen agreement, especially as far as the founding of detention camps for 'clandestine' migrants is concerned.[49] Some of its features are important. Despite the fact that it has been publicized by the government as 'the most advanced European law regarding immigration', the logic of expulsion and rejection prevails over that of acceptance. In fact it is a law that seems to follow the trend already manifested in the emergency decree of 1996, instituting a dualism of rights that discriminates against immigrants and is oriented toward repression and expulsion. Apart from continuing the hypocritical policy of 'programmed influx', which results in the systematic creation of new clandestine people, at the present time the law does not provide for any mass regularization. Thus it condemns approximately 250,000 clandestine people currently living in Italy to a precarious and frightening existence, as potentially they could be subjected to the new strict penal provisions provided for by the law. It establishes what are euphemistically defined as 'acceptance camps', that is administrative detention camps, where immigrants awaiting expulsion are interned and deprived of their personal freedom for no other crime than that of not possessing a residence permit. The law also grants certain rights. The possibility of obtaining an indefinitely renewable five-year residence permit is introduced, although the issuing of this document is conditional upon a series of strict conditions, first among which is the ability to prove that one is employed and has sufficient income to support a family. However, even this five-year permit is revokable and its holder is liable for expulsion at the first violation of even the most minor Italian law. Immigrants can lose all their rights, the prized five-year permit, and be expelled, simply for stealing a pack of French fries from a supermarket. Even with the new law, the foreigner's judicial position remains weak, and they are constantly subjected to police checks that never respect the principle of 'innocent until proven guilty' sanctioned by the constitution. The law does not provide for any system of permanent regularization of clandestine people, whereas the climate of suspicion and the panacea of expulsion as a remedy for all 'immigration evils' are continually re-emerging in public discourse.

Coping with the 'Extracommunitarian Invasion': the Political Myth of Border Checks

The tendency to simplify the 'immigration problem' in terms of police and military surveillance and to look at the arrival of the 'extracommuni-arian' as an 'invasion' of Italy is clearly illustrated in the debate on border controls. This debate has rapidly grown from a technical-military question to one of the great themes of Italian and European political debate.

For some time now the issue of Italian border checks has caused much debate among her European partners, and on many occasions it has appeared to represent a serious obstacle on the Italian road to European unification. The Germans have been particularly vocal in their admonitions of Italy's stance. The 2,000 km or more of Italian coast that stretches out into the Mediterranean has suddenly become a cause for concern for many north European governments. The 'Achilles' heel' of the Schengen agreement would appear to be the 'unofficial borders' facing the Channel of Otranto in the Adriatic that separates Italy from Albania, and the body of water surrounding the Sicilian islands, where Italian territorial waters extend 'dangerously' towards Africa.[50] In fact, after having signed the Schengen treaty, Italy found itself, along with Spain, representing the 'limes', the southern frontier of 'Fortress Europe', having been assigned the task of guaranteeing rigid control over the migratory fluxes towards its lands, as forseen by the treaty. With this in mind, in addition to introducing new systems of defence and border control, the Italian government conducted a policy of forming agreements with some of the migrants' native countries (with Albania, Morocco and Tunisia). This was aimed at obtaining the collaboration of the governments of these countries in the realization of two prioritized objectives: faciliating the expulsion and repatriation procedures for the 'undesirables', and that of exercising stricter control over those places in which such migration originates. Thus far the results are questionable, but beyond the relative success obtained regarding the containment of migratory fluxes, the political choices have contributed to reinforcing a distorted perception of the question of immigration within Italy.

In the last few years the Italian press has focused on the question of clandestine, fugitive and refugee entries, often exaggerating the figures. The tone has at times been apocalyptic and xenophobic, although, at the same time nothing was mentioned about the immigrants on board the fully loaded fishing boat that was shipwrecked off the coast.[51] The Italian government has unhesitatingly resorted to armed force on two occasions. In 1995 it brought troops onto the Puglia beaches. In 1997 it employed the military marine corps in an 'aggressive' patrolling operation of the Otranto channel in order to face an improbable invasion of 'boat people' with Albanian refugees on board. These patrolling operations in the waters between Albania and Italy brought forth their first result in March 1997 when an Albanian 'sea cart'[52] full of refugees was sunk after it collided with an Italian battleship, the latter carrying out the order to 'stop it at all costs'.[53] About one hundred Albanians drowned in the shipwreck, mainly women and children. The pretence was that of 'defending' what is considered one of the most 'permeable' borderlines. The islands off the coast of Sicily, in particular Lampedusa, represent the second area of weakness, being the closest landing point for boat people coming from Tunisia and elsewhere in the Maghreb. The practically futile employment of the military in the anti-clandestine operations has been underlined by military spokespeople themselves. They have emphasized that Italy's coasts are too great to be controlled and that it is too difficult to maintain such control over extended periods of time.[54] The paradox is that those frontiers, which are so frequently mentioned by the press and considered so highly permeable have only been witness to a relatively limited number of 'clandestine' immigrants. A larger number find access to Italy through borders that are considered 'safe', such as those with France and Switzerland. These are supported by a network of 'passeurs' that help them enter the country. The number of 'clandestine' arrivals, estimated as a little over 60,000 yearly, certainly does not create internal 'imbalances' of any kind, and in fact it fills an increasing negative population gap, especially in the northern regions. In this light the question of border control increasingly appears to be an instrument of political propaganda, used to reassure the indigenous population and at the same time intimidate the immigrant, through an increasing delegation of immigrant and refugee 'problem-solving' to police and military bodies.[55]

One analyst claims that

> the tendency to confer immigration policies on the police and the almost total halt of immigration, including that for humanitarian reasons, encourage an illegal type of immigration, easy to be criminalized because it is obliged to resort to the service of criminal gangs that exploit the frontier blocks'.[56]

The result of these conditions, as well as the fact that immigrants are rarely capable of benefiting from legal assistance, and as a result end up behind bars three times as often as Italians, is that today about 35 per cent of the national penitentiary population consists of immigrants.

Conclusion

Italy is a country of recent immigration where instruments of control and of temporary rationalization of immigration have been introduced after an initial period of deregulation. This has occurred in the course of its accession to Schengen. The initial phases of the process, where cycles of irregular immigration were partly regularized, seem to have come to an end. The 'see-saw' phase where the immigrant's destiny was part of a confused game between entrepreneurs and governments is drawing to a close. This game has frequently been determined by the 'invisible hand' of economy more than by political decision. Moreover, it has resulted in a repeated shifting of the immigrants from one condition to another, keeping them in limbo, in a state of uncertainty between work in the formal economy and in the informal one, between regular and irregular status. The immigrant's condition is especially marked by an unsettled state, being subject to economic fluctuations and to the consequences of political whim. Indeed, even regular immigrants have no guarantee of maintaining their status, and therefore their 'privileged' condition is real but precarious, and as such is little better than that of the clandestine immigrant. It is no coincidence that in the numerous rallies in the struggle for the recognition of their rights that took place during the second half of the 1990s, culminating in a number of national mass demonstrations (between 1994 and 1996) both regular and illegal immigrants have marched side by side in the streets.

A new and different era is beginning to take shape, and I will attempt to sketch its characteristics. Salvatore Palidda recently pointed out that:

> Aside from those who are beginning to integrate themselves through a regular status and have improved their economic and social condition, a large number of immigrants (in our opinion the majority) continue to live in a precarious condition, shifting from informal to formal status and running the risk of losing their regular status.[57]

In fact, as I have attempted to demonstrate, Italy is a country where the informal economy continues to play a major role, and according to some statistics it represents about one third of GNP.[58] The demand for irregular labour thus persists. A researcher writes: 'there are parts of the country where the number of regular immigrants more or less corresponds to that of the regularly employed but others where the difference is very significant'.[59] Furthermore, cases of new-slavery seem to be on the rise, especially in the south and in particular 'enclaves', such as the Chinese settlement in Tuscany.

In conclusion, the evidence seems to indicate a tendency towards dualism in the immigrant's condition. A minority is regularized and granted minimal rights. For the larger part, however, their fate in years to come seems to be that of perpetual precariousness, characterized by a subordinate condition and by unscrupulous employment without rights in particular sectors, especially in the black economy. This duality seems to correspond to aspects of regional localization and specialization, as shown by the prevalence of irregular workers in the south. Although, in the first phase, the processes of settlement and distribution were mainly determined by the difficulty experienced in passing the various borders, by geographical proximity – North Africans in Sicily, Albanians in Apulia, Slavs in Venetia – by the existence of friendly connections and by the presence of vast sectors of informal economy, now 'the local job markets are becoming the determining factors in defining the type and place of the immigrants' working settlement. It is these markets that drive immigrants to a specific geographical area and encourage them to concentrate in a specific productive sector.'[60] In short, there are many indications that we have reached a turning point, where, on one hand, immigrants tend to be concentrated in the developed northern regions[61] where their structural role in the economy is recognized and where they are granted certain rights. On the other hand, however, a large group of clandestine people continue to work in sub-segments of the job market where there are absolutely no regulations or controls. This is probably the reason why significant differentiations in immigrants' status are being introduced, as shown by the most recent legal provisions. Between those who enjoy a five-year permit, those who have only a one-year permit of stay and those who maintain a clandestine status, there seems to be a growing distance that may make the idea of a common fight and the identification of common objectives more difficult. The clandestines' future may be one of ever more segregation and isolation, with the formation of a large stratum of precarious workers with no rights, subject to severe exploitation and the threat of expulsion, and permanently experiencing social inferiority. That way many of them will have to abandon any illusions in the 'Bel Paese'.

Notes

1. More than 5,000,000 Italians emigrated between 1876 and 1900. Approximately 10,000,000 emigrated between 1900 and 1920. 3,500,000 emigrated between the two World Wars. Almost 7,000,000 emigrated between 1945 and 1970. The phenomenon started to wane at the beginning of the 1960s, and had significantly reduced by the 1970s, years that were characterized by a great return of migrants. During the early 1970s the number of migrants returning to Italy grew in relation to the number departing. It is worth noting that emigration from Italy has never ceased completely, having stabilized at 50,000 people yearly in the second part of the 1980s, and that the last few years have been marked by a significant intellectual emigration, by a 'brain drain' caused by difficult conditions in Italian universities. For a historical interpretation of Italian emigration, see: Various Authors (1974), *Cent' anni, 26 Milioni*, special edition of Il Ponte, XXX, n. 11–12.
2. Cf. Di Carlo, A. and S. (eds) (1986), *I luoghi dell'identità. Dinamiche culturali nell'esperienza dell'emigrazione*, Milan: Franco Angeli.
3. My argument is based on the research of Gambino, F. (1984), 'L'Italie, pays d'immigration: rapports sociaux et formes juridiques', in *Peuples Méditerraneéns* 27–8: 173–85.

4. Cf. Sergi, N. (1987), *L'immigrazione straniera in Italia*, Rome: Edizioni Lavoro.
5. Cf. CENSIS (Centro Studi Investimenti Sociali) (1979), *I lavoratori stranieri in Italia*, Rome: Istituto poligrafico zecca dello stato.
6. Torti, M.T. (ed.) (1992), *Stranieri in Liguria*, Genoa: Marietti.
7. Cf. Gambino, F. (1984), L'Italie, pays d'immigration : rapports sociaux et formes juridiques'.
8. Cf. Mazzon, S., Pace, E., Rossini, S. (1989), 'Percorsi migratori in un'area a economia diffusa' , in Cocchi, G. (ed.), *Stranieri in Italia*, Bologna : Istituto Cattaneo.
9. Cf. Jeffrey, E. (1993), *Race and immigration in Sicily*, UMI dissertation, who remarks that:

> 'The integration of immigrants at the bottom of a segmented labor market homogenizes and stigmatizes them; their vulnerability is the product not only of ambiguous legal status, but of the global pattern of inequality to which migratory patterns are linked', ivi: 73, but refer also: 125–9.

10. CENSIS, (1990), *Migrare e accogliere. Sintesi delle ricerche del Censis sull'immigrazione straniera in Italia*, press release presented to the Conferenza Nazionale dell'Immigrazione , Rome, 1 Giugno.
11. My argument is based on that of Marchetti, A. (1994), 'La nuova immigrazione senegalese a Milano', in Barile, G., Dal Lago, A, Marchetti, A., Galeazzo, P., *Tra due rive. La nuova immigrazione a Milano*, Milan: IRER: 241–366, esp.: 304–5.
12. 'Italy has arrived at zero population growth, its birth rate is the lowest in the world, it has a rapidly ageing population, and the regional demographic divisions between North and South are disappearing'. Cf. King, R. (1993), 'Italy reaches zero population growth' in *Geography*, Vol. 78, Pt. 1, n. 338, January: 63–9.
13. Cf. Bruni, M. (ed.) (1994), *Attratti, sospinti, respinti. I lavoratori immigrati nelle aziende bolognesi*, Milan: Franco Angeli.
14. Cf. Barbesino, P. (1996), 'Talking about migration : The State monitoring system in Italy', in Palidda S. (ed.), *Délit d'immigration. La construction sociale de la déviance et de la criminalité parmi les immigrés en Europe*, Bruxelles: Migrations, COST A2, Communauté Européenne: 73–82.
15. These figures are frequently corrected or revised, often by ISTAT, the Italian Statistical Institute, which has pointed out that the number of foreigners in Italy is habitually over-estimated. Cf. Vaccaro, C.M.

(1997), 'Immigrazione e sviluppo socio-economico', in *Studi Emigrazione/Migration Studies*, XXXIV, 126: 225–67, esp.: 227–8.

16. The statistics are taken from: *Anticipazioni del Dossier statistico Caritas sull'immigrazione* Rome, March, 1998.
17. These statistics seem to confirm the hypothesis on 'feminization of migration' expounded by Castles S. and Miller, M. (1993), *The Age of Migrations. International Population Movements in the Contemporary World*, London: Macmillan: 8–9.
18. Internal migratory movements have slowed. There is an increased tendency for Italians to live in their place of origin.
19. According to the order proposed by Zanfrini, L. (1997), *La ricerca sull'immigrazione in Italîa. Gli sviluppi più recenti*, Milan: ISMU: 70 ff.
20. In the Naples area, in Villa Literno, a heterogeneous and marginalized community of migrants is utilized for picking tomatoes. It is underpaid and forced to live in very bad santitary conditions, in campers and huts. The harvesters are recruited from a sort of international *caporalato* (illegal mafia recruiters), whose structure involves a number of hiring agencies based in the countries of origin.
21. Cf. Zanfrini, L. (1997), *La ricerca sull'immigrazione*: 72.
22. In some cases a perverse mechanism has apparently developed which leads to an interweaving of interests between the local workers and the immigrants, especially in some agricultural activities such as harvesting, where the immigrants work at jobs on the black market which are at the same time formally carried out by locals, cf. Palidda, S., Reyneri, E. (1995), 'Immigrazione e mercato del lavoro', in Chiesi, A., Regalia, I., Regini, M., (eds), *Lavoro e relazioni industriali in Europa*, Rome: La Nuova Italia Scientifica: 86.
23. Again, these trends confirm the hypotheses in Castles, S. Miller, M. (1993), *The Age of Migrations*: 8.
24. Zanfrini, L. (1997), *La ricerca sull'immigrazione*: 73.
25. Cf. Campani, G., Carchedi F., Tassinari A. (eds) (1994), *L'immigrazione silenziosa. Le comunità cinesi in Italia*, Turin: Fondazione Agnelli.
26. Reyneri, E. (1996), *Sociologia del mercato del lavoro*, Bologna: Il Mulino: 386.
27. Cf. Bruni, M. (ed.) (1994), *Attratti, sospinti, respinti. I lavoratori immigrati nelle aziende bolognesi*, Milan: Franco Angeli.
28. This thesis has been further developed in Petrillo, A., *Migranti e Città*, in course of publication.
29. Cf. Martiniello, M., Kazim, P. (1991), 'Italy: two perspectives. Racism

in paradise?' in *Race & Class*, 32 (3): 79–84; and Gallini, C. (1992), 'Dangerous games: Racism as Practised in Italian Popular Culture', in *Cultural Studies* (6) 2: 207–17.

30. Cf. Campani, G. (1993), 'Immigration and racism in southern Europe: the Italian case', in *Ethnic and Racial Studies*, 16 (3): 507–35; referring to riots in Genoa, summer 1993, cf. Rochu, G. (1994), 'L'Italie gagnée par la fureur xenofobe' in *Le Monde diplomatique*, janvier: 20–1; in Turin, cf. Griseri, P. (1996), 'Turin, ou le ghetto au centre', in *Le Monde diplomatique*, fevrier: 9.
31. Cf. Dal Lago, A. (1996), 'The impact of migrations on receiving societies. Some ethnographic remarks. In Palidda S. (ed.), *Délit d'immigration. La construction sociale de la déviance et de la criminalité parmi les immigrés en Europe*, Bruxelles: Migrations, COST A2, Communauté Européenne: 43–50.
32. Manifesto of the Lega Nord quoted in Biorcio, R. (1997), *La Padania promessa. La storia, le idee e la logica d'azione della Lega Nord*, Milan: Il Saggiatore: 151.
33. A summary of Dal Lago's ideas in id. (1997), *The impact of migrations on receiving societies. The Italian case*, research report presented to DG XII of EC, unpublished, but refer also to Biorcio, R. (1997), *La Padania promessa*.
34. Dal Lago, A. (1997), *The impact of migrations on receiving societies. The Italian case*, but refer also to Maneri, M. (1995), *Stampa quotidiana e senso comune nella rappresentazione sociale degli immigrati*, Ph.D. dissertation, Univ. of Trento.
35. Cf. Dal Lago, A. (1997), *The impact of migrations on receiving societies. The Italian case*: 48.
36. The sudden attention paid by the Italian press to the immigration question is well analyzed by Maneri, M. (1998), 'Lo straniero consensuale. La devianza degli immigrati come circolarità di pratiche e di discorsi', in Dal Lago, A. (ed.), *Lo Straniero e il Nemico. Materiali per l'etnografia contemporanea*, Genoa-Milan: Costa & Nolan: 236–72.
37. Cf. Palidda, S. (1998), 'La conversione poliziesca delle politiche migratorie', in Dal Lago, A. (ed.), *Lo Straniero e il Nemico. Materiali per l'etnografia contemporanea*, Genoa-Milan: Costa & Nolan: 209–35.
38. On the recurrent use of emergency legisation in Italy, refer to Ruggiero, V. (1995), 'Flexibility and intermittent Emergency in the Italian penal System', in Ruggiero, V., Ryan, M., and Sim, J. (eds), *Western Penal Systems. A Critical Anatomy*, London: Sage.

39. Dal Lago, A. 'The impact of migrations on receiving societies. The Italian case': 49.
40. Some time ago Etienne Balibar opened an interesting debate on the question, speaking of the spread of a 'post-racism' in Europe, cf. Balibar, E., Wallerstein, I. (1990), *Race, nation, classe. Les identitées ambiguës*, Paris: La Découverte.
41. For a long time the parlimentarians of the AN have insisted that clandestine immigration should be considered an offence punishable with a jail sentence. In autumn 1998 they presented a government bill to this effect.
42. Dal Lago, A. (1997), *The impact of migrations on receiving societies. The Italian case*: 29; for a more detailed discussion, see ibid.: 22–30. See also Campani, G. (1993), 'Immigration and racism in southern Europe: the Italian case'.
43. For example, the police in the different cities of Italy issue work permits for extremely varied lengths of time with little or no regard for official guidelines, and the same arbitrariness has applied to cases of family reunification.
44. There had not been any legislation in Italy concerning immigration for a long time. Before the decrees of 1986 and 1990 the regulations concerning immigrant entry and residence in Italy dated back to the Fascist Laws of public security of 1931. Until the beginning of the 1990s the juridical situation for non-EU foreigners was controlled merely by ministerial circulars. As a result, immigrant workers could scarcely benefit from judicial assistance. It was not until the end of 1986 that the first law which guaranteed equality of rights between immigrant and Italian workers appeared. This provided for the right to social and medical assistance, the right to preserve one's cultural identity, and facilitated measures towards the comprehensive regularization for illegal immigrants. That decree was however very limited since it concerned only officially employed workers, and many of the principles ratified by the law were destined to remain dead letters, as they lacked real executive backing. The law did not however alter the dispositions of 1931 with regard to immigrant entry, residence and expulsion.
45. 'The situation envisioned by the legalisation's proponents was the following: on the one hand, employers forced to hire immigrants illegally, but prone to hire them regularly if this is possible; on the other, immigrants forced to work as not registered wage earners because they lacked a residence permit, but willing to go on with the same job under a regular contract, after legalisation. Therefore quite

rigid requisites were settled to force an emergence both from illegal residence and underground economy'. Cf. Reyneri, E. (1998), *Migrinf: Italian field research report on migrants' insertion in the informal economy : The Impact of the 1996 Legalisation on the Insertion of Immigrants in the Italian Labour Market*, report TSER DGXII-EC: 105.

46. 'In addition to demonstrating, via documentation, their previous presence in Italy, immigrants had to have been irregularly employed in the last six months, to have an ongoing irregular labour position or a written job offer by an Italian employer, or to be the spouse or underage children of an immigrant holder of a residence permit. In any case of legalisation for job reasons a significant sum of money had to be paid to Social security: from over 870 ECU for a part-time housekeeper to almost 3,500 ECU for a full-time blue-collar manufacturing job. Payments were supposed to have been charged mostly to employers, but were in fact often paid by immigrants in their entirety. This obstacle was serious, as these amounts are up to two or three months' wages for an immigrant. Finally the procedures for the application were complicated and time consuming, so that some immigrants lost their irregular jobs because they spent too much time away from the workplace. In other cases some employers refused to legalise the work relationship as they were afraid of having to pay back social benefits. Cf. Reyneri, E., ibid.

47. The author of a detailed report on the latter regularization makes the following remark: 'In conclusion, there are three typical sequences, which help us illustrate the real effects of the legalisation process. These sequences are summed up in the table below. Unfortunately, we cannot indicate their relative frequency, but it seems likely that sequence B is the most common, although not much more frequent than the majority of legalised cases. The other two sequences should be about equal:

	Before	**Legalisation**	**After**
A	street vending, selling cigarettes odd jobs	fake work contract	street vending selling cigarettes odd jobs
B	steady but non-registered job	employer paid social security	kept the same job declared for permit
C	steady but non-registered job	immigrant paid social security	looking for new job

Cf. Reyneri, E., *Migrinf: Italian field research report on migrants' insertion in the informal economy*: 114

49. The ambiguity of this measure, directed not only towards the control of migratory fluxes coming from abroad, but also towards the management of immigrants already present on Italian soil, became evident immediately after the activisation of the first 'camps' in summer 1998. Immigrants who had just disembarked on Italian soil were not the only ones to be held there. Other 'irregular' immigrants, who were without documents, but who had been in Italy for some time were also held. This meant that the number of potential detainees was greatly enlarged.
50. Cf. Toller, L. (1997), 'Gli sbarchi di migranti senza documenti al sud: modelli di differenzialismo nella Fortezza Europa', in *Altreragioni* 6: 47–62.
51. This refers to a fishing boat, with three hundred people on board, which shipwrecked off the Sicilian coast on Christmas day 1996, causing about 300 deaths. The case was completely ignored by the Italian press, with the exception of the daily newspaper 'Il Manifesto'. The case has beeen accurately reconstructed by Quagliata, L. (1998) 'Scomodi Fantasmi', in *Altreragioni* 7: 127–34.
52. The pejorative nickname used by the Italian press to denominate boat-people.
53. 'Così la Marina causò il naufragio', 'And the Navy caused the shipwreck' titled by *La Repubblica* of 29 April 1998, but refer to the entire article by Mastrogiacomo, D. on p.11.
54. Toller, L. *Gli sbarchi di migranti senza documenti al sud: modelli di differenzialismo nella Fortezza Europa*: 52.
55. Cf. Palidda, S. (1998), 'La conversione poliziesca delle politiche migratorie', in Dal Lago A. (ed.), *Lo Straniero e il Nemico. Materiali per l'etnografia contemporanea*, Genoa-Milan: Costa & Nolan: 209–35.
56. Cf. Palidda, S. (1998), *Le risque d'une conversion pénale-policière-militaire de la politique migratoire italo-européenne*, unpublished report for the 'European Coordination for foreigner's right to family life', Première rencontre-débat: Pour une nouvelle politique européenne de l'immigration, Genoa 28 March.
57. Ibid.
58. Cf. Palidda, S. (1998), *Le risque d'une conversion pénale-policière-militaire de la politique migratoire italo-européenne*.
59. Ambrosini, M. (ed.) (1997), *Lavorare nell'ombra. L'inserimento degli immigrati nell'economia informale*, Milan: Quaderni ISMU: 21.
60. Sciarrone, R. (1996), 'Il lavoro degli *altri*, e gli *altri* lavori', in *Quaderni di Sociologia*, vol. XL, 11, 'La costruzione di una società multiculturale': 9–49, esp.: 41.

61. The process of distribution of the foreign population in the principle areas of Italy has changed as follows in the period 1990–1997: in the South the percentage of foreign presences has remained stable (about 11%), in the Centre it has diminished (from 41% to 31%), on the islands it has diminished somewhat (from about 9% to 7%), in the North the percentage has increased substantially (from 39% to 52%). In absolute terms, however, the immigrant population has increased in every zone, given that it has grown from 731,138 people in 1990 to 1,240,721 in 1997, cf: *Anticipazioni del Dossier statistico Caritas sull'immigrazione*, Rome, March, 1998: 3. For more details see Table 9.5.

Part III
Migrant Labour and Modern Capitalism

–10–

The Freedom to Move

Nigel Harris

Introduction

In 1944, Karl Polyani wrote that the history of capitalism from the late eighteenth century to the third quarter of the nineteenth century was a long drawn-out struggle to subordinate society to a completely self-regulating market. In his view, the simultaneously absurd and oppressive character of this endeavour was embodied in the attempt to make land and labour simply marketable commodities. However, from the depression of the years, 1873 to 1886, he saw a sustained and successful campaign to reverse this process and establish national (or State) regulation of land and labour as well as of finance and trade. In the case of labour, this process was embodied in the creation of strong trade unions that sought to regulate labour markets and, in alliance with the government, to regulate hours and conditions of work, and create measures of popular welfare, education and health.

From the vantage point of 1944, the achievements seemed impressive. The trade unions had moved from barely tolerated marginal organizations to one of the great institutions of state. With the settlement of the Second World War, many governments established more comprehensive systems of welfare than ever before, in effect guaranteeing a minimum level of livelihood for all.

Yet half a century later, what then seemed permanent accomplishments now appear as temporary victories, and those victories were only part of a larger process in which the Great Powers settled their domestic class struggles in order the better to fight each other. The other side of the coin to Polyani's triumphs of 1944 was total war. What we have called elsewhere (Harris 1995), the fully 'socialized state' in which the mass of inhabitants became citizens and, in return for complete loyalty to the state, were accorded both consultative and welfare rights – a kind of social contract – now appears as a temporary phase in the evolution of the system.

It is as if world capitalism needed a period of national incubation, and that for nearly a century up to about 1970, this was indeed what occurred – with all the attendant horrors of war implied by the unification of capital and the state within a system of competitive Great Powers.

The creation of the modern national State, however, opened a gulf between those who were legitimate citizens – members of the 'social homogeneity' – and the rest of the world, the vast majority of people. Access to full participation became a precious privilege, a route to what was presented as participation in the exercise of national sovereignty. It was not that national loyalty or sentiment was created by the change – they had existed to some degree and for various classes for a long time – but the sentiment was now armed with specific legal privileges and material benefits.

The project of building a national state of self-governing citizens in which all have rights and duties is now part of the past. It implied a strict control of the economic and political boundaries of the state, consistently discriminating between native and foreigner both in trade, in capital movements as well as in terms of people. The process of rapid post-war economic growth has forced the governments of the developed countries – and latterly, those of the developing countries – to decontrol if they are to enjoy the benefits of growth. For the best part of thirty years, the developed States have been dismantling the regulation of trade and currencies, capital and finance, and more recently, of domestic labour markets, conditions of work and the structure of social support (welfare, health and education). Thus, the profound difference between citizen and foreigners upon which the socialized state was founded, is being progressively blurred. Indeed, so great is the complexity of the system, no one can any longer be sure where a commodity is made or to what country a unit of capital belongs – or even if the question any longer makes any sense (although the newspapers and popular discussion still assume it does).

In periods of sustained growth the developed countries have always experienced serious labour scarcities – that is, their economies have rapidly exceeded the potential of the domestic labour market and spilled over to other countries. That has been an even more extreme phenomenon in the post-war period – labour demand in the developed countries has not only invaded areas of formerly non-labour (housewives, for example), not only drawn in new legions of immigrants, but also swept into production the labour forces of a mass of developing countries, particularly in east and south-east Asia. Indeed, what the labour demand of the developed countries started has by now assumed an autonomous drive, leading to the creation of a single integrated global economy (albeit, still far from full accomplishment). We can already envisage what has long existed for the higher professions (such as doctors, engineers, airline pilots), a range of world labour markets, setting the prevailing pay rates in each national economy. The full emergence of that process is still blocked by more-or-less elaborate immigration controls, some of the few systematic barriers remaining to obstruct the mobility of a 'factor of production' and a form of protectionism still accepted by liberals and non-liberals alike.

Thus, as governments have been driven – admittedly to different degrees – to end the old social contract with their citizens, to dismantle the socialized state, so also the emergence of global labour markets makes for continuously increasing rates of worker mobility – whether this means settlers, internal company movements, temporary migrants or whatever. Indeed, the operation of global markets is imposing a crisis on the state system, at its most dramatic in the old Soviet Union, but no less severe wherever the state structure is vulnerable – as in sub-saharan Africa, the Balkans, the Caucasus and former Soviet Central Asia, parts of the Middle East and so on. Now, the same violent process has been inflicted on those hitherto thought to be most invulnerable, in East and South-East Asia. The migration of finance between countries is one of the more obvious sources of instability, but the movement of unprecedented numbers of refugees across international borders is an even more painful index of that crisis.

In developing countries, the old project of national economic development – usually founded upon some aspiration to create a socialized State – has also come to an end. Growth now implies increased integration and specialization, not increased economic independence. The collapse of the vigorous movements of economic nationalism of the 1950s is one sign of the change – and the rise of alternative ideologies, pre-eminently religious fundamentalism, which try, at least initially, to reject the 'Western' aim of economic development along with secularism.

For the unskilled workers of the developed countries, the prospect is alarming. On the one hand, the old social contract has been unilaterally scrapped by what was supposed to be their own patron and protector, the state. On the other, the material foundations of their existence are radically contracting, represented by high levels of unemployment in Europe, and declining relative incomes in North America. The jobs on offer do not provide anything like an adequate subsistence, by the standards of society at large – and ill accord with the expectations of those raised to envisage quite reasonably that their earnings shall accord with the social norms and average levels of productivity. However, for those workers, immigrants, whose expectations are governed by a society of origin with far lower levels of productivity, such pay can be, by means of prodigious effort and abstemiousness, the means to attain some prosperity (and for their children, entry to upward mobility to the professional classes), and in some cases, the basis for a medium-sized business.

The prospects appear worse still : the entry into production for the rest of the world, in an open world economy, of – say – China and India seems capable of not only transforming world technology (by profoundly changing the factor endowment of the world economy) but also of making possible pay levels that will marginalize sections of the world's workforce far more drastically than anything Polyani envisaged (he, after all, was discussing market imperatives only in a relatively isolated national economy). Indeed, some observers think this process – equalizing wages between developed and developing countries – has already begun and that this accounts for the decline in the relative position of the unskilled worker in the developed countries (Wood 1994). The evidence is not clearcut, and the time period still short to draw such drastic conclusions.

The old working class, after the appalling experience of the nineteenth century, rejoiced at the new security offered by the state in a turbulent and dangerous world. The decline in this sense of security induces both periodic panic and continuing resentment at the harsh regime that has replaced it. At the other extreme, for the new cosmopolitan worker, nationality is no longer a sacred honour, but a garment to be donned or shed according to convenience; income and class also divide the cosmopolitan and the local. The freedom to move for one individual is the threatening insecurity of the other. Immigration controls are thus equivocal – as *The Economist* (18 April 1987) put it:

> universal immigration controls keeping people out are tantamount to a Berlin Wall shutting them in. It is time to recognize that the right to freedom of movement implies a duty to permit immigration.

The ideas that people of necessity are permanently located in one national entity, that the distribution of the world's population is complete forever, and only temporary anomalies now occur are also being challenged. It would be a curious outcome if the size and composition of the labour force of each country was exactly optimal, requiring no exchanges. In practice, world economic integration continually increases rates of mobility, so that in future it is going to be as difficult internationally to give an unequivocal answer to the question 'where are you from?' as it already is in developed countries. Native places are in decline and often the complexity of an individual's origin is well beyond the conventional mythology. The marks of identity may remain individual, ancestral, tribal, occupational – and even religious – rather than national.

The fears of the competition of workers from developing countries are misplaced, even though Western politicians are adept at reinventing this threat as a means to secure their power. The scale of trade is still relatively small for it to have had profound effects (cf. Lawrence and Slaughter 1993; Bhagwatti and Kosters 1994). In any case, the differences in the productivity of workers are so great, mere differences in wages tell us little either about where production should be located or the tactics of bargaining. There is no inevitable downward auction in wages, and the record for unskilled workers in Europe and North America is affected not only by labour-intensive imports but also the choices of employers in terms of technology and management. In any case, the figures do not make allowance for the change in numbers – the growth in the class of better paid and the shrinkage in those on low pay. In a well-ordered world, the pet prescription of economists would apply – as the incomes of the majority have increased, unskilled workers have a powerful claim for full compensation if they alone are bearing the costs of that adjustment that is benefiting everyone else; in the real world, the transfer rarely occurs.

The Structure of the World's Labour Force

The need for increased movement of workers as the world economy grows is exaggerated by the changing demography of the world's labour force. As noted earlier, the world's young workers are becoming increasingly concentrated in developing countries. This is shown in the distribution of those who enter the labour force – for example, for the developed countries (the OECD group), there are 13 under the age of 15 for every 10 over the age of 65, whereas in sub-Saharan Africa, the region with the fastest growth of population, there are 156 under the age of 15 for every 10 over the age of 65.

If the distribution of workers is changing, it is also true of the highly educated. In the late 1980s, Asia produced annually some nine million graduates compared to three-and-a-half million in the developed countries. Or to look at the issue from a different angle, between 1970 and 1985, the developed country share of particular categories of the world's educated people declined as follows:

- for high school enrolments, from 44 to 30 per cent;
- for College students, from 77 to 51 per cent (Johnston 1991: 121).

If we compare the 1986 output of the highest qualified workers in the United States (the world's largest producer) with six major developing countries (Brazil, China, the Philippines, Korea, Mexico and Egypt), then the gap is narrow or exceeded (and if we include others – India, Indonesia, Bangladesh, Pakistan – then the gap is reversed):

Table 10.1

In thousands

	Total College	*Scientists*	*Engineers*	*Ph.Ds graduates*
United States	979.5	180.7	77.1	394.3
The 'Six'	1,053.1	153.8	172.6	66.2

(UNESCO, 1988, Table 3–10, p.3–306).

Indeed, developing countries appear to be becoming major world suppliers of engineers and medical doctors to the developed countries – or rather, to the world. Students and staff from developing countries also tend to be predominant in these faculties in universities of the developed countries. In 1987, in US universities, 51 per cent of doctorates in engineering were awarded to students from developing countries (compared with 48 per cent in mathematics, 32 per cent in business studies, and 29 per cent in physical sciences) (Johnston 1991: 124). Coincidentally, these two faculties – medicine and engineering – are the strongholds of Muslim Brothers in Cairo University, as if simultaneously, these traditional spearheads of secular modernity are being globalized and localized.

The emergence of national specializations in the higher skills is already advanced, and this parallels specialization in the provision of unskilled labour. It could be that in the future all engineers working in developed countries will be recruited from developing countries, that consumers of medical services will go primarily to developing countries to receive treatment, and so on. Thus, developing countries will not be simply suppliers of unskilled labour to the world, nor will the developed countries be able to monopolize the higher skills. Nor are the flows simply of workers travelling from developing to developed – consumers will increasingly travel in the opposite direction. This is what a single world economy means.

Morality and Migration

The overwhelming majority of the world's population are foreigners, and all of us are part of that great majority for most people. Even for someone from China, 79 per cent of the world's people are foreign, and 84 per cent for that other population giant, India. For a small country like Britain, 99 per cent of the world's people are foreigners. The figures put in some perspective the awful egotism of nations who see themselves as the centre of the known universe.

The morality of discussions on immigration does not start from the interests of the world, the universal, but from the minority. There is no political lobby for the majority, no agency to press for internationalism. Yet in the shift from semi-closed national economies to an open world economy, the principles by which issues should be judged are also under revision – especially so in the field of labour where moralizing is most developed. Of course, this does not mean abandoning the specific interest of a people, regardless of how big or small it is, but rather placing that interest in a universal context. This is no more than following the standard practice in morality or the law – few try to justify murder on the simple grounds of egotism, but rather acknowledge that it is universally wrong to murder, even though in this case some exception is asked.

Yet all discussions of immigration policy start from the monopoly position of government, without even a nod at a universal interest. Public debate assumes a level of state egotism and particularism that would never be tolerated in an individual. No government is required to justify its immigration policy in terms of the interests of the world; no properly constituted tribunal is empowered to judge the state. Not even a forum like GATT or the World Trade Organization exists to apply common principles or adjudicate disputes. It seems that, for governments, people are very much less important than traded commodities – or else too important to allow foreigners to be involved in deciding their fate.

Yet the need for common policies is inexorably emerging. At the moment, virtually all governments cheat on the agreed rules for accepting refugees, and do so with impunity. Those who by geographical or other accident find themselves receiving a disproportionate number of those in flight – as Germany did in the early 1990s – complain and demand a sharing of the burdens. So far this has not led to any common position, and governments continue to subordinate issues of international compassion to often the most trivial questions of local parochialism. Yet sooner or later, common policies will be required to protect any individual power, at which stage the possibility of both developing some higher set of principles and bringing practice into some relationship with those principles may arise. Then building higher walls round the country – and the most shameless cheating – to avoid lending help to those in flight might give way to collective mechanisms either to make flight no longer necessary or help to accommodate all who wish to flee (on the reasonable assumption that no one embarks on such an intrinsically dangerous option without reasonable fears of disaster). Indeed, it seems that most people do not want to move, and if they are obliged to do so, do it with great reluctance and, if at all possible, return as soon as feasible. Only in the absurd fantasies of paranoid governments are foreigners assumed to be guilty until they can prove their innocence, assumed to be desperate at any cost to break in to the destination country.

A world economy cries out for a world morality and a world system of law, but the rise of the modern state subverted that universalism – in Christianity, the duty to love thy neighbour was displaced by one's duty to kill him if the state so willed. The military chaplain became the symbol of this subversion.

The Future

The regulation of immigration assumes that the norm is either a citizen or a foreigner, and the distinction is clear cut. The citizen has rights, normally lives at home and is relatively immobile; the foreigner has no rights (other than those agreed under bilateral agreements between governments), is mobile and temporarily in the country concerned. The transition from foreigner to citizen is difficult, but if made, then the former foreigner is presumed to become immobile with the acquisition of rights.

However, the norm is coming to include mobile workers for whom nationality is no more than a means to facilitate travel although these are still a very small minority. The rights of citizens are no longer needed, only the right to work. In Germany, with its rather more strict distinction between the two, the concept of *gastarbeiter* was the intermediate form. Those intermediate forms are now multiplying as the national economy needs to import a growing number of workers, even if only for a day or a week. The provisions must be rendered increasingly elastic to allow in those who are wanted but exclude those who are not, and immigration law becomes both opaque and hypocritical (at least Singapore is honest in its sharp distinction between a class of desired professional migrants and a class of resisted manual workers). Lionel Castillo, President Carter's Commissioner of the INS noted this paradox in US immigration regulations:

> The actual policy of the US government is quite different from its stated policy, which is the strict control of the border and strict restriction of entry. The de facto policy is to keep the door half open.

The half-open door allows the recruitment of foreign workers for particular jobs – New York hospitals advertise for nurses in the Irish or Philippine press, British hospitals send recruitment officers to the Caribbean. It allows a growing mass of workers to come frequently for short visits, like a type of international commuter. It allows the recruitment of seasonal unskilled workers – Caribbean workers to the apple orchards of Florida or the farms of western Ontario, Polish workers to Germany. It obliges all governments from time to time to acknowledge the failure of their controls by legalizing illegal immigrants.

Most of the legal exceptions are for the highly skilled. The unskilled – those who make possible the work of the skilled – must rely on illegality to help the output of the developed countries grow, and therefore, potentially, undergo the most pernicious regimes of oppression. In some cases – but sadly too few – trade unions have wisely campaigned to protect illegal immigrants since the toleration of bad conditions undermines the position of both legal immigrants and native-born workers.

In the present political climate, particularly in Europe, it is difficult to believe the numbers of unskilled foreign workers admitted could be expanded without public outcry – or rather, political challenge from the extreme right – even though the economic arguments for doing so are strong. Furthermore, the numbers of immigrants required to make up for the decline in the size of the labour force and, particularly, the decline in the younger age groups, would have to be large. Zlotnik (1991) estimates that over one million immigrants would be required in Europe annually for the first half of the next century to compensate for the declining rate of natural increase.

However, once we separate the question of citizenship from that of workers, and accept that in increasingly flexible economies, temporary workers are likely to be the most rapidly expanding sectors, the issue is no longer one of large permanent transfers. Indeed, if the immigration controls were less draconian, fewer immigrant workers would be obliged to seek citizenship. For the unskilled, the right of settlement is little more than a route to security and easing the crossing of borders. The form of immigration rules itself produces a high demand for the right to settle and secure citizenship (in the same way, state regulation forces the creation of an unregulated economy, the informal or black activity). For some, settlement also carries the right to bring in close relatives, but this may also not arise if there are rights to come and go at will. If there were less of a difference between resident alien and citizen – as in the United States – fewer would bother to move permanently. Furthermore, once a worker is obliged to settle in order to work, he or she then has a powerful interest in bringing in a spouse and children, and then the worst fears of the bigots are realized – the controls have forced a net increase in the foreign-born population.

Reforming the law and easing movement would make for a considerable increase in temporary migration without settlement or acquiring the rights of a citizen. In the future, this might allow foreign workers to tender for, for example, city or hospital cleaning services, for computer programming or data loading, coming for set periods per month while remaining resident at home. Agricultural subcontracts might be run in the same way. Construction companies might similarly be able to recruit foreign work teams (and foreign construction companies bid for contracts) on a project basis. Already entertainers, singers, dancers etc are hired on a seasonal basis on international circuits. Thus, the cheapness of foreign travel might make it possible for a variety of jobs to be turned into temporary subcontracts, legal – and legally regulated – tasks that allow people to remain living at home.

For jobs which cannot be defined in discrete time periods – pre-eminently, domestic service, staffing in hospitals, hotels and restaurants – longer term but still temporary contracts might be feasible (but 'temporary' does not mean without normal rights, or access to benefits such as pensions). Again, this might be organized by companies that bid to supply labour for set periods (as Korean companies did on Middle Eastern construction contracts) and organize the turnover and replacements. Having a company responsible for this means that, in principle, it can be legally obliged to operate according to the local standards of pay and working conditions and can be sued if it does not adhere to these standards. Government authorities have too little power to check individual workers, and the immigrant home country governments are even less well equipped to ensure tolerable conditions. Of course, the horrors of indentured and contract labour are notorious, but even those horrors are superior to unemployed hunger (and very superior to working conditions taken for granted in many developing – and some developed – countries) and they can be improved provided workers have the same rights to act against their employers as the natives do, and trade unions make it their business to facilitate this.

A company-organized system of immigration (whether organized by governments, voluntary organizations or private companies) would make normal immigration controls unnecessary. The market demand for workers as shown in the contract would determine the numbers. There would be no need for arbitrary quotas or limits, since in conditions of local economic contraction, no new arrangements would be created. It would also serve to undercut the constant need to reassure the citizens that whatever privileges supposedly attached to their nationality were not being arbitrarily ignored or diluted.

With no legal restrictions on migration, the second phase would involve proper – and fair – procedures to allow that minority which might wish to translate from temporary contract worker to resident (with a right to change jobs) and so to citizen, to apply to do this. Again, there is no reason to believe that, if immigration regulations are eased, the numbers moving would be large; but no doubt some would wish to marry locally or make some longer term commitment. The issue of continuing migration for work, while staying resident at home, would have become separated from the issue of nationality.

With increased movement, there needs to be an international forum where governments can negotiate mutual concessions on the restrictions to movement, as they do on trade in the World Trade Organization (WTO) – a general agreement on migration and refugee policy. Such a forum would also be a clear focus to reprimand governments that sought to use resident foreigners as scapegoats for domestic discontents or catspaws in foreign policy concerns. Such a body could seek to secure standard rights to protect foreign workers, procedures for entry and exit, standardized taxation rules, rules for the transfer of remittances and goods, pension transfer procedures and so forth (see *The Economist*, 16 March 1991; Straubhaar 1992: 478).

More jobs for developed countries will be done abroad. Together, through flexible working practices and eased migration controls, it may be possible, first, to avoid the disasters that seem implicit in the declining size of labour force and ageing in the developed countries, and second, to give growing access to workers in developing countries to earn and to learn in the developed countries. Both have a mutual advantage in such arrangements. Furthermore, the overall expansion of the economies of the developed countries as a result of expanded immigration might produce a general expansion of labour demand to the benefit of unskilled native-born individuals, allowing an upgrading of their position (as happened in the case of the Los Angeles garment industry – McCarthy and Valdez 1986).

It is a second best remedy, compromising on the essential underlying principle that the inhabitants of the world ought to be free to come and to go in the world as they decide – and that they can be as trusted to do so sensibly in this field as in any other activity beloved of advocates of freeing the market. The compromise is to seek a means which reconciles the fears and interests of the citizens, settled in one territory, and the need for the income and output of the world to be expanded and for workers to get work.

Such arrangements do nothing for the issue of refugee flows. Here different procedures are required to establish funds to offset the financial implications of sudden large-scale movements of those in flight, to mobilize the power to protect those who are persecuted and strengthen the volunteer agencies that currently are the most effective in reacting to emergency. Treating refugees as illegal immigrants which is what many governments are coming to do is full of absurdities – it denies the person seeking refugee status the right to work; the numbers applying go well beyond the existing bureaucratic capacity of governments (so those in flight are kept in limbo for long periods of time) and is of very high cost because to prevent the refugees working, they are interned. Seeking compassion, they are imprisoned for longer or shorter periods. Allowing those in flight to work would simultaneously relieve the public purse (and so the supposed resentments of the natives), allow the refugee to restore some self respect, and meet genuine labour needs.

Sooner or later the world's governments are going to be obliged to place a tax on themselves to establish a global fund to cover the transitional costs of refugee flight, funds available to bribe governments into a greater measure of compassion than is currently allowed. With an international agency responsible for refugees, it might become possible to link refugee skills with acknowledged labour deficits so that temporary work permits for those in flight become available in places that need the workers. So important could this become, governments might compete to gain access to refugee workers rather than currently turning all away. Would making it easier to flee encourage illegal immigrants? It might, but is that issue of such moment that it should allow the ending of the supposed compassion of governments – and the current brutal hypocrisy?

For worker migrants, the suggestions here imply an increasing separation of place of work and of residence, of 'home', a dissociation long established for long-distance commuting. Internationally, it is already common, with workers moving between countries on a regular basis. It is even more common in border areas, with daily commuters travelling between the US and Mexico, Poland and Germany, France and Germany, Hong Kong and China (although officially the latter two are now one country, border controls still operate). As transport grows faster and cheaper, geographical distance is becoming increasingly less of an obstacle to such movement, and in the future, we may expect people who live in Bombay to work in New York, or residents of San Francisco to go to an office in Shanghai.

Some countries might come to employ more foreigners than natives. At an extreme, the entire labour force might live outside the country, while the natives work abroad. Domestically this has long been the case – central business districts in important cities employ a labour force, most of whom commute from outside the employment area. In such cases, the idea of democracy – residents or citizens having the exclusive right to vote – has to be amended to give some rights of participation to those who also work there. At an extreme we can imagine a country that is no more than a junction in flows, where no one 'belongs', where there is neither polity nor electorate corresponding to the national economy. It would be a perverse embodiment of Marx's principle of a communist administration – simply the administration of things, a transport terminal, not people. However, unlike communism, this would be market driven, not subject to an egalitarian democracy. The sanction against its survival would not be an adverse vote by the citizens for there are none; but travellers would fail to use it. In less extreme cases, there will be many different types of ad hoc and messy arrangements to establish a democracy of users, whether resident or not, and there are many precedents already existing for such forms.

Prediction is hazardous, as the 1950s judgement of Brinley Thomas illustrates:

> migration is ceasing to be a major factor in the rise of per capita incomes, not because of legal barriers to movement but because of its reduced economic significance. (1958: 360)

The argument here has been the exact opposite. Global integration is making the movement of commodities and of finance greater and greater – movement increases far faster than output. The world economy, it seems, has by now passed the point of no return and we are set upon the road to the creation of a single integrated global economy, regardless of the wishes of governments or citizens. Indeed, any efforts to reverse the process spell catastrophe – and particularly for the central project, the employment at tolerable incomes of all those in the world who wish to work.

By whatever route, workers will come to secure the same 'liberation'. The costs are already apparent – as always, the poor and the insecure suffer the depredations. However, that was always true within the illusory security of one national state. One needs only the most cursory acquaintance with nineteenth-century Europe to see that. The promise now is a scale of growth that will allow all to get work. This will not touch the great historic inequalities of the world, let alone achieve universal justice;

that is a different political agenda, but those with work gain the confidence to pursue these other issues. The promise is also for the ending of the record of devastating war, which is the product of the heyday of national egotisms. Fierce nationalisms have reappeared even as economic integration proceeds – indeed, economic fusion seems to be making possible a greater degree of political fission and a downsizing in the scale of political management, but the disjuncture of political and economic power makes for a decreasing scale of war, and that is some advance on the epoch of world wars.

In the new world economic order, global markets are tending to swamp national politics. Governments have decreasing power to determine what happens in their domestic economies, so that the key focus of politics in the old order is declining. The old left became almost completely submerged in the issues of state power, so that the decline in public power robs them of the supposed means to change their world. But it is not the end of politics. Younger generations take for granted that issues of State power are only one element; there are a bewildering array of other issues, from the defence of the new rapidly growing working classes of the developing countries, to issues of human rights and the future of the world. There is no programme, as there was for the old left, linking diagnosis of current disorder, who is to blame, the means to transform matters, and a comprehensive programme to change the world. The means to change, the old state, is weakening before global markets, producing a sense of helplessness in those who used to work for change. It will be a long time before any similarly comprehensive programme becomes possible. However, it will be reconstructed, as the struggle for the freedom of the majority – including that freedom to decide collectively the material means of existence, rather than just what is left over after markets have settled all the important questions – is a stubborn theme of all human history. The transition to a global politics involves the painful destruction of the old national politics of right and left, of corporatism and state socialism. There remains an intellectual vacuum within which the old left shrivels, shell shocked by the completeness of its reversals. Trade unions in the developed countries are grateful to be still alive, preoccupied with individual grievances rather than collective action, with few aspirations beyond immediate interests. The bold promises of universal freedom on their banners mock the humdrum reality. The outcome of the long confrontation between capitalist nationalism and socialist internationalism sliced the wrong way, leaving confident capitalist internationalism and defensive socialist *étatisme*. Thus the world made mock of the dreams.

If the world economy in its new guise seems to be restoring elements of the economic order of the nineteenth century (particularly that surge of cosmopolitan growth between 1840 and 1870), the world polity seems to be emulating the order of fifteenth century Europe, a mass of principalities and city-states, based upon many different principles of foundation.

History does not repeat itself; it offers us only paradoxical echoes. The world today has no earlier parallels simply because of both the extraordinary wealth of the system and the even greater potential to overcome the severe material constraints on the lot of the majority of people. All endeavours to change that state of affairs are fraught with dangers, but the dangers are still less than those offered by the past. If it is true that 40 million people died in the Soviet Union in the second World War, that 12 million perished in the concentration camps, there is a long way to go before those triumphs of European civilization are superseded in the new world order.

An antiquated national political order is being dragged along by a world economy. There are many cruelties and injustices involved in that process. But within this, world interest and a universal morality are likewise struggling to be reborn after the long dark night of nationalism and the god-like state that incubated world capitalism. There are grounds for cautious optimism.

Bibliography

Archdeacon, T.J. (1992), 'Reflections on immigration to Europe in the light of US immigration history', *IMR*, Special No. 26/2, Summer.

Bhagwatti, J. and Kosters, M.H. (1994), *Trade and Wages: Levelling Wages Down?* Washington DC: AEI Press.

Harris, N. (1995), *The New Untouchables: Immigration and the New World Worker*, IB Tauris/Penguin.

Johnston, W.B. (1991), *Global Workforce 2000: The New World Labor Market*, Harvard Business Review, March–April, pp.115–27.

OECD (1991), *Migration : the Demographic Aspects; Democraphic Change and Public Policy*, Paris: OECD.

Lawrence, R.Z. and Slaughter, M.J. (1993), *Trade and US Wages : Great Sucking Sound or Small Hiccup?* Faculty Research Working Paper Series, John F. Kennedy School of Government, Harvard University.

McCarthy, K.F. and Burciaga, V.R. (1986), *Current and Future Effects of*

Mexican Immigration in California (R-3665-CR), California Round Table/Rand Corporation, Santa Monica, Calif., May.

Polyani, K. (1944), *The Great Transformation*, Boston Mass. (1957 ed.): Beacon Press.

Straubhaar, T. (1992), 'Allocational and distributional aspects of future immigration to Western Europe', *IMR* 98, Special No., 26/2, Summer, pp.462–83.

Thomas, B. (1958), (ed.), *The economics of international migration*, London: Macmillan.

UNESCO (1988), *Statistical Yearbook 1988*, Paris: UNESCO.

Wood, A. (1994), *North-South Trade: Employment and Inequality*, Oxford: Clarendon.

–11–

Capitalism and Migrant Labour

Gareth Dale

Introduction

The 1990s have witnessed an explosive growth in research on migration. In Europe, following North America, the subject has become strongly defined as a specialist subdiscipline. In the process numerous informative (and some ground-breaking) studies have been published. One can leave major libraries with armfuls of volumes covering such topics as Tunisian women in Milan, US policy on Mexican immigration, and the assimilation of Italians in Santiago. The expansion of migration studies has generated abundant empirical research; however, subdisciplinary specialization has tended to encourage a narrowing of focus and concomitant lack of attention to the overall social processes within which migrations occur. Glance at the index of most volumes on migrant labour in the modern world and you will find a range of categories that are invoked in the course of analysis: labour markets and mobility, wages and skills, (un)employment, (uneven) economic development, globalization, citizenship and rights, law and illegality, nation states, nationalism and racism. However, although frequently discussed in useful and insightful ways, such concepts tend to be handled as if self-sufficient, with scant regard to their interrelatedness.

Some scholars, the outstanding example being Robert Miles, do pay greater attention to higher order concepts, analysing migrations against a backcloth of theorized social change. Currently one of the most influential paradigms in such studies involves the counterposition of civil society (embracing human rights and private capitals) to the states-system. As if in an inversion of Hegel's *Weltanschauung*, the itinerary of civil society is depicted as universal whereas states are tethered to particularity. Capitals are posited as footloose, paying scant respect to borders. They represent the principles of fluidity and dynamism. Their movements stimulate those of labour; their interests therefore lie in its free mobility. With internationalization, the appropriate scale of labour mobility is *global*. Capital thus enhances the shifting and mixing of populations across the globe. It is a universalizing force, sowing a cosmopolitan future. Migration control is alien to its logic.

Nation-states, according to the paradigm, are geographically emplaced, static. Their *raison d'etre* is the maintenance of sovereignty over a demarcated territory. Their rule is sustained at one level through the monopoly of legitimate force, and at another by loyalty of 'their' population. The core of that loyalty is nationalism, which stems from culturally latent and politically constructed uniformity, defined in opposition to other nations. The forging and maintenance of national uniformity entails administration and surveillance, which ideally demands fixing the national population in place. States therefore have an interest in restricting the mobility of population. Immigrants represent a threat to national unity and, by extension, to state power. States erect walls and fences around peoples and territory, in defence of *Heimat*.

To this sort of problematic some would add a rider to the effect that, in the present world, global economic integration lends increasing weight to capitals *vis-à-vis* states. The result is increased labour mobility in the face of which states, their relative powers dwindling, will become impotent. Nation-states may even dissolve, with national citizenship evolving into world citizenship.[1]

This chapter dissents from the above approaches. It sketches an alternative conceptualization of the categories listed above (from labour markets to racism), suggesting that they are all, in determinate ways, 'internally related' (Ollman 1993) as moments of the developing social system known as capitalism. The argument is not novel, but draws on the works of Marx as well as contemporary Marxists – particularly Colin Barker, but also David Harvey and others. It proceeds along a 'spiral' path, beginning with a discussion of capitalism, its defining elements presented in bare abstraction; and proceeds through analyses of the regulation and mobility of labour, and the international system. In these sections – the bulk of the chapter – the regulation by states of people and territory is shown to be bound into the relations of production, class and property that define capitalism at its core; the accumulation of capital is shown to create and depend upon the disempowering and alienation of workers, their competition over jobs and resources, and the corresponding encouragement of divisive ideologies of nationalism and racism; and both the mobility and immobility of labour are shown to be produced by inherent tendencies of capitalism, rather than by separate dynamics of the 'economic' and 'political' spheres. The chapter concludes by discussing the implications of the preceding arguments for understanding the spatial economy of capitalism and the politics of migration and racism.

Exchange and Exclusion[2]

Marx's starting point in analysing capitalism is objects produced for exchange: commodities. Commodities have two properties: they are exchanged ('exchange values') before being used (what he calls 'use values'). The latter process is determined by their qualitative aspects; the former by quantitative comparison with other commodities, with 'abstract labour time' as the common standard. Each act of social production is validated through external comparison of the abstract labour ('value') contained within. Under generalized commodity relations, the coordination of the activities of producers occurs 'behind their backs', through unplanned exchange. Such interaction is, on the one hand, based upon interdependence – the mutual need of independent producers for one anothers' products. On the other hand, it is coercive, with competition forcing all producers to conform to prevailing prices or risk returning from the marketplace with their commodities unsold. The social basis of generalized commodity production is thus a systematic separation whereby interdependent producers assume the form of atomized units governed by relations of competitive antagonism.

For such a society to exist, some system of property rules must hold sway. Because exchange depends upon the alienability of commodities, ownership must be absolute, with others by definition excluded from possession. Generalized commodity production entails a system of private property, in which the whole world of use values 'is criss-crossed by innumerable property-fences, each in principle labelled "Trespassers Keep Out!"' (Barker 1998: 26).

Property fences are erected on the principle of mutual recognition among commodity owners, thus presupposing a practicable notion of right. Their exchanges involve consent – the right to buy from and sell to whomsoever they choose. Formally, exchange is 'free and equal'; it is necessarily a 'juridical relation, whose form is the contract' (Marx 1976: 178). As Marx continues, the possessors of commodities 'must place themselves in relation to one another as persons whose will resides in those objects, and must behave in such a way that each does not appropriate the commodity of the other, and alienate his own, except through an act to which both parties consent.'

However, equality is formal only. Equal rights define property relations that govern an unequal distribution of resources that is based upon a social division of labour in which producers relate to one another competitively, on the basis of the systematic separation of each *from the objects of their need* (Barker 1998: 27). Pressures toward the transgression of property rights are thus an ever-present potential. If the freedom and equality of commodity exchange is to be upheld and respect for property rights enforced, an apparatus of management and coercion is necessary. In short, property, and therefore exclusion and *force*, are essential to the commodity form. As Barker elaborates (1998: 28), 'without the continuous organization of means of violence, the very possibility of the world of "value" relations would dissolve. . . . "Economic" processes demand, as a vital presupposition, the consolidation of a system of "rights" and "freedoms" and a set of means by which they may be maintained.' These tasks, above all the constitution and arbitration of contracts and the enforcement of exclusion (right), require a segment of society to be 'separated out to act as the universal force that objectifies all particular rights' (Kay and Mott 1982: 61). In practice, such unitary authorities take the form of states.

Bourgeois states relate in contradictory ways to the sphere of commodity production. On the one hand, their tasks are specifically 'political' and public, involving authority over society as a whole. In this sense, their guiding principles contrast with those of commodity exchange. In Barker's words (1998: 30), 'the state's transactions with its subjects are not conducted according to the rules of the market, those famous principles of freedom, equality, property and [self-interest]. The freedom of the subject is always conditional; the state may declare its subjects free, but it also constitutes them as its creatures.' On the other hand, those authoritative relations are indeed rooted in a similar sort of absolute claim as private property, and operate according to cognate principles of possession and self-interest. States make exclusive claims to certain forms of authority over 'their' subjects, imposing their will upon people and things, usually within a framework of legal right. Their territory is spatial property; thus, like the fences around private property state boundaries are jealously guarded 'and maintained by force and the threat of force' (Barker 1998: 47). Consequently, each state is concerned above all to protect and 'build' itself, a project that requires the development of policies for managing society. These functions, in turn, depend upon creaming a surplus from the 'economic sphere' (via taxation), giving states a compelling interest in 'economic' organization and direction. In the process the laws of private exchange and property are qualified – just as the rights of private property qualify the powers of states.[3]

In short, the state is obliged to treat civil society at least partially as its own property. Private property can be conceived broadly, as a differentiated totality – in Barker's words (1983: 68), as a system of social exclusions whereby the real community of producers (worldwide) is denied access to the socially produced and defined means of production. Frontier posts, immigration officials, passports, import regulations, tariffs and so forth are all manifest aspects of private property – and of the processes of exclusion which Marx examined at their most fundamental level in his consideration of the 'commodity-form'. Certainly in this perspective, *state* property is not a negation of private property, but merely one of its forms.

Wage-Labour, States, Capital

The concepts discussed so far have been introduced at a high level of abstraction, as characteristics of 'generalized commodity production'. But, as used by Marx in *Capital*, such a system is synonymous with capitalism. For, if social wealth takes the form of commodities, then the 'factors' that produce that wealth are themselves exchanged. Production therefore depends upon money being advanced, and that, in turn, will only occur if profits are envisaged.

Marx's innovation was to solve the paradox of how profits can be systematically produced without violation of the rules of fair and equal commodity exchange. Famously, his answer involved the discovery of a special kind of commodity – the energy and intelligence of workers ('labour-power') – which possesses the apparently supernatural ability to produce a greater value of commodities than that required for its own production.

The initial relation between capitalists and wage labourers is as 'free and equal' commodity owners. The former own their labour power, the latter the instruments and conditions of production, which, when set in motion by labour, produce the goods. As commodity owners, wage labourers are posited as free subjects, owners of their selves. At least ideally, they can take their labour power to market and choose which employer to sell it to; after work they dispose over their wages howsoever they please. But, Marx's argument continues, they are also 'free' of instruments of production, and hence *compelled* to sell their labour power. Wage labour 'is therefore not voluntary but forced, it is *forced labour*' (Marx 1975: 326). At work, wage-earners' rights to self-ownership may be partially asserted, but technically they are mere tools in the hands of capital – indeed, the very instruments of its aggrandizement.

The contradictory 'freedom' of wage labour has a juridical expression. Wage labour is a peculiar sort of commodity (and therefore property), being embodied within a person with a will. Formally, workers and capitalists meet as equivalents, but in their exchange workers agree to submit their wills to the capitalist, so losing real subjectivity. Although Marx therefore describes the worker's freedom as an 'illusion', it is nonetheless one that does manifestly and juridically exist, and 'thus essentially modifies [the wage-worker's] relation [to appropriators of labour] by comparison to that of workers in other social modes of production' (1973: 284).

Thus, if the market appears as the realm of freedom and 'human rights' it does so on the basis of despotism. In Barker's rendition of Marx's account (1997: 36),

> the buyer and seller of labour-power meet together, as formally free contracting agents, in the market. They transact their business under conditions of legal equality, with each of them entitled to refuse to enter into a contract with the other, and each entitled to bargain over the terms of any contract they do make. But, once the bargain is struck, they move off into a quite different sphere of social relations, within the workplace. Here the buyer of labour-power demands the use of the property he has just hired, and sets the seller to work, as a worker. Now the relationships between them need to be described in a quite different language. . . . Marx turns to the political language deployed by the analysts of slavery and ancient empires, the language of 'despotism'. Within the workplace, the buyer of labour-power has become the 'master', the 'boss', while the seller has transmuted into the 'hand', the 'worker', the 'wage slave'.

Evidently, the worker's 'supernatural' ability is in reality the product of a distinctive set of social conditions, notably the commodification of the means of production and of labour power.

Here too, we discover the role of states to be less the antagonists of capital relations than forces vital to their emergence and continuity. In crucial ways, capital and wage labour are created and constituted through states. At the heart of Marx's account is the cleavage of social productive forces into objectified property on one side and producing but propertyless subjects on the other. Historically this severance first developed during an epoch of 'so-called primitive accumulation', a global colligation of processes centring on the expropriation of the English peasantry but also embracing 'the colonies, the national debt, the modern tax system, and the system of protection' as well as the 'discovery of gold and silver in America, the extirpation, enslavement and entombment in mines of the indigenous population of that continent, the beginnings of the conquest and plunder of India, and the conversion of Africa into a preserve for the commercial hunting of black skins' (1976: 915). It is only on the back of these coercive developments that labour power and means of production became commodified in a systematic and generalized way.

Plainly, states were not mere midwives at the birth of capitalism but the very muscles governing contraction. However, their indispensability to capitalist production relations does not rest at progeniture. They give legal form to the relations between capitals, and between capital and labour; they enforce law – arbitrating disputes, enforcing contracts, and punishing breaches.[4] In this regard, argues Bob Fine (1984: 153), the 'state is the juridic aspect of capital', and 'should be seen not as a thing but as a class relation'. States constitute and uphold the walls of property exclusion – crucially, the dispossession of workers, if need be through direct coercion. Further, they engage in shaping the coordinates of capital accumulation: regulating the production and circulation of labour, the media of commodity exchange, and so forth.

In this light it is clearly unhelpful to conceive of political and economic institutions simply as representing contrasting interests as regards the creation and management of wage labour. Although the interests of particular states and enterprises do constantly diverge, the two types of institution nevertheless also share an underlying unity. Claude Meillassoux points us, I think, in the right direction, by positing a division of labour between states and businesses in securing the conditions of exploitation:

> the development of wage-earning does not eliminate the costs of law and order necessary for the exploitation of labour, which are always, both at home and in the colonies, supported by the capitalist State. In no case can the resort to such political means be treated as extra-economic. They reveal a given differentiation of costs and labour . . . between private entrepreneurs and the capitalist State, to set up the structures which most effectively exploit labour and realise profit. (1981: 92)

Wage labour and capital are creations of their interrelation, but that relation is itself constituted through states. States, like capitals, depend for their existence upon the extraction of surplus labour, and must engage directly in that activity. They are themselves class relations, as well as the organizing forces of 'economic' class relations. Both states and capitals thus stand against wage labour 'as the alienated form of its own powers' (Fine 1984: 153).

Separation, Competition, Struggle

Thus far we have encountered two great antagonistic 'separations'. The first is of producing units from one another, expressed juridically in fragmented property relations, and which underpins (or exacerbates) a further fracture – of state from civil society. The capitalist class, worldwide, is riven and driven by competition, with individual firms compelled to expand, to invest, to outcompete rivals. States, being farmers of surplus extraction, are forced to intervene in, consolidate, and perpetually remould social relations in the interests of capitalist development.

The second involves the separation of objectified property (capital) from propertyless labour, and thus the sundering of productive capacities from human needs. It occurred (and occurs) 'originally' through the expropriation of peasants and their concomitant uprooting from communal, 'tribal' and/or kinship networks, and persists through the exploitation of workers by capital and the relative impoverishment of the former.

The two separations are internally related. Competition relentlessly forces capitalists to maximize accumulation, which involves, among other things, intensive management of the workforce. Mechanisms of control must be erected, greater security for and loyalty of employees may be sought, and attention may be directed to influencing external parameters such as state policies regarding employment, taxation, immigration, and working conditions.

Accumulation, in turn, underpins a set of tendencies towards increasing socialization of production. Driven by competition, capitals expand. Businesses merge, form alliances, and swallow rivals. Close bonds with states may be forged while expanding international trade and investment extend and integrate the worldwide division of labour. As a result, workers become combined (in the 'natural' or 'technical' sense) as the limbs of an ever-expanding and increasingly integrated (even 'globalized') collective labourer. But this is, in Marx's depiction (1973: 470), a collectivity of an alienated kind, whereby

> the overall process . . . [is] the work of the different workers together only to the extent that they are [forcibly] combined, and do not [voluntarily] enter into combination with one another. The combination of this labour appears . . . subservient to and led by an alien will and an alien intelligence . . . Hence, just as the worker relates to the product of his labour as an alien thing, so does he relate to the combination of labour as an alien combination.

In contradiction to the various forms of socialization of the processes of production of worldly wealth is the situation of workers outside that realm. Here they exist, in principle, atomized as individual consumers and commodity owners. Paradoxically, then, where workers collectively produce society they possess no real subjecthood, no real autonomy or property; only where they are practically powerless, as individuals spending their wages and 'free time', do they enjoy 'sovereignty' in their actions. The commodification of labour power delivers formal rights, but these come in a package deal together with social atomization and alienation, with commodity owners (including wage workers) posited as isolated subjects, their interdependency existing in the form of relations between their objects (including labour power).

If the argument thus far is credible, capitalist relations may be viewed as arising from and operating through a matrix of antagonistic separations. Divorced from the conditions of production, workers are dependent upon them (in the form of capital), above all for wages – those keys to the means of needs-fulfilment (such as survival and pleasures). The wage relation is the fundamental form of control of labour; as Marx put it, if 'workers could live on air, it would not be possible to buy them at any price' (1976: 748).

Secondly, there is the antagonism of capitals, reflected in (and based upon) that amongst workers on the labour market.[5] Here, the owners of labour power are rivals: victory for one spells defeat for another. Labour market competition means that occupational insecurity and the relentless compulsion to work hard, obediently, etc., although ultimately caused by the existential dependence of workers upon capital, *appear* (in part at least) in the guise of other workers and the unemployed.

Further fragmentations, of course, include those rooted in the technical division of labour, stratification along axes of pay and conditions, as well as seemingly 'natural' fault lines of gender, locality, nation and ethnicity. The result is a proliferation of cross-cutting status hierarchies through which the competitive aspirations of individual 'social mobility' can take on a political charge.

Workers alienated from one another, divided into competing individuals and groups, are ideal material for domination and exploitation. As Michael Lebowitz argues, '[w]hen workers compete among themselves, they press in the *same direction* as capital – the tendency is to *increase* the rate of surplus value! [Thus] the efforts of wage-labourers as *individuals* to act in their self-interest run counter to the interests of wage-labour as a *whole*' (1992: 66). He concludes that '*a necessary condition for the existence of capital is its ability to divide and separate workers*' (1992: 85).[6]

Conversely, the greater the degree of workers' conscious combination, the greater will be their ability to contest the dictates of capital. If powerlessness and subjugation to those dictates breed upon competition and division, then overcoming divisions is presumably a condition of successful resistance.

Mobility of Labour

If the generalization of the commodity form provides a suitable first step towards understanding the alienated, class-divided and competitive relations of capitalism, it also offers an approach into conceptualizing the mobility of commodities, including capital and labour power. For Marx, generalized commodity production centres on a process of 'real abstraction', in which all particular kinds of social labour are rendered commensurable via reduction to their common denominator, 'abstract labour'. Through production for exchange, commodities 'acquire a socially uniform status as values, which is distinct from their sensuously varied objectivity as articles of utility' (1976: 166). In capitalism, production is determined by relations of exchange value, which is 'a generality, in which all individuality and peculiarity are negated and extinguished' (1973: 157). This dynamic of homogenization is contrasted by Marx with pre-capitalist societies, in which the producer's 'productive activity and his share in production are bound to a specific form of labour and of product, which determine his relation to others in just that specific way.'

In Marx's view, if economic relations function through the comparison of quanta of abstract labour time, labour power itself must be universally alienable and generically applicable. This, in turn, implies universal mobility. As Marx puts it, '[i]ndifference towards specific labours corresponds to a form of society in which individuals can with ease transfer from one labour to another, and where the specific kind is a matter of chance for them, hence of indifference' (1973: 104). Wage labour is universal, generalized labour; in principle it can attach itself to any and every employer. Like money, it is in essence unrestricted in its activity and movements by customary norms, legal rules, political organizations and so forth. Wage workers are, in theory, indifferent to their occupations, and can retrain and relocate according to the demands of market forces.[7]

Like any other commodity, the circulation of labour power is, in principle, governed by the law of value. Wage workers, because the chief use value of their labour power to themselves is money, are, in theory, always 'ready and willing to accept every possible variation in . . . [their] activity which promises higher rewards' (Marx, in Harvey 1982: 381). The wage system enables labour to be allocated via the labour market such that the complex and changing needs of capitals can be met. This enables the supersession of petrified divisions of labour and the organization of cooperative labour on an ever-extending basis. As such, mobile labour power is essential to accumulation. In Marx's words, capital accumulation, in the modern age, constantly 'revolutionizes the division of labour within society, and incessantly throws masses of capital and of workers from one branch of production to another. Thus [modern] industry, by its very nature, necessitates variation of labour, fluidity of functions, and mobility of the worker in all directions' (1976: 617).

In addition to enabling the transformation of the division of labour, labour mobility intensifies competition by hastening the flow of capital into more profitable sectors. Accumulation is an inherently uneven and fluctuating process, with workers 'constantly repelled and attracted, slung backwards and forwards' (1976: 583) among positions within a firm, between firms and between branches of industry, and even from one country to another. In his brilliant discussion of this question, Harvey concludes that the 'versatility and geographical mobility of labour power as well as the "indifference" of workers to the content of their work are essential to the "fluidity of capital". . . . The more mobile the labourer, the more easily capital can adopt new labour processes and take advantage of superior locations' (p. 381).

If this appears to be an 'economic' argument it surely has political consequences. For capitalists it would appear to warrant support for policies of maximizing labour mobility, perhaps in conjunction with a philosophy of economic liberalism. It would justify the 'abolition of all laws preventing the labourers from transferring from one sphere of production to another and from one local centre of production to another [and the elimination of] all the legal and traditional barriers that would prevent [capitalists] from buying this or that kind of labour-power' (Marx, in Harvey 1982: 381). Capitalism, in sum, seems to generate processes of 'abstraction' in which the relations of qualitative properties are determined by quantitative yardsticks, thereby giving rise to a society in which all workers, being free and universally mobile, 'are alike in the face of capital' (1976: 364).

The Commodity's Double Edge

In reality, however, commodities are not unrestricted in their movements, workers are not alike in the face of capital, nor indeed are capitals alike in the face of workers. Commodities are not pure, fluid distillations of abstract labour; exchange values only exist through use values, and use values cannot create themselves out of thin air. Production and distribution take place in concrete space. They occur thanks to the organization in a complex social, technical and spatial division of labour of real people (with particular attributes) and physical means of production in actually existing places. All such conditions of production are in one sense 'concrete'. None exist in a frictionless world.

In this manner, Chris Harman describes capitals as follows (1991: 12):

> each individual capital has a twofold character. As well as being measurable in terms of exchange-value, it is also a concrete use-value – a concrete set of relations between individuals and things in the process of production. Each particular capital has its concrete ways of bringing together labour-power, raw materials and means of production in the production process, of raising finance and getting credit, of establishing networks for distributing and selling its output.[8]

Different moments and types of capital have different relations to material infrastructures. Some are more territorially rooted than others, but none exist 'in themselves' in a pure mercurial form, for the creation of value necessarily entails the interconnection of different capitals in relations of dependency and competition; such connections make up different moments of the pathway of capital in its process of self-expansion. Therefore even the most ephemeral forms of circulating capital are linked both into and against networks of more incarnated forms in a dialectic of the restless and the stationary, of flux and fixity.[9] Reflected in capitalists' orientation to policy, the emphasis of some, depending on circumstances, may be on forms of freedom of circulation whereas others may prioritize the need for secure conditions of production and reproduction.

If the distinction between use value and exchange value offers a way towards grasping the contradictory forces that shape the mobility of capital, the same holds good for labour power. The exchange value of labour power is expressed in its price, albeit determined at bottom by the labour time necessary for its production and reproduction. As an aspect of capital, the laws governing its production and distribution are 'embedded within those that regulate the mobility and accumulation of capital in general' (Harvey 1982: 380). But its use value (to capital) is something else entirely. First and foremost it is the capacity to labour to produce profit. It is hired to perform specific tasks, which depend upon definite combinations of energy, imagination, strength, particular skills and other abilities. Perhaps unfortunately for capitalists, these attributes are not stacked, disembodied, on supermarket shelves, but arrive at the workplace attached to walking, talking, living creatures.

In their aspect as living profit-making beings, wage workers pose a series of problems for capitalists. Capital-producing labour does not exist in nature but must be created. This can occur through the 'seduction' of workers from non-wage relations, in a process commonly involving migratory movements.[10] Where land is freely available for occupation, however, and where proletarians are scarce and labour markets primitive, coercive measures may take centre stage, in the interests of ensuring the supply of profitable labour, via the denial of workers' ownership rights over their 'own' labour power and restriction of its circulation.[11]

In circumstances where capitalist production is fully developed the supply and cost of labour power is regulated by the wage system and the production and absorption of a 'surplus population'. A cardinal moment of accumulation is the reproduction of workers; as Marx puts it, '[t]he labour-power withdrawn from the market by wear and tear, and by death, must be continually replaced by, at the very least, an equal amount of fresh labour-power' (1976: 275). Wages provide the means 'to reproduce the muscles, nerves, bones and brains of existing workers, and to bring new workers into existence' (1976: 717).

Regulating the level of wages and supply of labour is the 'reserve army' of the unemployed, a fluctuating product of two tendencies of accumulation. On the one hand, capitals are driven by the imperative of producing an ever greater mass of surplus value that, to be realized, demands greater quantities of labour power. In Marx's account, '[i]t is a law of capital . . . to create surplus labour, disposable time; it can do this only by setting *necessary labour* in motion . . . It is its tendency, therefore, to create as much labour as possible . . . This is why capital solicits the increase of population' (1973: 399). On the other hand, due to the imperative of maximizing productivity, 'It is equally a tendency of capital to make human labour (relatively) superfluous.' The outcome of these contradictory tendencies towards both increasing and decreasing demand for labour power is, as Miles explains (1986: 53), anything but spatially even, for certain sectors of the economy 'may be undergoing major reorganisation of the labour process, leading to the expulsion of large numbers of workers from production, while others are recruiting new workers'. Nor is the process temporally smooth. In Marx's account (1976: 785), the formation, absorption, and re-formation of a 'reserve army' of labour performs an active role in the business cycle. In times of crisis labour reserves increase, thereby enabling accelerated accumulation thanks to 'the possibility of suddenly throwing great masses of men into the decisive areas without doing any damage to the scale of production in other spheres.'

Contradictions in the Regulation of Labour Power

The regulation of labour through 'automatic' economic mechanisms, however, does not resolve all contradiction. For example, individual capitals require a pool of available labourers with particular attributes and certain kinds of price tags attached; to them, however, this pool is an 'externality', it is affected by employers' behaviour but its regulation is beyond the power of any private interest. It is therefore possible for the procedures of capital to contribute to the exhaustion of workers – the 'vital force of the nation' (Marx 1976: 348). The imperative upon capitals to raise the rate of exploitation results in pressures to lengthen and intensify the working day, reduce wages, skimp on safety measures, and make workers redundant. As a consequence, given their propertylessness, workers' lives tend to be intrinsically insecure and subject to pressures that cripple, reduce, or even kill them. In Marx's impassioned words, accumulation is a process that 'does away with all repose, all fixity and all security as far as the worker's life-situation is concerned' (1976: 618). Capital's 'blind desire for profit' drives 'towards a limitless draining away of labour-power' (1976: 348). With the tendency to create relative surplus population comes 'the misery, the sufferings, the possible death of the displaced workers during the transitional period when they are banished into the industrial reserve army!' (1976: 793). Thus the 'economic' forms through which labour power is regulated, distributed and priced, create what Harvey terms 'an endemic crisis of fluctuating intensity for much of the working class' (1982: 161).

Individual employers may seek to ameliorate such tendencies, for example through granting workers an allotment, or usufruct rights to a parcel of land, or tied accommodation. These provide the worker with a degree of security, and, by tying them to the property of their employer, provide the latter with a stable workforce. However, responsibility for workers' conditions of life and work, as well as for the regulation of the supply and price of labour power, are generally displaced onto the public sphere.

In this regard states mediate two 'economic' pressures. One is to maintain the supply, mobility (and 'flexibility') and to lower the price of labour power. Hence they may seek to ensure that the force of surplus population is brought to bear on workers, to 'encourage' the conversion of labour power into labour. On the other hand, states look to preserve and cultivate the workforce. The two underlying principles – social policy and profit making – may clash in detail, but share a singular basis. In the revealing words of a nineteenth century Poor Law commissioner, '[i]t is an admitted maxim of social policy that the first charge upon the land must be the maintenance of those reared upon it. Society exists for the preservation of property; but subject to the condition that the wants of the few shall only be realized by first making provision for the necessities of the many' (cited by Chris Jones and Tony Novack, in Corrigan 1980: 145).

States attend to the 'necessities of the many' in several key areas. First, the regeneration of the workforce must be secured. This takes place primarily through unpaid labour in the family household, which is therefore an institution that states are generally careful to shape and maintain. A second task involves direct measures to bolster the material security of workers, such as restrictions on the length of the working day, ensuring that an affordable infrastructure of sanitation, health, and housing is in place, and maintaining the 'reserve army' through social security schemes.

Finally, states appropriate many of the general tasks of 'tailoring' the attributes of the workforce to the needs of business. Capital is produced not by raw muscle but by labour power with specific characteristics – such as particular languages, literacy, experience, or skills. Productivity may be greatly enhanced through improvements in such fields as education, training, health. In general, more equipped workers are less replaceable, and in direct competition with fewer others. Accordingly, businesses may have to worry more about gaining access to and keeping hold of such workers. States may be obliged to attend to the detailed management of the domestic workforce, entailing investment in complex, durable and typically immobile social and physical infrastructures (cf. Harvey 1982: 398ff.).

Mobility and Immobility of Labour

Clearly the circulation of labour power cannot be understood separately from its production and reproduction. Clearly, too, the supply of appropriate labour-power to capital is not automatically spirited from within the accumulation process itself. Labour power exists as particular labourers with specific capacities; it is a notoriously 'inelastic' commodity, and provokes all manner of strategies for administering its production and circulation.

Accumulation depends upon the regulation of the workforce such that it is available, willing, and appropriately equipped. In the achievement of these ends contradictory tendencies in respect of labour mobility appear. One author who has touched upon these is Guglielmo Carchedi (1979: 57). After outlining the interests capitals have in free labour mobility he then asks 'But how can we explain the recurrent capitalist attempts . . . to bind the production agents to certain positions, locations, etc.?' The answer he gives is instructive, namely that

> both mobility and immobility can be ways in which capital attempts to increase the rate of exploitation and reinforces its rule over labour. The mobility 'enjoyed' by labour-power transforms itself into its opposite when labour-power transforms itself into labour, i.e. when it leaves the labour market and enters the production process. But, on the other hand, both immobility of labour-power on the labour market (e.g. in order to keep an abundant supply of labour power in certain branches or areas) and mobility within the production process (dismissals, dequalifications, promotions [etc.]) can be, and usually are, necessary to achieve capital's aims.

Employers may rely upon labour mobility but they generally also benefit from what Harvey describes as 'a stable, reliable workforce and captive labour supplies' (1985: 148), especially where they have invested in the education and training of their workforce. In this regard employers may gamble that the labour market permits such stability, but many will hedge that risk with schemes involving company pensions, promotion promises and other sub-market means of binding employees. Moreover, businesses may fund or support welfare and training programmes, and other examples of social infrastructure, and may well give backing to social and economic policies that in practice restrict the mobility of labour.

Similar contradictions also affect the policies of states. Although capitalist states have, historically, shouldered responsibility for the creation of nationwide labour markets, because all contracts are constructed through states in a system of many states, even the freest internal mobility inevitably comes up against national barriers. Moreover, conjoined to the management of free internal mobility is the coordination of welfare.[12] Bourgeois states have always been 'welfare states' – maintaining and constraining the material security of 'their' populations. They help to regulate and mobilize labour reserves, keeping them in place as a permanent threat to those in employment, or encouraging emigration in the hope that foreign exchange inflows will ensue. As discussed above, they attempt to shape, or directly manage, the institutions in which the reproduction and education of the workforce occur. In the process, powerful interests in the governance and indeed restriction of labour mobility arise. In the extreme, recourse may be made to outright emigration control, whether selective – such as the restrictions by the Turkish state on emigration by Zonguldak miners (cf. Collinson), or general, such as the Berlin Wall.

Clearly, the management of social reproduction invariably entails the transgression of another inherent imperative of capitalism – toward the free mobility of labour. These clashing imperatives find reflection in the twin poles of bourgeois political thought: liberalism, with its emphasis on free mobility, equality of opportunity, and universal rights, and conservative currents whose chief sympathies lie with institutions of social stability and control. Reflected in the literature of migration, conservatives tend to justify curbs on mobility in the interests of 'stability', whereas liberals – such as Julian Simon and James Hollifield – advocate the extension of rights and/or lowering of restrictions.[13]

From the arguments of the last few pages it appears that labour power is only in one aspect a universally exchangeable and mobile commodity. Comprising its other aspect are particular workers. They speak a language and may wish to remain in the area where it is spoken; they have particular skills that may chain them to an occupation or a branch of industry; their attributes and mobility are shaped and carefully monitored by spatially rooted institutions. Viewed historically, the rise of capitalism entailed the erosion of feudal ties of dependence, but generated in their place modern forms of spatial fixation – including that of workers to their employers and to states. As Nicos Poulantzas has expressed it, '[t]he direct producers are freed from the soil only to become trapped in a grid – one that includes not only the factory but also the modern family, the school, the army, the prison system, the city and the national territory' (1980: 105).

The Contrary Subjects of Labour Power

The discussion so far has been of labour-power as a bundle of muscles and other attributes of use to employers, with workers taking the stage, as in Marx's *Capital*, primarily as automata – 'personifications of economic categories' (1976: 92). However, labour power is peculiar. As Felton Shortall puts it, 'whereas all other commodities appear as objects that are not only *alienable* but also separable from their owners, labour-power, although it is alienable ... is *inseparable* from the subjective being of its bearer – the worker' (1994: 271). Workers are not merely subjects of capital, but are subjects in the human sense: they are active and conscious, involved in myriad social relations that find conscious representation in the form of 'identities'. Workers make sense of their social situation, expressing feelings, discussing meanings, deliberating actions. The attributes of energy, cooperation and imagination that are indispensable use values to their hirers are simultaneously use values to themselves, even enabling them to organize collectively against – or for – any or all aspects of the social order. In short, workers experience and interpret the economic, juridical and cultural relations mentioned above, and act upon them. They express hostility or sympathy towards the system of exploitation, towards workers occupying different rungs of the ladders of social status, towards foreigners, and so forth.

The methods used by workers to resist the ravages of exploitation bear upon the issues of labour mobility and the role of states. Workers engage in a tug of war over the value of their labour power, over the condition of the reserve army, and the rules and norms governing labour mobility. They may press for 'rigidities' in the labour market in so far as these protect their conditions, and oppose 'flexibilization'. Unions may gain influence over hiring and firing policy, may secure collective bargaining on a nation-wide scale, and may attempt to influence recruitment from the 'external reserve army' into the national labour market.

Second, workers, understood as 'creative subjects . . . perpetually roam the world seeking to escape the depredations of capital, shunning the worst aspects of exploitation, always struggling, often with some success, to better their lot' (Harvey 1982: 380). Although, as Harvey continues (1982: 384), '[c]apital in general relies upon this perpetual search by workers for a better life . . . as means to orchestrate labour mobility to its requirements'; migration nonetheless tends to reflect and reinforce an upward drift of workers' needs and aspirations. Migrants benefit from and contribute to the 'fructifying effects of living in the tension of two cultures' (Simon 1989: 100), and transmit those effects back home. In the process, migration develops the geographical and cultural interconnectedness of the working class, strengthening the potential for the erosion of local and national parochialisms.

Third, workers counter the destruction and disruption of what Harvey calls 'traditional support mechanisms and ways of life' by establishing 'networks of personal contacts', 'support systems and elaborate coping mechanisms within family and community', which may function as islands of solidarity (1982: 384). Workers exist in a complex system of social relationships in the realms of work, family, leisure, and so forth. These involve those interpersonal, cultural, and linguistic solidarities and commonalities that render labour power such a 'sticky' commodity: one which, thanks to the financial and psychological costs of moving, may often stay put even where that is, in market terms, an 'economically irrational' strategy. To paraphrase Michael Piore (1979: 52), most people work in a community setting, where each job is one of a series of interlocking social roles in terms of which individuals are 'identified' as persons by those to whom they relate, and through which they in turn define themselves.[14] Such identities tend to act as barriers to geographical mobility, though may also provide bridges for 'chain migration'. Their self-definition may refract antagonism to ruling classes. Or they may take divisive forms; as Harvey puts it, '[e]xclusion of other workers – on economic, social, religious, ethnic, racial, etc., grounds – may also be seen as crucial to the protection of the islands of strength already established' (1982: 384).

Finally, negotiating the trammels of exploitation may drive workers to illegal activity, such as theft, moonlighting or tax evasion.

In the light of these considerations it is apparent that the problematic of labour 'regulation' is not simply bound up with its production and circulation, but with the conscious reactions of workers to their social relations, including exploitation. The question of 'control' is raised again, this time from another angle.

Once again, one can point to a variety of 'economic' mechanisms that 'encourage' workers to sell their labour power at a convenient price, and which assure their submission to the laws of capital. These include the 'fragmentations' of the working class mentioned above, and the wage system, which operates in such a way as 'to prevent the workers, those instruments of production who are possessed of consciousness, from running away,' (Marx 1976: 719). They include the reserve army of labour, which 'weighs down the active army of workers [and] puts a curb on their pretensions' (Marx 1976: 792). And they include the spatial concentration of the labour process into workplaces where supervision is more effective.[15]

However, control can never be imposed by economic forces alone. Not only do the laws of capital tend to undermine the material bases of production, but workers can and do resist. In response, states become involved in wider tasks of social control – in effect, the management of workers' reactions to exploitation and alienation, whether those take the form of organized struggle, crime, interpersonal violence, or sundry 'deviance'. These tasks – sometimes summarized as 'law and order' – involve labelling, policing, and terrorizing. Significantly, they often involve, wittingly or not, the organization of forms of discrimination and oppression, involving the invention or buttressing of divisions amongst workers. Combined with the state's aforementioned responsibilities for welfare and education, they necessitate intensive activities of surveillance, registration and – crucially! – taxation. In turn, these impart states with a keen interest in ensuring a degree of stability of population.

In part due to their role in the regulation and policing of workers, capitalist states have become adept at intervention in all spheres of society, developing what Michael Mann (1988) terms 'infrastructural' power to a tremendous extent. Although recent decades may have seen a weakening of some powers of some states, others seem to be growing. For example, Mann suggests that over the last twenty-five years nation-states have continued to usurp erstwhile local powers, and 'have increasingly regulated the intimate private spheres of the life cycle and the family' as well as areas such as 'consumer protection and the environment' (1993: 118). Regulating migration, presumably, could be added to the list.

Abstract and Real Subjectivities

Workers are not mere hirelings of capital, but are subjects in their own right. Their real, concrete subjectivity, its expressions and suppression, have been discussed above. But workers also, in so far as they are 'free', possess formal, abstract subjectivity. They are constituted juridically – through states – as legal persons and owners of property (their labour power and, by extension, their own selves).

The two variants of subjectivity interact in significant ways. Workers, in general, positively value the rights that adhere to their status as propertied persons. Although formal, rights are eminently real, and bolster substantive claims and actions. Workers' organizations have historically been at the forefront of struggles for the extension and deepening of citizenship rights – in the forms of civil liberties, rights of suffrage and of industrial and political activity, as well as 'social rights' to welfare provision. In turn, the expansion of such rights generally furthers the capacities of workers to organize, to press for reform within the workplace and beyond.

However, the systems of formal rights, legal authority, and citizenship are simultaneously the juridicial clothing of the very relations of exploitation and domination that suppress and deny workers' real subjectivity. One notorious effect of this contradiction is that liberal principles are persistently subverted by the very states that proclaim them. Law may be simultaneously based upon abstract principles of equality whilst actually enforcing norms of inequality and discrimination in the pursuit of social control. Just as capitalism's 'abstract' tendency towards the universal freedom and equality of commodities is undermined by the exigencies of competition and the management of exploitation, so its 'abstract' tendency to the universal freedom and equality of citizens is subverted – essentially by the same concrete realities.

The juxtaposition of these two contradictions is not arbitrary. Where rights to property in the form of labour power are denied, legal and political rights are likely to be lacking, too. This is apparent when one considers systems of unfree labour, such as slavery in antebellum USA. Bonded labour in the American colonies initially developed as a method of ensuring labour supplies in a context where appropriate indigenous labour was scarce and 'free' land was readily available. It was not imparted with a radically racial character until the late seventeenth century, when numerous, frequently interracial, rebellions shocked plantation owners and other élites into establishing racial segregation as a means of incorporating white workers. These were vouchsafed legal privileges that cemented formal commonality with the white bourgeoisie, against enslaved blacks. As a number of historians, notably Theodore Allen, have shown, the racism of employers and officials was deployed as a deliberate – if often unspoken and sometimes only dimly recognized – instrument of social control. Even though labour competition was thereby attenuated, the erection of a racial division of labour was profitable, for it rendered white workers 'glad to hold what they have, rather than reach out for more' (Allen 1994: 158).

In this light it is worth noting that the American constitution, one of the great documents in the history of bourgeois right, implicitly made immigration a white-skin privilege by classifying Europeans as immigrants, Africans as imports. It was followed in 1790 by an Act which provided that 'any alien, being a free white person . . . may be admitted to become a citizen' of the US (Allen 1994: 185). White arrivals, often facing an insecure material future, were offered a solid place at the upper table of racial equals; they were implicitly enrolled – at least in their formal subjectivity – into a system that erected 'the social honor of the "poor whites" . . . upon the social *declassement* of the Negroes.' (Weber 1968: 391).[16] As Friedrich Engels remarked, 'it is significant of the specifically bourgeois character of these human rights that the American Constitution, the first to recognize the rights of man, in the same breath confirms the slavery of the colored races existing in America: class privileges are proscribed, race privileges sanctioned' (in Draper 1977: 268).

'*Specifically bourgeois character*?' What can Engels mean but that the development of capitalism underpins tendencies both to the greatest formal freedoms and the most repugnant inequalities; that the lofty ideology of civilization and human rights was built upon the sweat and blood of forced labour. Seldom has this contradiction been more clearly illuminated than by Fox-Genovese and Genovese (1983), in their argument that the origins of racism lay in the (initially barely conscious) response of bourgeois advocates of slavery to the contradiction in which they found themselves:

> The bourgeois apologists have had a point: capitalism . . . created a new and dynamic theory and practice of individual freedom and carried it . . . to the far reaches of an astonished world. Along with that freedom, capitalism also carried slavery, serfdom, peonage, genocide, and, in general, mass murder and cruelty on a scale previously perhaps beyond sadistic imagination and

> certainly beyond technological and political capacity . . . Thus the anomaly: capitalism, which rested on free labor and had no meaning apart from it, not only conquered the world; it created new ones, including systems of chattel slavery, on an unprecedented social scale and at an unprecedented level of violence. . . . Thus, slavery in a bourgeois world context required a violent racism not merely as an ideological rationale but as a psychological imperative. (1983: vii, 403)

Clearly, even the most hallowed laws of free competition, not to mention human rights, are forgotten if their transgression leads to the greater prize of the division of the exploited.

In short, citizenship and civil rights are not universal goods but in practice the *property* of states.[17] These are locked into relations of exploitation, which, in turn, depend upon mechanisms of oppression and social control. Citizenship and rights are used as instruments to divide, privilege, and control sections of the subject population. From the American constitution, to Joseph Chamberlain's 'Natal Formula' (which imposed proficiency in a European language as a hurdle for admission to Australia in order to maintain its 'whiteness' without disobeying the principle of equal standard), to the widespread denial of rights to 'undocumented' immigrants in today's world, liberties are selectively administered by states. Though formally universal they function in practice in particular, often discriminatory, ways.

Citizenship and Nationalism

If the first effect of the paradoxical unity of the systems of formal rights and exploitation relations is to refract rights into inequalities, the second is ideological. If relations of substantive inequality are manifested in the juridical form of equivalence, then distinctions between, say, owners of capital and wage slaves are flattened and shrouded. Both are citizens, equal before the law, and with an equal voice and equal vote in the political arena. And with abstract, universal law appearing as the arbiter of legal dispute, the coercive rule of particular interests adopts a mystified form as 'the authority of an objective, impartial norm' (Pashukanis 1980: 96).

That legality, citizenship and bourgeois democracy simultaneously expand the substantive capacities of workers and their organizations and yet subserve the 'economic' relations in which workers are shackled to capital, has had profound effects upon workers' movements. Historically, as the numbers, power and political experience of workers developed, their organizations tended to press for a fair share in the civic and political rights allowed to the privileged classes. But because all such rights, including the rights to association and political expression, are individualized and exist through states, however, their realization involves, as it were, an invitation of workers as individuals into their respective states. In most of the world, workers have fought for and received entry tickets to the political community, but only as aggregates of 'isolated individuals, without property and abstracted from communal solidarities' (Wood 1995: 211) and from their social existence as collective producers. Admittance of the masses, moreover, invariably occurred alongside the diminution of citizenship, which lost its participatory qualities as it became standardized and universal. In the process the 'nation' to which citizenship endowed membership became more and more *imagined*, as compared to the earlier commonwealth of the political nation which 'corresponded to a real community of interest among the landed aristocracy' (Wood 1995: 212). The democratic nation is thus based upon what Marx, anticipating Benedict Anderson, termed 'the abstraction of a community whose members have nothing in common but language etc., and barely even that' (in Sayer 1991: 82).

Seen from this angle, the rise of institutions of citizenship and democracy underwrote the creation of workers as isolated abstract persons, cells in the organisms of munificent states. The process involved tendencies both to the strengthening of national sovereignty (in opposition to dynastic or imperial rule) and thereby the 'legitimization' of state power, and to the integration of workers into a cross-class 'imagined community'. Bourgeois revolutions – in the narrow sense of the creation of popular and cohesive sovereign states – developed in relation to other nation states. In other words, 'the people' arose not only in opposition to dynastic or imperial rule, but also laterally, in reaction to other 'peoples'.[18] In a system of nation states, immigrant workers are by definition rendered vulnerable; as Portes and Walton put it, '[t]he very fact of crossing a political border weakens the status of workers' *vis-à-vis* states and employers (1981: 50).

In the *Communist Manifesto* Marx and Engels, assuming that socialist revolution would not be long coming, suggested that national differences and antagonisms were in the process of disintegration. In certain respects they were right; but continued capitalist development also furthered the consolidation of nation states. The rise of citizenship and democracy involved the positioning of workers' organizations within a landscape demarcated and defined by nation states, with the latter operating as a bargaining partner not unlike employers – conceding certain rights to workers and their organizations in a process whose boundaries are by definition those of national territory. In short, the extension of bourgeois subjectivity to workers involves their constitution as persons by states, in a negation of their social existence as collective subjects of internationally constituted relations of exploitation. In so far as collective subjectivity is recognized, it is at the political level, as threaded into national structures.

As the growth of the working class and its collective organization in unions and parties grew, ruling classes became increasingly concerned with the 'social question'. As Jones and Novack put it (in Corrigan 1980: 147), the '"condition of the people" became a major concern to ruling classes around the end of the nineteenth century, with intensified economic competition during the Great Depression'. Partly as a result of pressure from below, partly to promote fitter, more loyal workers and soldiers, rights were extended. Churchill, applauding the benefits of national insurance in 1909, lucidly expressed this argument:

> The idea is to increase the stability of our institutions by giving the mass of industrial workers a direct interest in maintaining them. With a 'stake' in the country in the form of insurance against evil days these workers will pay no attention to the vague promises of revolutionary socialism . . . it will make him a better citizen, a more efficient worker, and a happier man. (In Corrigan 1980: 166)

Apparently the creation of an infrastructure of national belonging underwrote ruling class attempts to institutionalize class struggle through shaping 'the consolidation of the subjectivity of labour' (Kay and Mott 1982: 139). In this light it can be seen why the period in which immigration control began to be (re)introduced on a widespread basis was in the decades around the turn of the century. It was a period of heightened international economic competition and political tension, and of increasing state supervision of industry and welfare. It was also a period in which ruling classes were urgently developing strategies to counter large-scale workers' movements and social democracy. Those movements were typically infused with an internationalist spirit – witness for instance the mass participation of Irish workers in the New Unionism in Britain, or the setting up of the First and Second Internationals. Regulation of national labour markets represented in part the attempts by states to counter internationalism through drawing lines of demarcation whereby nationals qualified for privileged rights and non-nationals for fewer or none – with states assuming the mantle of protector of the former against the foreigner.

Global Capitalism

The evolution of bourgeois rights and national sovereignty is connected to the emergence of what Charles Tilly (1993: 35) refers to as the 'consolidated state' – typically 'large, differentiated, ruling heterogenous territories directly, [and] claiming to impose a unitary fiscal, monetary, judicial, legislative, military and cultural system on its citizens'. Consolidation, Tilly suggests, accelerated in Europe from the eighteenth century alongside processes of 'circumscription' and 'control', whereby the capacity of states to demarcate and shape their territories and the people and social relations within grew dramatically. Bureaucratic apparatuses of rule, of surveillance and welfare provision and all-encompassing legal systems were constructed, producing a qualitatively new type of 'muscular' state (1993: 29), which reaches 'daily – and nightly – into the lives of most of [its] citizens'.

It is no accident that this revolutionary change occurred contemporaneously with the development of capitalist production and the rise of the world market. As mentioned earlier, the actions of states – including geopolitical rivalry – were crucial to the emergence of capitalism. Conversely, the rise of mercantile and, later, productive capital stimulated the consolidation of states. An intrinsically fragmented form of social relation, capitals, as we have seen, rely upon stable political and cultural infrastructures. Historically, these developed in regionally combined forms, upon the scaffolding of existing states, and forming socio-geographic centres for the struggle over global surplus value. The growth of capitalist production generated and/or exacerbated those contradictions that underlie state power – between states, between private interests, and between classes. States became increasingly consolidated structures of authority and organization serving to defend investments already sunk and promote accumulation of those capitals based within their bounds.

The *nation*-state evolved as ideally suited to the management and control of capitalist society. It posits relatively clear demarcations between private property and its own prerogatives; is internally uniform and well positioned to appeal to popular legitimacy; and is remarkably cheap, centralized, cohesive and strong, and hence well adapted to ensuring its own survival as well as that of capitals based within its borders.[19]

States dismantled local obstacles to the circulation of commodities, including labour-power, creating free – albeit administered and territorially circumscribed – markets.[20] They established structures for the creation of those standardized and interchangeable workforces that, as we have seen, are essential to the capitalist division of labour. And they appropriated other tasks, such as the minting and regulation currency. In all of these cases the operations of states (including the establishment of labour markets and welfare systems) are in one sense *national* – circumscribed by, or at least grounded within, state territory. It seems that the tendency towards 'nationalization' is inscribed in the development of capitalism; its triumph – contrary both to the predictions of Marx and to the retrodictions of many theories of globalization – is the globalization of the nation-states system in the latter half of the twentieth century, contemporaneously with the fullest encircling of the world by capitalist relations.

Though ostensibly parcellized, the framework of political society mediates commodity relations which are inherently transnational in potential. In Justin Rosenberg's felicitous formulation, insofar as 'capitalist relations of surplus extraction are organized through a contract of exchange which is defined as "non-political"' it becomes possible 'in a way that would have been unthinkable under feudalism, to command and exploit productive labour (and natural resources) located under the jurisdiction of another state' (1994: 129). The implications for the inter-state system are resounding. Each state is imbricated in a *world* society and economy whose movements it can influence but not control.

Not only, then, do capitalist states exist in relations of interdependence and antagonism to external powers, compelling each to stake forceful claims to definite forms of control over territories and the people and things within them. That is the case with any states system. In capitalism, however, 'the state's own stability and health are dependent upon social processes beyond its borders . . . Therefore in order to play the role of the state the national state must strive to burst through its own national character' (Wright 1997: 12). States' interests in maintaining power and supporting the processes of accumulation upon which they depend entail intervention not only within *but beyond* their home territories. Not only must they counter threats from other states, but are compelled to seek influence over property and populations beyond their home territories – massaging and manipulating external frameworks of rights, defending investments, and partnering and clashing with other states. In the course of responding to these imperatives, incidentally, nation states may well undermine the cultural homogeneity upon which basis they supposedly exist – notably through the encouragement of international flows of labour-power.

Thus, in Rosenberg's words (1990: 255), 'the political structure of nation-states is the channel for the projection of political *and economic* power across borders' (italics GD). States are inherently international, not simply through their mutual relations, but because they are dependent upon and threaded into the transnational circuits of economic life. As those circuits intensify and interpenetrate across borders, states are drawn into not weaker but denser interconnections and experience, if anything, *greater* pressure to exercise influence in the interests of accumulation. In the long run the internationalization of capital has developed in tandem with the globalization of the nation-state system, which 'involved, in practice, raising enormously the effective coercive power of the state' and the 'accumulation of permanently mobilised military power' (Rosenberg 1990: 255).

Uneven Accumulation

Geo-political and geo-economic competition produce tendencies both to the equalization of conditions of production and to their differentiation. The compulsion to organize production according to a singular law of value may determine the actions of capitals and, in different ways, of states; but both these types of capitalist institution in reality assume tremendously varied shapes and sizes and operate in sharply dissimilar conditions. That some forms of capital relations arose in one part of the world affected their rise in others. So, the extension of capitalist markets to non-capitalist areas could, for example, shore up pre-capitalist regimes, or indeed form the basis of capitalist systems of unfree labour, as in North America and the Caribbean. Capitalism did not merely originate in an irregular way, it is intrinsically uneven – the accumulation of value at one moment engenders devaluation at another, innovation in one centre threatens the viability of extant forms of production elsewhere.

A dialectic of combination and unevenness can be observed in the world system as a whole. On the one hand, the operation of even 'free' international trade produces powerful pressures, as Anwar Shaikh has persuasively argued – *pace* the sanguine axioms of classical and neo-classical economics – that produce a spatial mapping of the tendency toward the polarization of poverty and capital onto a widening gap between poor and rich nations (1980: 232). In turn, economic unevenness develops synergistically with the dynamic asymmetry of the states system; consolidated states with a stronger fiscal base are able to project power where others cannot. Colonialism and other forms of imperial power projection have tended to exacerbate global asymmetries, not only through plunder, conquest and the undercutting of local industries, but also through the denial or limitation of sovereignty across vast swathes of the world. On the other hand, the very ploughing of the law of value into all areas of the globe stimulates the emergence of countervailing tendencies, whereby the economic consequences of, or the political means of dealing with, 'backwardness' may induce the development of the technological or military muscle required to achieve a greater purchase on global surplus value. Thus, the early capitalist powers were joined by second and third waves, whilst recent decades have witnessed some regions of the 'Third World' achieving economic comparison with those at the top.

The upshot is a world combined more intensively than ever into one system, with each capital governed by a law of value that measures particular producers more firmly than ever against prevailing standards, and yet where the average organic composition of capital and value of labour power varies severely between regions. Similarly, at the political level, the generalization of the nation-states system has reached its zenith, with inter-state relations institutionalized in an increasingly dense manner, yet any investigation of the substantive content of sovereignty reveals awesome degrees of inequality.

It is a steeply differentiated yet constantly combined system, one where dynamic growth in one period gives way to deep crisis in another, where accelerated accumulation in one part coexists with the depths of stagnation elsewhere. In such a world, all varieties of transnational interlinkages, of deprivation and oppression, of aspirations, provide the bases for unprecedented flows of international migration. Yet at the same time states are as obliged as ever to keep a watchful eye not only on the objective conditions of accumulation (and the sluice gates to immigration) but on suppressing the collective organization and consciousness of workers.

The reason why immigration and refugee issues have surged up the political agenda in many countries since the 1970s, therefore, is not because these decades saw a spillage of rights issues into the political arena, as James Hollifield argues (1992: 29), nor because global economic integration combined with aggravated wars and poverty have spurred accelerated flows of migrants, as is commonly assumed. Rather, it is because resurgent economic crises have intensified the contradictions faced by states. On the one hand, intensified competition spurs employers' requirements for enhanced labour market flexibility – for which immigrant labour is ideal. On the other, in such periods questions of social control tend to become more pressing. Governments strive to uphold the ideology of 'social contract' even as its content is eroded through unemployment and austerity. The logic, commonly, is for less political capital to be derived from the compact's content, while greater emphasis is placed upon its exclusivity, on demarcation from those who enter from or lie outside – immigrants and foreigners.

Conclusion

Capitalism is a system based upon the exploitation of a large majority by a tiny minority; and is inherently crisis prone. As such, it depends upon the continuous decimation of working-class solidarity and the creation of cross-class community. It is certainly not far-fetched to note, with David Harvey (1982: 383), 'the importance of racism, sexism, nationalism, religious and ethnic prejudice to the circulation of capital', or indeed that the rule of capital rests upon the fragmentation of the working class, the repression of workers' aspirations, demands and solidarities and their refraction along trajectories of individual mobility, national and racial community. These are not empty claims. Historical evidence indicates that when workers' struggles rise, sectional, national and racial antagonisms tend to recede. When the sort of pitch is reached where the overthrow of bourgeois rule appears on the agenda, internationalist currents come to the fore – most famously in the Russian empire of 1917.

Does this, however, mean that xenophobia is best explained as a consequence of Machiavellian strategies of 'divide and rule' deployed by élites in the interests of social control? Certainly, many identities and oppressions of the contemporary world are rooted in calculated policy. Peter Taylor (1989: 116) gives the example of British imperial rule:

> British governors throughout the world 'officially' recognized various cultural groups in order to play one off against another. Official designation in administrative documents such as the census turned these groups into political strata competing for the favours of the Empire. Quite literally the British Empire was the great creator of 'peoples' throughout the world. The legacy of this policy remains with us today in such political rivalries as Hindus, Moslems and Sikhs in India, Tamils and Sinhalese in Sri Lanka [etc., etc.].

Nor are such strategies relics from bygone ages. Across the globe, élites seize upon national and ethnic differentiations, generating vulnerability of the oppressed *vis-à-vis* capital and states, and incorporating workers into cross-class alliances, i.e. into alignments of intra- rather than inter-class struggle.

Nevertheless, of the causes of racism and xenophobia only the conspicuous surface can be put down to intentional actions of employers and states. The soil in which modern prejudice and institutional discrimination grow is deeper, produced by the dynamics of capitalism considered as a totality. Some of these have been touched upon in this essay: labour competition appearing in the form of other workers; the alienation of workers' 'real' collective powers, endemic insecurity, and the corresponding appeal of 'communities' of race and nation; the construction of formal subjectivity along national lines; and the competitive struggles that have shaped the uneven geography of economic and political development, of colonial and imperial strategies of control.

Conversely, and as the chapters on England and Germany in this volume have shown, xenophobia can be undermined. This struggle may be assisted by liberal institutions of formal equality, but its core lies in the processes of the social coalescence and everyday solidarities of workers of different ethnicities, especially where working-class confidence is strong and where resistance to racism is organized. As Barker and Dale have put it (1999), questions, concerning racism are therefore inherent aspects of class conflict, 'for they affect the nature and quality of life and struggle within capitalist society and hence are of quite as much concern to "labour" as immediate questions about wages and working conditions within workplaces. Anti-racism is not "outside the scope" of the class struggle, but is part of a struggle to constitute a political force with the capacity to attack the very roots of its alienation.'

Notes

Thanks to Andrew Wright for critical remarks on an earlier version of this paper.

1. See for example the world citizenship manifestos of Kenichi Ohmae and Ulrich Beck. Also, though more tentatively, Nigel Harris (this volume).
2. This section draws heavily on Barker (1998).
3. Hence, writes Bob Fine (1984: 153), 'the private right of individuals to dispose of their property as they will turns into the expropriation of this right by the state as monopolizer of legal authority'.
4. See Miles (1987) for a concise discussion of some of these points.
5. cf. Weeks (1981: 160–3).
6. This may be obvious, but is worth emphasizing given the prevalence of such opinions as that 'capital has an interest in dividing the working class only when it is united and threatening' (Harris 1991: 87).
7. There are, moreover, processes that operate in practice to render

workers more commensurable, uniform and universally interchangeable – as if cut from one cloth. One example is 'deskilling', which lubricates labour mobility as the recalcitrant edges of craft specialism are sanded down. Universal literacy is another.

8. He adds, 'It inevitably turns for assistance in all of these tasks to other local capitals and to the state in which it is located.'
9. Even money capital, though extremely fluid (at least when simultaneously 'hard' and 'liquid'), can only exist thanks to its repeated transmutation into productive capital, as investments which are *sunk* into land, labour power, etc.
10. cf. Standing (1981); Miles (1993: 112–4).
11. For discussion of the contradictions involved in the creation of capital-producing 'unfree' labour, see Banaji; also Miles (1987).
12. In Britain, for example, the Poor Law Amendment of 1834 simultaneously directed policy towards freely mobile national labour and towards a centralized welfare system.
13. Interestingly, I have come across not one liberal author who advocates genuinely open borders. Do only Marxist internationalists consistently defend this liberal freedom?
14. This helps us to understand why migrants can be so beneficial to employers. '[M]igrants appear by far to be the most plastic, the most readily adaptable to the requirements of the labor market.' states Piore (1979: 90). They are generally more mobile than other 'marginal groups' such as youth and housewives, because for the latter groups 'the social roles and community settings to which they owe primary allegiance significantly constrain their adaptability to job needs. In virtually every case except the migrants, the geographic location is determined by factors external to the labor market.'
15. Spatial concentration is typically associated with major migration, whereby the capitalist, in the course of bringing workers 'under his command as wage labourers' seeks to 'draw them away from their home towns and to concentrate them in a place of work' (Marx 1973: 510).
16. Weber's discussion on this point is insightful, although his insistence that 'racial antipathy . . . was quite foreign to the planters' is presumably open to doubt.
17. As witnessed, for instance, by the small print in British passports: 'This passport remains the property of Her Majesty's Government in the United Kingdom and may be withdrawn at any time.'
18. The creation of nationality within a territorial state – real or projected – invariably takes an 'ethnic' form, equating a particular 'people'

with a particular territory. Whether the model of nation is 'universalist French' or 'particularist German', it necessarily entails exclusion of foreigners.

19. Just as the development of absolutism was key to the survival of the nobilities of late feudal continental Europe as independent ruling classes, so too the nationalization of the state seems to have played a similar role during the rise of capitalism, with geopolitics acting as selection mechanism.
20. In England the abolition of the Speenhamland system was central. As Thomas Mackay put it (1904: 15), the old Poor Law did not see that the 'migration of men was a necessary accompaniment in the changed course of trade'; it preserved the contradiction whereby '[c]apital was free to migrate, but labour was imprisoned in its settlement.' The old system penned labour reserves in the villages during a period where a key lever of accumulation was spatial concentration in industrial centres. The 1834 Amendment facilitated mobility to those centres.

Bibliography

Allen, T. (1994), *The Invention of the White Race*, London: Verso.

Banaji, J. (1977), 'Modes of production in a materialist conception of history', *Capital and Class*, 3: 1–44.

Barker, C. (1983), *State etc.* Unpublished notes.

Barker, C. (1997), 'Some Reflections on Two Books by Ellen Wood', *Historical Materialism*, 1: 22–65.

Barker, C. (1998), *Industrialism, Capitalism, Value, Force and States*, Paper given at Comparative Economic History conference, Wolverhampton University, June.

Barker, C. and Dale, G. (1999), 'Protest Waves in Western Europe: A critique of "New Social Movement" Theory', *Critical Sociology*, Vol.25.

Carchedi, G. (1979), 'Authority and Foreign Labour', *Studies in Political Economy* 2: 38–59.

Collinson, S. (1993), *Europe and International Migration*, London: Pinter.

Corrigan, P. (ed) (1980), *Capitalism, State Formation and Marxist Theory*, London: Quartet.

Draper, H. (1977), *Karl Marx's Theory of Revolution*, Vol.1, New York: Monthly Review.

Fine, B. (1984), *Democracy and the Rule of Law*, London: Pluto.

Fox-Genovese, E. and Genovese, E. (1983), *Fruits of Merchant Capital*, Oxford: OUP.

Harman, C. (1991), 'The State and Capitalism Today', *International Socialism* 51: 3–54.

Harris, N. (1991), 'A comment on *National Liberation*', *International Socialism* 53: 79–91.

Harvey, D. (1982), *The Limits to Capital*, Oxford: Blackwell.

Harvey, D. (1985), 'The Geopolitics of Capitalism', in D. Gregory and J. Urry (eds), *Social Relations and Spatial Structures*, Basingstoke: Macmillan.

Hollifield, J. (1992), *Immigrants, Markets and States*, Cambridge: Harvard.

Kay, G. and Mott, J. (1982), *Political Order and the Law of Labour*, Houndmills: Macmillan.

Lebowitz, M. (1992), *Beyond Capital*, Houndmills: Macmillan.

Mackay, T. (1904), *A History of the English Poor Law*, Vol.3, London: King.

Mann, M. (1988), *States, War and Capitalism*, Oxford: Blackwell.

Mann, M. (1993), 'Nation-States in Europe and Other Continents', *Daedalus* 122 (3): 115–140.

Marx, K. (1976), *Capital*, Vol.1, Harmondsworth: Penguin.

Marx, K. (1975), *Early Writings*, Harmondsworth: Penguin.

Marx, K. (1973), *Grundrisse*, Harmondsworth: Penguin.

Meillasoux, C. (1981), *Maidens, Meal and Money*, Cambridge: CUP.

Miles, R. (1986), 'Labour Migration, Racism and Capital Accumulation in Western Europe', *Capital and Class* 28: 49–86.

Miles, R. (1987), *Anomaly or Necessity?*, London: Tavistock.

Miles, R. (1993), *Racism After 'Race Relations'*, London: Routledge.

Ollman, B. (1993), *Dialectical Investigations*, London, Routledge.

Pashukanis, E. (1980), *Selected Writings on Marxism and Law*, London: Academic Press.

Piore, M. (1979), *Birds of Passage*, Cambridge: CUP.

Portes, A. and Walton, J. (1981), *Labor, Class, and the International System*, New York: Academic Press.

Poulantzas, N. (1980), *State, Power, Socialism*, London: Verso.

Rosenberg, J. (1990), 'A Non-Realist Theory of Sovereignty?' *Millennium* 19 (2): 249–59.

Rosenberg, J. (1994), *The Empire of Civil Society*, London: Verso.

Sayer, D. (1991), *Capitalism and Modernity*, London: Routledge.

Shaikh, A. 'The Laws of International Exchange', in Nell, E. (ed.) (1980), *Growth, Profits, and Property*, Cambridge: CUP.

Simon, J. (1989), *The Economic Consequences of Immigration*, Oxford: Blackwell.

Shortall, F. (1994), *The Incomplete Marx*, Aldershot: Avebury.

Standing, G. (1981), 'Migration and Modes of Exploitation', *Journal of Peasant Studies*, 8 (2): 173–99.

Taylor, P. (1989), *Political Geography*, Harlow: Longman.

Tilly, C. (1993), *European Revolutions, 1492–1992*, Oxford: Blackwell.

Weber, M. (1968), *Economy and Society*, Berkeley: University of California.

Weeks, J. (1981), *Capital and Exploitation*, Princeton: Princeton University Press.

Wood, E. (1995), *Democracy Against Capitalism*, Cambridge: CUP.

Wright, A. (1997), *On Holloway*, Unpublished notes.

Notes on Contributors

Kieran Allen teaches sociology in University College Dublin. He is the author of The Politics of James Connolly (1990) and Fianna Fail and the Irish Labour Movement (1997).

Mike Cole has, over the last twenty years, published extensively in the fields of education and equality. In more recent years, he has engaged in Marxist critiques of postmoderism, globalization and education. He is the co-editor of *Postmodernism in Educational Theory: Education and the Politics of Human Resistance* (1999). His PhD, completed in 1992, concerned the relationship between British imperialism, racism, migration and education.

Gareth Dale is currently completing a PhD on the East German revolution of 1989, at Manchester University. He teaches sociology and political economy, and has written on modern German history and, with Colin Barker, on social movement theory. He is on the editorial collective of '*Historical Materialism*', a journal of 'research in critical Marxist theory'.

Jon Gubbay lectures in Sociology at the University of East Anglia on research methods, political sociology and social stratification. His publications include *Economy and Class Structure* (with Rosemary Crompton), and 'A Marxist Critique of Weberian Class Analysis' (*Sociology* 1997) and he is the editor, with Chris Middleton and Chet Ballard, of *The Student's Companion to Sociology*. He is a long-standing member of the Socialist Workers Party.

Nigel Harris is an economist, professor at University College London and former director of the Development Planning Unit. Author of over a dozen books on issues of development and cities, he has worked over thirty-five years in many developing countries for the United Nations, World Bank, and governments etc. He is currently Visiting Professor in Cairo.

Mike Haynes is a lecturer in European Studies at the University of Wolverhampton. He has written extensively on long run patterns of change in Europe and has a particular interest in the transition in Eastern Europe.

Agostino Petrillo works at Genoa University. He has published articles about Urban Problems and German Sociology. His doctoral thesis is entitled *Origins of the City's Sociology in Germany : from W.H. Riehl to Max Weber* (1996) He is now working on urban insecurity and the situation of immigrants in European cities. A book about *Migrants and Cities* is to be published soon .

Jan Rath studied cultural anthropology at Utrecht University, where he specialized in urban studies. Since graduation he has taught political science and economic sociology. He is now Senior Researcher and Project Manager of the Institute for Migration and Ethnic Studies (IMES) at the University of Amsterdam. He is author of numerous articles, book chapters and reports on the sociology and politics of post-migratory processes.

Eugene Sensenig is Professor of History and Political Science at the University of Portland, Salzburg center, and Director of the historical photo archives of the Salzburg Ludwig Boltzmann Institute for Social and Cultural History. He has various publications in the fields of Cold War labour history, history of migration policy in Central Europe, social history, history of migration policy in Central Europe, social history of mining in the Eastern Alps; and extensive experience as an organizer within the immigrant communities in Austria.

Satnam Virdee is a lecturer in sociology in the Department of Government at the University of Strathclyde. His main research interests include racist and anti-racist collective action in trade unions, the political economy of racism, and racist violence. He is the author of several articles and monographs including *Racial Violence and Harassment* (PSI, 1995). He is currently undertaking an ESRC-funded ethnographic study of the racialization of school life and is writing a book on racism and resistance in English trade unions.

Khursheed Wadia teaches in the School of Languages and European Studies at the University of Wolverhampton. She has carried out research on the French Communist Party as well as on aspects of feminist activism in France and is currently co-authoring a book on women and politics in Fifth Republic France.

Index